Zentrum Moderner Orient
Geisteswissenschaftliche Zentren Berlin e.V.

Dissociation and Appropriation Responses to Globalization in Asia and Africa

■ Ed. by Katja Füllberg-Stolberg,
Petra Heidrich, Ellinor Schöne

Studien 10

Verlag Das Arabische Buch

Die Deutsche Bibliothek - CIP-Einheitsaufnahme

Dissociation and appropriation: Responses to globalization in Asia and Africa / Zentrum Moderner Orient, Geisteswissenschaftliche Zentren Berlin e.V. Ed. by Katja Füllberg-Stolberg/Petra Heidrich/ Ellinor Schöne. - Berlin : Verl. Das Arab. Buch, 1999
    (Studien / Zentrum Moderner Orient Berlin, Geisteswissenschaftliche Zentren Berlin e.V.; 10)
    ISBN 3-86093-211-X

Zentrum Moderner Orient
Geisteswissenschaftliche Zentren Berlin e.V.

Direktor:
Prof. Dr. Ulrich Haarmann

Kirchweg 33
14129 Berlin
Tel. 030 / 80307 228

ISBN 3-86093-211-X
STUDIEN

Bestellungen:
Das Arabische Buch
Horstweg 2
14059 Berlin
Tel. 030 / 3228523
Fax 030 / 3225183

Redaktion und Satz: Margret Liepach

Druck: Druckerei Weinert, Berlin
Printed in Germany 1999

Gedruckt mit Unterstützung der Senatsverwaltung
für Wissenschaft, Forschung und Kultur, Berlin

CONTENTS

Introduction   5

Shalini Randeria: Globalization, Modernity and the Nationstate   15

Joachim Heidrich: Globalization in Historical Perspective   25

Thomas Scheffler: The "Global Culture" Debate as a Challenge to Islamic Studies   43

Henner Fürtig: Universalist Counter-Projections: Iranian Post-Revolutionary Foreign Policy and Globalization   53

Dietrich Reetz: Mediating the External: The Changing World and Religious Renewal in Indian Islam   75

Anoushiravan Ehteshami: Globalization and Political Islam   107

Leonhard Harding: Africa in the History of Globalization   123

Zoya Hasan: Secularism, Legal Reform and Gender Justice in India   137

David Taylor: The Bharatiya Janata Party and Hindu Nationalism in India   151

Mushirul Hasan: Memories of a Fragmented Nation: Rewriting the Histories of India's Partition   167

Klaus Sagaster: Religion and Group Identity in Present Mongolia   185

Amr Hamzawy: The French Expedition, Egyptian Satanists and Lady Diana: Globalization and its Discontents   195

Armando Salvatore: Global Influences and Discontinuities in a Religious Tradition: Public Islam and the "New" Šarīʿa   211

David B. Coplan: Locations of Nation: Mobility and Locality in the Cultural Economy of Lesotho Migrants   235

Jean-Luc Vellut: Configurations of Space in Central African History   255

Annemarie Hafner: The Local and the Global in a Workers'
Milieu: The Example of Colonial Bombay   265

K.N. Panikkar: The "Great" Shoe Question: Tradition,
Legitimacy, and Power in Colonial India   275

Nicole A.N.M. Van Os: Ottoman Women's Reaction to the
Economic and Cultural Intrusion of the West: The Quest
for a National Dress   291

Perspectives on Globalization
(Summary of a Round Table Discussion)   309

Postscript

Ulrich Haarmann: The Effects of Globalzation on Asian and
Africa: Related Concepts, Language and History   317

Contributors   322

Introduction

This volume is the outcome of an international symposium on "Dissociation and Appropriation of Global Processes and Ideas: History, Religion and Local Culture in Asia and Africa" which was held in Berlin from 23 to 25 October 1997. The symposium was organized by the Centre for Modern Oriental Studies and sponsored by the German Research Foundation (DFG). Most of the contributions included in this volume are extended versions of the conference papers. Additional articles were submitted by visiting scholars who collaborated closely with the Centre in its ongoing research.

The Centre for Modern Oriental Studies is an interdisciplinary institute for research on the history, society and culture of the Middle East, South Asia and Africa. In 1996 it became part of the newly-formed "Verein Geisteswissenschaftliche Zentren Berlin e.V." (Registered Society for Research Centres in the Humanities). Current research work at the Centre focuses on "Dissociation and Appropriation in Response to Globalization: Asia, Africa and Europe since the 18th Century". In this programme local and regional perceptions, adaptations and consequences of global processes and ideas are examined in historical and comparative perspective. The geographical focus is on those regions of the South which are often underemphazised in debates on globalization, but share the experience of colonialism and postcolonial history.

Whereas the ongoing globalization debate has so far dealt mainly with the most recent period, the symposium attempted to broaden the scope of the debate by including other historical periods and by focusing on globalization from the perspective of Asia, Africa and the Middle East. This corresponds to the research profile of the Centre for Modern Oriental Studies. The scope of the symposium reflected the Centre's own approach in tackling the subject of globalization. It gives prominence to its historical dimension and to its local manifestations in Asian and African countries with particular emphasis on cultural factors, while considering the regional diversities of the globalizing processes involved.

The international symposium provided a forum for scholars associated with the Centre to exchange views on the responses to globalization in Asia and Africa with experts from other institutions who work on related subjects. Colleagues from India, South Africa, Tanzania and several European countries participated in the symposium both as contributors of papers and as discussants. The present volume contains papers submitted by scholars of various disciplines and gives an account of the major issues raised during the discussion as well as during the Round Table held at the concluding session.

A considerable body of literature on globalization appeared during the last decade and the subject emerged as one of the key topics in social science research during the 1990s. The wide-ranging publications available, representing diverse and rather controversial attitudes to the subject, opened up new perspectives on the global dimensions of economic, social and cultural processes. At the same time they demonstrated the need to foster a wider and more differentiated approach to the issue of globalization. Giddens' definition of globalization as "...the intensification of worldwide social relations which link distant localities in such a way that local happenings are shaped by events occurring many miles away and vice versa..."[1] served as the general point of departure for the symposium. The participants emphasized the dual nature of globalization as an objective and a subjective process and accepted the position that "globalization refers both to the compression of the world and to the intensification of consciousness of the world as a whole"[2].

The arguments and views submitted during the symposium enabled a comparison between different non-western indigenous positions with regard to global events, ideas and developments. The debate highlighted the manifold perceptions of globalization processes in Asia, Africa and the Middle East and the resultant reactions. The participants elaborated on manifestations of the individual and collective consciousness of different kinds of global situations.

There was general agreement in considering globalization as a multidimensional process which unfolds simultaneously on various levels. The perspectives on globalization, however, differed. While some participants conceived globalization mainly as a process of increasing global interdependence, others emphasized the obviously growing global asymmetries. Can we look at the global process as a phenomenon that just happens, or should we interpret the contemporary world as an arena embracing equally positioned players who meet and interact on a supposedly neutral platform? There are obviously winners and losers in the process. In this context, ways of resisting and influencing globalization "from below" were given prominence in the discussion. The differences in approach also surfaced on the question of a conceivable centredness and corresponding direction of globalization. While some participants stressed the existence of one or several centres, others emphasized the plurality of social and cultural flows in an uncentred world.

The symposium theme invited a debate on the dialectical nature of the relationship between the global and the local in the globalization process. Reference was made to Giddens' statement that "...local transformation is as much a part of globalization as the lateral extension of social connections across time and space"[3]. On the other hand, in order to highlight the contradictory nature of the appropriation of global influences at the local level, attention was drawn to the point made by Appadurai that "... globalization of culture is not the same as its homogenization..."[4].

Research results presented at the symposium testified to the fact that the tendency of socio-economic structures and cultural patterns towards homogenization over vast spaces in the course of globalization is accompanied by an increasing trend towards heterogenization. Particularization seems to be the twin brother of globalization. The dissolution and reconstruction of borders and boundaries was cited as a case in point. Key issues were the crisis of the nation state in the wake of the globalization process and the increasing significance of boundary-crossing transnational and international phenomena. The configuration of space and time has also begun to gain prominence in the debate. The question was raised repeatedly as to what distinction could be made between modernization and modernity and how both phenomena were linked historically in the processes which engulfed societies and cultures in the modern period.

The historical perspective in the globalization debate, which has concentrated on questions supposedly relevant for the twentieth century only, was underestimated for a long time - with rare exceptions such as the work of Bryan S. Turner[5]. More recent studies, however, confirm the importance of the historical dimension and the historical analysis of the globalization problem is gaining ground. In this context, the symposium tried to establish links between current processes of globalization and comparable phenomena in the past, which may have a bearing on shaping the future. The papers demonstrate how local actors perceived aspects of globalization at different periods of time and in variegated cultural settings.

A focal point was the cultural manifestation of globalization. In this context, contributors and participants in the discussion addressed the constitution, substance and changing of local cultures in history. Special attention was paid to the articulation of local cultures, tensions arising from globalizing processes, and the concrete reaction to the global in the local context as expressed in various forms of dissociation or appropriation. Case studies focus on individual and collective representatives of local culture who act within or between their cultural fields. A number of authors describe the changing attitudes of Asian and African actors vis-à-vis the external influences to which they were exposed during the colonial period. Such encounters have led, at times, to the reconsideration and reconstruction of traditional identities.

In the context of a more pronounced focus on cultural questions, several papers took up the role of religion in the globalization process. The authors elaborate on religion as a factor in local or national political movements and discuss the changes which occur in response to developments on a global scale. Some case studies analyse specific aspects in this context. They focus on local expressions of religiosity in Asian and African countries, on the role of religion in the formation of individual and group identities, particularly as an expression of an intended detachment from global influences. Other contributors are concerned with ideas of religious universalism as a counter-projection to global impacts which are mainly comprehended as an intrusion by the "West" into indigenous cultures.

The participants of the symposium noticed an increasing awareness of cultural differences and a strong urge towards cultural affirmation or re-affirmation at the local level. Feeling excluded from decision-making and unable to effectively influence global processes, local actors often attempt to disengage themselves from global developments. The more they fear the loss of their own cultural identity, the more they tend to affirm it. Despite widespread, especially verbal, rejection of external influences, numerous examples of the indigenization of global phenomena have, however, been observed. By blending such phenomena with indigenous value systems and world views, thus rendering their effects more tolerable, local actors go a long way towards appropriating the effects and symbols of globalization.

Although the symposium could address only a limited number of aspects, the issues dealt with reflected the complexity of the topic. The contributions to this volume demonstrate the intricacy of the appropriation of global processes or the dissociation from them in Asia, Africa and the Middle East. They display a great diversity in approach, ranging from a general discussion on the globalization debate to more regionally orientated papers. Several local case studies complement the picture.

The contributions by *Shalini Randeria* and *Joachim Heidrich* address the more general aspects of globalization. *Shalini Randeria* identifies the key notions of the topic and elaborates on the different theoretical approaches to globalization. She contrasts the Euro-American discourses on globalization with the perspective of most countries of the South. While the first tend to celebrate globalization, deny any centredness and concentrate on its cultural aspects, the latter, confronted with the adverse consequences of economic globalization, tend to characterize globalization as a "recolonization of the present and a colonialization of the future". The weakening of the nation state is another issue addressed in the paper. *Shalini Randeria* states that by comparison "the loss of political and legal sovereignty of the nation state has been much greater in the South". She, moreover, demonstrates that the nation state and its sovereignty is by no means weakened in all areas. She notes massive state intervention in most countries of the South in favour of global capital. Finally, she elaborates on the special features of cultural globalization.

Joachim Heidrich also discusses different perceptions of globalization. Recognizing that economy and culture are the domains most affected by globalization, the author defines the term as a concept for the qualitatively new phenomenon of transnationalization and internationalization, introduced by new technologies compressing time and space. Globalization brings about two contradictory processes. On the one hand, it tends to establish a global economy and global political structures. It also tends to universalize cultural elements and value systems which originated from industrially advanced countries in the West. On the other hand, it fosters new nationalisms and political separatisms, and strengthens cultural otherness and individuality. The author stresses that globalization is not just a process of the present but has its roots in the past. Linked to the transnationalization of the capitalist mode of production, this process has, from its beginnings, included both economic preponderance and political domination, as well as the universalization of Western concepts, values and institutions that characterize modern history. From this starting-point the author discusses perceptions of the globalization process and reactions to it in Third World countries.

In contrast to *Randeria* and *Heidrich*, *Thomas Scheffler* focuses exclusively on the cultural dimension of globalization. He is concerned with the emergence of the consciousness of the world as a single place, which is accompanied by a "global culture" debate. In his paper, *Scheffler* discusses how this debate challenges the Islamic world in general and Islamic studies in particular. The Islamic world is confronted by two conflicting tendencies. Firstly, global processes and ideas are regarded as a threat because they relativize, penetrate or supersede local cultures while, at the same time, providing new ways and means of vitalizing and empowering them. Secondly, the possible globalization of Islamic "particularism" is necessarily an ambivalent process because it presupposes a consciousness of global problems and an ability to address global audiences. Islamic studies will certainly be affected by changes in the Islamic world, which are bound to occur. In *Scheffler's* opinion, the former will have to transgress the spatial, linguistic and methodological framework of the "Orient". Islamic civilization can no longer be regarded as a world apart. Therefore, research on its various peripheries as well as on multicultural macrospace-building in Islamic history should be areas of growing interest.

Henner Fürtig traces universalist counter-projections to globalization in post-revolutionary Iranian foreign policy. He discusses the aspirations of the Iranian leadership - both during and after the period of Khomeini - to propagate a universalist Islamic world view. These ambitions were understood as a counter-initiative against "Western imperialism" and "Eastern communism" and became part of Iranian foreign policy after the Islamic revolution. The author examines the basics of this concept, which consist of the idea of Islamic unity, the export of the Islamic revolution, and the modified approach that Iran should set an example for the Muslims of the world to follow. Finally, he discusses the contemporary consensus of the seven principles, claimed to be Islamic and shared by all those dealing with foreign policy.

Dietrich Reetz demonstrates how two Islamic movements in colonial India respond to the challenge of modernity. In his paper he analyses the Deoband and Tablighi movements, both of which represent a broader trend in Islamic mobilization, aimed at reviving religiosity and piety in society. He discusses in detail the various aspects of change that affected these two Islamic reform groups and explores their different forms of response to the global impact. Their public intervention in the interests of Islam forced them to leave the "sacred" world. They engaged themselves in social and political transformation in order to achieve religious renewal.

A different perspective on the Islamic world is presented by *Anoushiravan Ehteshami*. He investigates the effects of globalization on political Islam. Firstly, he discusses the term "political Islam", demonstrating how Islam became politicized, and explores perspectives on radical Islam. Secondly, - and this was of particular interest during the symposium debate on globalization - he analyses the tension between the forces of political Islam and those that control and dominate the contemporary global system. He characterizes the Muslim world as a dynamic, rapidly changing, but politically, economically and geographically non-integrated group of mainly Third World states and globally scattered communities, which sees itself confronted with aggressive capitalist expansion that goes hand-in-hand with the spreading of Western organization, management and consumption patterns. The author explains that the West, led by the US, is not simply globalizing capitalism as a mode of production but trying to export it as a whole value system. This "concept of transculturalization" encounters resistance from both radical and liberal Muslims. Their response to globalization and cultural homogenization is viewed by the author as a strong desire to preserve the roots of their own world vision, their own value system and, in consequence, global diversity.

Leonard Harding discusses the effect of global processes on Africa from a historical perspective. Global influences over a longer period of history are, in his opinion, responsible for the failure of the nation state project in Africa at the time of independence. He exemplifies this failure by referring to two recent developments in Africa: the overthrow of President Mobuto and its aftermath in the former Zaire and the rise of the Islamic brotherhood of the Murides in Senegal. *Harding* names four major external influences that profoundly determined African history: the penetration of Islam, the Atlantic slave trade, the imposition of colonial rule and, finally, the end of colonialism which exposed African societies to new forms of economic and cultural dependencies and enforced the weakening and disintegration of state power.

At a time, when globalizing forces seem to be weakening the nation state in the countries of the South, *Zoya Hasan* points to the role the state has still to play there in the transformation of society. In her contribution she explores the debate on legal reform by analyzing the changing relationships between the state, the communities, and the women's movement. The controversy over the institution of a uniform civil code (UCC) to replace the existing personal law based on religion is at the centre of the debate. The paper describes the general contours of the UCC debate and stresses the conflicting aspects of secularism and minority identity, of equity, and of cultural difference. In this context, the issue of gender inequality and the status of women has gained in significance. *Zoya Hasan* is concerned with the various ways of conceptionalizing women's rights and puts special emphasis on the role of the state in promoting just gender laws.

Another global phenomenon, the upsurge of religious-based movements in the search for identity, is taken up by *David Taylor*. He analyses the outcome of the Indian parliamentary election in March 1998 that brought the Bharatiya Janata Party (BJP) to power for the first time. In a second step, the author explores the relations between the BJP and Hindu nationalism in India. The electoral victory of the BJP reflects an incremental change within the political system, a change that must be seen in relation to India's position in the process of globalization. The party, frequently characterized as Hindu nationalist, provides a form of identity that tries to blend the appeal of modernity with more traditional ties and networks. *Taylor* takes a closer look at the tradition of Hindu nationalist thinking and stresses that Hindu nationalism, although partly masked by the success of the nationalist movements under Gandhi and Nehru, was already part of the political discourse in India in the mid-nineteenth century.

On the occasion of the fiftieth anniversary of the partition of India, *Mushirul Hasan* examines the memories of a fragmented nation. Writing the history of an event that had a traumatic effect on the whole Indian subcontinent still seems to be dominated by community or religious-based discourses. The author pleads for a new approach that draws upon the intellectual resources made available by creative writers. By focusing on the human misery of all people involved, literature accomplishes to defeat the urge to lay blame, which keeps animosity alive. An analysis of partition and its consequences should be possible without drawing on religion or a particular community as the principal point of reference.

The role of religion in providing identity and a community feeling in a fast-changing world is also taken up by *Klaus Sagaster*. He analyses the relationship between religion and group identity in present-day Mongolia. Mongolians live not only in the Republic of Mongolia but also in Inner Mongolia, one of the five Autonomous Regions of the People's Republic of China, as well as in the Republic of Buryatia and the Kalmuck Republic, both of which are part of Russia. The author describes them as a numerically small people who share vast territories belonging to different states with other ethnic groups. He explores how the Mongols try to counteract the threats to Mongolian identity - language, culture, and religion. He emphasizes the increasing role of religion, notably of Buddhism, and the reactivated tradition of Genghis Khan as being important factors of identity-building.

The historical dimension of global action and reaction is again taken up by *Amr Hamzawy*. The author scoured Egyptian sources and mass media for examples. Comparing different events in Egyptian history, he demonstrates the perception of foreign threats to authentic values. First of all, he looks at the French expedition to Egypt and the reactions to it by al-Azhar scholars. He refers to al-Gabarti describing al-Azhar as the weapon of the Islamic *umma* against the Christians. Secondly, he analyses the attitude of the Egyptian media towards Satanism in 1997. He concludes that in rare unanimity the media of all persuasions - government and opposition, liberal and conservative – regarded it as a Western phenomenon which had permeated Egyptian society. Finally, *Hamzawy* describes the "romantic dream" of many Egyptians as a result of the love affair between Lady Diana and Doudi al-Fayed, which ended with their deaths in an accident in Paris. He analyses the subsequent press campaign and explores local perceptions which gradually purified Doudi and his partly westernized family, absorbed Diana into a local context, and presumed a Western conspiracy against both protagonists.

The impact of global, especially modern influences on religious tradition in Egypt is the concern of *Armando Salvatore*. He discusses the change in the perception of the religious norm, šarī^{c}a, effected by the modernization of state rule and the emergence of a modern press and a modern public sphere. The changing perception of šarī^{c}a demonstrates, on the one hand, global influences in the national context. On the other hand, the activities of reformers cannot simply be characterized as a local response to globalization. They are, as the author stresses, the result of balance and mediation between the global and the local. Therefore, the reform of šarī^{c}a constitutes a rewriting and reactivating of indigenous traditions in new guises under altered global conditions.

The theme of the global and the local is also taken up by *David B. Coplan*. He describes how the ongoing debate among the people of Lesotho in southern Africa on whether to remain an independent state or to support integration into South Africa, where many Basotho live and work, has raised the question of national identity. The author retraces the development of Basotho identity. He points out that the issue of national identity emerged in the context of Lesotho's involvement in the European colonial political economy. Labour migrancy, mostly to the South African mines, became a significant feature of the country's social and economic life and was, to a large extent, instrumental in defining Basotho identity.

Jean-Luc Vellut deals with the notion of space in the context of different historical stages of globalization. His historiographical paper elaborates on the changing interpretations of spatial concepts in the course of Central African history from the ancient period to the postcolonial era. His aim is to pinpoint significant instances where notions of space have played a structuring role in the major historical processes at work in vast parts of Africa.

Some authors explored individual cultural traits or studied debates which resulted from contacts with the West. Their research results demonstrate the intricacy with which external influences were appropriated and converted to an integral part of one's own culture. *Annemarie Hafner* presents a case study of the textile workers' life in colonial Bombay. The paper deals with the impact of colonial expansion and the capitalist mode of production on the social and economic life of Indian workers in general and the development of a "workers' culture" in particular. The interplay of global and local factors in shaping the workers' life is exemplified by two aspects: firstly, the regulation of working conditions by the introduction of factory legislation in accordance with international law, and, secondly, the changes in the workers' daily routine demonstrated by new food habits and new leisure occupations such as visits to the cinema. Dealing with the development of a specific "workers' culture" the author refers to the Indian workers' sense of belonging to the international workers movement, as expressed in the first May Day celebrations in India in 1923.

K.N. Panikkar's essay explores the complex problem of tradition, legitimacy and power in colonial India in the light of the "great shoe question". He investigates the controversies which resulted from the shoe regulation of 1854. Introduced under colonial rule, this regulation required the Indian population to take off their shoes on entering public places such as Government offices or judicial courts. Indians wearing European shoes were exempt. It was strongly contested by the Indians who regarded it as an infringement of their cultural rights. Whereas the British argued that the demand for "shoe respect" was not a colonial innovation but a traditional cultural practice, the Indians denied any uniform practice in this matter and highlighted the plurality of their tradition. *Panikkar* elucidates the mechanisms behind the shoe regulation and convincingly interprets British claims for participation in a traditional practice as part of the larger political project of colonial rule to appropriate indigenous tradition in order to legitimize its own power.

Last but not least, *Nicole van Os* looks into Ottoman women's quest for a national dress as a reaction to the economic and cultural intrusion of the West. In her essay she explains how Ottoman women's dress gave expression to their changing world views. During the nineteenth century, the Ottoman Empire was dominated by "modern" European states. Both civilians and the military demonstrated their sense of belonging to the modern world by wearing European dress. At the time, Ottoman women were attracted to Parisian fashion. However, growing resistance to foreign domination and internal despotism resulted in a political revolution and the search for a new identity, a modern, independent nation state. Ottoman women now felt the need to wear national dress and began a lengthy discourse on its design.

These individual contributions are followed by a summary of the Round Table discussion which concluded the symposium with a wide-ranging, controversial, but stimulating exchange of views on its general theme.

In a brief epilogue *Ulrich Haarmann* summarizes the reactions to globalization phenomena in non-Western countries as they emerged in the papers and became transparent in the deliberations at the symposium. He suggests accepting both the absence of any uniformity in the contributions and the controversial nature of the discussion as an intrinsic attribute of our subject and an incentive for future study.

The editorial team wishes to thank all scholars who participated in the symposium and those who contributed papers to the present volume. We express our gratitude to the colleagues at the Centre for Modern Oriental Studies who took the trouble of organizing the symposium. Finally we are indepted to Margret Liepach for the technical preparation of the volume.

Katja Füllberg-Stolberg, Petra Heidrich, Ellinor Schöne

Notes

1 Anthony Giddens, The Consequences of Modernity, Cambridge 1990, p. 64.
2 Roland Robertson, Globalization: Social Theory and Global Culture, London et.al. 1992, p. 8.
3 Anthony Giddens, Ibid.
4 Arjun Appadurai, Disjuncture and Difference in the Global Cultural Economy. In: Mike Featherstone (ed.), Global Culture. Nationalism, Globalization and Modernity, London 1994 (repr.), p. 307.
5 Bryan S. Turner, Orientalism, Postmodernism and Globalism, London-New York 1994.

Globalization, Modernity and the Nation State[1]

Shalini Randeria

Globalization appears to be rather like an Indian goddess: multifaceted and polyvalent with its shape, imagined according to one's desire and fears. For a start, it seems to me important to distinguish analytically between three different uses of the term "globalization"
- as a descriptive category subsuming a plurality of interwoven processes (some of which may, or may not be, all that new);
- as a new political rhetoric usually used to justify unwelcome policy shifts (e.g. the Indonesian Minister for Development who proclaimed in 1994, " No one can resist globalization in the area of infrastructures, it is like a war: kill or be killed"), or to stress one's superiority (e.g. the German politician, Edmund Stoiber, who emphasized last year that Bavaria with its unique combination of lap-tops and "Lederhose" was best equipped to deal with the challenges of globalization); and
- as a new paradigm in the social sciences which is replacing modernization theory.

As a descriptive term globalization refers to complex multidimensional processes of increasing transnational movement of capital, goods and people; closer ties via new communication technologies; a more complex international division of labour as a result of the dispersal of the production of goods and services to several different locations; a rapid spread of ideas and images as well as of patterns and objects of consumption; a growing awareness of risks and dangers that threaten the world as a whole; an increase in the number and importance of transnational institutions and globally interlinked political movements. The concept seeks to capture the interpenetration of these processes both horizontally and vertically at national, subnational and supranational levels.

Continuity or Disjuncture?

The trajectories and the impact of various processes of economic, political, legal and cultural globalization vary considerably in different regions of the world which have been in various ways asymmetrically integrated to different degrees into the capitalist world system since the sixteenth century. Interestingly, most of the sociological debates on globalization and modernity in their Northerncentrism overlook the historical continuities between colonialism and globalization in most countries of the South. They are, therefore, unable to analyse what is specifically new about the current global (inter)dependence.

In the academic domain opinion is divided on the issue of whether there is a historical continuity between processes of modernization and globalization. In contradistinction to Robertson[2] and Giddens[3], Martin Albrow in his recent book *The Global Age*[4] (the very title is chosen to contrast with the modern age), has argued that globalization is a requiem for modernity. Or, to put it otherwise, the ghost of modernization theory must be exorcised from debates about globalization.

Theories of modernity strongly reflect the particular experience of successful Western nation states. Rather than regarding globalization as an outcome of modernity as Giddens does, Robertson sees modernity as resulting from globalization. Neither, however, analyses the centrality of colonialism and imperialism in both processes. Featherstone recognizes that these theories are now being interrogated and from the point of view of societies outside Europe, these theories assumed to be universal may be seen as merely those of a "dominant particular". However, when Featherstone and Lash in their introduction to *Global Modernities*[5] claim that globalization can be regarded as the "triumph of the universal" and "an outcome of the universal logic of modernity", it sounds familiar to Northerncentric, especially as it is only the experience of Japan which is mentioned subsequently as highlighting the limitations of western-derived experiences and "particulars".

Jan Nederseen Pieterse[6] has argued against this view of globalization as universalizing, and more or less explicitly postulated as homogenizing, by regarding it as virtually synonymous with hybridization and the emergence of new heterogeneities. Anthony King[7] goes a step further when he argues that the new diversities, post-modern complexities and contradictions of Paris, London or Berlin can only be understood with reference to the global relations and modes of production embracing the colonies but with these cities at their core.

Similar to modernity's self-representation as a radical rupture from "tradition", globalization, both as an empirical phenomenon and as a new social science paradigm, is represented by many authors as a disjuncture from modernity. Modernization theory, it is argued, focused on the dimension of time, whereas globalization focuses on space; unlike the former which was normative and characterized by directionality, unilinearity and a teleological conception of progress, the latter is not. These Euro-American discourses which tend to celebrate globalization and represent it as having neither a centre nor directionality usually have cultural globalization rather than economic processes of liberalization in mind. Moreover, rather than postulate a plurality of interests in and perspectives on globalization processes which should lead one to analyze the positionality of various discourses on them, these authors tend to assume an archemedian point from which the totality of global phenomena can be captured.

Plurality of Perspectives

From the point of view of most countries of the South, the contemporary dynamics of these processes, and the political debates in their wake are a result of the deliberate pursuit of neo-liberal economic policies (beginning with Reaganomics and Thatcherism) and a fundamentalist ideology of the free market imposed through the IMF-World Bank programmes of structural adjustment to which different governments in the South have complied more or less willingly. Seen from the perspective of social movements and NGOs in most post-colonial societies, economic globalization, in particular, seems to be a recolonization of the present and a colonization of the future. So that globalization in their view represents post-colonial continuities rather than being a promising break into an exciting future.

But even within the periphery, there is a plurality of perspectives. For example, at a meeting of South Asian NGOs in 1997, for Indian NGOs the centre of economic and political power in the era of neo-liberal globalization remained in the West. For NGOs from Nepal and Bangladesh, however, the centre of "global" hegemony continued to be India. None of the South Asian NGOs shared the perception of a shift in economic power to the Asian-Pacific region, whose spectacular (if in retrospect short-lived) economic ascendancy is postulated in many Northern discourses on globalization as evidence of a decentred, or at least a polycentred, world.

But even within a country like India the contrast between diametrically opposed discourses on globalization could not be greater. For the class which trades in futures at national and international stock markets, liberalization is welcome as a challenge to corrupt and inefficient state structures and seen as a chance to participate in an increasingly global consumer and media culture. Whereas for small and middle peasants (e.g. those who have been burning down the experimental fields of the transnational agriculture giant Monsanto in India in early 1999) the latest WTO policies on trade liberalization mean a loss of livelihood and a threat to their very survival. For the one, the Indian state is too protectionist and not committed enough to privatization. For the other, it has liberalized too quickly and too much and has failed to protect the interests of its most vulnerable citizens who have been doubly hit by the withdrawal of agricultural subsidies and the dismantling of health and education services. Under pressure from the IMF and World Bank many of these services have been left to service-delivery NGOs dependent both on external donors and the Indian state through which these foreign funds are often channelled. It is, therefore, important to stress the differences in the nature, perception and interpretation of these processes which are neither unilinear nor uniform either across the globe or within societies.

The Dynamics of the Nation State

In the North and the South the nation state has been weakened and restructured in the process of globalization. However, not only has the loss of political and legal sovereignty as well as economic independence been much greater in the South, it has also meant an abject dependence on the IMF and World Bank in addition to transnational corporations and global financial markets. Since the conditionalities on which IMF credits are given are neither made public nor are they subject to legislative approval in the country concerned, these developments have eroded the legitimacy of the nation state even further. For example, the Brazilian government had introduced a highly innovative tax on financial transactions at the national level, based on the model of the Tobin-Tax and was using the huge revenue thus gained for a free health care system. After the 1998 financial crisis, it was forced to seek an IMF loan. One of the conditionalities imposed by the IMF was to substantially increase the amount of the tax which was no longer to be used for the health sector. It is remarkable that it is these very institutions which simultaneously propagate the virtues of democratization, decentralization, good governance and participatory development. Interestingly, these institutions are not keen to apply the framework of democracy internationally to their own working.

But it would be a mistake to conclude from examples such as these that there has been a weakening of the nation state and its sovereignty in all areas. If one looks at international migration, it becomes apparent that nation states remain powerful and are likely to continue to be able to legally and politically defend their territorial sovereignty. Of course, it could be argued that the very presence of so many refugees, asylum seekers, undocumented workers etc. reflects that nation states are not able to protect their boundaries as they would ideally like to in theory and in practice. However, an application of Ulrich Beck's concept of "world risk society"[8] to this phenomenon shows the differential risks of migrants, refugees and tourists. Only tourists, who face the minimum of risks among all the categories of people crossing international borders, are insured against them. The rights of refugees, asylum seekers, undocumented workers who are among the most vulnerable international border-crossers are protected the least by the international human rights regime. For, as a matter of principle, the sovereignty of the nation state is given priority over the protection of individual human rights of those migrating or seeking asylum.

As Saskia Sassen[9] has pointed, out the economic and political dimensions of globalization are closely intertwined in that most international migration has taken place, and continues to take place, between countries which were either linked through colonialism or military ties since 1945. Interestingly, however, the discourse on migration and that on economic globalization bear little resemblance to one another. The flow of persons across the nation states boundaries continues to be conceptualised in terms of citizenship, labour market and territorial sovereignty of states, if not the supposed ethnic purity of nations. Whereas the discourse on the transnational flow of goods and capital is in terms of the freedom of movement, economic rationality of investments and profit maximization. The arguments for removing barriers to the unhindered movement of capital flows is not applied to the movement of people.

The entire neo-liberal rhetoric of non-intervention by the state resulted in fact in a massive state intervention in most countries of the South in favour of global capital. It is not as if the nation state in these regions has been weakened per se. What has taken place is a restructuring of the state in order to weaken it vis-à-vis the interests of capital but not against labour. International institutions like IMF and the World Bank, as well as the entire UN system, need states which are strong enough to push through neo-liberal agendas in their respective countries and to keep in check the popular protests against these reforms. Rather than regarding globalization as a zero-sum game (more globalization means less of the nation state), it is important, therefore, to analyse differences in the processes of restructuring the nation state in different areas and its differential local impact. In the wake of these developments NGOs in many countries of the South are caught in a dilemma. Previously severe critics of the nation state, today some have turned into its defenders, needing a relatively strong state to mitigate the negative impact of liberalization policies on the poor. From being watch-dogs of the state, others have turned into its lap-dogs, receiving as sub-contractors international funding channelized often through the state and taking over the provision of services which are being privatized as part of structural adjustment programmes.

Cultural Globalization

In the conference many aspects of the processes of cultural globalization or rather "glocalization" (Ronald Robertson) have been discussed involving an analysis of the complex, and often contradictory, processes of integration and fragmentation, deterritorialization and reterritorialization, homogenization as well as heterogenization. I would just like to focus on aspects of the global flow of ideas and the production as well as consumption of global discourses in different localities and within transnational discourse coalitions (e.g. those of the human rights movement, indigenous peoples movement, but also fundamentalist movements or neo-liberal discourses).

Cultural gobalization does not imply the levelling of differences. On the contrary, it may even lead to an increase in differences at the local level. What is interesting, however, is the processes by which these differences are translated into a uniform global discourse of differences. So that cultural globalization in this context may be seen as the hegemony which enables the production of a common discourse which sets the agenda, determines what can be said or cannot, privileging certain perspectives and marginalizing others. It is the power to define the categories and standards to be applied universally according to which cultural differences world-wide may be perceived. Developmental discourses on ecology or population policy are good examples which illustrate my argument.

It is interesting in this context to trace the trajectories of concepts like "empowerment", "participation", "partnership", "sustainable development" or "reproductive health". These words are illustrative of what Ivan Ilich has called "amoeba words", words which can change their meaning and function according to context and which, therefore, enable quick international consensus despite differences of interests between nation states or between states, NGOs and international institutions. The concept of "empowerment", for example, was introduced into the global discourse on development by women's NGOs from the South who belong to the transnational network DAWN (Development Alternatives with Women for a New Era). Its rapid spread in all international and national documents shows that the vocabulary of development today does not come exclusively from the North or from the UN system. The concept was created as an alternative to a rather narrow western-liberal idea of equal rights and was originally intended to designate both the transformation of gender relations and of the social structures in which they are embedded. In the process of its long march through development institutions, donor agencies, the UN system, its very success has depoliticized it and undermined its emancipatory potential so that every institution may use it according to its own interests and continue business as usual.

Transnational Discourses

The problem of the translation of local social and cultural differences into a common global discourse become evident when we consider the "Chipko-movement" in the Himalayan region of India. In the international women's and ecology movements, this protest by poor peasants against the felling of trees by the state and industry is regarded to reflect the closeness of women (especially in the South) to nature and is used to empirically substantiate the eco-feminist position. One of the reasons for the global success of this discourse is that it offers an interpretative grid which can be globally used irrespective of context. It allows the specific experiences and struggles of Indian peasant women (or indigenous people in other parts of the world) to be translated into the language of a critique of patriarchy and technology emanating from sections of the western women's movements. The reception of local "ecology movements" at the regional, national and international level is possible through a series of translations by journalists, activists, NGOs and academics. In order to subsume the Chipko-movement under the idea of "feminist-ecological" movements, the messy local reality of diverse, often contradictory, discourses by a variety of different actors has to be homogenised through selection and idealisation of some of them.

The existence of two transnational discourse coalitions which are diametrically opposed to one another can also be studied with reference to the issue of population. The international women's movement is split on this question, a split which does not reflect a North-South polarization. There is a fundamental difference of opinion which centres on the question of whether "overpopulation" exists as a phenomenon and consequently as a problem. On the one side are those who believe the world is really "overpopulated" and this constitutes one of the most important global challenges to be solved through policies to reduce population ranging from state intervention to women's empowerment. On the other side are those who believe that the so-called "over-population" is a fiction based on ever changing arguments and standards throughout the last couple of centuries which has been used by nation states to legitimize a variety of political measures. In its most recent version this construct has acquired a global dimension, "global overpopulation" being postulated as a global challenge and hence a global responsibility. Feminists who radically oppose population policies point out that despite this change in the reference system, a fundamental dichotomy continues unchanged: there are two kinds of people in the one world - those in the North who are "diminishing" and those in the South who are "too many".

The international consensus formed at the UN-Cairo conference on "Population and Development" tried to steer a reform course between these two positions. Heralded as a historic landmark which signalled a paradigm shift in population policies from "demographic goals to democratic participation" and from policies driven by numbers to those sensitive to needs, it introduced the new buzz word "reproductive health" coined by US feminists. But one problem with this attempt to homogenize the discourse on population, and to reform the policies by providing them with a human face, became immediately apparent at Cairo. The term was translated into German to begin with as "Gesundheit der Fortpflanzung" before one settled on the cumbersome and nebulous "reproduktive Gesundheit". In Chinese it was translated as "man and women having a holiday on a farm" and the one-child policy continued, though now as a voluntary policy, as the Chinese government has since then been at pains to point out.

Critical Outlook

In the "global village" there are hardly any global answers. With the rise of "disorganised capitalism" (Lash and Urry[10]), there has been an increased interest in the "local" as the space of emancipation and of resistance. But how much autonomy does the local have in global capitalism? What would a "critical localism" (Arif Dirlik[11]) look like, or a "critical traditionalism" (Ashis Nandy[12]), if it were to steer clear of the dangers of romanticising a pre-modern past while wedded to the idea of social and cultural plurality and the 'local' as the space from which alternative visions of the future and alternative public spheres would emerge.

I am as sceptical of the "meta-narrative" of "globalization" as I was of that of "modernization". Both meta-narratives claim to have a universality which neglects the subjectivity of those affected by these processes and are, therefore, not in a position to conceptualize their agency. The problem with many forms of local protest and resistance to globalization which are being celebrated in many post-modern discourses is that though they struggle against western hegemony and capitalist oppression, they leave untouched indigenous and internal forms of inequality and discrimination. Transnational networks of NGOs and social movements with innovative forms of transnational action are important in this context as they contribute to a "contra-hegemonial globalization", to use Boaventura de Sousa Santo's term[13].

Notes

1   Many of the arguments on globalization here have been discussed in detail in my Globalisierung und Geschlechterfrage: Zur Einführung. In: Ruth Klingebiel/Shalini Randeria (eds.), Globalisierung aus Frauensicht. Bilanzen und Visionen, Bonn 1998, and those on the nation-state have been developed with reference to India in my paper on Vorbild Europa oder eigener Weg? Demokratie und Nationalstaat in Indien. In: Epd-Entwicklungspolitik (1997) 15/16.
2   Roland Robertson, Globalization: Social Theory and Global Culture, London 1992.
3   Anthony Giddens, The Consequences of Modernity, Stanford, Ca., 1990.
4   Martin Albrow, The Global Age: State and Society Beyond Modernity, Stanford, Ca., 1997.

5   Mike Featherstone/Scott Lash/Roland Robertson (eds.), Global Modernities, London et al. 1995 (reprint 1997), p. 2.
6   Jan Nederseen Pieterse, Globalization as Hybridization. In: Ibid., pp. 45-68.
7   Anthony D. King, The Times and Spaces of Modernity (or Who Needs Post-modernism?. In: Ibid., pp. 108-123.
8   Ulrich Beck, Weltrisikogesellschaft, Weltöffentlichkeit und globale Subpolitik, Wien 1997.
9   Saskia Sassen, Migration, Siedler, Flüchtlinge: Von der Massenauswanderung zur Festung Europa, Frankfurt/M. 1996.
10 S. Lash/J. Urry, Economies of Signs and Space, London 1994.
11 Arif Dirlik, The Global in the Local. In: Rob Wilson/Wimal Dissanayake (eds.), Global/Local. Cultural Production and the Transnational Imaginary, Durham-London 1996, pp. 21-45.
12 Ashis Nandy, Traditions, Tyranny, and Utopias: Essays in the Politics of Awareness, Delhi 1987.
13 Boaventura de Sousa Santos, Toward a New Common Sense: Law, Science and Politics in the Paradigmatic Transition, New York 1995.

Globalization in Historical Perspective

Joachim Heidrich

Globalization and global society have become widely used key concepts in recent years. As a corollary, endeavours have been made since the nineties to evolve an adequate methodology for analysing the contemporary reality, which the terms signify. Globalization as a paradigm is currently occupying the centre stage of the general political debate as well as of the scholarly discussion of current affairs conducted by representatives of various disciplines of human sciences.[1] Globalization at the conceptual level has meanwhile been recognised as a "fully 'emerged' theory in social sciences"[2]. Until now the subject of globalization has chiefly been the domain of sociology, and representatives of the discipline so far contributed the bulk to the already large body of relevant literature. Historians play a minor part in the debate. This paper emphasises the historical perspective of the matter. The historical approach, in the opinion of the author, focuses equally on a multifaceted contemporary and ongoing process and should not be interpreted in a reductionist manner as an attempt to merely study chronological antecedents or early stages of what is generally understood today by the term globalization.

The theme of the symposium accentuates the cultural and historical dimensions of the phenomenon at the ground level. Hence, the issues to be addressed centre chiefly on the images of the global as perceived in the experience of the local. The dialectic between identity, locality and globalization occupies a place of priority of any such deliberation – at least by implication. Globalization has been conceived as "a deeply historical, uneven, and even *localizing* process" of a long duration.[3] The complexity of the socio-cultural dimensions of globalization provokes and facilitates a multiplicity of approaches and interpretations. Basically, it is the nature and dimension of the current changes – social and cultural – that constitute the core issue. Its worldwide dimensions at various levels and its continuity posed a challenge to hitherto applied methods and gave rise to fresh attempts to tackle the reality. The consequences were far-reaching. The prevailing conceptual framework of endeavours to study social change in present-day conditions ascribes greater centrality to global *flows* – in mediascapes, ethnoscapes, financescapes and technoscapes, as Appadurai put it –, then to *national institutions*. Rejecting a "tradition which was strongly influenced by the process of nation state formation", the proponents of the attitude cited even conclude: "A central implication of the concept of globalization is that we must now embark on the project of understanding social life without the term 'society'."[4] The issue has been put against the specific background of the present "Third World" countries, i.e., posed in the context of the transition from colonialism to transnationalism. The problem then boils down to the question as to how today's global configuration of power and culture "is both similar and different vis-à-vis the historical metropolitan–colonial paradigm"[5]. The frequently quoted dictum "all that is solid melts into the air" which governs the present agenda poses a challenge to any attempt at reconceptualizing globalization from the viewpoint of the historian. This state of affairs in conjunction with the fact that a wide range of issues is currently subsumed under the category of globalization in the theoretical debate necessitates a few preliminary observations.

Globalization is chiefly used as an umbrella concept, and no monolithic definition of globalization is available. And yet, a certain commonality of the perception of the term exists. Those who may subscribe to rather diverse views otherwise will probably agree to perceive globalization as a multitude of ongoing processes of socio-economic, political and cultural internationalisation, which create an impact on national, regional, or local structures, and thereby distinguish themselves as a constitutive factor in constructing identities at various levels. One could further presuppose a certain agreement among scholars to look at the actual identities, localities and institutions that constitute the topics of investigation as mainly present-day constructions, composed of the cultural heritage available for political or personal reasons. There appears to be, however, a general reluctance among those who deal with aspects of globalization to address the question whose globalization it is, which classes, groups or gender are primarily affected or passed by. Relevant deliberations frequently tend to treat globalization in the abstract or at the sociological macro-level. On the other hand, there is an inclination to discuss concrete issues, which have been identified as manifestations of globalization in isolation from their social and historical environment. The situation calls for increased efforts to relink the globalization process with history when enquiries into rethinking the notion of globalization are made. In addition, more attention should probably be devoted to contextualize individual topics which are taken up for investigation by relating them to their respective social and historical fabric, in order to establish a sound basis for a meaningful comparison (including cross-cultural and transcontinental ones) of otherwise seemingly disconnected phenomena. The first prerequisite to accomplish the task of building up an appropriate conceptual framework would be to achieve a shared understanding of the premises involved. This brings me to the first point I would like to make. What do we actually mean when we talk about globalization?

I

The term globalization was initially used to identify the dynamics and perspectives of new economic factors and trends, i.e., of a new stage of globalizing capitalism. Outside the academic discourses, globalization is still mainly perceived as expansion of the free market economy and economic liberalisation. Globalization was, however, soon applied to a new stage of global interaction and exchange, to the intensification of global social relations, which brought about a close network interlinking distant localities. Simultaneously, *"[l]ocal transformation* is as much a part of globalization as the lateral extension of social connections across time and space"[6]. The same author identifies two kinds of "actors" in the new set-up: Whereas nation states are the principal actors within the global political order, corporations are the dominant agents within the world economy.[7] The emphasis is placed somewhat differently by the supporters of the view that anticipates the practical possibility of the emergence of a global society, which is imagined to be "borderless" and would overarch the older structures and institutions of the nation state. The institution of the nation state as a concept and as a historical reality has become a bone of contention. The debate on its continuing validity or its likely replacement by what is called civil society was brought to the fore also – as an unintended side effect – in the course of the much highlighted neo-liberal restructuring which is accompanied by the functional demise or retreat of the role of the state. Hence, the issue figures prominently in the literature on development problems.

For the limited purpose of this paper, a set of assumptions may be established as preliminary point of departure:
The term globalization is indicative of a new period in time;
1. Globalization as a concept points to a qualitatively new process of transnationalisation or internationalisation, brought about by new technologies which compress time and space.
The term connotes the institutionalisation of universal values.
2. Globalization as a comprehensive process acts as a vehicle of two contradictory trends: on the one hand, it tends to bring about a global economy, to establish transnational or global political structures, to universalise cultural elements and value systems, and, on the other hand, it simultaneously unleashes new nationalisms, political separatisms and strengthens perceptions of cultural individuality and otherness.

Economy and culture are currently the most affected and debated domains. The debate surfaced within the realms of systems theory and international relations. But meanwhile globalization has become a general frame of reference for all sorts of transnational events or transitional processes; it now even serves as a fundamental reference point for assessing intra-national transformations or for establishing policy concepts which aim at a deliberate transition or change of structures and institutions, in order to up-date the internal economic or political set-up (like economic and political liberalisation, democratisation of governance, "empowerment" of people). "The metaphors of globalization are also emerging at the centre of contemporary political discourses, and they are different from the Cold War metaphors of containment, peaceful co-existence, mutually assured destruction, and détente."[8] The termination of the East-West confrontation subsequent to the demise of the socialist super-power strengthened a strongly biased perception of globalization. The supposedly final elimination of a systemic alternative to capitalism and the subsequent equation of globalization (including the ongoing transitions in a number of former socialist countries) with the rapid onward march of the capitalist mode and its accompanying set of values on a world scale, revitalised the idea of a basically unilinear movement in history, even though the actual experience frequently contradicts such a simplified assessment. Closely linked to the attitude and informed by similar arguments was the idea of the final emergence of a unipolar world system – an idea that meets with a strong resistance from a considerable section of Third World intellectuals and politicians.

In common usage the term globalization carries the notion of an objective process that is about to usher in a new global order or a new system of global interaction at the levels of countries, peoples, and cultures. Because of its frequent and often rather indiscriminate use to describe all sorts of things one cannot escape the impression of an overstretching of the concept of globalization: it has meanwhile been elevated to the rank of another universalistic theory. In fact, globalization now seems to emerge as a substitute of earlier "grand theories" or metanarratives which, according to one strong opinion trend, are supposedly and deservedly on their way out. Although the contributors to the debate are inclined to take for granted the reality, features and meanings of globalization as a combination of irreversible processes, there are still competing interpretations of the concept. Despite its general acceptance, the term globalization continues to be understood differently by different people. It is, in fact, not a neutral term. "As a concept, globalization does not evoke a single image but rather an imagery of disparate meanings."[9] It is, as Aijaz Ahmed opines, "a highly ideological word and as such actually refers to quite a few things"[10]. This is particularly valid in regard to the assessment of the nature of the globalization process, its sources and its consequences in the so-called Third World or, more particularly, in the developing countries of Asia and Africa. A broad spectrum of phenomena observable in those regions is being subsumed under the caption of globalization. The state of affairs necessitates all the more the contextualization of the concrete situations described by it, in order to make the term a meaningful tool of cognition and to facilitate cross-cultural comparison, without allowing the contextual analysis to suggest a uniqueness or individualisation of the particular topic dealt with.

II

One influential school of "history-informed" thought visualises globalization as a correlate to modernity. If we accept this premise - and I am inclined to do so - then we would have to agree on a certain chronological frame within which phenomena occur that can be subsumed under the caption of globalization. Corresponding with the diverse explanations of the concept, opinions regarding the timing of globalization differ considerably.[11] Globalization is not a process merely of the present, but clearly has its roots in the past. "Modern" in conventional and Eurocentric understanding indicates a period and a discourse that had pre-eminence between the Renaissance or Reformation and the early twentieth century. Yet, in substance, the globalization process in a qualitative sense was basically linked to the transnationalisation of the capitalist mode of production as its trend-setting and major driving force. The process originated in (Western) Europe and implied the establishing of European or Western hegemony over large parts of the world not only in terms of economic preponderance or political domination. The universalising trend which stemmed from European Enlightenment thinking and which accompanied the emerging process of globalization also encompassed the extension of Western concepts, values and institutions - or, for that matter, European culture - beyond the boundaries of the area where it originated. It was subsequently imposed on peoples with a different cultural background. In chronological terms, the trend assumed universal dimensions in the aftermath of the industrial revolution in the late eighteenth century, from which it drew considerable sustenance, and in the wake of setting up modern bourgeois societies in the West which constituted the springboard for ideas of progress and development, freedom and equality of individuals, of a democratic pattern of society and governance, or of a civil society. I am inclined to side with those authors who conceive of universalization and globalization as different historical stages in the emergence and global expansion of capitalism. Is globalization then a "European" affair?

The course of events resulted in consequences which nowadays pose a challenge to scholars, both in writing contemporary history and as a heuristic problem. "The modern" or the period of modernity came to be equated with "the West". Modernisation or transition towards a supposedly higher stage appeared largely as a process of Westernization, or, at least as the necessity to emulate and implement patterns established in and by the "West". The concept was largely equated with development. It suffered from a major shortcoming. The underlying premise was that of a unilinear development from tradition to modernity. For large parts of the non-European world the new era was ushered in through colonialism. This implied establishing interrelations of inequality, but also a gross distortion in practice of ideals held out as fundamentals of a new type of advanced or modern society. In the strict historical sense, capitalist colonialism was as "modern" as the imperialism of the colonializers. At the same time, one cannot bypass an obvious fact. The nation state and the systematic capitalist production "have their roots in specific characteristics of European history and have few parallels in prior periods or in other cultural settings"[12]. Moreover, the very perception of modernity was grounded in the Western experience. The histories of the non-western societies, however, lacked the singular experience of "modernity" based on the European Enlightenment projects. In most cases, colonialism or the "colonial discourse" served as a vehicle for transmitting new ideas and institutions from "the West". The new social structures thus generated contradictions and social tensions, opening possibilities for social movements and ideologies of change. In this connection, elements of a "counter-culture" as a form of protest (to European imperialism and capitalist cosmopolitanism) emerged on the historical stage. The very tendency also provided the ground, at the conceptual level, for evolving a static and stereotyped image of "the other". This sort of foundationalism accompanied the period of colonialism and continues to engage scholars in the phase of so-called postcoloniality. At this stage the debate centred round the issue of an essentialized monolithic stereotype called "East" confronting an essentialized "West" to whom Said erroneously attributed a homogenised view of the Orient. More recently at the theoretical level we witness the rise of an altogether different paradigm of approach to contemporary affairs: the "cultural turn" or the culture-oriented globalization perspective which tends to disjunct the cultural sphere from the events in the socio-political and economic realm. Now "post-modernism licenses an anti-universalistic, indeterminate, decentring and thus relativistic interpretation of social existence, in which no particular identity or political view is – or can ever be – privileged"[13]. If we allow this methodological attitude to prevail, then another sort of reductionism will flourish. The door would be open to merely compare surface phenomena without asking for the historic conditionalities and significance of social or cultural configurations, structures, or social movements and events like revolutions which occurred over different periods of time and in different spatial contexts.

During the earlier phase the example set by the metropolitan countries was recognised as paradigmatic by the modernising forces in non-western countries. Britain in particular – it was after all at the centre of globalization for quite some time because of its dominant role as the leading industrial and commercial world power – constituted an outstanding example in this regard, at least till the early twentieth century. From then onwards a considerable section among the nationalist forces in Asia began searching for an alternative future based on a synthesis of indigenous traditions and such "modern" elements of alien origin which were identified as congenial to the aspirations of the local population. The process, it appears, was repeated with a certain time lag and in slightly modified form in Africa. After World War Two and during the decolonisation phase the earlier "Western" pattern was overlapped or even superseded by the example of the USA who were now looked upon in many of the newly emerging nations as the trend-setters in regard to modernisation. The fact that the USA had once emerged as an independent country from a successful anticolonial revolution was another reason why quite a few leaders of national liberation movements in the middle of the twentieth century tried to emulate the earlier American example.

If a linkage between globalization and modernity and a certain chronological frame were accepted, not every event of translocal dimension in history would then fall into a general category of globalization. Such is to say, for instance, about the spread of cultural traits through the migration of peoples in early periods of human history, about the expansion of Islam from its area of origin to other regions, or the transmission of mathematical knowledge from India to Europe through the Arabs in the early mediaeval age, as well as - more recently - the incorporation of technological knowledge achieved in the industrialised West into the corpus of contemporary learning of an Asian country. The inquiry into the concrete issues will certainly have to satisfy other criteria as well, apart from an equation of globalization with a particular period of time. The investigation should include a study of the varying capacity of the partners and participants of translocal interactions to influence each other. This depends to a large extent on how the actors in the drama were placed at the macro-level. For, "[t]he world is 'one' in some senses, but radically riven by inequalities of power in others"[14]. Similarly, significant events in the history of peoples, like revolutions, which occurred during different periods of time, should not be evaluated as manifestations of the onward march of globalism simply because they evoked transregional or world-wide responses. Their valorisation requires an analysis of whether they ushered in a new order on the spot or merely replaced one regime by another; in other words, whether they resulted in a genuine societal transformation and resulted in social development.

III

The very notion of globalization as an instrument capable of shaping mankind's future – as it is widely understood today - draws heavily on the experiences gained during the prolonged boom or the "Golden Age" of capitalism in the post-Second World War decades. One of the outstanding features of the period consisted in the rapid growth in the transnational operations of capital, which to a large extent obscured the role hitherto played by the nation states in international economic affairs. The nation state appeared to be fast losing its significance as the fundamental base or unit of development in view of the construction of regional communities and the strengthening of international institutions. Simultaneously, a tremendous upsurge in productivity coupled with the rapid increase of the level of mass consumption enabled an institutionalisation of relations between capital and labour in metropolitan countries, i.e., to establish a stable partnership between both, which held out the promise of minimising and finally controlling fundamental social contradictions in society – both at the national as well as at the international level. The image of globalization grew out of such preconditions and thus the factor came to be looked upon as a vehicle for resolving major challenges of the present age, particularly once the sharp international ideological rivalry subsided subsequent to the demise of the East-West confrontation and the end of the Cold War.[15] Those who support the "Golden Age" idea, however, usually bypass the fact that the positive consequences of the development of capitalism were confined to comparatively few advanced industrialised countries, whereas the much highlighted growth with a positive fallout on the social conditions circumvented entire continents. Globalization till today has been primarily a one-sided affair, so far as the sources, the operation of trend-setting forces and the accumulation of benefits are concerned. A contradictory tendency was set in motion: a trend towards establishing an increasingly integrated, yet simultaneously extremely differentiated global society.[16] The expectation of the nation state withering away was not corroborated by the developing countries' continuing need and efforts to utilise the state as an instrument for pursuing national interests. The crisis or breakdown of nation states, on the other hand, obviously fostered nationalism and chauvinistic ideological currents in quite a few places, including East European countries. Towards the latter part of the twentieth century the hitherto predominant imperialist world market has been replaced by the stage of global capitalism. At the conceptual level, it has even been suggested to perceive the present developments as "a complete, radical break, a *qualitative* change, in the historical development of capitalism", which started with the "world economic crisis" in the 1970ties and led to "a major transformation of the way in which production and distribution is organised. There is a new political economy in the making. But, in contrast to the past, this new political economy is not a political economy that first developed and became organised within one specific territorial space and next expanded outward; rather it is a political economy that is global from the very beginning."[17] This has consequences for our understanding not merely of economic issues like the creation of wealth and poverty. The new stage creates new hegemonies, tends to superimpose "global players" on the nation states, to undermine cultural traditions and peculiarities, and provokes resistance to all this while throwing up new contradictions – both at the global and national levels. A critical appraisal of older conceptions, including the Saidian perception of Orientalism, and a fresh perspective on the effects of globalization in the non-economic sphere is, therefore, called for.[18]

The assumption of an intrinsic connection between the process of globalization and the emergence, evolution and spread of capitalism would hardly encounter any serious contradiction. After all, the term globalization itself was originally used to describe the growing economic interdependence of individual countries, economies or regions on a global scale, which created a new network of global interrelationship and interdependence. The debate centres more on the multicausality of globalization and on the question which role other factors play in promoting and shaping its course. As a parallel development, there was the growing realisation of the global impact of negative features, which were capable of endangering the survival of mankind. Among such issues are the deprivation of people and unabated mass poverty in vast areas of the world, the threatening ecological disaster resulting from the consumer-oriented lifestyle in the industrially advanced countries and the population explosion in less developed countries, or the potential of unresolved regional or inter-state conflicts in the Third World for unleashing international confrontations. The concept of globalization became common currency and has been used unhesitatingly particularly since the nineties. It highlights primarily the spectacular globalization of capital in recent decades and the expansion of the capitalist market economy worldwide, which assumed proportions unprecedented in history. In this context, the term commodification has been coined in order to highlight the predominant feature as well as the determining factor which transgressed the boundaries of economics, engulfed all levels of the social and cultural life of the people and penetrated into every nook and cranny of the globe. The rapid spread of transportation and telecommunication facilities or the growth of a largely uniform consumerist culture, occasionally code-named "McDonaldisation", could be pointed out as glaring examples. But this as well as the rapid dissemination of patterns of fashion in clothing or music did not automatically result in a levelling down of cultural diversities. It should, however, be a matter of concern why even in this field patterns developed in countries of the West are usually projected as *the* up-to-date standard of universal validity, whereas certain elements or patterns of fashion derived from non-European/non-North American regions are being singled out as "ethnic" in every-day parlance of Western people, thereby relegating them to a secondary category of exotic stuff. In actual reality, the globalizing tendencies in the realm of culture frequently meet with resistance on the part of the underprivileged in the name of defending the "national" culture - which should not again easily be dismissed as reactionary, i.e., anti-modernist, or sheer reflection of foundational or fundamentalist aspirations. The universalising effect of globalization, particularly manifest as "Americanization", has to be examined as to how it confronts and affects the popular cultures, which are rooted in local communities that stick to their own interpretation of traditions and customs. The subject is charged with political implications, as recent examples of the emergence or re-awakening of ethnic identity consciousness tend to testify. Culture, after all, also surfaced as a political creation ("cultural nationalism") or can be instrumentalized in the pursuance of a political discourse and in the fight for power.

The new trend of development called globalization including its practical aspects like economic liberalisation and the unhindered operation of market forces did not bring about a large-scale harmonisation of either intercontinental, intersocietal, or even intrasocietal relations. Contrary to initial expectations and earlier optimistic forecasts, the gap between the advanced countries of the North and the so-called developing countries in the South widened, while among the Southern group of countries the process of differentiation made rapid strides. New "global players" entered the stage, which determine the direction of globalization and make it a rather one-sided affair. Foremost among the powerful "global players" are multinational corporations and international financial institutions. They are grounded in the economies of the advanced industrialised countries that - as a grouping of states – dominate the international commercial and financial relations. In this context, "global cities" have risen as the new power centres – and they, preferably, constitute the focus of the analyses of ongoing globalization. There is clearly a tendency of subordinating the weaker national economies to the norms set and the prescriptions issued by the "global players". The process involves impinging upon the sovereignty of independent states (for instance, through the imposition of structural adjustment programmes). As experience shows, globalization failed to usher in relations of equity and social justice. On the contrary, the very paradigm of globalization entails competition as a constitutive element that operates within an interactive network of unequals. As a consequence, the spoils are rather differently shared among the participants. The notion of space deserves much more attention in the globalization discussion. After all, locality is not obliterated by globalization. This is of particular relevance for assessing the impact of globalization on societies whose predominantly rural population may experience the negative fall-out from the globalization process in full measure, but are hardly able to take an active part in shaping it.

At the global level ("North-South") as well as at the level of individual countries, globalization has contributed to enhancing social differentiation and polarisation up to a dangerous mark. Empirical data contradict theoretical anticipations or ideals held out. The matter has become a subject of serious dispute, which concerns the very perception of globalization.[19] It would be difficult to imagine how any aspect or manifestation of globalization – whether in the cultural, political or social sphere – could escape the impact of that fundamental constellation in the present-day world. Any student of relevant topics will have to take cognisance of the situation.

IV

Several scholars attribute globalization as a typical feature to the twentieth century. They are inclined to look at it as the major factor for bringing about a genuine global history that tends to establish a global society – as distinguished from the earlier universal history which centred on the transregional and transcontinental interaction of people, cultures and countries and which saw the nation states as the chief agents or major players.[20] Another interpretation which draws both from social theory as well as from the sociological reality emphasizes that the processes of globalization "were set in high motion, reached their crucial phase of take-off, during the period lasting from about 1880 through the first quarter of the twentieth century"[21]. One could, in this connection, also cite as a precursor the opinion of Arnold Toynbee who periodized the beginning of the new age of Western history in the 1870s by locating at this juncture as simultaneous events the globalization of Western culture and the re-empowerment of non-western states.[22] The concept parallels the interpretation which established a coincidence between the crisis of hegemony of the West and the beginning of the use of Western and indigenous symbols by "people without history" to construct their own identity-spaces. In contrast, authors who favour the world-system's attitude perceive of globalization as a continuous process, which encompasses the past five centuries. They are not prepared to demarcate the establishment of transcontinental links or transcultural interaction and the configuration of universal relations since the age of Columbus and Vasco da Gama on the one hand, from the recent process of globalization, on the other. Yet even they concede a distinction. Representatives of the latter view while tracing the impact of globalizing forces across various centuries acknowledge that globalization being a complex process, assumed different forms at different times, and brought about rather different results in the core areas and in peripheral regions of an emerging world system.[23] Even authors who are critical about the current inflationary use of the very term globalization and who prefer to relate the phenomena understood by it straight to the rise of capitalism and its overseas expansion since the late fifteenth century, single out the "transnationalisation of economic life (as) one of the major developments in the late twentieth century"[24].

Should we not strive to be more precise when applying the term globalization, particularly when we talk about its manifestations in the non-economic spheres in the Asian and African context? How could we accommodate the problem in view of what a specialist of European history considers a major challenge to social history writing in the now outgoing century? Jürgen Kocka singled out the comparison of European and non-European societies as an urgent task facing scholars, particularly because of the prevailing sceptical attitude regarding the universal validity of the "project of occidental modernity"[25]. While pronouncing such doubts he obviously had in mind the rather different and even contradictory consequences which resulted from the process of modernisation in the area of its origin or in the peripheral regions of the world, respectively, as well as the differing perceptions of those historic events in the West and the East (or South, for that matter). One would be mistaken to delineate the trajectory of globalization in isolation and out of context of the forces that ushered in modernity as well as those later situations which now go by the labels of the postmodern and the postcolonial. The issue converges with questions raised during the debate on Orientalism. Hence, any attempt to tackle the issue will simultaneously have to examine the propriety or limitations of the cognitive tools hitherto used. The different levels on which globalization currently proceeds in the countries of those continents as well as the various manifestations it assumes in particular historical circumstances will have to be studied more closely.

V

Globalization perceived as a historical category links the present not merely with the past but also with the future. Recent studies authored by political scientists and devoted to the future of globalization usually emphasise the growing interdependence among nation states and focus on the increasing interaction at the social level between peoples on a global scale which is expected to promote the gradual emergence or building-up of a "global society". Some even fancy the vision of a "global civil society". But here we again enter an arena where diverse attitudes and arguments compete with each other.

Do we have to perceive globalization as a universal phenomenon which is distinguished by certain general features and which is capable of accomplishing similar results everywhere? Some authors use the term globalization without hesitation to describe current social and political transformations which recently assumed world-wide dimensions, for instance, the advance of democratic political systems and forms of governance. Democratisation has even been attributed as a corollary to development. In addition, cultural or civilizational criteria have been roped in. Even though there is a common agreement on the comparatively independent nature of such processes, a certain interlinkage with the ongoing technological and economic globalization cannot be negated. Contrary to what impressions based on superficial observation might suggest globalization obviously neither results in the imposition of a general uniformity nor does it generate large-scale homogenisation. The strengthening of economic and financial ties or the establishment of a dense network of global intercommunication did not automatically introduce harmonious interrelationships among the people, nor does it hold out the perspective of releasing less developed countries from their subordinate position. New problems have surfaced. Even at the economic plane, globalization in individual spheres progressed differently. Thus globalization of financial transactions and capital operations proceeded definitely much faster than the globalization of production. The global expansion of the capitalist mode of production and market economy entails at the same time the fragmentation of production and the management process at the ground level. Nowadays complicated technical gadgets consist of components manufactured in various countries that are then assembled together in units located somewhere else and from where the product finally receives its brand name. The arrangement involves the transnational training of experts as well as the stationing of so-called ex-patriate experts at foreign centres of manufacture and management. The system is based on an unequal relationship and somewhat obscures the older and simpler core-periphery pattern. This again raises doubts about the continuing validity of the core-periphery paradigm as a conceptual instrument for explaining the ongoing processes. The globalizing tendencies, at any rate, require for their functioning the removal of "national" barriers which obstruct the movement of capital and hamper the accumulation or transnational flow of profits which presupposes an adequate adjustment of the legal provisions in the countries where profits are generated.

At a different level, globalization is accompanied by the emergence or revitalisation of ethnic, cultural, religious or socio-parochial identities, which easily surface in modern society and can be exploited for political purposes. This is by no means an experience of lesser developed countries only or of the "countries in transition" from the former Second World; we only need to glance at political disputes centring on federalisation and autonomy in Canada, Great Britain, Belgium or Spain in recent years. This latter aspect should be seen in conjunction with what Larrain pointed out as the differing role played by globalization during different phases of modernity. Whereas "it could be said to be contributing to the success of certain versions of national identity" during earlier phases, "in late modernity it is eroding national identity"[26]. The nation state seems to be losing much of its earlier capacity to integrate various sections of the population. Promoting fragmentation within societies appears to be one aspect of globalization. In this context the much talked-about "failure of the nation state" should also be given a fresh look. On the other hand, ethnic minorities – and they have increased tremendously in number and strength during recent decades after the disintegration of the former colonial empires – who migrated in search of remunerative employment to Western industrialised countries, are no longer compelled to live in isolation from their "native" country and culture. Today's means of communication - themselves a product of globalization – enable ethnic groups like the Turkish workers in Germany to remain in constant touch with developments in the country of their (or their parents') origin through television. Furthermore, cultural traits or values, which originated in a particular region, are now being reproduced in diverse spaces of the globe where immigrant minority communities live in adequate numerical strength. They maintain a kind of cultural autonomy and do not necessarily enter the "melting pot". The outcome of the interaction of different cultures is yet difficult to predict and various interpretations are being offered. One influential view envisages globalization as a process of hybridisation "which gives rise to a global mélange"[27]. The idea envisages forms to become separated from existing practices and to recombine with new forms in new practices but expects the process to generate neither universalisation nor even multiculturalism. In my view, multiculturalism in a society seems to be the more likely pattern in the foreseeable future than the amalgamation of various traits. The emergence of uniform cultural entities may be as improbable as the re-emergence of ethnically homogeneous societies in industrially advanced countries of a type, which many of these countries could boast until a few decades ago.

VI

As a fall-out of globalization, people in Third World countries experienced what they visualised as an attack of Western values and norms on their own culture in the name of universalisation of modern standards. Obviously, in that sense the "West" continued its dominating presence even after the removal of colonial rule. The dissemination and penetration of new ideas and values of alien origin always tended to clash with local cultural institutions and behavioural patterns of a major section of the population. In the past the process provoked a search for or revitalisation of indigenous values and systems of knowledge. Coupled with the attempt to ward off the anticipated danger of extinction of the local culture, even under colonialism fundamentalist tendencies gained a foothold among subject people and obfuscated the anticolonial movement for renewal and national independence. In the post-colonial situation a continuing similar constellation gave birth to a pronounced urge for "cultural de-colonisation" which became quite strong in some countries like India, replacing genuine nationalist perceptions in the public consciousness to a certain extent. The proponents of that intellectual trend which trickled down to the level of everyday politics take a negative attitude to the heritage of European or Western Enlightenment, which they consider a mere ideological tool of Western colonialism and cultural hegemony. The explicit or inherent direction of a "de-Westernization" drive need not necessarily be anti-Enlightenment, but could be directed at establishing a different kind of consciousness and knowledge system which is grounded in indigenous traditions and supposed to be operated with the help of its own epistemology or independent system of cognition. The trend, in the first instance, reflects the present-day import of postmodernist thinking into the Third World, but it draws on indigenous sources as well. As an intellectual movement, however, it is not chiefly motivated by an endeavour to identify or comprehend the genuine "Otherness" within a multifaceted global civilisation. The proponents of the attitude appear to be more concerned with highlighting the individuality of their own culture or people, and in doing so are prepared to again counterpose a stereotyped Orient and Occident, discarding the idea of One World. Hence, the approach which in its extreme manifestations even envisages the construction of new "centrisms", looks like a repetition of the old concept of Orientalism inverted. The approach is equally rooted in failed expectations pronounced in the West regarding the imminent thorough restructuring of international relations guided by a spirit of global politics in a unilaterally structured world, the premises of which, naturally, were to be derived from "Western" experiences. In actual practice that belief has already been shattered. More significantly, the years since the end of the Cold War have witnessed the West pursuing a policy of disengagement vis-à-vis the Third World so far as the support of local endeavours for development and even efforts to construct a liberal democratic society are concerned.[28] The retreat added to the dilemma, which many developing countries are facing today.

VII

Is there no way out of the predicament? Instead of indulging in speculation, attention should be drawn to alternative proposals which were put forward by representatives of the Third World. Incidentally, earlier schemes to tackle current global problems from the viewpoint of Third World countries like the Report of the South Commission ("The Challenge of the South", 1990) did not evoke much response from outside the narrow circle of professional specialists in the "North." Yet there are alternative ideas and schemes which propose various paths of development and which favour paradigms other than the predominant West-centric approach, without advocating the dissociation of one part of the globe from the rest or opposing one region to another. Such schemes, at the same time, put the issue of cultural or civilizational differences or peculiarities in a proper place. I would like to refer to one recent example, which is closer to my own field of specialisation. In 1997 an international conference was held in India which brought together scholars from 18 Asian countries including Japan, apart from those of the host country, to discuss "Co-operative Development and Peace in Asia". The conference theme "was deliberately chosen in order to explore the paradigm of 'co-operation' as against the much-advertised paradigm of 'globalization and competition'"[29]. The conference was designed "to provide an opportunity to share our experiences, concerns, as well as hopes and aspirations". It was felt to be an appropriate way of commemorating the Asian Relations Conference held in March 1947 in India[30], which went on record as a stepping stone to and precursor of the idea of an independent, self-sufficient type of development of Third World countries.

Co-operative development as an alternative global perspective and a pattern to overcome inequities and inequality on the national, regional and international plane – such was the message, which emanated from the conference. The deliberations focused on the limitations of the West-centric paradigm of development with its urban-oriented, corporate and multinational-led concept and which by all indication has not only exhausted its potential for development on a global scale, but proved to be totally inadequate to be accorded universal validity. Against this background, attempts have been made to chalk out an alternative framework that not merely takes local traditions into consideration but also the socio-economic set-up of developing countries where agriculture still continues to contribute a major share to economic growth. At the conceptual level, the approach strongly supported a global perception of the issues raised, without indulging in speculations about a gloomy future of mankind, and by no means suggested disjuncting Asian countries from the rest of the world or replacing a West-centric paradigm by an Asia-centric pattern. Would it not be worthwhile to explore the potential of such submissions and to include them into considerations on the theoretical implications and practical consequences of globalization?

Notes

1   See Peter Schimany/Manfred Seifert (eds.), Globale Gesellschaft? Perspektiven der Kultur- und Sozialwissenschaften, Frankfurt/M. et.al. 1997, p. 8.
2   Mike Featherstone/Scott Lash, Globalization, Modernity and the Spatialization of Social Theory: An Introduction. In: Mike Featherstone/Scott Lash/Roland Robertson (eds.), Global Modernities, London et al. 1995 (reprint 1997), p. 1.
3   Arjun Appadurai, Modernity at Large, Delhi 1997, p. 17.
4   See ibid., p. 2.
5   Masao Miyoshi, A Borderless World? From Colonialism to Transnationalism and the Decline of the Nation-state. In: Rob Wilson/Wimal Dissanayake (eds.), Global/Local. Cultural Production and the Transnational Imaginary, Durham-London 1996, p. 79.
6   See Anthony Giddens, The Consequences of Modernity, Cambridge (reprint) 1997, p. 64.

7   Ibid., p. 71.
8   Proshanta K. Nandi/Shahid M. Shahidullah, Globalization and Development: The Emerging Dynamics and Dilemmas. In: Journal of Developing Societies, vol. xiv, fasc. 1, April 1998, p. 2.
9   Ibid., p. 3.
10 Aijaz Ahmed, Lineages of the Present, New Delhi 1996, p. 415.
11 See, for instance, the table provided by Jan Nederveen Pieterse, Globalization as Hybridization. In: Mike Featherstone/Scott Lash/Roland Robertson (eds.), Global Modernities, loc. cit., p. 47.
12 Anthony Giddens, loc. cit., p. 174.
13 Tom Brass, Post-Script: Populism, Peasants and Intellectuals, or What's Left of the Future? In: Tom Brass (ed.), New Farmers' Movements in India, Ilford 1995, p. 255.
14 Anthony Giddens, loc. cit., p. 154.
15 See Joachim Betz/Wolfgang Hein, Globalisierung und der Weg zur Weltgesellschaft: Herausforderung aus dem Süden – ein Problemaufriß. In: Nord-Süd aktuell, 3. Quartal 1996, p. 466.
16 Ibid., p. 468.
17 Ankie Hoogvelt, Globalisation and the Postcolonial World, Houndmills-London 1997, p. XII.
18 See Frank Schulze-Engler, McDonald's und die fremden Völker. In: Kulturwissenschaftliche Perspektiven zur Globalisierungsdebatte. Peripherie 69/70 (1998), pp. 192ff.
19 See, for instance, the sharp controversy which arose among the participants at the Round Table on "Globalization and Justice", held on the occasion of the Deutscher Evangelischer Kirchentag 1997: Deutscher Evangelischer Kirchentag, Leipzig 1997, Gütersloh 1997, p. 630ff.
20 See Manfred Kossok, From Universal History to Global History. In: Bruce Mazlish/Ralf Buultjens (eds.), Conceptualizing Global History, Boulder et al. 1993. W. Schäfer states rather determinedly: "Global history is the unwritten history of the twentieth century." See W. Schäfer, Global History: Historiographical Feasibility and Environmental Reality. In: Ibid., p. 47.
21 Roland Robertson, After Nostalgia? Wilful Nostalgia and the Phases of Globalization. In: Bryan S. Turner (ed.), Theories of Modernity and Postmodernity, London 1990, p. 50.
22 See Robert Young, White Mythologies: Writing History and the West. In: Keith Jenkins (ed.), The Postmodern History Reader, London-New York 1997, p. 75.
23 Jorge Larrain, Ideology and Cultural Identity. Modernity and the Third World Presence, Cambridge 1994, p. 155.
24 James Petras/Chronis Polychroniou, Critical Reflections on Globalization. In: Economic and Political Weekly, XXXII (1998) 36, p. 2249.
25 Jürgen Kocka, Perspektiven der Sozialgeschichte der neunziger Jahre. In: Winfried Schulze (ed.), Sozialgeschichte, Alltagsgeschichte, Mikro-Historie. Eine Diskussion, Göttingen 1994, p. 39.
26 Jorge Larrain, loc. cit., p. 155.
27 Jan Nederveen Pieterse, loc. cit., p. 45.
28 See the critical assessment by an author who takes a positive view of globalisation also in respect to the future of Third World countries: Shahid M. Shahidullah, The Third World After the Cold War. Global Imperatives and Local Peculiarities. In: Journal of Developing Societies, XII (1996) 1, pp. 119ff.

29 Soubrette Banners, For Co-operative Development and Peace in Asia – A Report. In: Man & Development, XIX (June 1997) 2, p. 1.
30 Ibid., p. 2. The invitation to the conference identified the preconditions and dimensions of the task facing the countries thus: "The countries of East, Southeast and South Asia have diverse cultural traditions, political structures and levels of development. They are all engaged in societal transformation in which science, technology, trade and investment are playing an increasingly important role. Some countries of the region are faced with religious and ethnic tensions compounded by historical legacies and socio-economic constraints. Released from the compulsions of the Cold War, all countries of the region are re-establishing economic and cultural linkages within Asia and with the rapidly changing global economy." See ibid.

The "Global Culture" Debate as a Challenge to Islamic Studies

Thomas Scheffler

"Globalization" is a generic term denoting the totality of social processes that contribute to "the compression of the world and the intensification of consciousness of the world as a whole"[1].

The Concept of the "Global"

The concept of the "global" contained a powerful image which inspired mankind in the wake of the first space flights in the 1960s. For the first time in human history, impressive photographs of the globe, i.e. the planet earth, seen in its entirety from outer space, became available to the terrestrial public. Unlike older conceptions of "the world" – such as *kosmos, universum, terra, mundus, dunya,* or *oikumene* – the image of the *globe* evoked intense representations of the unity and uniqueness of the planet as well as representations of its vulnerability and of its limits in space, time, and resources. It thus encouraged a new kind of holistic thinking that revitalized ideas of humankind as a global community and connected them to graphic ecological representations of the planet earth as *one* living organism.[2]

The implications of "global" thinking include *inter alia* an increasing awareness of global challenges and responsibilities, the relativization of the nation state and of ideological power blocs, a growing sensibility for transnational community-building, and an ethical re-evaluation of the position of man towards non-human beings such as animals and plants, a paradigmatic shift from an anthropo-centric to a bio-centric world view.

Globalization has many dimensions. The "global culture" debate deals with one of them, namely the cultural one.

Definitions of "Culture"

There is no universally accepted definition of the term "culture". In 1952, the cultural anthropologists Alfred L. Kroeber and Clyde Kluckhohn listed 164 different definitions of the terms "culture" and "civilization". In an additional footnote, the authors even assumed that the number of "definitions" spread over footnotes, quotations and other parts of their monograph might come closer to 300.[3] We may safely assume that since that time the number of definitions has grown considerably. For the purpose of our argument, however, four large bundles of meaning seem to be particularly important:

1. As opposed to *"nature"*, the term "culture" denotes those components of human life that are not biologically or genetically determined but produced or tranformed by man as a social being.

2. As a category of the *horizontal* "pseudo-speciation"[4] between human collectivities, "culture" denotes the specific traits that distinguish one group (or "culture") from other groups (or "cultures").

3. As a category of the *vertical*, normative classification of human groups, the term "culture" refers to an allegedly superior, particularly refined or advanced way of living. Used in this context, "culture" basically denotes "high culture", "elite culture", or "advanced culture" – as opposed to an "uncultivated", i.e. "primitive", "barbaric", or "backward" way of living.

4. As a category of the intrasocietal *division of labour*, "culture" denotes the sphere of production of immaterial values: e.g. the arts, sciences, religions etc. Used in this context, "culture" reflects the ancient juxtaposition of "mind" and "matter" (*Geist* and *Materie*).

Culture and Globalization

Culture is affected by globalization on all four levels:

1. As a result of global ecological thinking and the development of biotechnologies, the border between man and nature, human agency and natural processes becomes increasingly blurred (as is the border between man and machines).

2. The global mobility of people, goods, and ideas is making cultural boundaries increasingly fragile, "fractal", and difficult to maintain. Cultural identities are transformed and hybridized by the intermingling with elements of other cultures and are, in part, superseded by the development of a transnational "world culture". As the neologism "glocalisation"[5] suggests, even the fashionable evocation and reconstruction of "local", "autochthonous" and "particularist" traditions is deeply penetrated and facilitated by global considerations and imperatives.

3. Global consumer capitalism and the egalitarian pressures of civil societies are rendering distinctions between "high" and "low" cultures increasingly meaningless. On the one hand, the most salient cultural marker of today's global hegemony has been the so-called "McDonaldization" of the world, while, on the other hand, according to Stuart Hall, "the most profound cultural revolution (of the late twentieth century, T.S.) has come about as a consequence of the margins coming into representation – in art, in painting, in film, in music, in

literature, in the modern arts everywhere, in politics, and in social life generally ... Paradoxically, in our world, marginality has become a powerful space. It is a space of weak power but it is a space of power, nonetheless."[6] In view of the crisis of modernity, fashionable rediscoveries of the virtues of "primitive" and "backward" cultures or sub-cultures are not a rare occurrence. Even the spectacular economic successes of former "peripheries" like Japan and the East Asian "tigers" have (rather erroneously) been explained by their alleged traditional "Confucian" heritage.

4. The possibilities of audio-visual mass communication and the imperative to integrate fragmented mass societies by means of symbolic politics make the distinction between an *immaterial* realm of spiritual "culture" and the alleged *material* realms of "economics" or "politics" obsolete: film stars are entering politics and politicians are acting like film stars. Entertainment and information on political and economic issues are increasingly fusing into *infotainment*. Political and economic decisions are prepared and legitimized by scientific experts and "advisors". Cultural issues like trust, discipline, loyalty, motivation, or taste are widely acknowledged nowadays as important problems of the economy. Philosophy and spiritual holistic thinking have become part of modern management strategies.

As to the basic *direction* of global cultural change, three main lines of thinking may be distinguished:

a) *Homogenization*: In the nineteenth and twentieth centuries many influential philosophers, sociologists and political thinkers based their analyses on the long-term expectation (or fear) that the dynamics of modern society would render the world culturally homogeneous and politically isomorphic, implying the development of a *world society* and, finally, a world polity or a *world state*.

b) *Heterogenization*: Some of the very same authors conceded that the basic trend of fundamental homogenization might be accompanied by a rise in passing minor differences and rapidly changing fashionable distinctions in society. The reproduction of "structural heterogeneity" as a durable component of the modern world system, however, did not become an issue of academic discussion before the rise of marxist dependency and world system theories in the 1960s and 1970s. The "semiotic turn" of Western leftism and the rise of "postmodernist" and "deconstructivist" approaches finally took the debate beyond the confines of the core-periphery-dialectics of dependency theory. In a thought-provoking essay on "Difference and Disjuncture in the Global Cultural Economy" (1990) Arjun Appadurai suggested that the "new global cultural economy has to be seen as a complex, overlapping, disjunctive order, which cannot any longer be understood in terms of existing center-periphery models"[7]. According to Appadurai, it would be much more appropriate "to think of the configuration of cultural forms in today's world as fundamentally fractal, that is, as possessing no Euclidean boundaries, structures or regularities"[8].

c) *Macrospace-building*: Authors mainly interested in institutional medium-term solutions to the crisis of the nation state have shifted our attention to the development of larger, transnational, yet subglobal economic, political, and cultural *macrospaces* ("Großräume", "macroregions", "civilizations"). This line of thinking can be traced back to the geopolitical "*Großraum*"-thinking of authors like Sir Halford J. Mackinder, Friedrich Naumann, or Carl Schmitt. Its most recent and fashionable variant, however, is to be found in Samuel P. Huntington's work on the "Clash of Civilizations"[9].

Homogenization, heterogenization, and macrospace-building do not exclude but rather promote, transform and constitute one another. The common denominator of all three trends, however, seems to be the relativization of the nation state.

Global Culture and Islamic Civilization

Islam and Islams

These intertwined and conflictual processes affect the very heart of Islamic Studies, namely the supposed existence of an "Islamic civilization". If there ever was or is such a thing as an "Islamic civilization" – is it going to dissolve under the double strains of global homogenization and heterogenization? Or is it, on the contrary, going to reach some unprecedented degree of internal unification, be it as a truly *global* transnational community of believers or as a macroregional block of Muslim peoples on the level of a unified *dār al-islām*? How would this affect the traditional connection between "Oriental studies" and "Islamic studies"?

Under the thought-provoking headline "Islams and Modernities", Aziz al-Azmeh contended in 1993 "that there are as many Islams as there are situations that sustain it"[10]. In a critical review of al-Azmeh's book, however, Akbar Ahmed suggested in 1994 that the new possibilities of global communication might help to produce an unprecedented consciousness of Muslim *unity*.[11]

The debate whether there is not *one* Islam but *many* Islams dates back to the 1960s when sociologists, ethnologists, and historians of religion became increasingly aware of the local differences between e.g. "Moroccan", "Indonesian", "Indian", or "Egyptian" Islam.[12] At the time, speaking of many Islams mainly referred to the fact that the cultural meaning of Islam in everyday life was overdetermined by the national spaces into which it was inserted.

Although the founding fathers of modern Islamic Studies (such as Ignaz Goldziher and Carl Heinrich Becker) had never looked at Islam as a cultural monolith, the growing awareness of local differences in Islam posed a challenge to the assumption that the "world of Islam" could be understood as a meaningful unit by the mere exegesis of its theological literature.

The most elaborated response to this challenge has been Marshall G.S. Hodgson's suggestion to think of Islamic "civilization" as "a relatively extensive grouping of interrelated cultures, insofar as they have shared in cumulative traditions in the form of high culture on the urban, literate level"[13].

However, even if we accept Hodgson's proposal to locate the *unity* of Islamic civilization at the level of *urban, literate high culture*, we have to admit that the global cultural flows of the twentieth century are rendering the situation more complex, not the least by relativizing the meaning of "high culture", "urban culture" or "literate culture".

Today, large scale global migration and the development of audio-visual telecommunication media are creating a situation of cultural *mass liminality* that is involving millions of people simultaneously in two or more "mental worlds", thus promoting a culture of hybridity and borderline-intellectualism with considerable impact on the original local cultures of the migrants and media-users.

The links between culture and territory are becoming increasingly strained. As a genuine product of social interaction, culture presupposes some kind of "living together", a proximity or spatial "nearness" of the interacting beings. In the wake of large scale-global migration and global information flows, however, the tight and vital connections between culture and local face-to-face interaction, between group identity and territory, *dīn al-islām* and *dār al-islām*, "Islam" and "Orient" are becoming looser. On the methodological level, these developments may in the long run also affect the privileged nexus between Orientalist philology and Islamic Studies.

In the countries of the Middle East, the impact of global cultural flows is still mainly discussed in terms of "cultural imperialism", "cultural pollution" or "mental aggression", i.e. as a dangerous challenge from abroad calling for stronger cultural defence politics and more effective control of public and private spaces. On a larger scale, however, it has been one of the main arguments of the global culture debate that the same global processes, technologies, and problems that relativize, penetrate or supersede local cultures are also providing new ways to empower, vitalize and disseminate them. As Ulf Hannerz put it, "the transnational flow of culture can give the periphery access to a wider cultural inventory, providing new resources of technology and symbolic form to refashion and quite probably integrate with what exists of more locally rooted materials"[14]. Today, audio-visual media, computers and the internet are also used as media of the Islamic *daʿwa* in the West.

According to Roland Robertson "the globalization process itself – the rendering of the world as a single place – constrains civilizations and societies (including assertive national-ethnic solidarities) to be increasingly explicit about what might be called their *global callings* (their unique geocultural or geomoral contributions to world history). In a nutshell, globalization involves the universalization of particularism, not just the particularization of universalism."[15]

The globalization of Islamic "particularism" is certainly an ambivalent process. It presupposes, above all, an awareness to operate on a global level, an ability to address different global audiences, and a consciousness of growing global problems to be solved, e.g. the survival of the planet and the shifting relationship between humankind and nature with all their implications. In the scriptural self-representation of Islamic theologians, Islam already *is* the universal message of God to mankind irrespective of local, ethnic or national ties. In the perception of Western media, however, and in the everyday practices of many Islamic religious organizations, Islam still remains a vehicle for the demands and problems of Asian and African population groups. Much like the universalist religious rhetorics of European *nationalisms* in the nineteenth and twentieth centuries[16], "Islam" is often used as a vehicle of ethno-national demands or as a tool of neo-ethnic community-building[17].

Global Culture and Islamic Studies

All in all, however, we are witnessing the general subject of "Islamic Studies", namely the deeds and thoughts of Muslims, being increasingly transformed by global components beyond the spatial confines of "Oriental" countries. What does this mean for the development of "Islamic Studies" as an academic discipline?

Islamic and Oriental Studies: In nineteenth and twentieth-century Europe, Islamic Studies developed as part of *Oriental* Studies, i.e. as part of a *spatially* and *linguistically* defined discipline (and *not* as part of overarching *universalist* disciplines like theology or philosophy). Although important overlappings between "Islam" and "Orient" still remain and will do so in the foreseeable future, this classification is no longer self-evident. Considering the global presence of Muslims, the realm of Islamic Studies transgresses the spatial framework of Asia and Africa. This trend is also valid on the level of philological expertise: today, important inter-Muslim debates take place not only in Arab or Farsi but also in English and other non-Asian languages.

Specific and universal key concepts: On the level of *methodology*, classical Islamic studies usually looked at Islamic civilization as a relatively closed semiotic world apart. By and large, this approach reflected the language of the main *sources* of early Islamic studies, namely the "canonical" scriptures of Islam and their interpretations by Muslim theologians. At the same time, however, it was nourished (a) by the predominance of *nationalist* "Volksgeist" discourse in nineteeth and twentieth century Europe, which regarded it as self-evident that mankind lived on one planet but in different worlds, and (b) by the solid heritage of centuries of Christian theology and missionary work that conceived of Islam as a radical Other – and not as a continuation of the Abrahamitic[18] religious family.

In the late 1970s and early 1980s, encouraged by the success of Edward Said's critique of "Orientalism"[19], the discipline was then flooded by demands to replace orientalist "textualism" with the conceptual toolkit of "global sociology" and to apply universal key concepts like "class", "state", "elites", "market" etc. to the study of Asia and Africa as well as to any other part of the world.

Challenged by the unexpected rise of particularistic (communalist, ethnic or fundamentalist) movements in the 1980s and 1990s, these universal concepts, revealed their weak points, too. As Jacques Berque put it, "si on pense que la mondialisation abolira la spécifité des sociétés, comme on le dit parfois, on se méprend gravement et on s'expose à des résultats catastrophiques"[20]. The "global culture" debate rather suggests the need for approaches that explain cultural differences not as mere relics of the past but rather as a genuine part and result of ongoing overarching interactions.

Geocultural areas of research: As to the *spatial* focus of Islamic studies, two areas of research might be particularly relevant to the study of global change, namely (i) the study of the different *peripheries* of the Muslim world and (ii) the integration of multicultural *macro-spaces* in Muslim history. It is perhaps no accident that the most influential conceptualization of culture difference as a means of intercultural interaction has been the result of research among societies at the spatial periphery of the Islamic world. In 1969, the Norwegian ethnologist Fredrik Barth, a specialist on Pathan societies in Afghanistan and Pakistan, launched a momentous attack on the "simplistic view that geographical and social isolation have been the critical factors in sustaining cultural diversity". Two discoveries, Barth argued, were a glaring contradiction to this simplistic view:

> "First, it is clear that boundaries persist despite a flow of personnel across them ... Secondly, one finds that stable, persisting, and often vitally important social relations are maintained across such boundaries, and are frequently based on the dichotomized ethnic statuses. In other words, ethnic distinctions do not depend on an absence of social interaction and acceptance, but are quite to the contrary often the very foundations on which embracing social systems are built."[21]

The power of Barth's approach was not the least due to the fact that he had based his reconceptualization of culture difference precisely on examples from high mountain areas the geomorphology of which seemed, at first sight, to suggest that cultural diversity was rather a natural result of their physical inaccessibility and remoteness. Barth's basic line of reasoning, however, might also apply *mutatis mutandis* to those maritime "center-peripheries" of the Muslim world which were *easily* accessible to many parties, e.g. the regions of the *Levant*. Situated at the crossroads between three continents, at the intersection of vital lines of communication, of large empires and world religions, the coastal zones of the Eastern Mediterranean and their *hinterland* have remained an osmotic interface between European, Asian, and African cultures, a *periphery* and, at the same time, a dynamic and innovative *center* and, thus, a laboratory of "global culture" *avant la lettre*.

Purity, hybridity, and globality: Classical islamology has focused on studying the textual and linguistic essence of Islam in its purest, most classical and pristine *gestalt*, paying privileged attention to the historic core areas of Islamic history. Post-colonial or rather post-orientalist writers like Edward Said or Salman Rushdie, however, have time and again been celebrating situations of marginality, exile and *mélange* as global preconditions for intellectual creativity, independence and deeper insight into cultural processes.

Taking "exile" not only as an actual but also as a metaphorical condition, Edward Said argued "that to be as marginal and as undomesticated as someone who is in real exile is for an intellectual to be unusually responsive to the traveller rather than to the potentate, to the provisional and risky rather than to the habitual, to innovation and experiment rather than the authoritatively given *status quo*. The *exilic* intellectual does not respond to the logic of the conventional but to the audacity of daring, and to representing change, to moving on, not standing still."[22]

Speaking in defence of his novel *The Satanic Verses*, Salman Rushdie claimed that

> "[i]f *The Satanic Verses* is anything, it is a migrant's eye-view of the world ... *The Satanic Verses* celebrates hybridity, impurity, intermingling, the transformation that comes of new and unexpected combinations of human be-ings, cultures, ideas, politics, movies, songs. It rejoices in mongrelization and fears the absolutism of the Pure. *Mélange*, hotchpotch, a bit of this and a bit of that is *how newness enters the world*. It is the great possibility that mass migration gives the world, and I have tried to embrace it. The Satanic Verses is for change-by-fusion, change-by-conjoining. It is a love-song to our mongrel selves. / Throughout human history, the apostles of purity, those who have claimed to possess a total explanation, have wrought havoc on mere mixed-up human beings. Like many

millions of people, I am a bastard child of history. Perhaps we all are, black and brown and white, leaking into one another, as a character of mine once said, *like flavours when you cook.*"[23]

Certainly, the study of culture contact, of acculturation, inculturation, syncretism, and hybridity does not exhaust the range of challenges posed to Islamic Studies by the "global culture" debate. Processes of intercultural exchange have been a part of human history for thousands of years. Globalization certainly enlarged, accelerated, and intensified these processes. The new thing about *globality*, however, is "the consciousness of the (problem of) the world as a single place" (Robertson).[24] Hence, on the level of *text analysis*, one of the most fascinating subjects of Islamic studies might be the development of global thinking among Muslims. This applies particularly to the observation of the many transitions, fusions, and frictions between local and global Islamic discourses and between the media that are used to spread, channel and transmit different kinds of local and global knowledge in the Muslim world.

Notes

1   Roland Robertson, Globalization as a Problem. In: Id., Globalization: Social Theory and Global Culture, London et al. 1992, p. 8.
2   Cf. J.E. Lovelock, Gaia: A New Look at Life on Earth, Oxford 1979.
3   A.L. Kroeber/Clyde Kluckhohn, Culture: A Critical Review of Concepts and Definitions, Cambridge, MA, 1952, p. 149.
4   Erik H. Erikson, The Ontogeny of Ritualization in Man [1966]. In: Id., A Way of Looking at Things: Selected Papers from 1930 to 1980, ed. by Stephen Schlein, New York-London 1987, pp. 575-94 (pp. 579-80).
5   Roland Robertson, Glokalisierung: Homogenität und Heterogenität in Raum und Zeit" [1995]. In: Ulrich Beck (ed.), Perspektiven der Weltgesellschaft, Frankfurt/M. 1998, pp. 192-220.
6   Stuart Hall, The Local and the Global: Globalization and Ethnicity. In: Anthony D. King (ed.), Culture, Globalization and the World-System, Basingstoke 1991, pp. 19-39 (p. 34).
7   Arjun Appadurai, Disjuncture and Difference in the Global Cultural Economy. In: Public Culture, 2 (Spring 1990) 2, pp. 1-24 (p. 6).
8   Appadurai, loc. cit., p. 20.
9   Samuel P. Huntington, The Clash of Civilizations?. In: Foreign Affairs, 72 (Summer 1993) 3, pp. 22-49; id., The Clash of Civilizations and the Remaking of World Order, New York 1996.
10 Aziz al-Azmeh, Islams and Modernities, London et al. 1993, p. 1.
11 Akbar Ahmed, Review of al-Azmeh, loc. cit. In: The Middle East Journal, 48 (1994) 4, p. 735-37.

12   Cf. Wilfred Cantwell Smith, The Comparative Study of Religion in General and the Study of Islam as a Religion in Particular. In: Correspondance d'Orient, N° 5, Bruxelles 1962, pp. 217-31 (esp. 223).
13   Marshall G.S. Hodgson, The Venture of Islam: Conscience and History in a World Civilization, vol. 1, Chicago-London 1973, p. 91.
14   Ulf Hannerz, Culture between Center and Periphery: Toward a Macroanthropology. In: Ethnos, 53 (1989) 3-4, pp. 200-16 (p. 212).
15   Roland Robertson, Globalization Theory and Civilizational Analysis. In: Comparative Civilizations Review, 15 (Fall 1987) 2, p. 21.
16   For a collection of examples, see Arnold Künzli, Religion als Legitimation der Politik. In: Berliner Theologische Zeitschrift, 2 (1985) 2, pp. 358-82 (pp. 363-67).
17   Cf. Olivier Roy, Le néo-fondamentalisme islamique ou l'imaginaire de l'oummah. In: Esprit, (avril 1996) 220, pp. 80-107 (pp. 82-83, 99-101).
18   On the concept of the "Abrahamitic family" see Karl-Josef Kuschel, Eins in Abraham? Zur theologischen Grundlegung einer Friedenskultur zwischen Judentum, Christentum und Islam. In: Zeitschrift für Kulturaustausch, (1993) 1, pp. 85-97.
19   Edward Said, Orientalism, London-Henley 1978.
20   Jacques Berque, Au delà de "l'orientalisme" [interview with Thierry Fabre]. In: Qantara, (Oct.-Dec. 1994) 13, pp. 40-45 (p. 45).
21   Fredrik Barth, Introduction. In: Id. (ed.), Ethnic Groups and Boundaries. The Social Organization of Culture Difference, Oslo-Bergen-Tromsø 1969, pp. 9-38.
22   Edward W. Said, Intellectual Exile: Expatriates and Marginals. In: Id., Representations of the Intellectual. The 1993 Reith Lectures, London 1994, pp. 35-47 (p. 47).
23   Salman Rushdie, In Good Faith [1990]. In: id., Imaginary Homelands: Essays and Criticism 1981-1991, London 1991, p. 394.
24   Robertson, Globalization Theory and Civilizational Analysis, loc. cit., p. 23-24.

Universalist Counter-Projections: Iranian Post-Revolutionary Foreign Policy and Globalization

Henner Fürtig

World-wide fascination with the Iranian Islamic revolution is still alive. Since 1978/79, dozens of academic and journalistic publications have been printed about its course, and its various political, strategic, economic, cultural and religious impacts. The revolution in itself might have attracted many politicians and scholars but - in addition to this - it occurred in one of the most politically sensitive areas of the world.

As is commonly known, the Middle East is one of the cradles of mankind. It has been a source of many civilizational impulses throughout history and is the home of three monotheistic world-religions. As the border area of the three continents of Europe, Asia and Africa it is a traditional cultural bridge, too.

However, it was the establishment of a new global political order after the Second World War and the simultaneously emerging dominance of liquid and gaseous hydrocarbon as the most important source of energy and raw material for the industries of the developed countries, that enabled the Middle East, which possesses more than 60 per cent of this vital raw product, to start playing a key role in global politics. In the emerging East-West conflict, political, economic and military control of the Middle East as well as securing the grip on its most important raw products promised decisive advantages for either the East or the West. External factors such as the massive interference of both global camps coupled with attempts to recruit respective clients among the local elite had thus acquired great significance for the evolution and nature of the sovereignty of the regional states after 1945. In general, their development was decisively impaired and degenerated by this foreign interference.

In this regard, the Persian Gulf region gains special importance since the lion's share of Middle East oil is to be found in that area. Iran is not only one of the biggest countries of the region but also one of its main oil producers. Therefore, to influence the production and marketing of the region's oil, or at least to secure free access to it, the main global competitors concentrated their efforts to control and to lobby that country. These efforts coincided with Iran's own endeavours to gain a dominant position in the Persian Gulf, particularly under the Pahlavi dynasty rule. The hegemonial ambitions of Mohammad Reza Pahlavi were symbiotically connected to an American strategy to build up Iran as a corner-stone for securing its own interests in the Gulf area. As a result of this symbiosis, the Islamic revolution of 1978/79 not only liquidated the monarchy in Iran but had a strong anti-Western, namely anti-American approach, too.

It is of little importance whether or not the Iranian revolutionaries knew the word "globalization" when they toppled the Shah. What is important is that they considered the West to be the dominant power in the world and therefore responsible for all the existing injustices, inequalities and misfortunes in international relations. By trying to impose norms of political, economic, military and even cultural behaviour on mankind, the West was suppressing - according to their view - any development in the world that went against its interests.

In his last will and testament, the revolution's leader, Ayatollah Khomeini, wrote in 1983:

> "Among the gravest conspiracies ... has been the plot to alienate colonialized countries and make them look to the West ... as their model. So much so that those nations eventually lost their self-esteem and their trust in their own cultures ... (concluding) that their countries could not but become dependent ... More saddening, however, is that the (West has) checked the progress of the nations whom (it) attempt(s) to make consumption-orientated, and install a fear in us of (its) technological advancements and of (its) satanic power and destroy our self-confidence. This sense of self-nothingness and this feeling of dullness is inculcated in us by the big powers served to make us distrust our own knowledge and expertise and capacity in all areas and let us simply try to imitate the West ... blindfoldedly ... even though (this) might be totally absurd and ridiculous..."[1]

In an interview with the journal of the Revolutionary Guard, Khomeini added:

> "(The West) claims that civilisation, science and development are peculiar to (it) and they - especially Western and more recently American - are the 'superior race' while others are of lower races; therefore, their progress is the result of their 'noble race' and these other people's backwardness stems from their being an imperfect race. (They) ... are still on the way to perfection which, after millions of years, will gain proportional perfection; therefore, the effort for our own progress is useless ... In other words, we don't have anything and must beg everything from either East or West, be it science, civilisation, law or development."[2]

The revolution's attempt to interrupt the one-sided dependency on the West meant a tremendous strategic defeat for the United States. For the next ten years at least, American Middle East policy was designed to compensate for the losses inflicted on it by the Iranian revolution. Not only did Iran, with its enormous geographic area, its large population, its material resources and its military strength have to be written off by Washington and the West in a more general sense, but the emerging Islamic Republic of Iran took another - even more surprising - step by evading the East-West formula, i.e. it did not lean towards the Soviet Union and the Warsaw Pact.

On the contrary, it began a specific foreign policy of its own, fighting "Western imperialism" as well as "Eastern communism" while simultaneously propagating an independent "Islamic" foreign policy. At this point at the latest, it becomes clear that the Iranian revolution of 1979/80 was not merely an upheaval against a hated dictator but one of the "great" revolutions of modern times. All fundamental social and political change, be it 1789 in France or 1917 in Russia, has been characterised by universalist efforts and the claim to have set new norms of social, political and cultural behaviour with global validity.³ It was Crane Brinton, in his classic "The Anatomy of Revolution", who made the pattern that these "great" revolutions "as gospels, as forms of religion... are all universalist in aspiration" common wisdom.⁴

The lack of change in the regions surrounding Iran was considered a challenge by the revolutionaries. They wanted to bring about the same conditions there as in their own country. Victory over former rulers, seen to be invincible before, seemed to be a "miracle" which was sufficient legitimisation and an incentive to presuppose success not only in the region but in the whole world. Since this "miracle" became reality only after disregarding formerly valid rules and laws, the revolutionaries were convinced that they were legitimised to act beyond the recognised norms of diplomacy and international law when pursuing their political aims. Depending on the type of the respective revolution, it became one of the most important tasks to fight for the international standing of civil liberties, socialism or - in this case - Islam.⁵

Khomeini's Universalist Aspirations

The Iranian revolutionaries saw themselves duty-bound to explain to every single Muslim that nationalism, socialism, communism and capitalism, all Western imports, had been tried and found wanting. Instead of these Western ideologies, Islam, indigenous and comprehensible to the Muslim masses, literate and illiterate, was shown by Khomeini and his disciples to be a viable belief system, even when opposed by a military formidable monarch supported by a superpower.⁶ According to Iran's revolutionary leader, there was, therefore, only one way left for mankind to escape the negative impacts of Western and Eastern ideological imports, and that was to rely on Islam as the only indigenous worldview not affected and thus not degenerated by Western ideas and thoughts. Only Islam could stop the vicious circle of the formerly oppressed becoming the new oppressors because the eternal laws of Islam are valid for all people.⁷ In this sense, Khomeini never changed his credo: "Rely on the culture of Islam, resist Western imitation, and stand on your own feet."⁸

Without doubt, Khomeini felt himself and the Iranian revolution obliged to reintroduce Islam in the sense of Prophet Muhammad, that is as a revelation for the whole world. His universalist approach was at least as total as he thought the West's universalist schemes were. He firmly declared:

> "The Iranian revolution is not exclusively that of Iran, because Islam does not belong to any particular people. Islam is revealed for mankind and the Muslims, not for Iran ... An Islamic movement, therefore, cannot limit itself to any particular country, not even to the Islamic countries; it is the continuation of the revolution by the prophets."[9]

Time and again he emphasised the responsibility of the Iranian Islamic revolution to spread Islam's message.

> "The Islamic Republic intends to implement the ordinances of the Qur'an and those of the messenger of God in all countries. Iran is the starting point. It intends to demonstrate to all countries that Islam is based on equality, brotherhood and unity."[10]

Islamic Unity

In Khomeini's view, the source of the Muslim world's problems is the estrangement from the divine path of Islam, its adoption of corrupt ways of either the East or the West and its disunity, which is partly due to the intrigues of the oppressors. Their salvation would be a return to Islam, the establishment of a truly Islamic government and the overcoming of division to achieve unity.

> "There is no difference between Muslims who speak different languages, for instance the Arabs and the Persians. It is very probable that such problems have been created by those who do not wish the Muslim countries to be united ... They create the issues of nationalism, of pan-Iranism, pan-Turkism, and such isms, which are contrary to Islamic doctrines. Their plan is to destroy Islam and Islamic philosophy."[11]

Khomeini, on his part, tried to enforce the unity of all Muslims, making the *umma* the only legitimate concept of Islamic politics. He strongly denied any particular nationalism among Muslims or even Muslim nation states based on language, ethnicity or geography.[12] Thus, in the end, national boundaries would become obsolete in an Islamic society, since Islam would demand the creation of a single state (*yek kešvar-e hamegānī*), uniting all people under one flag and one law.[13] Consequently, the initial years of Iran's post-revolutionary foreign policy were dominated - apart from of Khomeini - by a group of clerical leaders and laymen who considered national borders simply a heritage of colonialism.

In their opinion, the Islamic world used to be united but was later disintegrated by the two aggressive elements of Western culture, i.e. nationalism and colonialism. This led to racial and national hatred between different Muslim nations and overshadowed Islamic cultural values. By espousing the powerful "Islam does not know any borders" concept, they could well justify themselves and legitimise their actions.

The struggle for the unity of the *umma* was therefore laid down in the constitution of the Islamic Republic, too.

> "Based on the ordinances of the Qur'an, that 'Lo! that your community is a united one and I am your Lord, so worship me' (XX:92) the Islamic Republic of Iran is to base its overall policy on the coalition and unity of the Islamic nation. Furthermore it should exert continuous effort until political, economic and cultural unity is realised in the Islamic world."[14]

Article 10 reads:

> "All Moslems form a single nation, and the government of the Islamic Republic of Iran has the duty of formulating its general policies with a view to the merging and union of all Moslem peoples, and it must constantly strive to bring about the political, economic and cultural unity of the Islamic world."[15]

The revolution's leader often said that "nobody could defeat one billion Muslims if they were united". Thus, the Muslims and other oppressed groups and nations should cooperate in order to change the global balance of power and to put an end to their subjugation and exploitation.[16]

As mentioned before, in the early days of the revolution the entire Iranian leadership spoke with one voice in this regard. The then Speaker of Parliament, Hojjat ol-Eslam Ali Akbar Hashemi Rafsanjani, declared in a Friday prayer in 1982:

> "If the Islamic world would have acted on the basis of Islam and the words of the Prophet, it would be the most powerful force in the world. I don't exaggerate when I say 'the most powerful force' ... Some of you may ask:' Bigger than America? More powerful than the Soviet Union? Stronger than China?' I say 'Yes!' Right now, we would have been stronger than China, stronger than the Soviet Union, stronger than America and all their satellites if we only would have been able to establish a global and united Islamic government."[17]

In the early 1980s, it was seen as a betrayal of the revolution to act merely for the benefit of Iran. To work for the domestic development of the country alone would lead to the destruction of revolutionary values and the existing model of the Islamic revolution.

Therefore, continuous aggression against values dominating the existing international system and efforts to overthrow neighbouring regimes were the main objectives of the Iranian leadership. For this purpose it was ready to use military force, guerrilla attacks and intelligence, and to arm the national liberation movements in order to jeopardise "non-Islamic" regimes. It would agree with national development only in the context of creating a series of revolutionary movements in Islamic nations and of threatening the international interests of the Western system.[18]

Export of the Revolution

These efforts were summarized in the conception of *ṣodūr-e enqelāb*, the export of the revolution, which became the overall credo of early post-revolutionary Iranian foreign policy.[19]

> "For its part, postrevolutionary Iran saw its neighbours not as independent nation states but as parts of the Islamic world for which the 'Islamic republic' and 'Islamic revolution' had duties in mind which included what others would call 'intervention'".[20]

It was Ayatollah Khomeini once again who was most outspoken in this regard.

> "We should try hard to export our revolution to the world. We should set aside the thought that we do not export our revolution, because Islam does not regard various Islamic countries differently and is the supporter of all the oppressed people of the world. On the other hand, all the superpowers and all the powers have risen to destroy us. If we remain in an enclosed environment we shall definitely face defeat."[21]

Khomeini felt the Islamic revolution was obliged to spread its ideas all over the world, to pave the way for the ultimate establishment of an Islamic world order when the Mahdi, the Twelfth Imam, appears.

> "We will export our revolution to the four corners of the world because our revolution is Islamic. The struggle will be continued until there is everywhere the call: 'There is no God but God, and Muhammad is his prophet'. As long as people are being oppressed all over the world our struggle will be continued."[22]

Khomeini repeated these ideas several times, directing them to different audiences, to allow for no misunderstanding. For example, he told a group of Iranian youth before travelling abroad:

> "Today we need to strengthen and export Islam everywhere. You need to export Islam to other places, and the same version of Islam which is currently in power in our country. Our way of exporting Islam is through the youth, who go to other countries where a large number of people come to see you and your achievements."[23]

The leader of the Iranian revolution, however, did not assign this task only to the youth but considered it the duty of every Muslim citizen in his country and of all its institutions. Also, according to him, it was not exclusively the responsibility of the Ministry of Foreign Affairs to pursue these political aims. In the early days of the revolution a so-called Liberation Movements Bureau was even assigned to the Ministry to co-ordinate the efforts of exporting the revolution. To increase its importance, the Bureau was soon put under the authority of the Supreme Command of the Revolutionary Guard Corps (*Pāsdārān*). For the Pasdaran, created as a kind of praetorian guard for the clerical regime to counterbalance the uncertain attitude of the regular forces, it became - according to the constitution - one of their most important tasks to fight for the expansion of the rule of the *šarī˓a* in the world.[24] Nevertheless, other individuals and organisations also continued their independent efforts to export the revolution by creating their own networks and structures.

In 1984, the Intelligence Ministry established yet another bureau from which to orchestrate Iran's Islamic activity abroad.[25] Because Khomeini's version of the Islamic revolution did not recognise international laws and frontiers, i.e. Islamic peoples were all one, he felt free to use the already existing links between different religious communities across the Muslim world, and to create new ones, to establish a world-wide Islamic network with Iran at its centre. Therefore, these efforts were not only directed at the region around Iran itself but at communities as far away as the Maghreb or even South East Asia, including Indonesia and the Philippines. The policy included all the means of enforcing revolutionary political and ideological ideas - arms, financial support, training, international congresses, propaganda, radio programmes.[26]

Nevertheless, it should also be mentioned that Iran indeed saw itself dutybound to export the revolution and to support all peoples struggling for independence and freedom but Khomeini also reminded them that "a right is something you have to fight for. The people must rise for themselves and destroy the rule of the superpowers in the world"[27].

But not only revolutionary Islamic idealism drove the Iranian leadership to export the revolution. Pragmatic considerations also led to the conclusion that an utmost level of admiration and influence within the Islamic world might safeguard the young revolutionary state which felt exposed to a variety of internal and external challenges.

For example, the Iranian leadership soon became aware of the economic, political and military weaknesses of its Islamic Republic and had to conclude that the export of the revolution would not be accomplished in one step or within a very short period of time. Furthermore, the response from the Muslim addressees of the export idea was not at all encouraging. This situation added to the further differentiation of the Iranian leadership; a more moderate and pragmatic policy began to take shape. The export of the revolution was to be well balanced between peaceful coexistence and opportunism. In other words, the Islamic Republic was to inflict blows to "puppet and dictatorial states" if national interests required and the situation permitted; if not, it was to continue peaceful relations.

Of course, Ayatollah Khomeini and his followers could not propagate this shift in their politics officially. But they tried to downplay the apparent threat contained in their declamatory policy to export the revolution without, however, disavowing it altogether. In late September 1982, Khomeini for example declared, "by exportation of Islam we mean that Islam be spread everywhere. We have no intention of interfering militarily in any part of the world"[28].

Setting an Example

As a modified approach, the Iranian leadership began to propagate that the Islamic Republic of Iran was to set an example for the Muslims of the world to follow instead of actively exporting its revolution. Its mere existence should convince Muslims of their revolutionary responsibility. It should encourage them to follow suit and topple their respective dictatorial, pro-Western and non-Islamic regimes.

At first the revolution should succeed internally, laying the ground for propagating its values and objectives internationally. The success and stabilisation of the Islamic revolution in Iran would inevitably influence other suffering Muslims living in a world of advanced systems of telecommunication. "When we say we want to export our revolution we mean we would like to export this spirituality and enthusiasm we see in Iran ... we have no intention to attack anyone with swords or other arms ..."[29], Khomeini elaborated.

The attempt to be recognised as a model by the Muslims was not new in itself but it gained momentum as the vision of an immediate export of the Islamic revolution gradually vanished. Right from the early days of the Islamic revolution, Iran had presented itself as the centre of that aspired world-wide drive for Islamic unity, as a model all Muslims should follow, as an alternative to the existing Arab/Islamic regimes.

Mohammad Javad Larijani, Deputy Chairman of the parliament's foreign policy committee, went so far as to even advocate the acceptance of the *velāyat-e faqīh* (rule of the jurisconsult) principle by other Muslims.

"... we have and have had the velayat, both during the Imam's (Khomeini's) time and during Ayatollah Khamenei's. This velayat is a righteous jurist ruling the entire Islamic nation. Muslims may not even realise that we have such a jurist ruling here, but this does not undermine the reality of this guardianship. Of course, it affects the ruling jurist's effectiveness, but not the principle. As long as this guardianship exists, the velayat is responsible for the Islamic world, and it is the duty of the Islamic world to protect the ruling jurist ... As long as our country is the seat of the true ruling jurist, we are responsible for the whole Islamic nation, and the Islamic nation is duty-bound to safeguard the Umm ol-Qura."[30]

In a more general sense, A.N. Memon wrote enthusiastically:

"... Iran, as an Islamic republic, has inspired numerous Muslims to advocate changes in their own governments. The Iranian Revolution has become a symbol of defiance against the West. Iran has superseded Saudi Arabia as the leading voice among many Muslims seeking an alternative to Western culture."[31]

The former Foreign Minister Velayati even used the word "Mecca" in connection with Iran's revolution to show that the centre of gravity in the Islamic world had shifted to Iran.

"Iran's friends and foes alike perceive Iran as the country that is the centre and Mecca of the aspirations of all Muslims ... Iran is a model for the fifty Islamic countries. This is because the domineering powers have not have very pleasant experiences regarding Iran."[32]

Becoming a source of inspiration and emulation for all Muslims, which was not unattainable in the Middle East and in the Persian Gulf region where Muslims are dominant and politically active, would result in increased political strength and diplomatic manoeuvrability for Iran. The revolutionary Iranian leadership could refer to the many miseries in the Islamic world to gain respect and sympathy. The absolute majority of Muslims around the world, including those in the oil-rich Middle East, live under conditions of economic hardship and/or political oppression. Regardless of the real Iranian influence among Muslims, the revolution had a great impact on them because it supported the anti-status quo posture of the suppressed Muslim majority. Thus its popularity was also a result of the acutely inept economic policies of the existing governments in the region.[33]

However, apart from this and from Iran's assertion that it is the only country in the world where Islam has officially become the foundation of society and government, thus implying that it is the duty of all Muslims to support it, there were other reasons for Muslims to admire the Iranian revolution. Among them were Iran's uncompromising stand with regard to the Palestinian issue and the question of Jerusalem and its strict adherence to an independent and non-aligned foreign policy, both of which have great appeal for many Muslims.

The Long Shadows of Khomeini's Heritage

Once convinced of the much greater usefulness of this more sophisticated policy, Khomeini dropped the more aggressive overtones from the propaganda of the Islamic Republic for the time being. In 1981, he told a group of Iranian ambassadors and chargés d'affaires who had been recalled to Tehran for consultations:

> "It does not take swords to export this ideology. The export of ideas by force is no export. We shall have exported Islam only when we have helped Islam and Islamic ethics grow in those countries. This is your responsibility and it is a task which you must fulfil. You should promote this idea by adopting a conduct conducive to the propagation of Islam and by publishing the necessary publications in your countries of assignment. This is a must. You must have publications. You must publish journals. Such journals should be promotive and their contents and pictures should be consistent with the Islamic Republic, so that by proper publicity campaigns you may pave the way for the spread of Islam in those areas."[34]

Thus, other Islamic countries were to get the impression that living under the threat of exporting the Iranian revolution meant books, journals, leaflets, radio and TV commentaries, conferences, mass rallies but not tanks and missiles, not even guerrilla warfare.[35]

After Khomeini's change in propaganda tactics, it was not surprising that other leading functionaries of the Islamic Republic followed this directive, too. The then President of the Republic, Hojjat ol-Eslam Ali Khamenei, while pointing out that "the foundation and the idea of this revolution is not limited to our country and this nation,"[36] stated that

> "Foreign Ministry officials are the apostles of the revolution. The nature of an official despatched abroad by a government demonstrates the nature of his government. If our diplomatic representative in all his dealings, including with people and government officials of the country to which he is despatched, adopts an Islamic approach, then he will be utilising the best method to demonstrate the role of the Islamic Republic of Iran."[37]

Later, when he was already the ruling Faqih, Khamenei declared on the occasion of the beginning of the Iranian year 1372 (21 March 1993):

> "The Islamic Revolution of Iran has taken place and was simultaneously exported throughout the world. The revolution was exported once, and that is the end of the story."[38]

The Iranian Prime Minister of the eighties, Mir-Hossain Mussavi, added:

> "We have declared time and again that we have no intention of interfering in other countries' internal affairs, but what is shaking the Islamic world

is a movement springing from this revolution among the Moslem masses of the world and, naturally, each people will shape their movement according to their own peculiar circumstances. They will force their governments to tread this path and, if not, naturally they will be confronted by the people's moves."[39]

The influential Hojjat ol-Eslam Rafsanjani, President of the Republic from 1989 to 1997, became active in this regard, too. While agreeing with Khamenei when declaring that "from early on when the revolution succeeded we realised that a revolution is not a phenomenon which would stay limited within one border,"[40] he later specified:

> "The phrase 'exporting the revolution', if it is mentioned here, means that we introduce our revolution and (that) anyone who wishes to use our experience can do so. But interference and physically exporting (revolution) has never been our policy."[41]

Voices that legitimised the Iranian concept of exporting the revolution by pointing at the "permanent Western approaches to export its value-system throughout the world," and thus declaring the Iranian efforts a simple countermeasure became a minority.[42]

But it might not have been mere pragmatism which led to this remarkable change in the Iranian policy of exporting the revolution.

> The "reluctance to export the revolution by force of arms has deep roots in the Shi'a theory of war and peace, which holds that wars to spread Islam can only be waged by the Imams. And since the Shi'a world has been without an Imam since the Twelfth Imam was occluded, no expansionist wars can be waged."[43]

Trial and Error

After the death of Khomeini in June 1989, power was - more or less - shared between President Rafsanjani and the new ruling Faqih, Ali Khamenei. Both had the approval of the late Ayatollah and tried to continue the foreign policy course set by him in the late 1980s. They encouraged further changes in the revolutionary rhetoric. Even more moderate considerations crept in. Khamenei, for instance, repeatedly stated that other nations need not adopt Iran's structures but they should imitate its attitude: steadfast, unyielding, uncompromising, an inflexible spirit in the face of global power and world domination. The new ruling Faqih nevertheless made clear that Iran regarded the defence of all Muslims throughout the world and Islamic sanctities everywhere as among the great tasks of its great mission.[44]

Simultaneously he hastened to declare that he would not deviate from the lines set by Khomeini, insisting that divisions in the Islamic world, as well as deviation from true Islam by some states, were the root cause of failure. Every state that was subservient to the United States and abetted its designs to weaken Islam was a traitor to be eliminated. Khamenei compared the Islamic revolution to "a permanent volcano" and said that the revolution was still alive.

Today's Iranian President, Mohammad Khatami, was cited in 1990 in support of Khamenei: "Today, Islam in the world is primarily defended by the Islamic Republic of Iran under the leadership of Ayatollah Khamenei."[45]

In general, however, after a decade of revolutionary zeal without adequate success, the post-Khomeini leadership started to look for new answers to the burning question of how foreign policy objectives could be achieved. The already mentioned Mohammad Javad Larijani asked:

> "Should Iran pursue what it wants through the promotion of national liberation movements in the manner done by the communists or should it engage in plotting coups d'état as was practised by the U.S. or other Western powers? The answer to both options is clearly and forthrightly negative ... our understanding of the Islamic renaissance values its generative potential *within* various countries."[46]

Compared with Khomeini's approach, which envisioned a complete merger of all Muslims within an organic *umma*, this new approach suggested that the Iranian government handle the issue flexibly and be more sensitive to the adverse impacts of this objective. The post-Khomeini foreign policymakers - at least within the government - no longer subscribed to the utopia of a Muslim world without national frontiers. Instead, they advocated more and more Muslim solidarity.

> "Theoretically, this reflects a shift from a monist concept of Umma to a more complex and pluralistic concept in which the principle of ethnic and national difference ... is respected."[47]

But one should not conclude from these changes that the post-Khomeini government's commitment to sustain and spread Islam was less firm than that of the previous leadership.[48] It revised and refined the methods employed to fulfil the mission. At least six factors, three of them internal and the other three external ones, should be summarised for this tactical adjustment.

Three main internal aspects limited Iran's foreign policy ambitions: First of all, the country's Persian character. Despite the government's attempt to minimise Iranian nationalism, the Persianness of Iran has limited its ability to reach the Arab masses. On the contrary, ethnicity and nationalism have proved to be much stronger than the appeal of Islamic universalism.

Secondly, Iran's Shia nature. This has also hindered Iran's ability to appeal to larger groups of Muslims beyond the Shii minorities. Indeed, in some cases, Iranian activities have brought Sunni fundamentalist groups closer to their governments. Iran has been forced to focus most of its attention and efforts on these areas where the existence of Shii majorities or sizeable minorities creates a relatively more receptive environment for its visions and influence.

Thirdly, the financial and economic limitations of the country.[49]

Among the external factors, it should be mentioned first and foremost that continued attempts to subvert governments in the name of "true Islam", particularly when applied to the Gulf region, were incompatible with efforts to forge economic ties with those same governments, which was much more important for the survival of the Islamic Republic. Secondly, emphasis on spreading Iran's brand of Islam can be too easily exploited by Iran's detractors who tend to accentuate the differences between Shiism and Sunnism.

And thirdly, experience has shown - especially in the Gulf region - that Iran's revolutionary call to topple existing governments has had limited appeal. Nevertheless, the post-Khomeini leadership continued to insist that Iran's "Islamic responsibility" transcended national borders. Yet, it appears to have accepted - tactically, pragmatically and perhaps temporarily - international boundaries. However, this has neither implied nor required Iran's abrogation of responsibility to assist Islamic societies within other states in their struggle for "true Islam". Iran's 1990 budget reportedly allocated $ 120 million in support of Islamic groups and movements. This amount was increased by 20 per cent the following year.[50]

Resistance of Reality

The remarkable influence of the Islamic Republic of Iran among Muslims and Islamic movements cannot be denied. It enabled Tehran to use the latter as power boosters and barraging tools, as identifying and legitimising tools and as sources of strategic purpose and direction.[51] But contrary to many allegations and/or expectations as well as the Iranian assumption of being the centre of the Islamic world there was never an institution such as "Islamic Comintern", headquartered in the holy city of Qom to instruct Muslims and direct their activities according to a grand strategy worked out by the Iranian leadership to spread the revolution.

Iran's record of influencing Muslims has rather been characterised - like many other aspects of its post-revolutionary life - "by a great deal of parallel, and often contradictory, actions by a host of official and semi-official organisations and groups. Similarly, Iranian activities in regard to the export of revolution rather than following a strategic blueprint have been marked by what could be called tactical opportunism. Thus, Iran seems to have concentrated its efforts in areas where local conditions have created opportunities for it to expand its influence."[52]

Nevertheless, even ten years after his death, Khomeini's legacy of the overall universalist nature of Iran's foreign policy is still valid. As one of the basic marks of its identity, the Islamic Republic cannot afford to conceal it. If Islamic foreign policy is a reflection of Islamic belief, having a global mission with a message for the people of the whole world and thus unable to accept limits or remain bound within the framework of national, regional, ethnical or geographical structures, how can the responsibility of an Islamic state then be limited to its borders? But, as already mentioned, Iran's leadership had to learn its lesson, and was forced to adapt its foreign policy objectives to the real world.

In the decade between 1979 and 1989, when the majority of the Iranian revolutionaries felt themselves a part of the mighty revolutionary wave, no one really noticed the overall declamatory character of Khomeini's foreign policy statements or dared to ask questions about commonly recognised Islamic propositions concerning international relations. But as soon as the situation in Iran began to normalise, both politicians and clerics painfully felt the widening gap between the pursuit of Islamic foreign policy and the pressure to secure the interests of Iran as a nation state in a world becoming more and more complex. In particular, diplomats and members of the Foreign Ministry were asking questions as to how Islamic foreign policy could be handled in detail.

With increasing frankness they accused the religious jurists of Iran of not providing sufficient and satisfactory answers despite the importance and sensitivity of the issue.[53] Contemporary *foqahā'* and Islamic scholars would either deal with foreign policy matters in a very cursory manner or would pursue extremely idealised principles impossible to implement in the present world such as collecting tribute (*ğezye*) from those who refuse to convert to Islam, rejecting present borders between countries, insisting on the religious duty of directing others to do good or enjoining others not to commit anti-religious deeds.

According to Iranian foreign policy specialists, also "befriending God's friends" (*tawalli*) and "avoiding God's enemies" (*tabarri*) is not possible in the foreign policy arena due to conflict with existing international law and the interests of certain powers.

On the other hand, those directly involved in Iran's day to day foreign policy do not feel themselves legitimised to call their pragmatism Islamic foreign policy. Be that as it may, in contemporary Iran both its clerics and diplomats seem to have reached at least one common denominator in the seven basic principles that should not be left out in a foreign policy claiming to be Islamic. These are:

Protection of dār al-islām. Both clerics and laymen within the Iranian leadership have agreed upon the protection of the Islamic system as the most important and fundamental principle in the foreign policy of Islam. Thus, the Foreign Ministry and the diplomats are obliged to keep this vital principle in mind throughout their activities and should not move towards a practical path that undermines it.

Glory, Protection of Independence and Rejection of Dominance. The second important and basic principle in the foreign policy of an Islamic government should be the glory and the authority of Islam and its government. The experts among the Iranian politicians know that the relevant texts on this principle were compiled and arranged when the Muslims were at the height of their power, when their domain was spreading, and other states were conquered by them. Thus, the principle reflects the honour and glory of the Islamic state at a time of powerful presence in the global arena. Under present circumstances, the Iranians are therefore concentrating their foreign policy efforts on the second part of the principle, i.e. the rejection of dominance by non-Muslims (*nafi-ye sabīl*). It forbids any relations that lead to the dominance of foreigners over the destinies of Muslims such as giving concessions, specific powers or exclusive economic and commercial rights that promote foreign dominance. Articles 152 and 153 of the Islamic Republic's Constitution refer especially to this principle. According to most clerical leaders of Iran the principle of *nafi-ye sabīl* is one of the fundamental commands and rules of Islamic jurisprudence and has priority over other rules.[54] But despite the importance of this principle, there is an ongoing dispute among the Iranian leadership over the feasibility of implementing *nafi-ye sabīl* under the conditions of an accelerating globalization, leading to "mutual dependence among countries" and making "concepts such as independence and absolute (national) sovereignty obsolete ... in the not too distant future"[55].

Interest (maṣlaḥat). The third principle is grouped around the rules of ability (*vosʿ*), no harm (*lā żarar*) and avoidance (*taqiyye*). The *vosʿ* rule connotes the fulfilment of one's duty according to one's ability. The *lā żarar* rule means choosing the easier way if the more difficult one implies the possibility of losses.[56] The *taqiyye* rule suggests going along with an opponent in order to ward off harm and injury.[57] There is a deep rift within the Iranian leadership on the question of whether *maṣlaḥat* primarily refers to the Islamic Republic of Iran or the whole Muslim *umma*, on the extent of *vosʿ*, the amount of noticeable *żarar* and the necessity of *taqiyye* in the contemporary era. In general, Iran's acceptance of UNSCR # 598, which led to a cease-fire with Iraq in 1988, is seen as a convincing example of applying the *maṣlaḥat* principle by the Iranian government.

Establishment of Relations, Coexistence and Cooperation with other Countries. According to the present Iranian leadership, there is no other way to implement the above mentioned major principles than to establish cooperative relations with other countries, in order to avoid isolation, strengthen the Islamic state, and relay its message to the people of the world. The IRI should have an active and authoritative presence in the global arena.

Support for the Rights of the Muslims and the Oppressed throughout the World. According to Article 154 of the Iranian constitution, every citizen of the country and all its institutions are obliged to "support the righteous struggle of the downtrodden in face of tyranny all over the world"[58]. The Iranian leadership is sure that all its relations with Muslim and non-Muslim opposition movements throughout the world are legitimised by this principle, including material and ideological support. Although the Iranian leaders dealing with the country's foreign policy are well aware that their uncompromising attitude towards the rights of the *umma* and the world's oppressed has fostered their prestige among Muslims, they also know that such a policy has many harmful effects for Iran, too. Because their support for political movements in other countries is often answered by the governments of those countries with extensive pressure and boycotts, Iran has to consider the pros and cons of the various foreign policy principles, especially that of *maṣlaḥat*.

Invitation and Propagation (daʿvat). In Islamic jurisprudence, there is no major disagreement among the *ʿulamā* on the obligatory nature of *daʿvat*. But the Iranian clergy has not reached a final conclusion as to whether this obligation should be imposed on each and every individual in society.[59] Some of them definitely believe that *daʿvat* has priority over other principles in foreign policy, both in terms of timing and value.[60] In that sense, it would be impossible to direct the responsibility for the propagation of and invitation to the Islamic faith exclusively to specialised organs such as propaganda, cultural and media organisations. Therefore, given the sensitivity and importance of propagation and the Koran's emphasis on it, most of Iran's *foqahāʾ* consider it one of the foreign policy principles of the Islamic Republic and thus one of the main duties of the country's diplomacy. Seyyed Ali Qaderi, for example, stated:

> "The first social duty of any prophet after mission is invitation - this principle constitutes the essence of Islam's foreign policy ... Avoidance of invitation not only confronts Dar al-Islam with the danger of extinction, but also carries punishment in the next world."[61]

Gaining the Endearment of Others. The principle of giving financial or non-financial assistance to other countries should not be confused with the fifth principle, i.e. the support of Muslims or oppressed people. This seventh and last approved principle intends rather to gain the affinities of other countries or to moderate their views in relation to the Islamic Republic of Iran and its policies (*ta'līf qolūb*). Donations or interest-free loans to countries like Syria, North-Korea, Sudan or the former PDRY can be seen in the light of this principle.[62]

Although these principles of the Islamic Republic's foreign policy have been agreed upon by the majority of the country's leading personalities, there is still no common opinion about the rank of each principle in relation to the other ones.

Especially diplomats know that the realisation of Islamic ideals and sacred objectives, such as support for the rights of the Muslims and the deprived, and invitation and propagation, is a large and dangerous responsibility, with its own particular effects, for instance the threat of becoming isolated. Thus, none of them is really sure whether the efforts to realise one or more of the above mentioned principles might harm others. Iran's foreign policy is therefore caught in a trap between pretension and reality.

But, taking into consideration what little is really known about the nature of the Islamic Republic of Iran and its leadership, one can predict - at least for the time being - that it will not try to resolve the conflict by relying completely on either idealism or pragmatism. By accepting reality, Iran's leaders will proceed more cautiously, they will opt for a step by step strategy, permanently testing to what extent their foreign policy principles are tolerated by the international system.

The ordinary observer may mistake this shift for normalisation, in the sense of a pragmatic, nation-focused foreign policy. But we should know better. As long as the system of the *velāyat-e faqīh* remains the foundation of the Islamic Republic of Iran, the country will have a universalist message for us all.

Conclusions

Not only the outcome of the Arab-Israeli conflict but also regional developments along Iran's northern and eastern borders as well as in the Persian Gulf will decisively influence Iranian behaviour. In addition, much will depend on the development of Islamic radical movements elsewhere. Although Iranian diplomats such as Kamal Kharrazi, previously ambassador to the United Nations and now the new Foreign Minister, constantly emphasise that Islamic revivalism is bound to the respective countries and situations, and thus perhaps inspired but not controlled by Iran[63], the remarkable success of these movements might encourage the Iranian leadership to repeat its demand for hegemony in the Islamic world more frequently.

Iran's future behaviour will definitely be influenced by the reaction of the West, particularly the United States, as well.[64] Western capitals might be on the right track to criticise, for instance, Iran's human rights record or to fight terrorism organised by some Iranian radicals, but it will only strengthen these very elements within the Iranian establishment by continuing an undifferentiating policy of containment in the long run.

Resulting from the heterogeneity of its system of power and the continuing existence of parallel power centres, Iran will, as in the past, seek to normalise ties with its most important neighbours while cultivating and maintaining its options for subversion and agitation. Mohammad Khatami will probably try to start his presidency with a foreign policy that keeps Iran from deepening the rift with its neighbours and intensifying its isolation.

The question still remains as to what degree the Islamic revolution in Iran really has influenced the Islamic world and to what degree it will probably continue to do so. Will there be repetitions of what happened in Iran?

In the first flush of victory after the overthrow of the Shah, Iran was giddy with its own success and utterly confident that it could reshape the world in its own image. As mentioned before, it rejected traditional diplomacy, traditional economics and even traditional ideology in the pursuit of its own version of universal Islamic rule. The Islamic state supported terrorist groups, seized American hostages, rejected any dependency on either East or West, turned up its nose at the United Nations and earned a reputation as a maverick state in the Western hemisphere.

But - just to repeat it - this is a common experience for revolutionary societies. The toppling of the old regime, which had seemed impossibly powerful and well entrenched, is typically regarded as a miraculous event. It is no wonder that the revolutionaries expected a spreading of their doctrines and ideas everywhere. Most genuine revolutions carry the seed of new ideas that transcend the locality and the parochial circumstances that first permitted it to take root and flourish.[65]

But coming back to the question raised at the beginning, the answer is relatively easy: the Iranian revolution has not spread and fundamentalism has been contained. But at best this is only half the answer, because it adopts too small a timescale. Revolutions and revolutionaries, whether Islamic or otherwise, are impatient, and expect other peoples to imitate them immediately: in this regard they become disappointed just as quickly as their opponents become relieved.[66] When a transformation of the international system proves to be exclusively difficult, dangerous or expensive, the proselytising impulse usually wanes and is progressively subordinated to more traditional objectives. Thus, the activities of the revolutionary state gradually come to resemble those of a conventional country.[67]

In that sense, the Iran of 1999 is less of a threat to its neighbours and to the international system than the Iran of 1979/80 was. Ideologically, much of the early boisterousness of the revolution was eroded by the relentless pressure of economic realities and the unforgiving demands of governing a large country with severe problems. At present, Iran is much less likely to undertake adventurous and costly intervention in the affairs of its neighbours than it was in the early eighties.[68] At least this is the situation at present. Nobody can exclude the possibility of radical and adventurous foreign policy steps by Iran in the event of a substantial economic crisis.

And there is the timescale to be remembered. The international impact of a revolution is not evaluated in a few years but in several decades. It was Chou En-lai who suggested that the effects of the French Revolution continue to be felt two centuries after the event.[69] Thus, the impact of the Iranian revolution can only be analysed completely by future generations. Even now the impact has been substantial, though no other state - except perhaps Sudan - has become an Islamic Republic such as Iran. It is only necessary to look at the rise in Islamist political consciousness in a range of countries, or to recognise the increased interest in Islamic clothing, Islamic literature, mosque attendance, etc., to see how far Iran has influenced the political behaviour of Muslims.

> "Whether or not Islamist forces of the Iranian variety do come to power in the following years or decades, the impact of the revolution and of the broader trend with which it is associated is undeniable."[70]

Summarizing these aspects, it has to be stated that despite the more pragmatic - or rather, national - Iranian foreign policy since the beginning of the nineties, religiously motivated universalism will retain its importance as long as the Iranian Republic and its leadership identify Islam as the precondition and the essence of its statehood.

Notes

1 Imam's Final Discourse. The text of the political and religious testament of the Leader of the Islamic Revolution and the Founder of the Islamic Republic of Iran, Imam Khomeini. In: The Iranian Journal of International Affairs, Tehran 1 (1989) 2&3, pp. 328-329.
2 Message of Revolution (Islamic Revolution Guard Corps), Tehran (1983) 21, p. 6.
3 See B. Baktiari, Revolutionary Iran's Persian Gulf Policy: The Quest for Regional Supremacy. In: H. Amirahmadi/N. Entessar (eds.), Iran and the Arab World, London 1993, p. 72.
4 C. Brinton, The Anatomy of Revolution, New York 1965, p. 196.

5 G. Sick, Iran: The Adolescent Revolution. In: Journal of International Affairs, New York 49 (1995) 1, p. 146/147.
6 See G. Linabury, Ayatollah Khomeini's Islamic Legacy. In: H. Amirahmadi/N. Entessar (eds.), Reconstruction and Regional Diplomacy in the Persian Gulf, London-New York 1992, p. 33.
7 See Farhang Rajaee, Islamic Values and World View: Khomeyni on Man, the State, and International Politics, Lanham et. al. 1983, pp. 80-81.
8 Message to the Pilgrims. In: Hamid Algar (ed.), Islam and Revolution. Writings and Declarations of Imam Khomeini, Berkeley 1981, p. 304.
9 Eṭṭelāʿāt, Tehran, 3 November 1979.
10 Quoted in: Rajaee, Islamic Values..., loc. cit., p. 83.
11 Quoted in: H. Amirahmadi/N. Entessar, Iranian-Arab Relations in Transition. In: Amirahmadi/Entessar (eds.), Iran..., loc. cit., p. 3.
12 See S.K. Anderson, The Impact of Islamic Fundamentalist Politics within the Islamic Republic of Iran on Iranian State Sponsorship of Transnational Terrorism, Ann Arbor 1994, p. 152.
13 R. Khomeini, Kašf-e asrār, Tehran 1980, p. 337.
14 Constitution of the Islamic Republic of Iran, Tehran 1979, Principle 11.
15 Quoted in: J. Calabrese, Revolutionary Horizons. Regional Foreign Policy in Post-Revolutionary Iran, London 1994, p. 27.
16 See S.T. Hunter, Iran and the World. Continuity in a Revolutionary Decade. Bloomington 1990, p. 40.
17 Hoṭbe-ye namāz-e ǧomʿe-ye Tehrān. Vol. 4, Tehran 1989, p. 185.
18 Echo of Islam, Tehran, (1996) 142/143, p. 42.
19 See also W.G. Millward, The Principles of Foreign Policy and the Vision of World Order expounded by Imam Khomeini and the Islamic Republic of Iran. In: N. Keddie/R. Hooglund/E. Hooglund (eds.), The Iranian Revolution and the Islamic Republic, Washington DC 1982, pp. 189-204.
20 S. Chubin, Iran and the Persian Gulf States. In: D. Menashri (ed.), The Iranian Revolution and the Muslim World, Boulder 1990, p. 74.
21 FBIS, Daily Report, Middle East and Africa, 24 March 1980, Vol. V, No. 058, Supplement 070.
22 Rāhnemūnhā-ye emām, Tehran 1979, p. 28.
23 FBIS, Daily Report, South Asia, 9 March 1982, Vol. VIII, No. 046.
24 G. Sick, Iran..., loc. cit., p. 148.
25 J. Calabrese, Revolutionary..., loc. cit., p. 144.
26 F. Halliday, The Politics of Islamic Fundamentalism: Iran, Tunisia and the Challenge to the Secular State. In: A.S. Ahmed/H. Donnan (eds.), Islam, Globalization and Postmodernity, London-New York 1994, p. 101.
27 Bayānāt-e Emām Ḥomeinī be monāsabat-e yekom sālgerd-e enqelāb, Tehran 1982, p. 5.
28 Tehran Times, 30 September 1982.
29 Quoted in: F. Rajaee, Iranian Ideology and Worldview: The Cultural Export of Revolution. In: J.L. Esposito (ed.), The Iranian Revolution. Its Global Impact, Miami 1990, p. 68.
30 Quoted in: M. Mohadessin, Islamic Fundamentalism. The New Global Threat, Washington D.C. 1993, p. 38.
31 A.N. Memon, The Islamic Nation. Status & Future of Muslims in the New World Order, Beltsville, MD, 1995, p. 150.
32 Resālat, Tehran, 15 February 1993.

33	See H. Amirahmadi, Iran and the Persian Gulf: Strategic Issues and Outlook. In: H. Zanganeh (ed.), Islam, Iran, & World Stability, New York 1994, pp. 116-118.
34	Soruš, Tehran, March 1981, pp. 4-5.
35	See also M. Muhajeri, Islamic Revolution. Future Path of the Nations. Jihad Sazandegih, Tehran 1983, p. 175.
36	A. Ḫāmeneʾī, Čahār sāl bā mardom, Tehran 1985, p. 354.
37	FBIS, Daily Report, South Asia, 11 March 1982, Vol. VIII, No. 048.
38	Kayhān Hawāʾī, Tehran, 4 April 1993.
39	Tehran Journal, 10 October 1981.
40	Peyām-e šāhedān, Mashhad n.d., p. 8.
41	BBC SWB, 3-4 February 1993.
42	See I. Sangar, Nofūd-e Amrīkā dar Īrān: Bar-rasī-ye sīyāsat-e ḫāreǧī-ye Amrīkā va ravābeṭ-e bā Īrān, Tehran 1989, pp. 33-35, 59.
43	Hunter, Iran..., loc. cit., p. 41.
44	See S. Chubin, Iran's National Security Policy. Capabilities, Intentions & Impact, Washington DC 1994, p. 12.
45	Eṭṭelāʿāt, Tehran, 28 June 1990.
46	M.J. Larijani, Iran's Foreign Policy: Principles and Objectives. In: The Iranian Journal of International Affairs, Tehran 7 (1996) 4, p. 756.
47	K.L. Afrasiabi, After Khomeini. New Directions in Iran's Foreign Policy, Boulder et.al. 1994, p. 203.
48	See also M.H. Fayyāżī, Bar-rāsī-ye ʿavāmel movāṯīr dar dast-yābī va ʿadam dast-yābī be ahdāf enqelāb-e eslāmī. In: Faṣlnāmeh ḥuqūq va ʿolūm-e sīyāsī, Tehran 2 (1992) 2, pp. 47-60.
49	See Hunter, Iran..., loc. cit., p. 180.
50	See Calabrese, Revolutionary..., loc. cit., p. 145.
51	Amirahmadi, Iran..., loc. cit., pp. 117-118.
52	S.T. Hunter, Iran and the Spread of Revolutionary Islam. In: Third World Quarterly, Washington DC 10 (1988) 2, p. 740.
53	See A. Ghazvini, On the Foreign Policy of Islam: A Search into the Juridical Dimension of Iranian Foreign Policy. In: The Iranian Journal of International Affairs, Tehran 7 (1996) 4, pp. 780-796.
54	See A. Šakūrī, Oṣūl-e sīyāsat-e ḫāreǧī-ye eslām. In: Feqh-e sīyāsā-ye eslām. Vol. 2, Tehran 1982, p. 387.
55	Ghazvini, On the Foreign..., loc. cit., p. 786.
56	See A. al-ʿAlawī, Al-Taqīya fī riḥāb al-ʿālamayn al-šayḫ al-aʿẓam al-Anṣārī wa-l-sayyid al-imām al-Ḥumaynī, Qom 1994, p. 4.
57	See M. al-Anṣārī, Al-Taqīye, Qom 1994, p. 11.
58	E. Amīnī (Āyātollah), Sīyāsat-e ḫāreǧī-ye hokūmat-e eslāmī, Tehran 1985, p. 7.
59	See Šakūrī, Oṣūl-e..., loc. cit., p. 360.
60	See ʿA. Qāderī, Ṭarḥ-e tahqīq-e mabānī-ye sīyāsat-e ḫāreǧī-ye eslām. In: Maǧallāt-e sīyāsat-e ḫāreǧī, Tehran (1989) 1, p. 226.
61	Ibid., p. 228.
62	See Šakūrī, Oṣūl-e..., loc. cit., pp. 501-514.
63	See U.S.-Iran Review, Washington DC 1 (1993) 2, p. 1.
64	See F. al-Mazidi, The Future of the Gulf. The Legacy of the War and the Challenge of the 1990s, London—New York 1993, p. 3.
65	See Sick, Iran..., loc. cit., p. 147.
66	See Halliday, The Politics..., loc. cit., p. 96.

67 See Sick, Iran..., loc. cit., p. 147.
68 Ibid., p. 165.
69 Ibid., p. 147.
70 Halliday, The Politics..., loc. cit., p. 97.

Mediating the External: The Changing World and Religious Renewal in Indian Islam

Dietrich Reetz

Developments in colonial India, particularly during the active phase of the national and anti-colonial movement in the 1920s to 1940s, are a prime example of rapid political and economic change and the challenge they pose to social and cultural forces. Religious groups were drawn deep into the overall process of polarisation. The role of Islamic movements in a predominantly Hindu country ruled by a Christian colonial power was a particularly precarious one. This is the point of departure for an inquiry into the strategies of two Islamic movements in colonial India to deal with the pressures of modernisation. The two groups were the Deoband movement, named after the religious seminary in the north Indian town of Deoband, and the *Tablīghī Jamāʿat*[1], aimed at renewing Muslim religious beliefs and practices. They are treated here as representing a much broader trend of Islamic mobilisation in colonial India aimed at reviving religiosity and piety in society. Although Islam was a minority religion of roughly 22 per cent of the population[2], representing a broad medley of social groups, and linguistic and ethnic identities, it drew its significance from the fact that its influence was concentrated in geographical areas where more than half the local population adhered to Islam[3]. It gained additional importance by receiving political representation in legislative bodies. Constituencies in India were traditionally diverse. Legislative representation in India gradually developed from indirect elections where electoral bodies were constituted either territorially by district or local boards or by special interest groups, such as chambers of industry and universities. The constitutional reforms act of 1892 recognised the representation of religious communities in legislative bodies in principle and the Act of 1909 formally introduced separate constituencies for Muslims. These were widely regarded as political manoeuvres to contrast the anti-colonial movement led by Congress with potentially more "loyal" groups.[4]

Islamic mobilisation in colonial India was characterised by a variety of forms. The spectrum ranged from established bourgeois parties appealing to a Muslim constituency,[5] to sectarian and revival movements,[6] and spontaneous and militant forms of mass mobilisation.[7] Within this framework the Deobandis and the Tablighis were "middle of the road". They represented movements which were created with the objective not of fighting for political power, but for religious renewal. And yet, they were drawn into nationwide currents of political and social change, forcing them to take public positions.

It is argued here that the public intervention they sought in the interest of religion led them to reach out from the "sacred" to the "secular" public domain.[8] In order to affect change for a religious renewal they had to engage in social and political transformation. Thus, they acted as "Agents of Change" not only and not so much for religious conduct as for the strata of Muslims they mobilised who looked to their religion as a source of identity and orientation in a fast-changing environment. "Agents of Change" are understood here to be cultural brokers who inhabit the intermediate space between the indigenous cultural norm and western (colonial) influence.[9] The term looks beyond forces spearheading capitalist transformation such as established parties, entrepreneurs, and trade unions, forces which directly adapted western values and institutions but left them basically intact. Although western institutions underwent significant mutation at their hands, these forces and structures were still western. They contributed little in terms of cultural mediation and brokerage. Within the scope of the project, the concept of "Agents of Change" is extended to the more traditional elements not usually associated with change or transformation since they often remain deeply committed to their local culture and mostly conservative tradition. It is still underestimated that cultural and religious forms of public mobilisation in Asia and Africa have been a key element in mediating external transformation processes through their ability to translate new values and institutions into the local idiom. In the process, external influences and their local interpretation often underwent significant alterations. This approach draws on the increasingly active discourse on the intersection of cultural and political landscapes in a globalising world where clear-cut sureties are few and intermediate stages abound. It was inspired by Homi Bhabha and his study of the "interstices" of cultures[10] and continues work on the meaning of networks, cultural brokers and friends.[11] It is meant to contribute to the understanding and emancipation of social and cultural agents who live in more than one world continuously and concurrently, participating in transformation and bringing it about not in a linear fashion but in a roundabout way, being both selfless and selfish in turns.

It is proposed to discuss here what aspects of change affected the Deobandis and the Tablighis, what change did they aim at, and what changes did they undergo themselves. Through this, it is intended to clarify their concept of change and their role in this process. The argument will concentrate on the twentieth century when public and political mobilisation became especially pronounced in British-India in the course of the national movement against colonial rule, marked by the movements for non-cooperation and civil disobedience starting in 1919.

Islamic Mobilization in India

When the Deoband seminary was founded in 1867 it responded to the perceived need of the Muslim community in India to improve the knowledge of Islam among its members. Muslim dynasties had ruled over India for many centuries. But ever since Unitarian tendencies took root under Emperor Akbar (1542-1605), who sought to promote inter-religious dialogue and to placate the Hindu majority, Islamic scholars had demanded a renewal of Islam, allegedly fearing their community would resolve in majority Hinduism which had successfully assimilated many religious movements in its fold before. Particularly the practices of the mystic Muslim orders of Sufism had resonated well beyond the confines of Islam, helped by their emphasis on sensual experiences through music, poetry and dance. Scholars like Shaikh Ahmed Sirhindi (1564-1624) sought to redirect Sufism back to its orthodox beginnings and to re-establish the authority of Islamic knowledge based on the Quran and the Sunnah, the revealed book of Islam and the written tradition of the Prophet and his companions. This reform tradition was continued by Shah Waliullah (1703-1962). Without exception, the reformers of Indian Islam understood by reform not modernising Islam in an abstract sense but rectifying and correcting its religious practice, to bring it into closer conformity with the original sources of Islam. The Deobandis were one of several *seminary movements.* Other important seminaries in Indian Islam, with affiliated mosques and seminaries across India, were the Firanghi Mahal, established around 1700, and the Nadwat seminary (1908) in Lucknow, the *Madrasa manzar al-Islām* (1904) of the Barelwi school of thought, in Bareilly, all in the United Provinces (U.P.) of north India.

The Tablighi Jamaat came into existence in 1934 to counter the reconversion efforts of the Hindu reformist movement Arya Samaj.[12] It was one of many *faith and revival movements* in Indian Islam which were not connected with any particular seat of religious learning. They displayed a great variety of approaches all meant to improve the position of Islam or of Indian Muslims in general. Yet, their outlook was often regional and sectarian. The radical *Ahl-i ḥadīth* ("people of the tradition"), starting in the 1880s, rejected conventional orthodoxy as embodied in the four medieval law schools of Islam and pleaded for an exclusive return to the Quran and the Sunnah. The *Ahrār* movement (of the "noble" - 1930) similarly argued in favour of a purification of Islam. Both of them, sometimes violently, opposed a reformist sect by the name of *Ahmadīyya*[13] which was constituted after its founder had claimed to be the awaited saviour and messiah. Although the latter movement was considered liberal with bourgeois leanings, its attitude was one of deep-felt religiosity. All three vehemently fought against Hindu and Christian conversion efforts. A fourth one, the *Khāksār* (the "humble"), founded in 1930, strove to exercise physical prowess and militant self-esteem for Muslims in alleged defence against inter-communal violence.

Separating seminary and revival movements is, to a certain extent, artificial, since seminary movements fully shared the goals of revival movements for a renewal and the purification of Islam. The distinction is, therefore, more symbolic in nature, to help understand the different currents of Islamic mobilisation in India. A functional distinction becomes visible in the attachment of the seminary movements to the institutions and structure of a seminary whereas the revival movements were largely leader-centred. The seminary movements, therefore, did not strictly or exclusively focus on the personality of the principal or vice-chairman but were built around a more collective leadership. In contrast, the revival movements critically depended on and were defined by the activity of their founder-leader, as in the case of Allama Inayatullah Khan Mashriqi for the Khaksar, Maulana Muhammad Ilyas (1885-1944) for the Tablighis, Ghulam Mirza Ahmad (1835-1908) for the Ahmadiyya, Sayyid ʾAtaʾullah Shah Bukhari (1891-1967) for the Ahrar, and Maulana Nazir Husain for the Ahl-i Hadith. Another consequence of this distinction between institution-building and personal leadership is the degree to which emphasis is put on religious knowledge or spiritual guidance. One could say, particularly looking at the Deobandis and the Tablighis, that the seminary movements by virtue of their vocation stood for increased religious knowledge, whereas the revival movements significantly cherished spiritual guidance provided by a mentor, or *sheikh*, who would initiate adherents into one or several of the Sufi orders. But it is important to note that in the reform movements of Indian Islam both elements were always present in one form or another ever since scholars like Sirhindi and Waliullah attempted to join these two currents of Islam. It is interesting to see how the principles of religious knowledge, of spiritual and moral guidance became structuring elements of the reformist discourse in Indian Islam.

The Deobandis and the Tablighis were exemplarily well-suited to demonstrate this dialectic. Their concept of change was very much related to the comparative importance they attached to religious knowledge, or to spiritual guidance and moral renewal. For them, reform was *Islāh*, correcting a misguided practice. Reform was not meant to make improvements in terms of changes or innovation, which has come to be a contemporary meaning of "reform." It was understood that Islam as a revealed religion was in no need of improvement but was to be practised properly. The correction of the prevalent religious practice mainly meant the purification of Islam from syncretic customs inherited from Hinduism. In their opinion, this required increased religious knowledge, renewed morality and faith. Such changes, it was assumed, would go a long way in solving not only the problems of faith and the hereafter, but also of this world, and would provide a recipe for the ills of both the sacred and the secular realm.

The Deoband Movement

The Deoband seminary or *dāru'l ʿulum* ("house of religious learning, or knowledge") was founded for the purpose of Islamic and Arabic education. In the first 45 years of its existence it educated 1000 students, providing Arabic and Islamic courses at Secondary and College Level. The circumstances surrounding its establishment have been described in great detail in Barbara Metcalf's classical study of 1982.[14] It should be noted here that its very inception embodied change. By creating separate buildings and departments for various educational activities, with hostels where students could stay during the week, it departed from the tradition where students received instruction from teachers in a more private setting, often in the corner of a mosque or even at home. The set-up at Deoband obviously copied western models such as English colleges. Doctrine-wise, it followed a rather conventional syllabus for Islamic instruction, the famous *dars-i nizāmī*. This collection of Islamic readers was compiled in the eighteenth century at the *Firanghi Mahal* seminary in Lucknow. It was named after its author, Nizamu'd-Din (d. 1748), and based on Arabic grammar, logic, philosophy, mathematics, rhetoric, the study of the Islamic law schools (*fiqu*), and theology.[15]

In the twentieth century, issues agitating the ʿulama[16] of Deoband in their seminary affairs have so far received little attention in academic literature. The centenary history publication of the seminary[17] draws on a mass of data and details and provides a unique insight into the workings of this institution. The conflicts and campaigns of these theologians and their students furnish interesting evidence on the different ways in which currents of change and conservatism swept through the seminary during the heydays of anti-colonial discontent. Broadly speaking, these issues were

- the ascent of materialism and science and the declining interest in spiritual and moral values;
- national education as opposed to western and colonial education and the role of religion therein;
- student politics and agitation within the confines of a religious educational institution such as Deoband;
- participatory principles and majority rule within the body politics of the seminary.

Science and Religion

Reflecting the contemporary political and intellectual discourse in the west, which was mirrored in the Indian media, the role of scientific and materialist thinking was an important issue. This discourse was partly fed by a rapid succession of stunning scientific discoveries and their breathless reception. Foremost among them perhaps was the relativity theory of Einstein. Increasingly the question was being asked as to what was left of the dominion of God if supposedly the answer to all cardinal questions of existence was within reach of mankind. Another source of this discourse presumably was the hotly-debated advent of Soviet Russia and its political philosophy of materialist thinking, combined with increasing hostility towards religion and religious institutions under Stalin.

In 1359 AH (1940),[18] the long-time vice-chancellor of the seminary, Qazi Tayyib, delivered a lecture on "Islam & Science" at the Aligarh Muslim University (A.M.U.), the start of a whole series of lectures there to boost the reputation of the scholarship of the ʿulama of Deoband. At the largely secular, although Muslim-oriented university, ʿulama, as freely admitted by the Deobandis themselves, were held in rather low esteem as far as their academic qualifications were concerned. The official Deoband centenary history volume noted:

> "As a result of these lectures, the academic underestimation and mistrust prevailing in the university regarding the ʿulamā was removed. From that time onwards the relations between the *dar-ul ulum* and the A.M.U. have been on the increase from day to day and the distance that existed *inter se* these two great academic institutions has now, thank Allah, been much reduced."[19]

In his lecture, based on an "authentic *athar*"[20], Tayyib, discussed in theological terms the "human energy and capacity and its sway and domination over material powers." "After making it clear that the spring of human powers is the soul," the Deoband history noted, Tayyib "argued in a very subtle manner about spiritualism, theology, the Being of Allah and His Attributes." In asking questions such as "What is the relation between Islam and material wisdom? What are the harms of pure materialism?"[21] he apparently wanted to provide ammunition to counter the numerous arguments about the growing irrelevance of religion in the face of an increasing impact of science on people's lives.

Education and Identity

The second issue of national and religious education derived directly from the first one. On several occasions Deoband scholars intervened in the debate on the character of education required for a liberated India. This was a truly national debate in which Gandhi and many contemporary Indian leaders and educationists of all confessions participated. The origins of the debate went right back to that famous Minute on Education in 1835 by Thomas Babington Macaulay (1800-1859) in which English-language education was made mandatory in India. English education opened channels for communication and kept India abreast with global trends. But ever since it started, leaders of public opinion in India had believed that it also bestowed India with a sense of servility towards British and English-language culture. A truly free and independent India required a national education policy of its own including the elevation of its native tongues. The search for the meaning and contents of national education united religious leaders, ethno-nationalists and socialists. It was therefore no coincidence that one of the first major campaigns in the anti-colonial struggle from the twenties to forties was the boycott of English education and the creation of national educational institutions.

Rejecting the western legacy of the Aligarh Muslim University which came into being through heavy colonial patronage, all-India Muslim leaders such as Muhammad Ali (1878-1931)[22] initiated the creation of a national university. In the beginning this amounted to makeshift open-air public university classes at Aligarh during the *Khilafat* campaign.[23] It was intended to put pressure on the trustees of Aligarh University to give up the government grant-in-aid as part of the movement of non-cooperation with British colonial institutions. Eventually his initiative laid the foundation for the *Jamia Millia Islamia* in Delhi, an Islamic university which, somewhat contrary to the expectations of its founder, grew into a secular national university for Muslims in independent India.[24] One of the founding fathers was the *Shaikh-al Hind* Mahmud al-Hasan (1851-1920), a spiritual leader of Indian Muslims who was closely associated with the Deoband seminary. He delivered the presidential address at the foundation ceremony for the *Jamia Millia* in 1921. Other occasions on which Deoband divines formulated their position on national education were advisory missions to Afghanistan and the Muslim-Indian principality of Qalat where the rulers asked for their opinion on suitable national education and its compatibility with religious instruction. On all these occasions Deoband ʿulama argued in favour of a curriculum in which "the religious sciences would be given due weight along with modern sciences and social necessities". This was thought necessary to remove "that gulf of 'educational dualism'" so that, as the Deoband historian puts it, "by the gathering of both the old and modern educational tendencies at one point of union, an effort be made to create the unity of knowledge and thought in the community"[25].

In other words, religious instruction was considered a national duty, a prerequisite to achieve national unity. Otherwise, unity would supposedly be threatened by the dominant western education and orientation of an elite which was increasingly about to turn its back on religion. Interestingly, also from today's perspective of endless infighting, this issue was considered relevant for Afghanistan as well, not only by the Deoband divines, but also by an influential faction of the royal Afghan household.

Agitation and Democracy vs. Paternalism

The third and fourth issues, those of agitational student politics and of participatory majority rule, threw an illuminating light on the transformation of the seminary itself. Although remaining highly conservative on doctrinal points of social relations (such as the role of women etc.), political intervention by the Deoband seminary, both teaching staff and graduates, has been equally pronounced over the years and based itself on a long tradition. The political activism of Deoband was substantiated with reference to its purist and pan-Islamic antecedents in the eighteenth and nineteenth centuries, the highlights of which were the struggle of the so-called *mujāhidīn* or freedom-fighters under Sayyid Ahmad Bareilly (1736-1831) and the uprising of 1857-58 against British colonial rule in which Muslims played a prominent role. This interventionist and purist doctrinal discourse went back to Shah Waliullah. Due to their purist notions this school of thought was called the "Indian Wahhabis" or "Nejdis", with reference to the movement of the Muwahhidun, or "monotheists," commonly referred to as "Wahhabis". Yet doctrinally the Deoband seminary remained within the confines of the Hanafiyya law school, or *fiqu*[26], which differed notably from the Wahhabis over the relationship to Sufism[27]. The latter was completely rejected by the Wahhabi school but partially accepted by the Waliullahi school in a purified version. The Deoband seminary stood firmly in the Waliullahi tradition. Purism itself is a form of interventionism as it seeks to correct religious practice. This perhaps partly explains why this school of thought also actively engaged with the British colonial power. The Wahiullahi tradition opposed the British for undermining the rule of Islamic law by virtue of their legislative and executive actions while ruling over India. It sought to restore the priority of the Quran as a primary source of tradition *vis-à-vis* the British, and even more so for ordinary Muslims who were advised against the creeping dilution of local Islamic customs and rituals by Hindu and Sufi practices. There was a fear that Indian minority Islam would become extinct if it did not guard the purity of its faith. A contributing factor to anti-British feelings on the part of the Waliullahi tradition was the fear that Christian missionary efforts allegedly aimed at eliminating all other religions in India, a fear shared by many religious revival and reform movements in India, also among the Hindus and the Sikhs.

It is therefore easy to see why Mahatma Gandhi (1869-1948) started his massive non-cooperation movement in 1919-20 on a religious Muslim campaign issue, the fate of the Turkish Caliph after the end of Word War I. Indian Muslims campaigned for the defence of the Turkish-Ottoman Khalifat when the Ottoman empire was about to disintegrate after its defeat in the war - as was suspected, with a good measure of British support. This was dictated mainly by British-Indian politics. Indian Muslims strove to shore up their position *vis-à-vis* the British and to assert their minority rights strongly, completely disregarding the critique of the institution of the Khalifat by Turkish Muslims who abandoned the Khalifat, and from dependent Ottoman territories striving for independence from Turkey. It was only natural that Deobandi divines were a party to this movement, some of them like Mahmud al-Hasan, its instigator and prime mover.[28]

This in itself could not but politicise and radicalise internal seminary affairs. The issue of priority for political or educational involvement remained topical throughout this period, that is from the twenties through the forties. Adherents of a more conventional academic vocation for Deoband were defeated in the seminary. Even the chancellor of the seminary, Maulana Sabbir Ahmed Usmani, was forced to resign in 1942 on the grounds that he considered political activity for staff and students at Deoband harmful to their educational goals.[29] His resignation was equally a result of the amputation of the powers of the chancellor in favour of the vice-chancellor. The chancellor was made the constitutional authority of the convening body with little or no decision-making power. Interestingly, these decisions were brought about by a majority decision of the Majlis, or decision-making congregation of the seminary. A similar development denoting the advent of majority rule within the seminary was the abolition of the position of patron in 1354 AH (1935).[30] The patron used to be an eminent personality from public and religious life. At the time it was held by Maulana Shah Muhammad Ashraf ʿAli Thanawi (1863-1943), an outstanding Islamic theologian and scholar in the tradition of Deoband who had published extensively on Islamic law and other doctrinal issues. The opposing Majlis faction argued that the patronship was an expression of the "helplessness" of the Majlis and "unneedful". It wanted to make "the majority opinion as the pivot of decision"[31]. A resolution of the Majlis finally accepted Thanawi's resignation and requested him "to cast his shadow always on the Dar al-Ulum with his pious invocations and lofty favours"[32].

Violent student politics entered Deoband in a big way in 1344 AH (1926). A students' party came into being with the name *Lujnat al-Ittehād* ("Unity Committee") and took exception to certain practices in the kitchen and in the administration of the seminary. During the annual examination, the administrative officer was manhandled, for which five students were rusticated. The students' party was declared illegal, considering it a "source of interference in the administration"³³. Unexpectedly, the disturbances not only revived the following year but engulfed the whole faculty, with one of the teachers, Maulana Anwar Shah Kashmiri delivering two speeches at the local mosque in support of the students' demands, joined by a number of other teachers.³⁴ Strikes and manhandling instances, which would seem to be at variance with the self-proclaimed ethos of the seminary, nevertheless recurred. The response of the administration was twofold. The dissenters among the students and teachers were dealt with firmly through strictures and censures, not dissimilar to colonial government attitudes, easing them out over time. The practical issues were diffused by the new vice-chancellor, Tayyib, when he took office in 1348 AH (1929) and regularised administrative affairs, introducing *en lieu* a meal ticket system.³⁵

Inspired Activism

A picture of Deobandi thought and action during this century would be incomplete without a brief account of the activist campaigns since 1900 which were inspired by the Deobandi school but took place mainly outside the confines of the seminary. The first Deobandi off-spring came into being in 1911, an organisation of the graduates and alumni of Deoband, the *Jam ͑īyat al-Ansār*.³⁶ It was organised by Mahmud al-Hasan who had been one of the first students at Deoband and served as its principal (*sadr-e-mudarris*) and superintendent (*sarparast*) since 1890 and 1905 resp. Its declared objectives were to arrange for religious instruction and the teaching of Arabic to Muslim students in government schools and colleges; to arrange for the placement of well-trained imams in mosques; and to promote the publication of inexpensive religious books and pamphlets.³⁷ Hasan involved one of his old students in this project, a former Sikh, Maulana Ubaidullah Sindhi (1872-1944), who had an equally activist temperament. In 1913 they both also organised a Quranic school in Delhi, the *Nazārat al-Ma ͑arif al-Quraniyya*, aimed at English-educated Muslim boys whose religious education was found wanting or nonexistent. Despite the obvious educational thrust of both endeavours, it was felt that the organisers were pursuing other objectives as well. Sindhi stressed the need for reforms within the Deoband seminary, with emphasis on the activist teachings of Walliullah and Shah Ismail Shahid, on public speaking and writing. Sindhi later went on to hold radical social views, merging Islamic millenarianism with socialist ideas which were becoming more popular during World War I, as an outflow of the Russian revolution of 1917. The anxiety of Muslim intellectuals in India was caused by the Tripolitan and Balkan wars of 1911-12 which saw a conflict emerging between the Caliph residing in Turkey and the Christian ruler of India. Islamic solidarity with the Turkish Caliph resulted in opposition to the

British and, by extension, to British rule in India. Hence polarisation and tension deepened between the cautious non-political and pro-British line of the Deoband administration and the activities of the group around Hasan and Sindhi. The latter was externed from Deoband as an "infidel" and both were engaged in a political intrigue aimed at securing a naive alliance against the British between the Islamic ruler of Afghanistan and Indian Muslims. It was later called the "silk letter conspiracy," after a bunch of letters written on yellow silk was intercepted, leading to the arrest and externment of Hasan in 1916 while Sindhi went underground.

Deobandi divines were joined in these activities mainly by Muhammad ʿAbdul Bari (1879-1926) from the Firangi Mahal seminary, who had organised a medical mission to collect money to help Turkish participants and victims of war activities. This was followed by the introduction of an albeit short-lived organisation to mobilise Indian Muslims for the protection of the holy places of Islam during the war activities, the *Anjuman-i-Khuddam-i-Kaʾaba* ("Society of the Servants of the Kaʾaba", the holy shrine of Islam in Mecca) in 1913. Other prominent Indian Muslims who participated in these activities beyond the allegiance to a particular seminary were Dr. Ansari and the brothers Shaukat Ali (1873-1938) and Muhammad Ali.

A more successful endeavour in terms of longevity was the founding of the *Jamʿīyat ʿal-ʿUlamā-e-Hind*, an organisation of Islamic scholars in India, in 1919. It continued to exist after independence and its branches are still active in India and Pakistan. It was meant to formalise arrangements for an increased role of the more radical ulama in religious and political affairs and cooperated closely with Gandhi and the Indian National Congress, particularly during the Khilafat campaign of 1919-24. Gandhi and Indian Muslim theologians called on the Indian public to mobilise against the dismemberment of the Ottoman Empire after WWI and against the removal of the Caliph. They made it the first stage of the civil disobedience campaign, turning it into a huge mass movement of non-violent resistance against British rule.[38]

The common denominator of these endeavours was the activist view grounded in the tradition of Shah Waliullah and the Indian *mujāhidīn* movement of the beginning of the nineteenth century. It was a concept that sought to establigh the true Islam, holding colonial rule by a Christian European power as much responsible for the plight of Islam in India as every single Muslim who failed to live according to the dictates of religion. Gaining control over religious (Islamic), political and social institutions was considered imperative for clearing the way to erect the kingdom of Allah on earth.

The Tablighis

In contrast, the movement of the Tablighis, also called the Tablighi Jamaat, proposed a different approach in dealing with the challenges of a changing society, concentrating on the individual and his inner perfection. Although Tabligh literally means "mission", it was not exactly a missionary movement since it was not primarily aimed at conversion but at keeping Muslims within the fold of the Islamic faith. Hindu and Muslim élites were particularly shaken by the so-called Moplah riots in 1921-22 in which Muslim peasants on the West Indian Malabar coast rose in revolt against their mainly Hindu landlords and proclaimed a short-lived "Khilafat Republic". Their militants subjected local Hindus to violent attempts at conversion and killed a considerable number of them. In response, radical Hindu and Muslim leaders intensified their efforts to organise co-religionists to resist conversion and practise self-defence on the basis of their religious community. Hindu campaigns of *Shuddhi* ("purification") and *Sanghahan* ("Unity") were countered by Muslim campaigns of *Tablīgh* and *Tanzīm* ("Organisation"). These militant movements were led by former "non-cooperators" who had grudgingly cooperated in that previous anti-colonial campaign. The Shuddhi and the Tabligh campaigns clashed over conversion, notably of the Malkana Rajputs in the districts of Agra and Saharanpur in the western United Provinces. Tabligh efforts were headed by Khwaja Hasan Nizami and Maulana Abdul Bari. The Sangathan and the Tanzim campaigns aimed at strengthening communal religious institutions and their defences. Both were led by prominent Punjabis, Lala Lajpat Rai (1865-1928) and Dr. Saifuddin Kitchlew (c. 1888-1963).[39] Tension soon rose and the years 1923-24 were marked by a spate of bloody inter-religious riots.

While the Tabligh efforts of the 1920s responded to the intensified Shuddhi campaign, the latter had already started in the 1880s.[40] Beyond the Moplah violence it was a reaction to the perception of a relentless growth in the Christian and Muslim communities at the expense of the number of adherents to Hinduism. This sense of alarm was heightened by the decennial publication of census figures showing much higher population growth rates for Muslims and Christians than for Hindus.[41] Orthodox Hinduism, which accepted membership by birth only, did not know of any ritual for the return of converts who would otherwise remain permanently excommunicated. The Shuddhi campaign provided such a ritual of purification. Although the Arya Samaj pursued a constructive agenda of social reforms not limited to doctrinal issues, critics often accused it of a negative attitude, primarily thriving on controversy between caste Hindus, Christians and Muslims.[42] The Shuddhi campaign concentrated on Punjab and parts of the United Provinces, it peaked around 1900 and at the beginning of the 1920s.

Maulana Muhammad Ilyas introduced the Tabligh movement out of concern for the Meo hill tribes in the Mewat region near Delhi, who adhered to syncretic practices with strong Hindu influence.[43] Strengthening their faith in Islam meant providing them with religious schools, instructing them in the five pillars of Islam, teaching them the Islamic way of conducting prayers etc. This task was compounded by the low level of development and education among them. Ilyas started his movement by sending out groups of Mewati students for *daʿwat*[44] as travelling preachers. He sent them to the centers of Muslim learning in western U.P., notably to Kandhela, from where Ilyas hailed.[45] These were areas inhabited by people known for their experience in Islamic doctrine and rites. At the 1941 convention of the movement as many as 20,000-25,000 people assembled at Nuh in the Gurgaon district of Assam.[46] While the orthodox ʿulama had been cautious at this outburst of public piety, the growing mass appeal of the movement forced them to adopt a clear position. From 1940, students and staff of the Nadwat seminary in Lucknow participated openly, and in 1944 principals of a number of Islamic seminaries and academies from Deoband, Delhi, Saharanpur and Lucknow convened to debate what part their academies could play in Ilyas' movement.[47] This close relationship between the Tablighi Jamaat and some reformist Islamic seminaries was embodied by Sayyid Abul-Hasan ʿAli Nadwi (b. 1913) and Muhammad Manzur Numani from the Nadwat Seminary in Lucknow. Both wrote a number of devotional tracts on the life and ideas of Muhammad Ilyas and the concept of his movement.[48]

Beyond this immediate objective Ilyas' movement aimed at strengthening existent faith wherever it became weak for whatever reason. Its main aim was spiritual revival. This made it akin to similar religious movements of the quietist, pietist or puritan variety known from European and Christian history. Renewal was to be achieved through increased observance of the Islamic ritual, obeying the commandments of God mainly by conforming to the requirement for prayer five times daily. In Islam Tabligh activities refer to the traditional Quranic institution of *daʿwah* (arab.). Its root meaning is "invitation," assuming an invitation is extended to non-believers to embrace Islam and to believers to join in prayer.

The institution of *daʿwah* in particular relates to the Quranic verse "Call unto the way of thy Lord with wisdom and fair exhortation, and reason with them in the better way"[49]. It closely interconnects with the institution of jihād, variously translated as "holy war" or "exertion in the way of God". Non-believers are to be called upon to clarify their position towards Islam, either to embrace it or to submit to its rule (and to accept the tax on non-believers). *Daʿwah* as such is an opportunity to be offered to them before they are conquered in the name of Allah. That *daʿwah* can be directed at non-Muslims and Muslims alike has been the subject of a long and contentious debate both in and outside of Islam.[50]

Some historical instances of *daʿwah* movements had strong political implications. They usually denoted a propaganda or mobilisation campaign for allegiance to a particular *imām*. The *daʿwah* served the "Abbasid dynasty when it came to power and the Ismaʿilis in their Quarmatians movement which challenged the ʿAbbasids in Syria, Iraq and Bahrain in the ninth century. For political purposes any sympathiser could execute this propaganda, but in doctrinal matters it was carried out by the *dāʿīs* or preachers.[51] In this context, the *daʿwah's* ability was noted as communicating rapidly over a large area, relying on its travelling operatives as well as on a network of local cells. This particular feature of its communication technique also proved to be instrumental in the modern activities of Ilyas' Tabligh movement. Although it is not clear that he was influenced by historical precedent, he insisted that his Tabligh efforts were moulded on the Quran and the companions of Muhammad.[52]

The main source of information on the activities of this movement in the 1930s and 1940s is its devotional literature written mainly by Abul-Hasan ʿAli Nadwi, Manzur Numani and Shaikh al-Hadīth Muhammad Zakariyya (b. 1898). It contains accounts of the life of Muhammad Ilyas, his letters, his so-called sayings or pronouncements and treatises on the principles of Daʿwah and Tabligh.[53] The collection of religious texts compiled by Zakariyya, the son-in-law of Ilyas, under the title of *Tablīghī Nisāb* is the only authoritative foundation for the philosophy of the movements, with all other tracts not officially owned by the Tablighis. And since the former contained well-known orthodox Islamic texts, Tablighi leaders maintain that there is nothing new in their movement, that the mode for Tabligh and Daʿwah was set by the companions of the Prophet themselves, devising ways and means of extending the influence of Islam and propagating it through preaching.[54] From the beginning, the Tablighi Jamaat maintained its character as a grassroots movement of laymen with minimal administration.

From the literary sources a concept of reform emerges directed at religious practice, and the personal and social behaviour of Indian Muslims which partly resulted from the pressures of the time and partly from long-term objectives. Here one can broadly distinguish between
- religious reform,
- moral and personal perfection,
- social concerns and
- political consequences.

The Meaning of Religious Reform

Ilyas himself preferred his movement to be called a faith movement seeking religious renewal.[55] This was more in consonance with his striving for an all-encompassing approach to the reactivation of Muslims and implied an activist approach to his co-religionists. He wanted to change their way of life bringing it into conformity with the basic commandments of Islam. But his activist approach differed from that pursued by the Deoband seminary, although he maintained close links with that institution ever since he was a student there. While students and faculty members from Deoband supported active intervention in anti-colonial politics, Ilyas' emphasis was on the hereafter and a withdrawal from this-worldly concerns.

Religious reform was at the heart of his approach. As far as his understanding of Islamic doctrine was concerned, he mainly followed the Deoband and Wahhabi tradition, calling for the correction of a misguided practice. Where Deoband emphasised knowledge and purity of doctrine, the religious knowledge recommended by the Tablighis primarily concerned the ritualistic aspects of Islam. Where Ilyas demanded a purification of Islamic practices, he targeted not only Hindu "corruptions" in Islam, but also European and Christian influences. Ilyas though did not distance himself aggressively from Hindus or Islamic sects outside the Indian Sunnite mainstream such as Shias and Ahmadiyya in particular, as other Islamic reformers had done.[56] His emphasis on the *practical* knowledge of Islam brought him closer to the Sufi tradition of focusing on the proper ritual for a union with God.

On one hand, his intent was to turn the gaze of Muslims to the world hereafter, while on the other hand, he demanded that Muslims should turn inwards to seek the path of self-perfection.[57] His practical bent became obvious when he pointed to the devil and demanded the propagation of the advantages of paradise "so that the followers can imagine the merits and rewards of joining the Tablighi movement and may forget the worldly loss caused by their engagement"[58]. The way to self-perfection was to be closely modelled on the life of the Prophet. His advice was

- to seek comfort in simple life like Muhammad[59],
- to be ready to make sacrifices for religious purposes[60],
- to be always hospitable to fellow Muslims[61],
- to make obedience to God the primary occupation in life, all other activity such as bread-earning being secondary[62].

A key strategy for him to reach these goals of faith, devotion and self-perfection was the acquisition or strengthening of religious knowledge (*ilm-e-dīn*). This in turn should lead to an intensified religious practice, particularly keeping the regular daily five prayers, and *remembering God* through repeated recitation of his name and of key verses of the Quran (*zikr*) a practice perfected mainly by the various Sufi orders in combination with techniques of breathing and trance.[63] However, Ilyas preferred the so-called quiet *zikr* where His name is not invoked loudly, where the emphasis is not on outward features but on internal devotion.

It is not surprising that this agenda, aimed at restoring the "Golden" era of the Prophet, religious sincerity and the customs and practices of the Prophet's community, also served the intent of *uniting* the various factions of Islam in a common recourse to faith and to the original sources and practices of Islam, or what they were understood to be. In verse 102 he emphasised that the Tablighi movement's foremost aim should be to try to become the source of reconciliation between different Islamic groups which should drop their doctrinal differences.[64] In verse 164 he talked about the "main aim of the Tabligh to bring all Muslims around one nucleus that is the spirit of the religion"[65].

Model Conduct and Preaching Technique

The idea of improving the conduct of the members of the Tablighi Jamaat extends beyond the religious aspect to civil affairs and, in particular, to personal character-building. The concept of being a good Muslim has to be internalised as well as practically lived.

Ilyas' movement is marked by a system of the minutest instructions on how to behave as a Tablighi.[66] This is a multi-layered formula including a complete canon of preaching technique, ethical and civilised behaviour in a group environment while on a preaching tour and a moral code of conduct in everyday life. At times it borders on group therapy and attempts to mould or model its members in detail. The obsession with detailed instruction partly stems from the belief that to restore the conditions and terms of the life of the Prophet and his companions is a major step towards becoming a good Muslim. The need for these instructions lies partly in the nature of the movement. Since it is by and large a movement of laymen, new members or adherents are schooled in the ways of the Tabligh by other lay members. Large numbers of rural and lower middle-class men are drawn into the movement and introduced to an urban etiquette of behaviour. Conduct is also central to the success of the movement since by definition it wishes to convert or mobilise by example and not by pressure. In reality this is often undermined by considerable organised moral pressure. The rounds (*gāsht*) in market places and neighbourhood areas are obviously meant to intimidate "anti-social" elements, corrupt, immoral and un-Islamic practices as they understand them. It has an air of religious policing, as practised by the latter-day Taliban in Afghanistan and in Iran after Khomeini's revolution. Such an approach cannot be considered Islam-specific, as neighbourhood watch has become an effective tool of crime prevention in the United States and Britain, and is also occasionally fed by religious motives. In character formation special emphasis is put on self-denial and a self-effacing attitude, but also on self-control. This is expressed in advice such as

- to refrain from showing off while doing good[67],
- that one should exercise self-assessment and not hurry to pass judgement on others[68],
- or, to spend money in the right way, balanced, within the limitations set by God and without being stingy[69].

The technique of self-denial has proven to be a very effective strategy to deal with ideological/religious adversaries. It leaves the onus of being wrong on the other and claims high moral ground for whatever one demands. Its practical importance becomes visible in the instructions for preaching. There Ilyas demanded
- to show patience and yet passion, to be humble,
- to interact with the local pious and intellectual people,
- to accept hardship on the road of preaching,
- not to get disheartened by a negative response, or by not getting the right attention even from the pious and learned.[70]

He advised them to impart simple and basic knowledge about the Islamic ritual so as to give people the feeling that they now know how to observe the five pillars of Islam correctly, to which prayer and *Zikr* as a means of seeking union with God are clearly central. This included knowledge
- on how to do a correct recitation of the names of God and of certain Quranic verses[71], how much *Zikr* and why[72],
- on what to focus on in preaching, for which he suggests three points: to submit to the will of God, to believe in the day of judgement, and to highlight the principle of requital that every act will be rewarded or punished on the day of judgement[73].

The fundamentals of the Tablighi work were summarised in the so-called *sath batein*, seven matters or sayings, sometimes also reduced to six. They show interesting parallels with the preaching instructions of the Arya Samaj (see table, p. 92). From this comparison it can clearly be seen that such instructions for preaching are not Islam-specific either. It is a technique equally cherished by missionaries of other religions, notably the evangelical churches of America. It similarly shows to what extent the concerns of the Tablighis were influenced and shaped by their potential adversaries, that is the Arya Samaj which they and their colleagues at Deoband studied in great detail. Yet the approach of the Tablighis also aimed at wider goals of moral improvement. In their technique of self-reflection and moral improvement, of pressure by exemplary conduct, the Tablighis shared the cultural legacy of South Asia's many religions. Around the same time as the movement came in to existence, M. K. Gandhi, leader of the anti-colonial movement in India, had exemplarily shown by his *satyagraha* technique how effective non-violent pressure can be.

Table

Tablighi Jamaat	Arya Samaj
1. Kalima Profession of faith in Allah as the only God, and in Muhammad as his Prophet, in Allah as the sole guardian and helper in distress who is present everywhere and sees and hears everything (*hazir-o-nazir*), as expressed in the *Kalima* verse of the Quran.	1. God is the primary source of all true knowledge, and of all that is known by its means.
2. Namaz Regular prayers, five times a day, every part of the worshipper's body is engaged in an exercise of obedience to His commands.	2. God is All-truth, All-knowledge, All-Beatitude, Incorporeal, Almighty, Just, Merciful, Unbegotten, Infinite, Changeless, Without a beginning, Incomparable, the Support and Lord of all, All-pervading, Omniscient, Imperishable, Immortal, Exempt from fear, Eternal, Holy and the Maker of the universe. To Him alone is worship due.
3. Ilm and Zikr Acquire religious knowledge to know and observe Allah's commands. Continuous remembrance of Allah and his Prophet so as to intensify one's devotion to Him, with special Quranic verses for various details of life, like falling asleep, waking up, meeting people, having the meals, setting out for a journey and returning etc.	3. The Vedas are the books of all true knowledge. It is the paramount duty of all Aryas to read them and to instruct others in them, to hear them read, and to recite them to others.
4. Ikram-i Musilmeen Respect every Muslim. Every Muslim must be considered as one's real brother and must always be given affection, sympathy and sincere attention at all times, particularly when in need. No controversial matters or points of secondary importance are to be discussed at any time.	4. All persons should remain ever ready to accept the Truth and to renounce untruth.
5. Ikhlaas Pure intentions, sincerity, self-appraisal.	5. All actions ought to be performed in conformity to virtue, *i.e.* after due consideration of right and wrong.

6. *Tafrigh-i waqt* Spare time as much as possible for inviting others, and by implication oneself, to the commands of Allah and the ways of the Prophet. This may involve leaving home and family for a specified duration, in the way of the Prophet and his companions, who ate leaves or a single date and walked barefoot long distances. It does not mean giving up everything else in one's profession and employment. Minimum schedule: once a week a *gasht* (walk, talking rounds) in the locality, around the mosque; once a month a tour of full three days to a locality, town or village other than one's own; once a year a tour of forty days (*chilla*) in a distant area; once a life a tour of four months in a given place or area.	6. The primary aim of the Arya Samaj is to do good to mankind, i.e. to ameliorate the physical, spiritual and social condition of all men.
7. *Tark-i layani* Abdicating the pointless, which is telling lies, backbiting, picking quarrels, any thought or deed which takes the believer away from the commands of Allah.	7. All ought to be treated with love, justice, and due regard to their merits.
	8. Ignorance ought to be dispelled and knowledge diffused.
	9. No one ought to remain satisfied with his own welfare. The welfare of the individual should be regarded as included in the welfare of all.
	10. In matters which affect the well-being of all, the individual should subordinate his personal liking; in matters that affect him alone, he is to enjoy freedom of action.

Source: Mohammad Talib, The Tablighis in the Making of Muslim Identity. In: Mushirul Hasan (ed.), Islam, Communities and the Nation: Muslim Identities in South Asia and Beyond, Delhi 1998; Kenneth Jones/Arya Dharm, Hindu Consciousness in the 19th Century Punjab, Delhi 1989, p. 321.

Social change

Within the parameters of this concept, social and political concerns were understood to derive from religious reform, character formation and preaching. Yet concentrating on the world hereafter, he could not dissociate himself and his movement from social reality in British India. His main advice to a member of the Tablighi Jamaat was to do his work in society as a good Muslim, help other Muslims, and particularly help poor Muslims. Although he did not take an explicit position on secular matters, some of his sayings suggest what attitude he had towards issues such as education, women and poverty.

Education

In keeping with views shared by the Deobandis Ilyas argued that education should be mainly religious. True education (in religious terms) for Tablighis should conform with the time of the Prophet, modern education was seen as a deviation.[74] Only religious education was seen to restore a sense of identity other than western. Again, this combined with the sense of a civilising mission. He supported efforts and concepts directed at providing the masses with basic education as propagated by Zakir Hussain (1897-1967) through the Jamia Millia, a public educational institution for Muslims.[75]

Role of Women

Women were expected to stay at home and look after the children, to create a model household. The most influential publication in Indian reformist Islam on this subject was *Perfecting women* (Urdu: *bihishti zewar*) by the Deobandi theologian Thanawi, which for generations was - and is - a bedside table book for most Muslim wives in India.[76] Although this was a conventional and conservative approach, within the Tabligh movement it included emancipatory elements as well. Women could run their own study circles, and occasionally, they would go on tour, although this was generally discouraged. Looking at the role of women in recent forms of Islamic mobilisation in Iran and also in Turkey, it becomes clear that women do not contend themselves for long with a subordinate role and use Islam also as a means of emancipation within religion to go on to emancipation in society.[77]

Wealth and Poverty

The relation to rich people was ambiguous. While the Tablighis needed their support they definitely wanted to reform them in the spirit of Islam. Therefore, Ilyas stipulated that the Tablighis should not ignore wealthy people because they need guidance in religious matters.[78]

Poverty alleviation should be organised mainly through *zakat*. For true and wealthy Muslims he considered the customary amount of *zakat* insufficient, sympathisers can give their dues, advanced followers should renounce their worldly possessions in favour of the movement.[79] Renouncing one's possessions is played down nowadays as it occasionally creates considerable difficulties when men desert their families and force the dissolution of the household on them in order to go on unlimited preaching travel. Wives are known to have strongly protested to leaders of the movement that this should not be condoned. A preferred interpretation today is, therefore, that nobody should escape his duties in the place in society where God has put him. Businessmen should demonstrate the Islamic way of life to the business community, teachers to the educational community etc.[80]

Ilyas wanted to encourage the interaction of people belonging to different sections and classes of society, e.g. religious scholars, people with English/western education, traders, and the poor since this would have "a good impact on the Tabligh movement". It was hoped this would contribute to enhancing the understanding of the Tablighis' approach and would in turn help the ʿulama deal with the social diversity of the movement, a tacit acknowledgement of the mental isolation in which the ʿulama sometimes live. Such social intercourse would lay the foundation for the co-operation of all classes as desired.[81]

While being in favour of reforming the moneyed and landed classes, the Tablighis did not advocate plain egalitarianism. All members of a Jamaat, a group of travelling lay preachers, should relate to each other morally and ethically on an equal footing. Yet, social harmony was not to be confused with equality. Hierarchical structures were important in the conduct of the Tablighi tours where Tablighis were advised to obey the elders[82] who play a central role in the conduct of the affairs of the Tablighi organisation.

The existing social order is treated as God-given and should not be altered by man, yet beyond social status, religious knowledge is the main criterion for belonging to a social group. Ilyas distinguished three classes of Muslims who should play their role in the Tabligh movement in the place Allah has put them.

> "There are three classes of Muslims: (1) the backward (*pasmandah*), (2) the reputable/dignified people (*ahl-e-waqār*), and (3) the scholars of religion (*ʿulamā-e-dīn*). Those groups should play their role (in the spreading of Islam) according to their place/ right (*haqq*), the ordinary people marked by mercy and service, the dignitaries marked by veneration/honour, the religious scholars, by respect. Accordingly, religious work (*daʿwat*) should be directed at them."[83]

His political views

Ilyas expressly stated that the Tablighi Jamaat does not involve itself in politics. Here again he markedly differed with the activist stance of the Deoband seminary. Yet, looking close at his positions it becomes clear that he shared many of the basic assumptions of the Deobandis about politics and Islam, notably in relation to colonialism and the west, to the "adversaries" of Islam in general. As in other matters, Ilyas' position was derived from his focus on the other-worldly aspect of Islam. In answer to the question of why Muslims in British India have difficulty getting positions of power and authority in government, he referred to the need to focus on God's kingdom which is the world hereafter.

> "How can the administration of this world be entrusted to you if you did not mould your personality and your life with regard to the defence of the commandments and deeds of Allah (to the extent where you are capable of it and do not face any disability). When trusting the believers with the governance of this world Allah's will is that his intentions and commandments reign supreme in this world. If you could not achieve this within the limits of your own capabilities what hope is there from you for tomorrow if the world is entrusted to you?"[84]

His underlying sympathy with the anti-colonial movement became clear when he touted the loyalists and influence-seekers for the sake of opportunistic gains who should be influenced to turn back to the path of faith and religion.[85] He was critical of the system of examination in Government-sponsored educational institutions since through its secular emphasis it exerted "a negative impact on religious knowledge"[86].

Ilyas' emphasis was on withdrawal from politics and strengthening the faith in its many facets. His movement was non-political in the sense of being apolitical to the point of almost having an aversion to politics or political actions. Yet its political impact cannot be truly measured by its intentions and declarations. Its impressive gain in influence among Indian Muslims in the late thirties and forties, and even more so today, raises questions of vast political implications. The way in which this movement was and is tied in with social and political change was accentuated by its desire to ameliorate and alleviate the spiritual and moral privation of the rapidly "urbanizing" middle and lower middle classes. Social and cultural dislocation of these strata was the background against which they acted and from which they obtained their sense of direction. Their major field of activity were the district towns and the townships of the big cities. The response of the local people was known to be ambivalent. While some were ardently enthusiastic about them, many reacted with indifference and mild ridicule. With many they had the reputation of simpletons, often including half- or uneducated youths with burning religious fervour.

The seemingly passive political position of the Tablighis proved to be potentially explosive at times and its consequences were fraught with ambiguities. Before independence, the movement was criticised for leading part of the Muslim community away from active involvement in the anti-colonial movement, and more specifically from the movement for the creation of the separate Islamic state of Pakistan. More recently the political nihilism of the Tablighis was strongly denounced by the politicised Islamic groups, notably the *Jamāʿat-i Islāmī* (Islamic Party), founded by Maulana Syed Abul Ala Maudoodi (1903-1979) in 1941. The latter strongly believed in the creation of an Islamic polity. The Tablighis were attacked for their stand on Afghanistan where they refused to support the involvement of militant Islamic groups from Pakistan. Given the fact that this position was maintained despite considerable pressure it is difficult to call the Tablighis non-political. As such the Tablighis perhaps exerted a certain moderating effect on political radicalism among Indian and Pakistani Muslims.

At the same time, their attempts at recharging the religious faith of people at large strengthened the environment for Islam-based politics since it raised the self-awareness of Muslims and increased their religious focus. Dual and multiple membership in movements was and is typical of South Asia. While banning politics from its own ranks, the Tablighis never refused to allow any Muslim to go on tour with them and would never question his antecedents whether he belonged to the Jamaat-i Islami, or to more radical and militant groups like the infamous *Harkat-ul Ansār* in Pakistan[87], a militant Islamist outfit which is accused of being at the back of part of the Afghan militancy as well as of that in Indian Kashmir. They took spiritual refuge in the Tablighi preaching tours to rekindle their faith just as others go to prayer. In fact it strengthened a sort of "catholic" attitude where you remain unburdened by a sin as long as you repent.

The Tablighis remain a product as well as an element of change. Although they claim otherwise, the change they desired was not towards restoring tradition as it was known. They constructed a new religiosity of the industrial age for which its counterparts in the western world were well known, including groups such as the Salvation Army, Jehova's Witnesses, or the New Age religious cults.

Summary

The Deobandis and the Tablighis demonstrated that reformist Islam in South Asia was indeed interventionist. It aimed at change both of society and of the individual. It needed to do so by nature of its reformism which is never content with what it finds, reaching out from the "sacred" into the "secular". It was intervention not explicitly intended to help modernisation to bear fruit but rather to counter its effect on Muslim India. Yet to do so it had to engage with modernisation and society so deeply, had to "pollute" itself by the mundane to such an extent that it could not achieve its desired sacral "purity" without adapting itself to the world around.

The Deobandis and the Tablighis acted as "Agents of Change" to the extent that
- they were themselves affected by changes, facing consequences of social transformation and acknowledging their impact;
- they followed their own agenda of change, partly as a response to the social and political transformation and partly on their own intiative;
- they underwent changes themselves, went through a process of adaptation, relocation and redefinition.

From the perusal of their major concerns and activities during the period under study it appears that the Deobandis and the Tablighis were mainly affected by
- social transformation and the attending circumstances of a market-oriented bourgeois way of life such as the rise of materialism and non-religious ideologies, "spiritual deprivation", the marginalisation of religious institutions and professional religious functionaries;
- competitive and participatory public institutions and political mobilisation, partly replacing hierarchichal and heridirary decision-making by egalitarian approaches and merit-based selection for participation in the public arena;
- cultural alienation resulting from structural hegemony of western and colonial concepts and policies leading to an intense quest for a true national identity of the multi-ethnic and multi-religious society in India encompassing all social and political forces in colonial India.

These changes in Indian society obviously had a secularizing effect, or so it was feared, increasing laxity in religious matters. This would undermine the cohesion of religious communities and also community-based decision-making. The ʿulama who constituted the core of the activists of both movements explicitly acknowledged the increasing competition in the public arena from other religious communities. They had to accommodate the restructering of the political system as pursued by the constitutional reforms projects of the British who introduced more elements of representative participation through the gradual extension of elective principles. And they had to come to terms with the aspirations of the nationalist forces regarding the envisioned polity of an independent India for which schemes and concepts were advanced and in which the

ʿulama definitely wanted a secure place and perhaps increased influence in decision-making compared to the colonial period.

From these pressures a separate agenda of change arose, pushed by the ʿulama and aimed at
- a revival of a spiritual perspective and practice in the daily life of Indian Muslims, strengthening religious knowledge, faith and conduct, constituting the "internal", pietist thrust of Islamic mobilisation;
- a renewal of religious institutions, demarcating the Muslim community more distinctly from other communities, defending Muslims and Islam against secular and competing religious commitments to the point of claiming a privileged position for minority Muslims as the best possible defence, constituting the "external" dimension of their agenda.

Islam was to be made the major, and for some the sole determinant for the national and cultural identity of Indian Muslims. Islamic mobilisation was to secure a strong and lasting position of influence for the ʿulama, "relaunching" themselves after the turn of the century as a major activist force in the public arena of Muslim India. This goal was not identical with the campaign of the Muslim League or the Pakistan movement. Although objectives regarding the role of Islam in politics were close or overlapping, the role of the ʿulama in the League's activities remained limited, and differences over the direction of political and social change after independence continue to this day, particularly in Pakistan. They found their most prominent expression in the so-called Objectives Resolution initiated by the ʿulama and moved by Prime Minister Liaqat Ali Khan in March 1949, reposing final sovereignty over Pakistan in God where the authority delegated by Him to the state of Pakistan was a "sacred trust" to be exercised through the people "within the limit prescribed by Him"[88]. It was meant to offset the more liberal and almost secular directions given by the leader of the Muslim League and the founder-father of Pakistan, M. A. Jinnah (1876-1948), in his late speeches in 1947-48 before his untimely death, expressing strong faith in the institutions of elective democracy.[89]

Yet engaging with change, the ʿulama could not help changing themselves. They became more conscious of nationalist politics, more populist, less divorced from social and political reality, acknowledging and accepting some of the basic elements of the western system, such as elections and participatory democracy, although often they would interpret them according to their needs.

The mode of response to change by both of them was disparate, one was active, the other passive. Whereas many of the Deobandis (though by no means all of them) considered it imperative to challenge the external political and social institutions, the Tablighis concentrated on the individual and its reformation as the securest way of achieving final deliverance.[90] In terms of western-inspired modernisation, the Deobandis could partly be considered as an "agent" since they paved the way for Muslim orthodoxy, for orthodox Muslims into the modern nationalist polity of independent India/Pakistan. The Tablighis represented the "antidote" to modernisation, responding to the consequences of change which is equally indispensable in any process of transformation.

In terms of results of change their impact is difficult to quantify. They shared with other Islamic movements in South Asia a certain mismatch between some extraordinary claims, a distinct short-term failure or inability to accomplish practical goals and a medium- to long-term success in moulding and forming the political ethos of a Muslim élite. Activists coming from movements with a highly local, doctrinal or particularist agenda went on to play a role in mainstream politics.[91] Muslim politicians such as Maulana Maududi, Zakir Husain, who later became President of India, and Maulana Azad acknowledged having been influenced by the reformist tradition of Deoband or by the sincerity and fervour of the Tablighis.

In spite of these peculiarities and their often marginal position it would be wrong to treat these Islamic groups outside the general discourse on change and transformation. Their contribution to change or response to it was as legitimate as that of forces from the political mainstream like parties, trade unions etc., whether one agrees with their recipes and attitudes or not.[92] It is neither possible nor useful to determine unequivocally whether they were dangerous or helpful for the process of transformation. Their sustained capacity to unleash significant social and political forces was proven during the pre-independence period of anti-colonial resistance. And if anything, it is undiminished today. They have been part and parcel of the dialogue between indigenous culture and global influences. This makes it all the more important not to castigate or label them in any way but to involve them increasingly in a dialogue on common concerns.

The intention was not to prove that they were "Agents of Change" because in one way or the other, depending on how broadly one defines change, every socio-religious movement is an "agent of change". The intention was rather to do away with stereotypes in relation to historical change and progress, to show in what way religious groups such as these were involved in change, what kind of agents they were and what kind of change they were after. Their mode of operation in localizing global influences, adapting or responding to western concepts will be difficult to understand without their historical background, notably in pre-independence days when cultural modes of operation in the global political field were established with lasting effect.

The two movements demonstrated that irrespective of how "obscure" and strange these groups may look to the discerning public gaze in the west, their political, social and cultural functions are not dissimilar to phenomena in the history of the west. In many parts of the western world religious mobilisation has been mediating change for a long time and is still being called upon as a major source of legitimacy for power and morality. To understand the effects of global processes on Asia and Africa it remains pertinent to take a close look at their interaction with the more well-known processes of social and political polarisation and change. Both groups are hugely relevant today, the Deobandis in Pakistan and Afghanistan through the Taliban, the Tablighis in the whole of South Asia. Understanding their current incarnations as part of this global interaction seems impossible without looking at their historical inception. Cultural and religious aspects of the current globalisation can only be meaningfully studied when their historical roots are taken into consideration.

Notes

1   Urdu: missionary society, henceforth used in anglicized transliteration: Tabligh, Tablighi Jamaat etc.
2   According to the 1921 census, the share of Muslims in the population of India, including provinces, states and agencies was 21.74 per cent. Government of India, Census of India 1921. India - Report. Vol. 1, Part I, Calcutta, p. 123.
3   Of 15 Indian provinces listed in 1921, the Muslim population exceeded 50 per cent in the North-West Frontier Province (N.W.F.P. - 91.62 per cent), in Baluchistan (87.31 per cent), Punjab (55.33 per cent), and Bengal (53.99 per cent). Amongst the 18 listed states and agencies, the same is true for the Kashmir State (76.75 per cent) and the adjoining confederations of states or agencies in the N.W.F.P., Baluchistan, and Punjab. Beyond their nominal share of between 10 and 20 per cent, Muslims played an important role in the political and cultural life of the United Provinces (U.P.), Bombay, Madras and the Hyderabad State. Ibid.
4   On the evolution of political representation for Muslims and other communities, see Farzana Shaikh, Community and Consensus in Islam: Muslim Representation in Colonial India, 1860-1947, Cambridge 1989, chapter 2 (Participation or representation?) and 3 (Muslim attitudes to representation), pp. 49-118.
5   For the Muslim League and Muslim parties in the provinces of today's Pakistan, cf. Ayesha Jalal, The Sole Spokesman: Jinnah, the Muslim League and the Demand for Pakistan, Cambridge 1994; Ian Talbot, Provincial Politics and the Pakistan Movement, Karachi 1990; Tazeen Murshid, The Sacred and the Secular. Bengal Muslim Discourses 1871-1977, Delhi 1995.
6   For a classical overview, see W. C. Smith, Modern Islam in India: a Social Analysis. Delhi 1985 (reprint).
7   On radical and mass mobilisation, see Gail Minault, The Khilafat Movement: Religious Symbolism and Political Mobilization in India, New York 1982; Conrad Wood, The Moplah Rebellion and its Genesis, Delhi 1987; D. Reetz, Hijrat - The Flight of the Faithful: A British File on the Exodus of Muslim Peasants from North India to Afghanistan in 1920, Berlin 1995; idem, On the Nature of Muslim Political Responses: Islamic Militancy in the North-West Frontier Province. In: Mushirul Hasan (ed.),

Islam, Communities and the Nation: Muslim Identities in South Asia and Beyond, Delhi 1998, pp. 179-200.
8   On the issue of Islamic intervention in the public domain in connection with interreligious violence, see Sandria Freitag, Collective Action and Community: Public Arenas and the Emergence of Communalism in North India, Berkeley 1989.
9   On the concept of "Agents of Change" as pursued by the research group from which this manuscript emerged, see Dietrich Reetz, Akteure des Wandels und die Globalisierung - zur Einführung. In: Dietrich Reetz/Heike Liebau (eds.), Globale Prozesse und "Akteure des Wandels". Quellen und Methoden ihrer Untersuchung - ein Werkstattgespräch, Berlin 1997, pp. 5-17.
10 Homi Bhabha, The Location of Culture, London 1994.
11 Jeremy Fergus Boissevain, Friends of Friends: Networks, Manipulators and Coalitions, Oxford 1974.
12 *Āriā Samāj* (Sanskrit): "Society of Nobles". Founded 1875 by Dayananda Saraswati (1824-1883).
13 Named after its founder Mirza Ghulam Ahmad (c. 1839-1908).
14 Barbara Daly Metcalf, Islamic Revival in British India, 1860-1900. Princeton 1982.
15 Ibid., p. 31.
16 ʿ*ulamā* (Arab./Urdu): religious scholar, divine, one possessing religious knowledge, part. about Islamic law and its various schools, derived from *ilm*: knowledge, science.
17 Sayyid Mahbub Rizvi, Tarikh-i Darulʿulum, Diyoband (Deoband). Translated into English by Murtaz Husain F. Quraishi. 2 vols. Deoband 1980-81.
18 *Anno Hijri*: Year of the Islamic Calendar, starting with the exodus of the Prophet and his followers from Mecca to Meddina in 622 AD.
19 Rizvi, Tarikh-i Darulʿulum, Diyoband, loc. cit., vol. I, p. 235.
20 *Athar* (Arab./Urdu): Islamic tradition as source of religious knowledge, usually that of the prophet's companions or successors, whereas one emanating from words or deeds of the prophet himself is called *Hadīth*.
21 Rizvi, Tarikh-i Darulʿulum, Diyoband, loc. cit., vol. I, p. 234, note 1.
22 Muhammad Ali wanted to combine "the separate elements of the common Indian nationality and Islamic *millat* and brotherhood." However, this meant there was no place for Hindu and Muslim students to live and study together: "Only those people can do so for whom religion does not have any value, who consider religion to be a useless thing." Mohammad Sarwar, Mazamin-e Muhammad Ali. Part I, Delhi, n.d., p. 254. Quoted in: Mushirul Hasan (ed.), Communal and Pan-Islamic Trends in Colonial India, Delhi 1985 (2nd rev. ed.), p. 97.
23 Khilafat movement - Indian religio-political movement initiated by Mahatma Gandhi and Indian Muslim leaders in 1919 in defence of the Turkish Sultan and the Islamic institution of the Caliph, i.e. the head of the world Muslim community, after the Allied Powers including Britain threatened to punish Turkey in post-World War I peace negotiations for its participation in the war on the side of the German and Austro-Hungarian empires.
24 Muhammad Ali, for instance, revived Shibli's discourses on the Quran in the first days of the Jamia and ensured that "our day began with a full hour devoted to the rapid exegisis of the Koran". Quoted from: Mushirul Hasan, My Life: A Fragment: Mohamed Ali's Quest for Identity in Colonial India. In: Id. (ed.), Islam, Communities and the Nation, loc. cit., p. 77.
25 Rizvi, Tarikh-i Darulʿulum, Diyoband, loc. cit., vol. I, p. 233.

26 Hanafiyya: one of the four mainstream legal traditions in Sunni Islam, developed from the teachings of the theologian Imam Abu Hanifah (c. 700-767).
27 Islamic mysticism taking recourse to varied rituals intended to bring about a direct union with God which include certain prayer techniques, devotional poetry, music and dance as well as the worship of Saints.
28 Cf. Gail Minault, The Khilafat Movement, New York 1982, pp. 103-104 and *passim*.
29 Rizvi, Tarikh-i Darul ͨ ulum, Diyoband, vol. I, loc. cit., p. 240.
30 Ibid., p. 222.
31 Ibid.
32 Rudad-e Majlis-e Shura (Proceedings of the Advisory Council), 30th Rajab, 1354 AH, quoted in: ibid.
33 Rizvi, Tarikh-i Darul ͨ ulum, Diyoband, vol. I, loc. cit., p. 210.
34 Ibid., p. 211.
35 Ibid., p. 220.
36 Old Boys' Association, lit. "group of friends/helpers"; *ansār* - companions of the Prophet from Medina.
37 Minault, The Khilafat Movement, loc. cit., p. 28.
38 For a more detailed account of this Islamic activism, see Minault, The Khilafat Movement, loc. cit., chapters 1, 2.
39 Minault, The Khilafat Movement, loc. cit., pp. 192-197.
40 Cf. R. K. Ghai, Shuddhi Movement in India, Delhi 1990; K. C. Yadav/K. S. Arya, Arya Samaj and the Freedom Movement 1875-1947. 2 vols, Delhi 1988; G. S. Saxena, Arya Samaj Movement in India, 1875-1947, Delhi 1990.
41 Proportional share of the religious communities in 1921 and its change over 1881 (in per cent):

Hindus	Buddhists	Jains	Sikhs	Muslims	Christians	Tribal	Others
63.41	3.56	0.37	1.03	21.74	1.5	3.09	0.2
- 15	- 19	- 25	+ 41	+ 9	+ 105	+ 19	- 10

Computed on the basis of: Census of India 1921 - Report, Vol. 1., loc. cit., pp. 122-23.
42 Cf. J. E. Llewellyn, The Arya Samaj as a Fundamentalist Movement. A Study in Comparative Fundamentalism, Delhi 1993, pp. 103-108.
43 Cf. I. S. Marwa, Tabligh Movement Among the Meos of Mewat. In: M.S.A. Rao, Social Movements in India, Delhi 1979, pp. 79-98; Abdul Shakur, Tarikh-i Mewat, Delhi 1919.
44 Urdu: invitation, mission, propagation of Islam.
45 M. Anwarul Haq, The Faith Movement of Mawlana Muhammad Ilyas, London 1972, p. 111.
46 Mumtaz Ahmad, Tablighi Jamaat of the Indo-Pakistan Subcontinent: An Interpretation. In: Rashid Ahmad/Muhammad Afzal Qarshi (eds.), Islam in South Asia, Lahore Institute of Islamic Culture, 1995, p. 65.
47 M.A. Haq, The Faith Movement, loc. cit., p. 95.
48 Cf. Sayyid Abul-Hasan ͨ Ali Nadwi, Life and Mission of Maulana Mohammad Ilyas, Lucknow 1983 [2nd ed.], pp. 169; Muhammad Manzur Numani, Malfuzāt Hazrat Maulānā Muhammad Ilyās, Lahore, n.d., pp. 152ff.
49 Sura XVI: Verse 125. Quranic translation quoted here after: The Meaning of the Glorious Qurʾān, by Muhammad Marmaduke Pickthall, Hyderabad-Deccan 1938.
50 Poston, Islamic da ͨ wah in the West, loc. cit., pp. 11ff.

51 Cf. B. Lewis et al., The Encyclopedia of Islam. New Edition. Vol 2, Leiden 1991, pp. 168-170. For a historical profile of daʿwah activities see Larry Poston, Islamic Daʿwah in the West: Muslim Missionary Activity and the Dynamics of Conversion to Islam, New York 1992, pp. 3-26.
52 Numani, Malfuzāt (M.), loc. cit., nos. 1, 2, 4, 21 [Sayings quoted according to their numbered listing].
53 Cf. Sayyid Abul-Hasan ʿAli Nadwi, Makātīb, Hazrat Maulana Shah Muhammad Ilyās, Karachi 1982 (1st ed. 1952); Muhammad Ilyas, Irshādāt-o Maktubāt. Compiled by Iftekhar Faridi, Delhi 1980; Manzur Numani, Daʿwat-e-Tablīgh', Lahore, n.d.; Maulana Muhammad Zakariyya, Tablīghī Nisāb, Delhi 1975 (various editions); see also note no. 45.
54 Interview with Prof Masood, activist of the Tablighi movement, at its Delhi headquarters in Nizamuddin on 26 October 1998.
55 Manzur Numani, Introduction. In: Nadwi, Muhammad Ilyās aur unkī dīnī daʿwat, loc. cit., pp. 30-31.
56 Cf. Numani, Malfuzat, loc. cit., no. 3. Ilyas shared the concern to remove innovations (bidʿat) from Islam which were introduced under European/Christian and Hindu influences. He particularly denounced imitation (taqlīd) of the manners and customs of European Christians [M. 124]. He condemned saint worship (pir parasti) typical of Sufism and the Barelwi tradition [M. 25].
57 Ibid., M. 73, 18.
58 Ibid., M. 67.
59 Ibid., M. 12.
60 Ibid., M. 15.
61 Ibid., M. 14.
62 Ibid., M. 22.
63 Ibid., M. 35.
64 Ibid., M. 102.
65 Ibid., M. 164.
66 For an account of the routine of Tablighi work which has changed little over time, cf. S. Ziauddin, Tablighi Movement in India: Organisation and Functioning Style. In: Islam and the Modern Age, Delhi, Jamia Millia, November 1996, pp. 264-283.
67 Numani, Malfuzat, loc. cit., no. 6.
68 Ibid., M. 9.
69 Ibid., M. 13.
70 Ibid., M. 25-30.
71 Ibid., M. 49.
72 Ibid., M. 68, 69.
73 Ibid., M. 56.
74 Ibid., M. 84.
75 On the interest taken by Zakir Hussain in the work of the Tablighi Jamaat and his personal relationship with Muhammad Ilyas, cf. Sayyid Abul-Hasan ʿAli Nadwi, Purāne Charāgh. Vol. 2, Lucknow 1980, pp. 62-84, here p. 69.
76 Barbara Daly Metcalf, Perfecting Women: Maulana Ashraf ʿAli Thanawi's Bihishti Zewar. A Partial Translation with Commentary, Berkeley 1990.
77 Cf. Maulana Majaz Azami, Guidance for a Muslim Wife, Delhi 1993.
78 Numani, Malfuzat, loc. cit., no. 5.
79 Ibid., M. 51, 62, 64.

80 Interview with Prof Masood, a Tablighi activist, on 26 October 26, at the *Tablighi* Centre, Delhi, Nizamuddin West - D.R.
81 Numani, Malfuzat, loc. cit., no. 104.
82 The elders are called in Urdu the *Buzurg*, by a Persianised expression, in Pakistan, and *Bare*, in plain Hindustani Urdu, in India.
83 Numani, Malfuzat, loc. cit., no. 135.
84 Ibid., M. 10.
85 Ibid., M. 11.
86 Ibid., M. 8.
87 The News,. 9 October 1997, Islamabad edition, reports about double membership in the *Harkat* and the *Tablīghī Jamaʿat*.
88 Cf. M. Rafique Afzal, Political Parties in Pakistan 1947-58, Islamabad 1976., p. 134.
89 Cf. Mohammad Ali Jinnah, Speeches: Indian Legislative Assembly 1935-47, Karachi 1991.
90 In a way, both represent the external and internal variant of missiology as discussed by Poston, in particular in chapter 3, External-Institutional Versus Internal-Personal: Fundamental Strategies of Religious Proselytization. In: Poston, Islamic Daʿwah in the West, loc. cit. pp. 49-63.
91 Cf. my monograph, Hijrat: The Flight of the Faithful, loc. cit., pp. 76-85, where I make a similar argument for the activists of the regional Hijrat movement in 1920 when peasants and local activists left for Afghanistan in hope for a better future and in protest against colonial rule of the "infidels". Minault shares this argument, as far as the agitation for a Muslim University is concerned which resulted in the 1920 Muslim University Bill. The latter fell much short of the declared objectives of the movement although "it nevertheless had served as an important vehicle for Muslim political mobilization". Minault, The Khilafat Movement, loc. cit., p. 54.
92 There is a strong opinion, particularly in Indian historiography, that religious movements in Islam, but also in Hinduism, mainly furthered 'communalism,' *i.e.* religious antagonism, and hindered transformation. The argument appears to be justified where it questions the claim of religious organisations to speak for all Indian Muslims or Hindus and deplores militancy and violence. But it is difficult to sustain where it ignores or minimizes the role and potential of religious organisations in political and social transformation. Cf. Mushirul Hasan, Legacy of a Divided Nation, London 1997; Bipan Chandra, Communalism in Modern India, Delhi 1986; Sumit Sarkar, Writing Social History, Delhi 1997.

Globalization and Political Islam[1]

Anoushiravan Ehteshami

The "Fundamentals"

In a nutshell, this chapter focuses on two sets of issues. Firstly, the ways in which Islam has become politicised, and has been deployed as a political tool in the hands of Muslim political actors. In this regard, the analysis focuses on the re-emergence of Islam as a sociopolitical force in the world.[2] Secondly, the chapter will try and idenfity the causes of the tensions, which are now plain for all to see, between the forces of political Islam and those who control and dominate the contemporary (economic and political) international system. In this sense, it is also about exploring the inevitable linkages which seem to tie the domestic and the external - linking political Islam at home to the prevailing areligious and hierarchical international environment.

Jansen has asserted that "Islamic fundamentalism is both fully politics and fully religion"[3]. The "duality" in nature that he identifies is highly explosive, because on the one hand it enables the Islamists to use religious authority to challenge the legitimacy of Muslim rulers and established Islamic hierarchies, and, on the other, to adopt the secular political wherewithal and methods with which they can shake the main pillars on which the modern world has been built, and in which so many of our lives are rooted.

In terms of Muslim politics today, the assertion made by Eickelman and Piscatori, that as individuals and societies "struggle to make sense of the global processes of rapid social, economic, political, and technological change, standard conceptual maps of the social and political world become obselete and the necessity of new guide-posts obvious"[4] remains a valid point of reference for this chapter. The tensions in the relationship between political thought and ideology in the 1990s perhaps testifies to the problems that these commentators have highlighted. But until a new set of acceptable guides are ready and widely available, the conceptual vacuum will be filled by all types of "mappers", some of which have already tried to draw up a series of sign-posts to the new brave world of post-Cold War international relations.

Some of the cartographers of our age, perhaps not unlike many of their predecessors who had lived in rather uncertain times, have become profits of doom. One, for instance, warns of the global consequences of an emerging new cold war based on "the resurgence of parochial identities based on ethnic and religious allegiances"[5]. While another points to the resurgence of religion and sees in this a direct threat to international stability.[6] Clearly, these mappers, along with the army of actors and activists who are the subject of this chapter are feeling the need to make sense of the complexities of the new international order. But a crucial difference separates the two types: while members of the first group (intellectuals like Huntington, Juergensmeyer and Fukuyama) try and draw the map of the new age, the Islamic activists (who are part of the second type) try and seize the moment - the opportunities created by the demise of the Soviet system - in order to redraw it.

It is therefore not surprising to hear the often repeated view that one of the main elements of the post-Cold War conflict lies in the struggle between militant Islam originating in the Middle East region the Western-dominated international system led by the United States and subscribed to by the West's allies in the Middle East. Although most of the world's 1.1 billion Muslims live outside of the Middle East and North Africa (MENA) region, and not every person living in the Muslim Middle East is in fact a Muslim, the politicization of Islam is said to be most evident in this region. But Islam does not have just one voice in today's complex world, nor is political Islam a monolithic force. Contrary to the public image of Islamists in the popular media, the radical Islamist groups are not Soviet-type Leninist parties reincarnated, despite the fact that extensive, and historical, links do exist between individuals and some groups (like the Muslim Brotherhood) across the Arab world.

Actually, the very term "political Islam" is itself shorthand for a diverse set of opinions, in an environment where the Islamic groups themselves have many fundamental differences with each other. These movements do not represent a single political force - neither at home nor internationally. Furthermore, we can discern that Islamists are still split doctrinally between those adhering to the majority sect of Islam (Sunnis) and the minority ten per cent of Shiis, though in terms of tactical planning and political campaigns it may increasingly be possible to find individuals and groups who can comfortably straddle the two main streams of the faith.

Before digging any deeper, however, we need to clarify the terminology used to describe politicization of Islam. I use the term Islamic fundamentalism to mean the emotional, spiritual, political responses of some Muslims to an acute (and on-going) set of social, economic and political problems which have gripped the Muslim Middle East. For reasons that will become clear later, Western countries and their commercial flagships are singled out for sustained criticism and attack by the so-called fundamentalists. This is as much a result of fear of whole-sale "Westernization" of their cultures, as a reaction to decades of direct Western intervention in the MENA region.

The term political Islam, on the other hand, is used here to indicate the Islamists' desire, political programme, and their political and military campaign to establish an Islamic order. This objective they have been pursuing on two (related) levels: through challenging the status quo in their own countries; and, through their increasingly transnational network of contacts in the Arab and Muslim arena in general. In this context, one may well be able to identify the early shoots of a regional-wide "pax-Islamica" in the Middle East and North Africa, even though the eyes of the Islamists remains fixed on attaining state power in their own countries. So, although the two terms have increasingly come to be used interchangeably, and to refer to the same phenomenon, it is important for empirical and methodological reasons that we draw a clearer distinction between them and also try and apply the terms more rigorously.

Perspectives on Radical Islam

I would argue that there are five ways in which the phenomena of radical Islam, or what Taylor has called "neofundamentalism" can be perceived.[7] The first way is to see it as a response to the monumental crisis of the nation-state in the Middle East, which has been caused by a combination of factors in the economic, political and social realms, all which have come to challenge regime legitimacy. It is not very difficult to list the most important amongst the factors which have been causing tensions in state-civil society relations; social deprivation, lingering poverty, corruption, nepotism, reliance on the West for security and defence, dependence on the West for economic assistance, diminishing degree of political legitimacy, little regard for the rule of law, problems of stability associated with unclear political succession procedures, and unaccountable and unresponsive political systems. These problems have been compounded in recent years by rapid population growth, urbanization, and environmental degradation. Radical Islam, therefore, could be said to be an extremist response to a general crisis.[8] As Taylor puts it, "the Islamic reconstructionist response to the sociopolitical criris in the Middle East represents the attempt of Muslims to retrieve their own religious heritage and make it the foundation of a new public order"[9].

The second approach views Islamic fundamentalism as a form of cultural nationalism. A passing, and badly misperceived, revival which poses little danger to the West[10], but is a vital part of the cultural renewal of Third World peoples. Fundamentalist movements are seen as no more than a response to the process of globalization, which in all of its aspects - economic organization and processes, culture, and politics - challenges standards and ways of life of non-Western societies.

Another perspective regards the phenomena in the rubric of "clash of civilizations" between *dār al-islām* and the now dominant Christian-Western world. Samuel Huntington, for one, has argued that conflict between civilizations is likely to replace ideological and other forms of conflict.[11] And it is not just Western commentators who have been making such arguments. Note the words of a prominent Tunisian lawyer (Abdelwahab Belhawi), which were uttered well before Huntington's warning of a clash of civilizations had become public.

"Colonialism tried to deform all the cultural traditions of Islam", said Belhawi, "I am not an Islamist. I don't think there is a conflict between religions. There is a conflict between civilizations."[12] This line of reasoning could lead to the conclusion that the conflicts of the twenty first century will more than likely be between the "West and the rest", between Islam and the West. In Huntington's own words: "The central axis of world politics is and will be the interaction of Western power and culture with the power and culture of non-Western societies."[13]

The fourth school regards radical Islam as a new and "authentic" force for positive change in the Muslim world. The slogan, "Islam is the solution", is heard across the Middle East and North Africa, particularly in those countries where the Islamists have been engaged in challenging the ruling regime (Algeria and Egypt), as well as in those where Islamic groups have been able to use the political process to advance their own cause (as in Jordan, Kuwait and Yemen).[14] Part of the evidence for the "Islam is the solution" thesis stem from the electoral success that Islamist parties and groups have had in organised elections. Undoubtedly, where they have been engaged in parliamentary politics, the Islamists have registered notable victories. Jordan's Muslim Brotherhood won 22 of the 80 seats in the House of Representatives elections in 1989 and 16 seats in the 1993 elections; the Al-Islah (Reform) Party in Yemen won 62 seats of the 301 contested seats in the parliamentary elections of April 1993; the Lebanon's Hezbollah (Party of God) movement has had several MPs in the Lebanese parliament since the early 1990s; and, the Kuwaiti Islamists have become the most influential political bloc in the rejuvenated Kuwaiti national assembly since the small sheikhdom's liberation from Iraqi occupation in 1991. Their success is not limited to the Arab world either; the Refah (Welfare) Party in secular Turkey won 21.3 per cent of the popular vote in Turkey's parliamentary elections in December 1995 and 158 seats in its 550-member national assembly.

The two cases which digress from the above pattern are Iran and Afghanistan, but for very different reasons. In sharp contrast to the above examples of reformist activities, in the hands of the Taliban, the Afghani struggle for Islamic authenticity has taken an extreme and violent form, causing a tremendous amount of hardship for the ordinary Afghanis. Here, the Taliban interpretation of Islam has increasingly become part of the problem, and in no way the solution for the ills of the country it was meant to be. In Iran, whose leadership has been highly critical of the Taliban in Afghanistan, the opposite trend seems to hold true. Here, civil society has been getting stronger and the clerics' presence in several institutions has been declining. In the parliament, for example, their number has dropped from 137 in 1980 to 50 in the 1996.

The final perspective in this line-up not only rejects Huntington's clash of civilizations thesis, but is equally dismissive of the potential power of the

Islamic radicals - the "Islam is the solution" school. There are several seams to this perspective: the first challenges the Islamists' ability to make a lasting impression on the Middle East or beyond. One critic speaks of the "failure of political Islam" to bring about any fundamental or lasting change to the existing order in Muslim societies: "The influence of Islamism is more superficial than it seems."[15]. The second seam in the same school argues that the tide of militancy has crested; the Islamists' power may be on the wane and the extremists on the defensive. In this camp also are those who regard the prospects of an Islamic confrontation with the West as extremely unlikely, and the confrontation between Islam and the West as no more than a "myth", which is "used to legitimize, to mislead, to silence, to mobilize"[16]. The third seam of this school is based around the argument that the Islamic threat itself is largely misunderstood. The challenge of the Islamists, this strand holds, is much more benign than realised; it "need not always result in a threat to regional stability or Western interests"[17].

These arguments used by the above authors are not mutually exclusive. Indeed, several of these perspectives do borrow from each other, and many of the ideas that they advance are products of cross pollination. But, in terms of contextualising the forces of radical Islam they do offer different analysis, prespectives and approaches.

The Muslim World in the International System

The Muslim world is a dynamic, non-integrated, rapidly changing and evolving group of mainly Third World states and globally scattered communities, where about one-third of all Muslims are minorities in the countries in which they live. The Muslim world is a complex world of states and communities whose intricacies can best be illustrated through an examination of its geographical, political, economic and cultural diversities. When viewed through this prism, it seems a disunited set of entities within which pan-Islamism holds little water.

The Muslim world is spread across the three continents of Europe, Africa and Asia, with sizeable Muslim communities in the Americas, India and China. The Middle East region and south-east Asia form the heartlands of this faith; Saudi Arabia is the birthplace of Islam, and Indonesia the most populace Muslim country (with around 90 per cent of its 188 million people Muslim). The geography of the faith, however, has been experiencing some changes in recent years. The emergence of a Muslim-dominated Bosnian entity in former Yugoslavia and the regeneration of Muslim Albania in southern Europe are recent additions to what has been Turkey's lonely spot in Europe as the continent's only Muslim state. These states' collective European presence is already being felt in inter-state and inter-communal relations in the Crimea, the

Balkans and eastern Mediterranean regions. Much of it discouragingly negative so far since the end of the Cold War.

Further east though, the emergence of Muslim republics in the Caucasus and Central Asia has practically transformed the map of west Asia. Five new Central Asian republics have been joined by Azerbaijan in the Caucasus. These states are not Muslim in the classic sense of the word, where Islam would be the dominant cultural influence. Culturally and linguistically these states have been permeated by Slavic influences, and are in any case much more in tune with secularist Turkey and still far removed from the traditionalist Islamic forces in the Arab world. But their emergence does represent an expansion (or more precisely recovery of Muslim territory from Orthodox Christendom) of the Muslim world in geographical terms, and in terms of a quantitative growth in the number of independent Muslim states operating in the international system. This fact can be ascertained by the growing number of member-state participants at the organization of Islamic countries meetings.

The birth of these six new states and the addition of their 70 million people to the Muslim world will, in the fullness of time, begin to have an impact on the direction and policies pursued by the established Muslim states. Their presence will also influence the orientation and ethos of such hitherto Arab-dominated international Muslim organizations as the 54-member Islamic Conference Organization.

Another important feature of the geographical expansion of the Muslim world in the 1990s is that it is almost exclusively taking place outside of the Arab world. The new Muslim entities are all non-Arab states, and the only notable geographic change in the Arab world stems from the establishment of Palestine Liberation Organization's control over a part of the Israeli-occupied Palestinian territories.

The expansion of the Muslim world outside of the Arab network of states is already creating new opportunities for co-operation among the non-Arab Muslim actors of the Middle East. The expansion of the Economic Co-operation Organization (ECO) by its founding members (Iran, Pakistan and Turkey) in the early 1990s to incorporate all of the independent Muslim republics of the former Soviet Union plus Afghanistan shows this trend well. It is not often known that this new economic-oriented organization, comprising ten members, is the largest regional organization in Asia. It boasts of over 300 million people within its huge geographical space and bountiful natural resources. The ECO's territory holds much water and agricultural land, as well as hydrocarbons, gold, lead, zinc, coal, copper, and uranium, amongst others. At the very least, ECO possesses the material basis for eocnomic development in west Asia.

Equally diverse are political structures of Muslim states. The popularised image of the political systems of the Muslim world do not do justice to the varied pattern and the intrinsic complexities of political organization in Muslim societies. Several Muslim leaders, for instance, identify themselves as believers and actively incorporate the tenets of Islam into their policies. In the pro-Western monarchies of Morocco, Jordan and Saudi Arabia, the kings of these countries weave their families' histories closely to those of the Prophet Muhammad and his ancient tribe. In Iran, the spiritual leader of the republic, Ayatollah Khamenei, is a senior Shia cleric whose black turban is supposed to indicate direct line of descent from the Prophet's family. In Afghanistan, the Taliban leadership, still a "student movement" of sorts, enjoy the fruits of office precisely because they claim to have the right Islamic credentials for governing.

Muslim states, therefore, are highly dynamic entities, many of which constitute core components of key strategic regions in the international system, such as the Middle East, South-East Asia, and Central Asia. As they do not form a single force in the international system they inevitably find themselves bunched together at certain junctures and pressures, giving the impression of unity, and rather stung out at others, appearing to be disunited. But the fact that they are *different* types of states cannot be dismissed easily.

So, in providing a yardstick for understanding the political structures of the Muslim world, I propose to use a framework which divides political organization in the Muslim world into four broad categories. These being:
- the traditionalist monarchical Muslim states;
- the modernist Muslim states;
- the revolutionary Muslim states; and,
- the secularist Muslim states.

It is clear from this rather unorthodox list that Muslim peoples are governed by quite different and, at times, competing political systems. The differing nature of the Muslim states' political systems, though enriching in international political terms, has in the past adversely affected their relations with one another. Today, these differences have an even more direct bearing on the policies of Muslim states towards each other. This problem is nowhere more evident than in the Middle East, where radical secularist regimes and radical Islamist regimes have been trying to co-exist with the traditionalist monarchies of the region for some time.

The problem of incompatibility, in terms of international politics, is much larger than this, however. It is, at times, one of deep-seated disputes and violent confrontations. Just in the 1990s, for example, Muslim Iraq invaded and attempted to annexe Muslim Kuwait; Muslim Sudan confronted Muslim Egypt; Muslim Saudi Arabia engaged in a protracted border dispute with Muslim Yemen; Muslim Iran forcefully rejected the credentials of revolutionary Muslims of Afghanistan; and, Muslim Syria engaged in high politics in fear of the intentions of Muslim Turkey towards it.

It is worth underlining this simple point again: when we look around us we find that there is no one political system prevailing in the Muslim world; nor do we find harmony amongst the states. One finds modernising and fast-developing Muslim regimes (like Malaysia, Indonesia and Turkey), some of which function as authoritarian regimes; secular (Central Asian states, Algeria, Egypt, Syria, Tunisia and Turkey) and Islamist (Afghanistan, Iran, Sudan) republican regimes; "moderate" Islamic regimes and monarchies (like Pakistan and Morocco); and, Islamic monarchies whose external policies may be non-confrontational but their domestic realm conforms with traditional Islamic norms. Within each of these categories, moreover, one can spot a range of differences, both amongst the traditionalist and modernist regimes. They cohabit, and interact, first and foremost, as members of a much wider international community.

Economically too the differences between Muslim states is quite marked. The newly-industrialising Muslim countries, for instance, are spearheading part of the Third World challenge to Western domination of the capitalist world economy. Muslim states in this category include Tunisia, Morocco and Turkey in the Middle East and North Africa, and Malaysia, Indonesia, and possibly Pakistan in Asia. Then there are two other types of economic states in the Muslim world; the survivor, or "make-do", economy - which is the prevalent form in much of Muslim Africa; and, the stagnant or under performing Muslim economies - which is characteristic of some of the Arab world's economies. Accounting for more than a dozen Muslim states and many millions of Muslims in Asia and Africa, these groups of countries either suffer from a natural resource deficiency, or else find that their economies are unable to respond to the multitude of pressures which are now days generated at the global level. They simply do not have the means to assess, let alone respond, to the challenges that a globalised international system poses. Tragically, in most of these cases, poverty continues to prevail, despite a liberalization and opening up of the economy.

A number of other Muslim economies, on the other hand, have been doing quite well out of the systematic collection of "rent". By and large these economies have prospered because they have been blessed with huge hydrocarbon deposits, which has been the main source of their wealth and income in the twentieth century, and will likely be in the next century as well. Furthermore, the ranks of the Middle Eastern oil states has been expanded in the 1990s by the gradual arrival on the international hydrocarbons scene of potentially big players such as Azerbaijan, Kazakhstan and Turkmenistan. The combined reserves of Kazakhstan and Azerbaijan, for example, is said to exceed 50 billion barrels of oil, or could even be as great as 200 billion barrels. Such reserve figures will mean many billions of dollars in revenues, and may indeed herald a new oil bonanza in another Muslim-dominated geographical zone.

Not surprisingly, therefore, several of these new Central Asian states see themselves as leading regional economies of the twenty first century, with potential to emerge as new "tigers" of Asia. The economic ambitions of these newly independent states is likely to catapult them to prominence as some of the next century's main hydrocarbons providers. But their arrival as large hydrocarbon exporters may bring them into a devastating competition with the established Middle Eastern hydrocarbons exporters, all of whom are, of course, Muslim states.

Despite their many differences, however, the vital point is that all Muslim states are part of the same international capitalist division of labour and exist and function within this same global order, but at different levels within it. Drives at creating a Muslim economic common market have been made, most recently the D-8 Group of some of the largest Muslim economies which was founded by the Islamist government of Turkey, but in the absence of a solid economic or political Muslim international division of labour, which could act as a unifying force for the Muslim world, it is unlikely to succeed. Today, it seems, religion and history, the only threads that bind this multitude of states and communities together, weave too loose a net to be able to keep all the Muslim states within it.

Muslim States and Globalization

Although the contemporary world may be regarded as being more open and "pluralistic", as well as more boundaryless, it is also a more divided and differentiated one, politically, economically, and technologically. In the new global economic order the forces of change are all-powerful, and the nation-states' apparently insurmountable problems are mirrored in the increasingly violent challenges it faces from minorities as well as those groups who find themselves (or think that they are) disenfranchised or neglected. In this brave new world, "globalization" of capital (spearheaded by giant Western corporations and their brands) can be argued to be responsible for some of the problems associated with dislocation and deepening crisis in the developing world in general, which naturally includes much of the Muslim world.

The cultural battles between Western companies and their brand names on the one hand, and Muslim consumers and their governments on the other, is not the only impact of the capitalization process in the Muslim world, however. Capitalism has brought with it many irreversible developments, and like other societies the Muslim ones have remained vulnerable to these immensely powerful forces of change. One can draw attention, for example, to the ways in which market forces have caused alienation and accelerated rural to urban migration (which in turn has intensified cultural dislocation). Today, great Muslim metropoles - Cairo, Istanbul, Karachi, Tehran - all bear the scars of rapid labour migration from the countryside to the city, and endure the tensions which surface on a daily basis between city authorities and the often destitute labourers who find themsleves cut off from family, without work, and a long way from the social safety net that used to give them security in their hour of need. Such shantytown neighbourhoods, as have sprung up around every Muslim metropole, provide a deep reservoir of supporters for Islamists of all hue. Already, at certain junctures these groups of dislocated individuals have played an important role in tipping the balance in favour of Islamist activists. Note the Iranian revolution and the way in which the Islamists were able to mobilise Tehran's shantytown dwellers against the might of the Pahlavi state. In such circumstances, one can argue that alienation is an absolute problem, as it in fact causes almost complete separation of the labour migrant from the social setting that predominates the city.

Alienation as a social problem also touches those in work, thus affecting even more lives than the millions of shantytown dwellers. It causes problems in the work place, where the process of work tends to lose its purpose for many employees, and where traditional values and customs are constantly challenged. Such apparently mundane issues as members of the opposite sex working in close proximity to each other, for example, acquire explosive undertones.

Also, it is evident that capitalist production bombards and eventually fractures socially and economically supportive extended family units. Such units, one needs no reminding, are vital to the renewal of Muslim cultural values - and are seen by Muslims the world over as the central plank in their fight against moral degradation. Capitalist production, which is now the prevalent mode of production in the world, does not require extended families or their influence. Training the next generation and preparing other members of the family for engaging in the same profession, or for tilling the land, is no longer a function that an extended family network can usefully undertake. A typical employer today would, of necessity, require suitable individuals to employ and will have no interest in the rest of the individual's family. Training, if required, will be done by the firm itself or by another agency on its behalf. Extended family relations have no place in a world where employees are the total sum of single units. In search of work, individuals are forced to leave behind not only their traditions but also their families. The socialising function of extended family structures, moreover, is also lost. Vital customs and value systems fail to be transmitted, while new (often imported) habits are acquired and internalised. In these circumstances, it is no wonder that Islamists argue that the global capitalist order is not only an enemy of the Muslim but also of his family.

In more general terms, capitalist expansion brings with it Western models of organiation, management and progress indices as well. While most of us accept these models and indices, and indeed find ourselves functioning by them, it should still be recognised that, in essence, these are all value systems designed to measure success, efficiency and achievement. These indices and models have little or no regard for traditions and cultural norms. They work, their proponents argue, precisely because they are "scientific". They work for they are universal and acultural. But, in the last analysis and for all practical purposes, the adoption of such measures of development do cause change in social relations and values, which is not only sometimes unwarranted but rather destabilising. In the context of the Muslim world, moreover, where social justice is important and where an alternative, albeit imperfect, set of rules for conducting economic activity already exists, only using the Western criteria and models can cause a social and political backlash. Evidence for such a backlash is apparent in the vionent and uncompromising responses of Indonesian and Malaysian Muslims to their countries' economic problems in the late 1990s. Not surprisingly, Islamists in both countries have been busy fishing in these muddy waters. But in reality theirs is a kneejerk reaction to a clash between cultural values and economic necessities.

More forcefully still, capitalism introduces and feeds divisive forces which arise from economic competition and rivalries (in trade, investment and production for example) among the Muslim states. These forces capitalism naturally generates. Moreover, capitalist production not only causes atomization of the economic potential of Muslim states, but also the separation of their resources by pulling them into quite distinct, and ultimately separate, regional markets and organizations. Here, as Brian Beeley has noted, "connections between Muslim countries are attractive because they do cut across the established links"[18].

There is even more to it than this, however. A desire for Islamic unity has come to represent an alternative to the colonial division of the Muslim Middle East into separate political and economic entities. But this same desire has brought into sharp focus the tensions which have arisen in recent years between individual rights and collective duties, as well as between the Muslim peoples' responsibilities to their faith on the one hand, and their country on the other. In these circumstances, the struggle of the Islamists against the state has been threatening the state's legitimacy, and indeed its very right to exist. In effect, the Islamists have, through their actions, been challenging the very basis of the existing international system - the system of territorial-based states. This partly explains their difficult relationship with the West, the proponent of the state-based international relations. In the current scheme of things, it should be noted, the Islamist alternative appears as a direct challenge to state-based nationalism which has characterised the Muslim world's post-colonial experiences in the twentieth century.

One should spare a thought for the state at this point: having gained autonomy of action from colonial powers and having secured sovereignty and independence of the nation's territory, the state now finds itself under attack not noly by the Islamists at home, but also by the very forces which are shaping the international system - the forces of globalization. No sooner had the state gathered the resources to check the power of the Islamists at home it had to find new ways of containing the overwhelming power of globalization, which also directly challenged the territoriality of the state as well as its functional arena.

Introducing and extending Western capitalist consumption patterns is another feature of globalization as manifested in today's truly global production methods and systems. As mentioned already, most Muslim societies find this aspect of globalization objectionable and potentially threatening to their sociocultural survival. But another problem, that of the aggravation of state-civil society relations caused by the disruption in the balance of power between the state and civil society, is a more serious issue to highlight. In a nutshell, I am arguing here that, by actively de-legitimising the state (as it is forced to forego its traditional role of social provider), Western patterns of development - privatization of core economic sectors, liberalization of trade and economic relations - in fact sow the seeds of instability. Could not one argue that the crisis of the Arab state may, in part at least, be caused by these global forces?

With this background, we need now to ask the question, how do the Muslim world and the international system interact? Here, I want to identify several problem areas pertinent to the question. Firstly, we can all see a widening technological gap developing, which tends to set the West and the Muslim world apart. Indeed, at times it appears that the West and the rest of the world are travelling at different speeds and that the Western world is managing to change orbit and travel along the time continuum at a higher and more efficient level. This technological gap finds expression in the industrial and manufacturing techniques gap that is visible even to the untrained eye, such as mine! One serious result of this technological deficit is that the Muslim world has increasingly become a net consumer of Western production techniques, which, apart from anything else, has had a knock-on effect on labour as well as production relations that prevail in every corner of the Muslim world.

The second aspect of interaction between the Muslim world and the Western-created pattern of production and consumption, is a worsening food security. This problem has been worsened by grave economic inefficiencies in the Muslim world itself and rapid population growth. One result of this problem has been further dependence of Muslim countries on the efficient food producers of the world - who are of course in the West, most notably the United States. Accompanying concerns about the food security gap in the Muslim world has been the fear, openly expressed by many Muslim activists, that such extensive food dependence might in fact encourage the Western powers to use the "food weapon" in one of their multitude of political disputes with Muslim countries. This might sound a far fetched argument to most of us, but the fact is that it is being aired in the Muslim street, which is itself, as you know, already riddled with exotic tails of conspiracies being hatched against Muslims!

To recap, in the Middle East at least, the long-term impact of the globalization process has been the conversion of the Arab world (the Muslim heartland) into net consumers of Western products, production techniques and labour-capital relations, and the reduction of these states' role to that of suppliers of cheap labour for international producers and relatively cheap strategic inputs (i.e., hydrocarbons) for international consumers. To make matters worse for the Arab state, copying production techniques from the West in the late twentieth century has entailed accepting the decentralising force of today's modern technologies - in that they can not be controlled centrally. This means that adoption of modern capitalism's production techniques is itself centrifugal, running the risk of undermining the ruling elite's grip on society, and weakening the bureaucracy's control of the national economy.

Transnational Capitalism and Radical Islamic Politics

Herein lies the root of the problem. Briefly, the tensions between radical Islam and the West, which has become a major concern of contemporary world politics, stems from the fact that the former, arguably representing a form of cultural nationalism, is having to respond to the "process of world-wide Westernization and ... the means used to uproot the planet"[19]. The latter, on the other hand, is being guided today by the West's "civilising mission" - a sense of righteousness which has been strengthened by its moral and political victory over Soviet Communism - and its conviction that the end of the Cold War has heralded the transculturalization of capitalism. That is to say, the US-led West is not content simply to globalise capitalism as a mode of production - which is no mean achievement in itself! - but to export it as a set of values, indeed a whole value system.

The concept of transculturalization, therefore, indicates a process through which the planting in non-Western settings of a culture, which is deeply rooted in western Europe and its associated "Western heartlands" of the United States and other settler-colonies, is achieved. The end product, many have observed, may be homogenization of culture under Western economic hegemony.[20] The final triumph of the so-called "Coca Cola culture" syndrome.

For radical and liberal Muslims alike, therefore, globalization of capitalism is causing cultural dislocation of such a magnitude that salvation appears only be found in the safety of the all-encompassing faith that Islam is. After all, if

Islam is a whole way of life and part of the very fabric of Muslim societies - which it is - then it stands to reason that attempts to preserve it from the vagaries of international capitalism will necessarily bring it into the confrontation with those who act as vanguards of the faith. Today, it is the radical Islamists who have taken it upon themselves to fight global capitalism, whose very being and logic, let alone behaviour and culture, is based on capturing new markets and profiting from efficient production and exchange of goods and services world-wide. In political economy terms, therefore, the Islamists' response to globalization and cultural homogenization could be viewed as no more than a deep desire to preserve the roots of a distinct world view. In other words, they are having to fight for *indigenization* in the face of deepening globalization and "standardization". An on-going fight, in short, for global diversity.

In the Muslim Middle East, in the meanwhile, the secular state's inability to overcome the endemic crisis prevalent in society, which in turn has increased its reliance on the West, has already unleashed its own anti-thesis: protest in the form of political Islam. This strain, however, does not, and cannot, offer a cure for the ills associated with Muslim societies' growing Westernization. Nor is it a wholesome medicine by itself! But, the fact that it is being received by the masses as a reliable form of medicine for the panic-ridden patient - i.e., the society - not only provides it with political space but also considerable ammunition with which to fight the "enemies of Islam" - imagined or real, at home or abroad - with messianic vigour. Herein, perhaps, lies the very root of the problem of Islamic fundamentalism for international relations.

Whether regional and international responses to the Islamists will eventually form the nucleus of a new structure for containing this problem remains to be seen. Some argue that co-optation and accommodation will eradicate the Islamist threat as a combination of these policies will, inevitably, force the Islamists to change their violent stance against the state and re-enter peaceful political dialogue. Others maintain that the only way to remove the Islamist threat is to defeat its proponents on the battle field, wherever they happen to challenge the status quo. When choosing a strategy though, it seems that the West and its regime allies in the Muslim world and the radical Islamists are looking at one another through the same looking glass. But, for a range of reasons, the parties see very different mirror images of each other. Not until the images in the mirror have begun to tally with the image of the self will there be room for constructive engagement, however. But, in reality, as the images are being mediated by the faceless forces of globalization today little chance of a genuine compromise seems likely. This much is depressing clear in the aftermath of the US embassy bombings in Kenya and Tanzania in August 1998 and Washington's violent response to the bombings. Its attacks on targets in Afghanistan and Sudan have provided further ammunition for the very Islamist forces which it had tried to defeat. The statement of the Islamic International Front for Fighting Jews and Crusaders, issued soon after the US missile attacks, sounded ominous: "Holy struggle operations will continue until American forces withdraw from the land of Muslims." In today's world, where global forces shape economies as well as societies, this is much easier said than done.

Notes

1   This article is based on the work entitled *Islamic Fundamentalism and Political Islam*, which appeared in White, Little and Smith (eds.), Issues in World Politics, London 1997. This article has benefited from the constructive comments of colleagues at the Centre for Modern Oriental Studies, Berlin, to whom I owe a debt of gratitude.
2   M.Z. Husain, Global Islamic Politics, New York 1995.
3   J.J.G. Jansen, The Dual Nature of Islamic Fundamentalism, Ithaca 1997. Press, p. 1.
4   D.F. Eickelman/J. Piscatori, Muslim Politics. Princeton, NJ, 1996, p. 136.
5   M. Juergensmeyer, The New Cold War? Religious Nationalism Confronts the Secular State, Berkeley 1993, p. 2.
6   S.P. Huntington, The Clash of Civilizations. In: Foreign Affairs 71 (1993) 3.
7   A.R. Taylor, The Islamic Question in Middle East Politics, Boulder, CO, 1988.
8   R.H. Dekmejian, Islam in Revolution: Fundamentalism in the Arab World, Syracuse, NY, 1995.
9   Taylor, loc. cit., p. 72.
10 Cf. Husain, loc. cit.
11 Cf. Huntington, loc. cit.
12 J. Walsh, The Sword of Islam. In: Time, 15 June 1992, p. 30.
13 S.P. Huntington, The Clash of Civilizations? In: Peaceworks 1995, No. 4, p. 6.
14 S.A. Sidahmed/A. Ehteshami (eds.), Islamic Fundamentalism, Boulder, CO, 1996.
15 O. Roy, The Failure of Political Islam, London 1994, p. 26.
16 F. Halliday, Islam and the Myth of Confrontation: Religion and Politics in the Middle East, London 1995, p. 6.
17 J.L. Esposito, The Islamic Threat: Myth or Reality?, New York 1992, p. 211.
18 B. Beeley, Islam as a Global Political Force. In: A.G. McGrew/P.G. Lewis et al., Global Politics, Cambridge 1993, p. 304.
19 S. Latouche, The Westernization of the World, Cambridge 1996, p. 72.
20 M. Featherstone (ed.), Global Culture: Nationalism, Globalization and Modernity, London 1990.

Africa in the History of Globalization

Leonhard Harding

For quite some time almost everybody has been talking about globalization and its effects on the international community and the world economy. Obviously, people are anxious about fundamental changes affecting their lives in a radical way they cannot foresee and, what is worse, they feel unable to influence. Some of these changes became obvious shortly after the breakdown of the Soviet Union, when international alliances were restructured and the US, with its economic, military and technological power remained unchallenged. In the background of this unprecedented rise of one single superpower a rapidly spreading political ideology is active, the ideology of the free flow of ideas and information and of the free market. Many economists see the market as the most efficient means of regulating the economy, of stimulating production and exchange, of creating growth and wealth all over the world.

For others, a kind of existential anxiety is growing, culminating in the fear of an outright new imperialism of the world's superpower.[1] Many people are indeed scared by the predominant role economic factors play in the decision-making of democratic governments and by the social consequences of a world system which seems to be ruled by one superpower or rather by economic and financial interest groups organized in multi-national societies. These large unpersonalized companies withdraw from the control of democratic governments and their political directives. And they have begun to rule the world.

These consequences apply to all countries, but particularly to the non-industrialized world. Africa e.g. is continually losing its position in the world economy and subsequently its political weight and voice in the international fight for influence.

This symposium attempts to analyse the conflicts arising from the clash between globalizing factors and the reactions of African and Asian societies that want to build up just and democratic societies, to expand their economy and to defend their cultural heritage. This conflict is of vital importance; some might say it has already been lost for the Africans and many Asians, others are more positive, they are looking for alternative models of organization.

In this contribution, entitled "Africa in the History of Globalization", I do not want to present a complete picture of what globalization means, a specialist in international relations would be better qualified for this; nor shall I try to define what effects globalization has on the African continent; this is a subject for a large international conference of experts in many spheres. For the same reason, I shall not describe how African societies are trying to cope with the consequences of globalization. I simply want to look at a major event of recent years in Central Africa, the overthrow of President Mobutu and its aftermath, and at a long-term process in Senegal, the rise of the Islamic brotherhood of the Murides to a "state in the state", and try to give an interpretation against the background of globalization. In my interpretation, I shall put these developments into the broader perspective of African history and analyze them as the final stage of a secular trend of weakening or even disintegration of state power.

I shall begin at the end of the story, stating that the nation state project of the independence period in Africa has failed.

Recent Developments in Central Africa and in Senegal

The events of 1997 in Central Africa are a powerful demonstration of how and to what extent the state and other powers changed their roles.

The collapse of Zaire[2] was caused by the mismanagement of the Mobutu regime and its consequence, the passive resistance[3] and internal emigration of large parts of the population who simply no longer cared about the state and its political and social norms; an "alternative society, with parallel social and religious institutions alongside official ones"[4] had emerged. On the other hand the Zairean state "has opted out and simply ignores much of what is going on"[5]. But this was a long process the outcome of which was uncertain. The final breakdown was due above all to a shift in power outside the African continent: When the east-west confrontation drew to a close, western powers and international capital no longer needed President Mobutu; for decades he had been considered a guarantee of political stability and western interests in a strategically important region. When the so-called communist threat came to an end and the broad movement of democratization in Africa took shape, fostered by the World Bank, the International Monetary Fund, the US, and finally France which had enormous interests in Central Africa[6], President Mobutu lost his strategic position. The US began quite openly to support first the political opposition in Zaire, then the "Conférence Nationale" which sought a restructuring of power in Zaire, and finally, when the internal democratization process had failed, the US supported the military opposition lead by Laurent Désiré Kabila. The US government gave substantial logistic and military support to Kabila in the double perspective of helping establish a democratic regime which would be able to end the political and economic chaos in this strategically crucial region and secondly of paving the way for American business and investment interests in the Zairean mining and oil industry. In fact, US-dominated companies were the first to court Kabila.

This intrusion of foreign political and economic interests in Central Africa did not cease after the new regime was in power in Kinshasa, on the contrary. After the overthrow of President Mobutu fighting broke out in Congo-Brazzaville, the northern neighbour of Zaire. It was not a civil war, still less an ethnic conflict although the different armed units and their leaders were organized along ethnic lines. It was a battle for power between General Denis Sassou-Nguesso, the former dictator of the Congo, and Pascal Lissouba, the democratically elected President. Both were supported by powerful, but contesting foreign interests. General Sassou-Nguesso was supported by the petrol company Elf Aquitaine, a French state-dominated company with clearly defined metropolitan interests. American interests, represented by the predominantly American oil company Gulf Oil, had their eye on the new oil fields at Pointe Noire in Congo-Brazzaville and hoped that President Lissouba would end the unilateral orientation of the Congo towards France and accord them some of the very promising new concessions. President Lissouba was willing to grant these, but General Sassou-Nguesso used French support to oust the elected President from power. In other words, this was not a tribal war, not even a civil war, it was more an oil war, conducted by and for foreign interests.

But the situation became still more complicated when at first UNITA troops from the Angolan rebel movement of Jonas Savimbi and then Angolan army troops intervened on behalf of Nguesso; UNITA hoped to be rewarded in oil capital and safeguard Congo-Brazzaville as a retreat area as well as a transit for arms and diamond smuggling. To understand these interests fully one has to bear in mind that UNITA was originally supported by the United States in its struggle against the so-called marxist government of Angola which in turn had called in Cuban troops to protect the enclave Cabinda, exploited by the American Gulf Oil Company. But because UNITA did not ply to the 1994 Truce of Lusaka, ending the civil war in Angola, and had continued fighting to safeguard its power base in northern Angola instead, it became increasingly isolated and desperately needed new retreat areas and transit roads, all the more so since with the downfall of Mobutu it had lost his protection. But the search for new allies in General Sassou-Nguesso and the region of Pointe Noire proved a complete failure because Angolan government troops had intervened on behalf of Nguesso as well and brought him to power, ousting the influence of UNITA in the region. At the end of this power struggle UNITA was seriously weakened whereas Angola had become a regional power centre extending its influence into the francophone zone.[7]

And there is a third power group now, acting for the first time in Africa: African mercenaries, from Mobutu's presidential guard, from the Rwandan Hutu militia responsible for the genocide in Rwanda, and from Angolan UNITA fighters. These people are politically homeless, they are ready to fight for whoever pays them, and that's what happened in the oil war of Brazzaville.

These developments in Central Africa show three fundamental changes in the political landscape of Africa:

1. in this region, the nation state has lost its power and function, it has become meaningless and is looking for a new role;
2. other forces, oil or mining interests, have become the new centres of power, replacing the state and deciding the future of the people;
3. these new predominant forces do not particularly care for democratic structures, human rights or for economic and social development; their main interest is profit, irrespective of the political regime which might formally be in power.

In other words: in Central Africa the effective power of the nation state has to a large extent shifted to multinational organizations or to other power groups.

The second example, less spectacular but more typical for long term developments and particularly for the appropriative reactions which occurred in society, is the recent past of Senegal.

The Senegalese state[8] has proved to be unable to fulfil two basic functions: it is unable to enforce its legislation in all parts of the country; large sections of the population have shifted their loyalty to other authorities, to the marabouts of the islamic brotherhoods in particular. Touba, the religious capital of the brotherhood of the Murides and the seat of the Khalif, has informally assumed an extraterritorial status where Senegalese legislation is not enforced, where Senegalese police are not present and where state schools have been closed and replaced by islamic schools.[9] The state is furthermore unable to foster economic development, to control the economy and to provide basic services. The economic basis of the country is one of the poorest in Africa: soils are poor, mineral resources extremely scarce, and the most important economic activities are peanut production, fishing and services. Many basic services in health care, education, energy and public transport have been reduced steadily for the last 10 or 15 years, and employment in the public sector has been reduced at the same speed.

Several serious consequences of this failure touch the moral roots of the state: an informal economy is spreading and provides a modest income for many people, largely outside the control of the state, and the common disillusionment over the collapse of basic state services has turned into a growing disengagement by the people and a desperate search for new organizations able and willing to provide basic services and create a feeling of solidarity.

The islamic brotherhoods seem to have taken over this function. The Tidjania and the Murides have become powerful centres of prayer, of production and of services.[10] Members give part of their income to their religious leader, the marabout, in exchange for the provision of a piece of land or of other forms of material or spiritual assistance. The brotherhoods have thus created new communities, bound together by mutual solidarity and loyalty; belonging to such groups is considered helpful, whereas citizenship rights in the Senegalese state simply confer a juridical status.

In economic terms, the brotherhood of the Murides has organized the peanut production since early colonial rule and developed a network of commercial relations in Senegal, West Africa and other parts of the world. This includes a specific financial transaction system, the so-called KARA-exchange[11], which provides facilities for immediate capital transfer without excessive red tape between Senegal, the United States, Europe and Asia. A great number of these productive activities and international exchanges are organized outside the knowledge and control of the Senegalese state.

In political terms, the brotherhoods have assumed the task of nation-building in a modified form: solidarity within the islamic community binds people together regardless of ethnic and social origin; community-building has replaced nation-building and is, it seems, responsible for the relative political stability and unity of Senegal.[12]

This case study of Senegal demonstrates that state authority is not of major relevance to large parts of the population and that new forms of authority and new centres of power have taken over some of the essential roles of the state. In the minds of many people, the brotherhoods successfully fulfil the tasks necessary for the proper functioning of society, at least at the local level.[13] This does not mean that these functions are fulfilled in any satisfactory way; but given the failure of the state, the brotherhoods are seen as an alternative. This development of state, society and economy in Senegal must be seen within the framework of the world capitalist system. Senegal is strongly influenced by specific links to its former colonial master and the French economy, and this dependency reduces effectively the political options of the state.

Both case studies, Central Africa and Senegal, show how global influences affect the state in Africa, how people appropriate this new situation and how they look for alternatives given that the state seems unable to fulfil its basic functions.

Historical Perspectives

Although we consider globalization to be a recent phenomenon, the African experience shows that it is not as new as theorists might suppose.

African people have never been isolated from one another or from the outside world. It is true that demographic structure, distance and climate were serious barriers to regional or interregional integration, and that no common ideology was active in uniting most of the continent as Christianity had done in Europe or Islam in the Arab peninsula and North Africa, but internal migration in different directions took place on a huge scale and touched the whole continent. On the other hand, long-distance trade in very large regions, which included crossing the Sahara, as well as overseas trade created contacts between different peoples and linked coastal societies to the outside world. But these exchanges were not yet based on what we call globalizing factors, since African rulers continued to control them. Nevertheless, on the whole African societies were not linked by a common ideology, a common religion or a common political structure and were more isolated than societies in mediaeval Europe.

At the same time, they were more autonomous than European societies: in many centralized African kingdoms or empires the rulers and the ruling classes had links to other regions and to the outside world; they often had common economic interests and tried to control long-distance trade routes, the production of gold, salt or iron and the slave trade. Sometimes they were linked by common ideologies as well, if they were Muslims; these interests were centred around a world-wide Islamic culture. But it seems that in all these states the different peoples were allowed to preserve their own identity and their political autonomy as long as they paid tribute.[14]

This background of relative isolation and internal autonomy was interrupted by several waves of foreign penetration.

The first major breakthrough of direct outside influence on a larger scale took place when Islam began to penetrate the northern and western parts of Africa, and later the eastern parts, introducing elements of a foreign culture with an alien political philosophy and other forms of political organization, with a new cosmology, new value systems, new ways of life and with new and repeated contacts to other parts of the world. Wherever Muslim rulers established their authority, existing political structures were destroyed and replaced by those visualised by Islamic law. Culturally speaking, the pilgrimage of West African rulers to Mecca since the thirteenth century, the establishment of centres of Islamic learning in cities like Timbuctu and the links to other centres like Cairo opened the way for a continuous flow of Islamic religious and political thought between Africa and other Centres of Islam. But unlike Christianity in Europe, the religion of Mohamed had no means of compelling an entire society into the same mould; large parts of the society remained untouched or hardly influenced by Islam which was seen for centuries as the religion of the ruling elite. So Islam had to comply with African societies and form new ways of Islamic civilization, and in this form of appropriation traditional African systems could survive.

The second wave of foreign penetration was stronger and had deeper effects; it began when the Atlantic slave trade was established thus enlarging the flow of slaves to the north and the east. Although local or regional forms of slave trade already existed, the export of slaves overseas introduced new power relations: external interests and a growing demand for black labourers and followers began to influence and often enough to dominate coastal rulers; their authority and their power dwindled away or, at the very least, were weakened; large parts of West Africa were balkanized in the subsequent wars. Even the institution or role of chieftaincy was transformed in the process: from protector of his people and mediator between the living and their ancestors the chief often became a link in the chain of human trade and exploitation. By the same process, traditional value systems and institutions were pushed aside and new concepts of social justice and moral economy took their place, bound to the demand of the outside world and economic considerations. At the same time, foreigners began to settle in coastal areas, establish their political overrule, invest their capital and spread their ideas, interests and ways of life, even participating in the emergence of a new culture, as happened in East Africa when the Suaheli culture was born.

A third transformation was introduced by the imposition of colonial rule: Foreign economic and other interests began to dominate in Africa; significantly, one of the first things the Europeans did was to depose local rulers and bring the political autonomy of existing states to an end. It was replaced by the colonial state. This was the beginning of a period in which Africans had no political authority and in which political borders were radically transformed by the colonial powers. Any form of continuity of political rule was stopped and any form of adaptation of traditional forms of rule to democratic ones was interrupted. In a second step, the economic interests of the colonial powers began to transform local economies and subject them to their own needs and to the conditions of the world market.[15]

This political and economic power shift was followed by a serious attack on prevailing systems of values. Many traditional values were challenged by a whole range of competing and combined influences: military force, superior technology, western schools and christian missions. All of them can be seen as part of a steadily growing influx of new and challenging information.

The effect of these transformations was cultural destruction, political bondage and economic exploitation.[16] But at the same time on the ruins of what had been destroyed a kind of "mental liberation" was initiated; in the perspective of "global processes" colonialism might therefore be called "the most important liberating factor that the African mind has experienced in historical times", as Ali A. Mazrui put it in an extremely provocative formula.[17]

For him, this process contains two elements: 1. liberation of the mind from tradition in its conservative sense of protecting and maintaining the world of the ancestors against fundamental changes[18], and 2. exposition to and encounter with other cultural systems. Both parts of this influence can be, and in fact were, highly destructive, but out of this destruction something new can be born and, in fact, did come to life.

In economic terms therefore, colonialism was not only the exploitation of African societies and the alienation and destruction of local and human resources, it can also be seen as the opening of the productive capacities of African producers to a growing demand from local, regional and international markets. The fact that this access to the world market occurred during the colonial economy period and is still in many respects, restricted and regulated to the disadvantage of African producers in the current world economic order, does not invalidate this interpretation completely, yet it shows the narrow limits of such a view.

On the political and cultural level, the post-colonial experience of the recent years has shown that large parts of the African population have accepted and integrated basic democratic concepts and values into their own system of thought; the "national conferences", the growing pressure of African forms of civil society and the "anger" of the masses with their political leaders are all examples of the penetration of global values into the minds of African societies.[19]

A fourth fundamental change has submitted African societies to even wider and more unlimited powers. The globalization of the last two or three decades and the breakdown of the Soviet Union, the end of East-West confrontation and the formation of the European Union put a definite end to privileged colonial or postcolonial relations and other kinds of "chasse gardé"[20] and from now on expose African societies, their culture and their economies, to unlimited international competition. This can be seen as the logical end of the process of mental liberation which had begun in the colonial period; now, in its final phase, this process is itself being liberated from narrowing colonial limits and is going to be exposed to political, economic and cultural influences of the globalized world system.

What is new in this fourth stage is the basically economic nature of the new power structure and the emergence of information as a second leading power, and both are uncontrollable. These phases of foreign penetration were different stages of globalization in world history, related to the progressive articulation of the world economy. They have affected African societies in different ways, intensifying cultural contacts on the one hand and subjugating local cultures on the other, linking different economies and at the same time exploiting the weaker partner. In political terms the results are somewhat similar: foreign influences did not strengthen the political structures or revitalize political concepts, on the contrary, state power was weakened throughout all theses phases.

It is true that in Africa nation states have never existed, with the possible exception of Egypt and Ethiopia; many political leaders at different places and at different times have tried to seize and maintain power and elaborate appropriate political ideologies. But it seems that they never succeeded for a longer period or on a larger geographical scale. Local forces were able resist such tendencies and maintain their autonomy, even if they were integrated into large empires. It is significant in this respect that no national consciousness, no national language or national religion was imposed or could be imposed on the masses of the population. This was partly due to what Path' Diagne has called the "communaucratic nature of power", the "dyarchic structure of state power" in African societies, or the "differential character of the state"[21], terms by which he wants to stress that the African state did not know the concentration of power in one or very few hands, that power was always divided.

The influence of foreign intruders in all four phases has certainly strengthened these autonomistic tendencies in replacing existing power structures, transforming political concepts, corrupting the political culture or undermining the political authorities, the main effect of which was to weaken state structures and to foster Balkanization.

This might not seem evident in the case of Islam which after all created large empires with a common political philosophy and a common ideology; but a closer look at the internal power structure reveals that for centuries Islam remained the life style of the ruling classes and that large parts of the population continued to live according to their own value systems or to systems of a highly adapted form of Islam.

In the case of the slave trade, of colonial rule and of globalization the disintegration of the state is apparent, and as the examples of Zaire and Senegal point out, even after independence the project of a nation state has not been successfully realized. This means, seen in a historical perspective, the nation state has not been the proper organization for African societies and under the pressure of globalization the African state today tends to skip the nation state phase which, after all, was a European experience, not a universal phenomenon.

Conclusions

If these four stages of globalization in Africa can be seen as a process of continuous weakening or even of disintegration of state power, it is correct to suppose that globalization means the end of the nation state.

Globalization can be defined as a process in which the flow of capital, information, ideas and values becomes the predominant factor in international relations and in domestic policy. Internationally, a new world order is being created, comprising those regions and peoples which participate actively in the globalized system and marginalizing the rest. On the national level, the most obvious consequences of globalization are fundamental changes in the organization of the state, of the economy, of society and culture.

The state is no longer the sole actor, not to mention the main one, in international relations and the power structure of national territories; different societal forces have taken over some of its functions and prerogatives. Under the pressure of this broad process of globalization the "world of states" has been transformed into a "world of societies".[22]

If we accept such a definition of globalization, we have to admit that the nation state project of the independence period in Africa has failed. It had the intention of transforming the colonial state into a modern state centred round a nation, as European states were the political organization of nations; multicultural African societies were to be knit together to form nations; nation-building and state-building were thought to be one complex and combined process.[23] Yet, at the end of this century it is obvious that the power that the nation state should have established, monopolized and exercised in international relations and in the organization of the national territory, has been weakened steadily. The intervention of international organizations, the United Nations, the World Bank or the International Monetary Fund is merely the political side of a fundamental change in international and internal power relations. The failure of the democratic system, the rise of social conflicts and of ethnic confrontations, civil wars, the disaster of the economy and the crisis of indebtedness and, finally, the breakdown of educational and health-care institutions are different aspects and manifestations of this failure of the African nation state.

It is due, on one hand, to internal problems of economic organization and development, to the multi-ethnic structure of the society and to bad governance and, on the other hand, to fundamental changes in the world economy and the international system, particularly to the rise of multinational enterprises and the unlimited growth in the flow of capital and information.

After nearly 40 years of independence, the African nation state has lost its fascination, power and function.[24] If the state is to survive, a new role has to be found. Globalization has brought about these fundamental changes, it affects states all over the world, and it affects the state as an institution. What its role under the new conditions will be, is not yet clear, and it is less clear still, what the consequences will be for society. The state might be reduced to what Helmut Willke has called "to supervise or revise fundamental decisions taken by other organisations on a world-scale"[25]. This will affect the African states in two ways:
- the nation state project of the independence period has failed; the African state will miss-out, will skip the phase of the nation state and proceed immediately to assume the function of a mere supervisor, trying to channel global interests on their way into and out of the national territory;
- the greater part of the population and the society as a whole are affected by this change insofar as the state under the conditions of globalization is

almost exclusively interested in those parts of the population and of the territory which are linked to the world market and the world system; the rest of the population, mass poverty, hunger, rural development, education, healthcare and other social services and needs will be of marginal interest to the state; they will remain more and more within the responsibility of local communities in what is already called "community development projects"; they might include the construction of hospitals and even of universities, which will be in the charge and under the control of these communities.

The frightening aspects of this development are: 1. it will be more and more difficult to control the new internationally organized capital and its flow; it will be just as difficult to control the flow of information; 2. cultural and human values such as fundamental human rights, international law or democratic rule will risk being pushed aside; 3. cultural values of the different peoples and continents, their traditions and value systems, will be threatened by a new world culture; 4. there will be no central authority any more, responsible for social justice and development within each country. Territorial borders will cease to have the importance they used to have.

A more hopeful outlook may foresee the emergence of specific forms of appropriation: new organizational forms, e.g. "networks of practical initiatives and projects on the basis of independent groups"[26]. In other words: self-help organizations on a community or religious or even ethnic basis may assume a steadily growing responsibility.[27]

Notes

1   See Benjamin R. Barber, Culture McWorld contre démocratie, Denis Duclos, Naissance de l'hyperbourgeoisie, Herbert I. Schiller, Vers un nouveau siècle d'impérialisme américain. In: Le Monde Diplomatique, August 1998.
2   For the general problem of "collapsed states" see: I. William Zartman (ed.), Collapsed States. The Disintegration and Restoration of Legitimate Authority, Boulder 1995. See in particular Herbert Weiss, Zaire: Collapsed Society, Surviving State, Future Policy. In: Ibid. For the state collapse in Central Africa, see: René Lemarchand, Patterns of State Collapse and Reconstruction in Central Africa. Reflections on the Crisis in the Great Lakes. In: African Studies Quarterly 1 (1998) 3 (special issue "Crisis in the Great Lakes"). See also the regular documentation in "Le Monde Diplomatique".
3   See Elikia M'Bokolo: Aux sources de la crise zaïroise. In: Le Monde Diplomatique, May 1997: "La richesse du Zaïre se trouve dans l'inventivité de ces pratiques populaires qui ont permis aux masses de 'survivre' malgré une atroce paupérisation."

4   Janet MacGaffey, The Real Economy of Zaire. The Contribution of Smuggling & Other Unofficial Activities to National Wealth, London 1991, p. 154.
5   MacGaffey, loc. cit., p. 158.
6   For the French turn see the speech of President Mitterrand at the Conférence de la Francophonie in La Baule on 20 June, 1990. In: La Démocratie B contre-coeur. In: Le Monde, 24 July 1997.
7   See e.g Philippe Leymarie, L'Angola - Nouvelle puissance régionale. In: Le Monde Diplomatique, 24 November 1997.
8   For a broader discussion see Momar Coumba Diop/Mamadou Diouf, Le Sénégal sous Abdou Diouf. Etat et Société, Paris 1990.
9   The schools were closed at the end of 1996.
10 For the role of the Marabouts, see Jean Copans, Les Marabouts de l'Arachide. La confrérie mouride et les paysans du Sénégal, Paris 1980; Moriba Magassouba, L'Islam au Sénégal: demain les mollahs?, Paris 1985.
11 More details, see Leonhard Harding/Laurence Marfaing/Mariam Sow (eds.), Les opérateurs économiques et l'Etat au Sénégal, Hamburg—Paris, 1998.
12 Villalón describes this process of "nation-building" by the brotherhoods in: Leonardo A. Villalón, Islamic Society and State Power in Senegal. Disciples and Citizens in Fatick, Cambridge 1995; see also Lamine Sanneh, The Crown and the Turban. Muslims and West African Pluralism, Boulder 1997.
13 The sociologist study of Ndiaye tries to present the specific morality of Senegalese traders and entrepreneurs and the role of Islam and solidarity: Malick Ndiaye, L'Ethique Ceddo et la Société d'accaparement, ou: Les conduites culturelles des Sénégalais d'aujourd'hui. Tème 1: Le Goorgi, type moyen de la société sénégalaise urbaine post-indépendance, Dakar 1996. Tème 2: Les Moudu Moudu, ou l'éthos du développement au Sénégal (forthcoming).
14 It is a common theme in African history that non-islamic empires or emperors were more interested in tribute than in a common ideology or a common "national consciousness". Even the great annual ceremonies in the capital were conceived less as a means of ideological integration than as powerful demonstrations of the ruler's power. All the chiefs or provincial governors had to be present and represent their people.
15 A side-effect of this new world-orientation was that the transport problem, one of the major problems of precolonial African production, was overcome.
16 See e.g. one of the most critical interpretations of colonialism in the famous "Discours sur le Colonialisme" of Aimé Césaire, Paris 1955. A similar view is: Peter P. Ekeh, Colonialism and Social Structure. Inaugural lecture, Ibadan 1993. The Nigerian historian Ade Ajayi sees in the period of colonism only "an episode". Colonialism: an Episode in African History. In: Colonialism in Africa. Vol. I, Cambridge 1969, pp. 497-509. See also A. Adu Boahen, African Perspectives on Colonialism, Baltimore-London 1987.
17 Ali A. Mazrui, Borrowed Theory and Original Practice in African Politics. In: Herbert J. Spiro (ed.), Patterns of African Development. Five Comparisons, Englewood Cliffs 1967.
18 In this context, see D. Etounga-Manguelle, L'Afrique a-t-elle besoin d'un programme d'ajustement culturel?, Paris 1990; Célestin Monga, Anthropologie de la colère. Société civile et démocratie en Afrique noire, Paris 1994; Jean Copans, La longue marche de la modernité africaine, Paris 1990. For a similar approach, see Jean-François Bayart/Achille Mbembe/Comi Toulabor, Le Politique par le Bas en Afrique Noire. Contributions à une problématique de la démocratie, Paris 1992.

19 Célestin Monga, loc. cit., tries to redefine civil society under the conditions of post-colonial Africa: "La société civile en Afrique noire est constituée de tous ceux qui gèrent la colère collective" (p. 104). See also John W. Harbeson/Donald Rotchild/Naomi Chazan (eds.), Civil Society and the State in Africa, Boulder 1994, and Eghosa Osaghae (ed.), Between State and Civil Society in Africa, Dakar 1994.
20 See the series of 5 articles in Le Monde on "France-Afrique, Les Liaisons Dangereuses". Le Monde, 22-26 July 1997, and Philippe Leymarie, En Afrique, la fin des ultimes "chasses gardées". In: Le Monde Diplomatique, December 1996.
21 For Diagne there is a fundamental distinction between the European and the African concept of power and state: "L'Etat différentiel négro-africain est l'antithèse même de l'Etat-nation indo-européen, ethnocide et réducteur de l'autre." Pathé Diagne, 1981. 1986. Le pouvoir en Afrique. In: UNESCO. Le concept de pouvoir en Afrique. Paris, p. 46.
22 Ernst-Otto Czempiel uses the terminology "Staatenwelt" and "Gesellschaftswelt" to explain this transformation. See: Ernst-Otto Czempiel, Von der Staatenwelt zur Gesellschaftswelt. In: Frankfurter Allgemeine Zeitung, 25 February 1995; id., Innovationen statt Kanonen, ibid., 22 November 1997.
23 A good introduction is: Abebayo Olukoshi/Liisa Laakso (eds.), Challenges to the Nation-State in Africa, Uppsala 1996.
24 The nation state project had been criticized long before; for the transition of the political discourse from the nation-state in Chinua Achebe's *Things fall apart* (1958) or Camara Laye's *L'enfant noir* (1953) to the idea of a state based on global human values in Yambo Ouologuem's *Le Devoir de Violence* (1968), see Kwame Anthony Appiah, In My Father's House. Africa in the Philosophy of Culture, New York 1992. pp. 137ff.
25 Helmut Willke, Supervision des Staates, Frankfurt/M. 1997.
26 Joachim Hirsch, Der nationale Wettbewerbsstaat. Staat, Demokratie und Politik im globalen Kapitalismus, Berlin 1996.
27 See the discussion "Ethnic and religious identities re-visited" in: Olukoshi/Laakso (eds.), loc. cit., pp. 28ff.

Secularism, Legal Reform and Gender Justice in India

Zoya Hasan

In the past decade, religion and gender have become intertwined in the political turmoil in India. One issue at the centre of debate is whether religion based personal law be continued or a uniform civil code [UCC] be instituted. The UCC, that is, the legal unification of different religious communities - refers to the ideological deployment of uniformity with the dual agenda of improving the status of women and integrating communities through a set of uniform laws. At different historical moments, therefore, the UCC has been projected as the most salient emblem of a modern homogeneous nation in contradistinction to personal laws perceived as the symbol of difference. The state's commitment to a UCC was expressed in the Directive Principles of State Policy of the Constitution. But five decades after Independence public opinion remains sharply divided. Religious personal law in matters of marriage, divorce, maintenance, inheritance and child custody continue to be binding on the followers of different communities.

As various analyses have shown, the enterprise of instituting common laws was confounded from the outset by the dispute over the desirability as well as the feasibility of introducing legal uniformity in a socially stratified and heterogeneous society.[1] The UCC debate underscores the conflicting pulls of secularism and minority identity and the tensions between the demands of equity and cultural difference. The gender inequality reveals the centrality of the gender question in contemporary critiques of the state. By the same token, increased women's participation and politicization engendered the formation of a public and collective identity for women which has distanced itself from definitions of separate gender roles within the private and public spheres. Instead women's groups are focused on gender justice which cross-cuts power relations between modernity and tradition, secularism and religion, as well as between men and women and women themselves.

This paper explores the controversy over legal reform through an analysis of the changing relationships between state, communities, and the women's movement. It attempts to unravel some of the strands in the tangled web of interconnections between community identity and gender. It maps the general contours of the debate and the shifts in these interrelationships in the post-Ayodhya period. Its specific focus is on the role of the state in the promotion of gender just laws and the various ways in which women's rights have been conceptualised.

State, Community and Minorities

Until recently, the scholarly literature tended to treat gender, community identity and state as unchanging. Those studying identity construction often focus on the social and cultural domain, rather than on the state. Students of the state, on the other hand, are less inclined to examine the processes of identity formation.[2]

The debates over the UCC reveal that it is untenable to draw a sharp line of distinction between community and state on the question of religion or gender. This is on account of the structural, administrative and ideological linkages between the two.[3] Religious communities under discussion have been constituted in relation to the state and, more importantly, by political processes connected to the state. Moreover, successive governments have been involved in the internal affairs of religious communities and in the maintenance of places of worship and other kinds of religious establishments. Thus the interface between community and the state extends to the sphere of law. This has, consequently, led to a triangular relationship between personal laws, community representatives and the state.[4] The state has been asked to protect religious boundaries in two different ways: through the demand for the exemption of minorities from the application of the criminal procedure code made by religious spokesman, and through the demands for a UCC, made by, among others, the Hindu communalists.

The demand for a UCC, first made by the All India Women's Conference in 1937, figured prominently in the nationalist and early feminist agendas in the 1940s and 1950s. Today, however, none of the major women's organizations support it, though one can discern a wide spectrum of positions. More recently, however, the UCC has acquired political salience in part because gender just laws are conspicuous by their absence, and in part because India's new ruling party, the Bharatiya Janata Party, a right-wing authoritarian formation, has appropriated what was otherwise a feminist demand. The Congress and the Left, on the other hand, are opposing it, though for different reasons.

The principal focus of contention are the laws relating to marriage, divorce, maintenance, inheritance and adoption. As is well-known, the Hindu family laws were changed in 1955-1956 through the Hindu Marriage Act, the Hindu Succession Act, the Hindu Minority and Guardianship Act and the Hindu Adoption and Maintenance Act. Yet, there was no attempt to secure, as was suggested by the Directive Principles of State Policy, a UCC or initiate moves towards legal reform of personal laws of the minority communities.

The Congress government was unwilling to press for similar changes in laws of the minority communities or legislate a UCC. The question of personal law had come up for debate on several occasions in the Constituent Assembly. Muslim members emphasised the unchanging nature of Muslim personal law and that it cannot be changed by the state, and changes, if any, should be initiated by the Islamic community. As this line of reasoning confirmed government suppositions, it was effective. In the process of these negotiations, Muslim political leaders represented both Islamic law and their own community as more unified than they actually were, or ever had been. They succeeded in establishing that legal codes and religion are interlinked and that personal laws form an integral part of the socio-religious identity of Muslims.

In such a situation, the government remained non-interfering in the regime of personal laws. Jawaharlal Nehru was reluctant because he felt his government in the aftermath of Partition should avoid any step that would offend the religious susceptibilities of minorities, especially the Muslims, instead he wanted to assuage Muslim anxieties regarding their status in Independent India. Nehru said, "If anybody brings forward a civil code bill, it will have my extreme sympathy. But I confess I do not think the time is ripe in India for me to push through it." Although he considered a UCC for the whole country essential, Nehru was apprehensive that any imposition on minorities, without their consent, would be imprudent. Hence, the policy of merging religious communities in a single citizenship remained a pious hope enshrined in the Directive Principles. But given the changeable nature of cultures, Nehru the architect of this policy, expected these provisions and concessions to the minorities would themselves be subject to change. He hoped that Muslim communities would, in the fullness of time, respond to the winds of change. Meanwhile he insisted they should have the right to when.

Nehru's expectations have not been fulfilled. The last fifty years have witnessed inconsiderable effort toward reform. By contrast, the two decades preceding Independence saw considerable reformist activity, albeit of a type which stressed return to pristine Islam and the need to observe *Shariat* in everyday life. Nevertheless, there was agreement among reformers, which included a coalition of the ulama, middle class reformers and Westernised politicians, that the status of Muslim women required amelioration.[5] Often reformers recommended eliminating custom, in some cases they advocated legislative enactments in order to bring personal law closer to the scriptures, but a series of legal changes, which included the Muslim Dissolution of Marriage Act of 1939, led to some improvements in women's rights in the context of family relations.[6]

After Independence, Muslim political leaders were able to hold off the legal advance of women's rights by taking shelter under the special provision for minorities and its overall significance in a multicultural heterogeneous society. The Constitution provides for the religious liberty of both the individual and associations of individuals united by common beliefs, practices, and discipline. This has given rise to tensions between two different conceptions of rights - the rights of individuals and the claims of communities. Through the special provisions for the scheduled castes, scheduled tribes and other backward classes, the Constitution introduced the principle of positive discrimination in favour of the poorest and lowest in the social order - especially those excluded from the caste system. The grant of universal rights to all was offset by the recognition of injustice suffered by particular groups, especially the scheduled castes in the form of reservation of government jobs and educational institutions for members of these groups.[7]

The implicit recognition in the Constitution that religions have both sustained and legitimised caste and gender discrimination led the state to be at once a reformer of injustices based on religion and protector of religious freedom. The minorities were granted some degree of control over their own affairs, including the right to express their cultural particularity. This took two forms: the inclusion in the Fundamental Rights of the freedom of religion and safeguards for minority rights, including the right to maintain their own educational institutions.[8]

The incorporation of these rights was undoubtedly influenced by the context of partition, when the state endeavoured to gain the trust of Muslims communities that opted to stay in their country of birth. The spectre of Hindu-Muslim communalism hung over the subcontinent when India became independent. The partition meant that Pakistan might become a homeland for Muslims, but India would remain a home for Hindus, Muslims, Christians and others, and though Pakistan was a Muslim state, there were more Muslims in India than in Pakistan. One way of facilitating the integration of minorities was to recognise them as members of religious communities. From the standpoint of universalism and egalitarianism such group-specific rights were a violation of liberal principles, but in India they were seen not as privileges, but primarily as safeguards against larger majority groupings. It did, however, express a recognition of minority identity in the legal structure of the state. Hence, personal laws, which were often disadvantageous to women, were allowed to function without any reform. While these safeguards are important, no effort has been made to ensure that they are not monopolised by the most conservative elements within the minority. The controversy over the Shah Bano judgement is a case in point.

Community Identity and Women

The turning point in the debate on gender justice was the famous Shah Bano case. The Supreme Court in a landmark judgement delivered in April 1985, granted a small maintenance allowance to Shah Bano a seventy three year old divorcee, to be paid by her husband Mohammed Ahmed Khan under the provisions of the Criminal Procedure Code. Ahmed Khan had argued in an appeal to the Supreme Court that since he had fulfilled his obligations under Muslim Personal law by paying her an allowance for three months of the *iddat* period and *meher* as well, he was not bound to maintain her any further. The Supreme Court, however, ruled that criminal laws override personal laws and are applicable to all, including Muslim women. This judgement sparked off a political furore. To soothe ruffled feelings, the Rajiv Gandhi government enacted a legislation, the Muslim Women (Protection of rights on Divorce) Bill, 1986, to explicitly exclude Muslim women from the purview of the Criminal Procedure Code, to which all citizens otherwise have recourse.

Spearheading the crusade against the Shah Bano judgement was the All India Muslim Personal Law Board which was outraged by the judgement and joined a campaign to repeal it. There were a spate of public meetings all over the country to oppose the judgement and the danger it posed to minority identity. As against this, the campaign in favour of the judgement was much smaller. To understand why this was so and why the issue became so very heated one has to look at the context in which it arose. The 1980s witnessed a steep rise in communal violence all over India, both Hindu-Muslim and Hindu-Sikh. Hindu communalism was acquiring increasing legitimacy in the eyes of the state and was further strengthened by the public response to the Ramjanmabhoomi movement. The lack of any noticeable opposition to the Ramjanmabhoomi movement among Hindus, compared to the outrage against the new legislation, left large sections of Muslims feeling vulnerable. For its part the government showed no sensitivity to Muslim sentiments over the campaign against the Babri mosque, in contrast to the extraordinary concern for Muslim feelings on the Shah Bano case. This was in part because the plan was to pragmatically accommodate both Hindu and Muslim communal sentiments.

The controversy around the judgement and the public as well as the parliamentary debate, tended to focus on the conflict between the right of the religious minority to cultural autonomy and to a separate civil code as an important guarantee of its identity, and on the other hand, the claims of the state legitimised through representative institutions to articulate and realise the common good.[9] The critics ignored the important question of women's rights which remained confined to feminists and Left parties. The Muslim leadership focused on legal issues that linked women and family life to Islamic legal identity and defended the definition of the Muslim community as a legal entity. The government defended the legislation on the ground that it conformed to the wishes of the Muslim community and should be conceded irrespective of the opinion of other communities or society at large. The Law Minister stated that:

"We have to tread very carefully for the Muslim personal law is linked to the Muslim religion in the mind of Muslims... We must look at it from the point of view of Muslims and then try to find out what is the law which governs the Muslims and which according to them is not merely a law of man's making and law ordained by God. This is the belief of Muslims."[10]

The primacy of community rights over citizenship was once again endorsed by the state which willingly limited the application of its own laws to exclude citizens from the rights available to others. The controversy signifies the important role played by official state discourse in safeguarding community identity. The Congress party legitimised it, in terms both of state policies and strategies of mobilization. In the absence of a reformed divorce law, Muslim women were unequal vis-à-vis men and were now rendered unequal vis-à-vis women from other communities who have access to the law in respect of maintenance. To be sure, these issues raise questions that are not easily reconciled: the claims of rights of women and of individuals as against those of cultures and groups. The problem is undoubtedly compounded by the substantial purchase of community identity in the polity.

However, the recent debate among social scientists on notions of community makes it clear that community identity is not natural or primordial. Communities are constituted in distinct ways at different historical junctures. Thus it is well known that personal laws are constructions of the twentieth century.[11] As with the Hindu Code Bill, the Shariat Act of 1937 and the Dissolution of Muslim Marriages Bill, 1939, demarcated the boundaries of the Muslim community. Nonetheless, the historicity of community construction does not deny the reality that these identities exist and they matter to large numbers of people. Yet, it is a fact that community identity can be punitive and there is little evidence to show that communities are committed to internal democratization of gender differences. Personal laws deny women the rights that communities claim for themselves vis-à-vis the state: autonomy, selfhood and access to resources.

From the women's standpoint, the difficulty lies in marking the identity of the community exclusively by defining its women. Failing to define the community in broad terms, the Muslim leadership conflates religion and culture identifying only one area as the essence of cultural identity which boils down to personal laws. By defining community identity entirely with reference to a strict code of laws, legal change is ruled out because the survival of cultural identity depends on a codified identity. But the reform of personal laws does not mean the end of community or community identity, because there are a vast array of things which constitute the identity of the community, including language, religious rituals, pilgrimage to Mecca, fasting and prayers.

Hindu Communalism, Minorities and Women's Rights

Over the last few decades the state has had to steer a precarious course between the norm of secularism and the norm of religious pluralism. Secularism in India simultaneously posits disengagement of religion from the public arena and the need for the state to regulate religious practices, either by non-intervention, for example, declaring certain areas of jurisprudence to be the prerogative of religious leaders or by intervention, for example, ensuring financial accountability of religious trusts.[12] The critique of the state in this context is either that it intervenes too much as when the government passed the Muslim Women's Bill or too little as in its reluctance to enact a UCC. This is the peculiar predicament of the state to understand which we have to keep in mind, not only India's composite cultural tradition, but also its present demography and heterogeneity. The presence of social pluralities makes it difficult to conceive of a stable political arrangement without religious tolerance and secularism.

The conflicts between the two positions mentioned above coexisted for four decades after Independence. There were moments when the contradictions came to the fore, but not many appear to have been troubled by the their disagreement. At any rate, these discordances were not widely contested and they did not appear to be seriously divisive.[13] The relative accommodation was upset in the late 1980s, which has much to do with changes in India's politics: the growth of communal politics and the controversies surrounding it.

In the changed political context many have asked why action has not been taken to bring about the fulfilment of the constitutional ideal. It has become a source of political conflict and polarization, it revealed deep cleavages between secularists and the Hindu organizations in general and between them and women in particular. It also created a major area of tension between the Hindu nationalists and the minority communities.

Epitomising a long term tendency in politics and society, the design of Hindu nationalism, in contrast to pluralistic nationalism, stands for emphasising the distinctness of Hindu civilization, playing down horizontal divisions among Hindus and integration of all castes, communities and sects into a homogeneous whole. In some respects Hindu nationalism is different from fundamentalism. Whereas fundamentalism rejects the separation of religion and state, Hindu nationalism accepts this separation in principle. Partha Chatterjee argues that:

> "The persuasive power, and even the emotional charge the Hindutva campaign appears to have gained in recent years do not depend upon its demanding legislative enforcement of ritual or scriptural injunctions, a role for religious institutions in legislative or judicial processes, compul-

sory religious instruction or state support for religious bodies, censorship of science, literature and art in order to safeguard religious dogma or any other similar demand undermining the secular character of the existing Indian state."[14]

This has crucial implications for women.[15] By virtue of its supposed commitment to secular principles, the BJP can uphold constitutional protection of sexual equality, and in fact adopt a high moral posture to castigate secular governments for being pseudo-secular owing to their indulgence of minorities. "Personal law", Uma Bharati argues, "defies the spirit of the constitution."[16]

Politically, this criticism and the appropriation of women's rights was made for the wrong reasons. Until it came to power in March 1998, the BJP raised the issue mainly to draw a parallel between the Congress party's capitulation to Muslim conservatives in the 1950s and then again in the 1980s on the Shah Bano case. The rationalization of Muslim personal law by the Congress government was capitalized upon to build a critique of secularism and minority rights. It became a rallying point for a campaign against secularism and the 'pseudo-secular' state run by the Congress party. It attacked the Muslim desire to conserve a separate identity, and demanded that Muslims should shed their special ways of life and culture and accept a uniform civil code. The latter was basically an advocacy of homogenization, it was a way of saying that "you must be like us and give up your alien cultural attitudes and customs".

In the course of this campaign, Hindu nationalism took upon itself the mission to reform the oppressive and backward laws of the Muslim community.[17] Muslim women were portrayed as "unfortunate slaves" of the "evils of Islam" and Muslim men as "the most backward and aggressive" operating outside the national mainstream, and sympathetic to an international conspiracy to undermine Indian/Hindu civilization and culture.[18] Easy divorce and polygamy were singled out for special attention.

The striking aspect of the Hindutva discourse was not stereotyping of Muslims - a necessary feature of communal politics - but the way in which Muslim women were used for the denigration of secularism. Thus, their campaign against the Muslim Women's Bill, shifted its emphasis from women's rights to a full blown critique of secularism, ridiculed as "pseudo-secularism". The emphasis on the oppression of Muslim women was displaced by a sharp attack on the protection of minority rights and how it constituted a violation of constitutional principles of legal equality. Women's right was a subsidiary theme in the more crucial struggle against social and cultural pluralism. The Hindu right dismissed cultural pluralism by setting the equal treatment of women in opposition to secularism. Indeed, any recognition of cultural difference was considered a violation of the constitutional guarantee of equality, besides perpetuating minority privileges. The transmutation of these arguments into a national common sense helped catapult the BJP to the political centre stage in the 1990s.[19]

By decrying actions of successive Congress regimes on the issue of family law, the BJP seeks to demonstrate its own commitment to constitutional principles. The BJP uses the language of legal and constitutional rights to pit woman's rights against minority rights. Feminist legal scholars point out that Hindu nationalism interprets secularism to mean that Muslims and Hindus should be treated alike, thereby disregarding the vulnerabilities to which Muslims as a minority are subject.[20] This is because Hindu nationalists unlike their counterparts in many Muslim countries identify their principal enemies as internal rather than external.[21] By comparison Islamic fundamentalism in the Middle East, for example, is inseparable from the nationalist opposition to Westernization and modernity in its various guises. Nilufer Gole notes that veiling in Turkey embodies the battleground for two competing conceptions of self and society, Western and Islamist.[22] Similarly, Valentine Moghadam observes, that fundamentalists in Iran consider the veil an antidote to the virus of "Westoxication" and "Euromania".[23]

Until the BJP-led government decided to conduct a series of underground nuclear tests, Hindu nationalists had not expressed any open anti-Western sentiment. Rather their target were the "outsiders" located within the nation, that is Muslims whom they regard as foreign even though Indian Islam is no more derivative than Chinese, Tibetan, Thai or Japanese Buddhism. Yet the idea that Islam is foreign is axiomatic for Hindu nationalists and their agenda of removing the protective safeguards for communities and regions in order to produce a uniform homogeneous code.

It is clear that the ideological consensus formulated by the state on issues of secularism and minority rights during Nehru's regime has given way to a politics of intolerance that now pervades the culture. The controversy over the UCC provides the BJP with a crucial means of challenging the ideological legitimacy of the secular state. The compulsions of coalition politics have forced the BJP government to shelve the immediate introduction of a UCC. Meanwhile in the Hindu nationalist discourse the UCC continues to be a touchstone of what it means to be an Indian and a struggle over what the conditions of belonging are.

Women's Groups and Gender Justice

In the larger body politic, gender construction, identity formation, and citizenship continue to be formulated within the rhetoric of binary opposition. Salient among these are: universalism\difference; uniformity\plurality; state\community. Rather than accept them as a logical and necessary opposition, these categories need to be historicized and subjected to closer scrutiny. Women's groups have attempted this by taking a fresh look at the process and mechanics of gender construction, especially the role of the state in this process.

From the 1940s until the early 1980s, there was a general consensus that the state should legislate gender just laws for all communities. This was part of the larger understanding that the state ought to play an important role in the progressive social and political transformation. However, by the mid-1970s this consensus broke down with the economic and political crisis of the state, engendered by the failures of development planning and socialism. The mass discontent brought about a radical rethinking in the women's movement on the role of the nation state. There was a growing disquiet with state initiated legislation in areas of marriage, divorce, maintenance and inheritance, including the Hindu Code Bill.[24] The reform of Hindu laws did challenge religious elites, but it had culminated in the promulgation of laws that were not entirely just to women.[25]

Though the state is theoretically committed to ensuring the rights of its citizens it has been constrained by the dilemma of whether to initiate reforms from above or support reforms from within. Significant initiatives to reform personal laws have been thwarted as often by the state as by pundits, mullahs and priests. Even the strategy of reform from within in the case of Christian community met with prevarication from the state.[26] The legal reform of personal law becomes a bargaining counter for the state which retains the power to decide whether or not to reform personal law of any community.

The decisive shift came in the wake of the Ayodhya movement and the dramatic growth of the BJP whose ambition is to establish a singular citizenship by obliterating the legal recognition of religious and cultural differences. Hence, their excessive focus on Muslim personal law. The feminist groups are ill at ease with the UCC's rather incongruous appropriation by the parties of the right, particularly because in their hands it becomes a rhetorical device to attack minorities. This created a dilemma for feminist politics and more generally for secular democratic politics between two conflicting norms: the norm of religious tolerance and the norm of equality between men and women. The women's movement remained committed to equality, but it did not want changes forced upon personal laws by the militant Hindu communal forces who saw the Muslim resistance to the UCC as an sign of its inability to integrate into the nation. Aware that legal change cannot be isolated from the wider political contradictions in the context of communal politics, women's groups began to seriously rethink the demand for a UCC.[27] This gave rise to two kinds of approaches, one proposed that the present historical moment of heightened religious identities requires working within them, while the other foregrounded gender justice by delinking it from national integrity.[28]

From the early 1990s, the opposition to uniform laws was marked by a simultaneous critique of the UCC and personal laws. It signalled an acknowledgement that gender justice needs to be delinked from uniform laws. Groups which earlier supported uniform legislation jettisoned it in favour of common, gender just or egalitarian, as against uniform laws. It is worth noting that the term uniform was practically dropped within the women's movement, even by those groups who endorse state legislation.[29] The change is visible in the repudiation of the UCC by all political parties, the BJP excepted. The change is most explicit in the case of the All India Democratic Women's Association, the largest women's organization in the country. AIDWA, like other feminist groups, has had to reckon with the political climate vitiated by communal politics and religious identities. Not too long ago the AIDWA promoted common laws, but at this juncture it champions a gradual approach to legal reforms in recognition of the difficulty of pushing change in the present communal climate, encouraging community initiative and demanding fresh legislation with regard to matrimonial property and the custody of children.

A number of proposals have been mooted by women's groups to enlarge the scope for gender justice. Some groups, such as the Bombay-based Majlis, prefer to maximise the space for women within communities, which means reform within personal laws, rather than legislation by the state. Then, there are others who want to devise genuinely egalitarian or secular laws and allow people to opt for it.[30] The Forum Against Oppression of Women, Bombay, has evolved such a code.[31] Working Group on Women's Rights, Delhi, put forward a proposal that blends state legislation in both private and public domains and also provides the option of a return to personal laws.[32] This option would turn the regime of personal laws into something voluntary and yet leave open the possibility of transformation of community through its own initiatives, rather than by the state.

All these initiatives uphold unequivocally the principle of gender justice which cannot be indefinitely postponed. It is by seeking rights as citizens that women aspire to actively redefine the contours of the debate and shape new laws. "The legitimacy of new common laws", as Kumkum Sangari argues, "should be based on secular and democratic horizon that seeks justice for women within a wider egalitarian project. As such it cannot be formulated by the state or the BJP, or through a consensus of religious communities."[33] Such laws can only be made from a non-religious location, and they would have to take into account both similarities and differences and allow the individual's right to choose where to belong. In sum, common laws have to be based on a principle of access to inalienable rights that are the same for all.

Notes

1 See for example, Kumkum Sangari, Politics of Diversity: Religious Communities and Multiple Patriarchies. In: Economic and Political Weekly, 23 December 1995, and Archana Parasher, Women and Family Law Reform in India, Delhi 1992.
2 See Chapter 1 by Amrita Basu in: Patricia Jeffrey/Amrita Basu (eds.), Appropriating Gender: Women's Activism and Politicized Religion in South Asia, New York 1999, pp. 2-5.
3 Kumkum Sangari, Politics of Diversity: Religious Communities and Multiple Patriarchies. In: Economic and Political Weekly, pp. 3294-3296.
4 See essays in Zoya Hasan (ed.), Forging Identities: Gender, Communities and the State, New Delhi 1994.
5 Gail Minault, Women, Legal Reform and Muslim Identity. In: Mushirul Hasan (ed.), Islam, Communities and the Nation: Muslim Identities in South Asia and Beyond, New Delhi 1998, p. 139.
6 Ibid., pp. 140-142.
7 On the social commitment of India's constitution, see Granville Austin, The Indian Constitution: Cornerstone of a Nation, Oxford 1966, pp. 50-74.
8 Donald Eugene Smith, India as a Secular State, Princeton 1963, pp. 100-134.
9 Niraja Gopal Jayal, Secularism, Identities and Representative Democracy. In: Mushirul Hasan (ed.), Islam, Communities..., loc. cit., p. 161.
10 Lok Sabha Debates, Fifth Session, Eighth Lok Sabha, Vol. I, XVII, Government of India, New Delhi.
11 Despite centuries of Muslim rule the community did not adopt the Shariah as the basis of law, consequently women's rights in the Shariah were seldom complied with or enforced. As a result, the opportunities of exercising their Quranic prerogatives, especially in claiming ownership of landed estates and property, were denied to women. Until the introduction of the Shariat Act in 1937, legal and social codes observed by Muslim communities in different parts of the country were varied and diffused. Thus began an effort by the ulama to work for a complete supersession of non-Islamic customary practice and compulsory enactment of an Islamic legal system. The enactment of the Muslim Personal Law Shariat Application Act, 1937 signaled the acceptance by the state legal system of the principle that in all personal matters, such as marriage, divorce, maintenance, inheritance and custody, Muslims would be governed by the Muslim personal law. Similarly, the Dissolution of the Muslim Marriages Act, 1939, represented yet another attempt by the ulama to rectify what they perceived to be a lacunae in the existing laws which had left Muslim women without the option of divorce, except through apostasy from Islam. For the first time, this Act gave Muslim women the right to seek judicial dissolution of marriage. See A.A.A. Fyzee, Outlines of Muhammedan Law, Delhi 1974.
12 Nivedita Menon, Women and Citizenship. In: Partha Chatterjee (ed.), Wages of Freedom. Fifty Years of the Indian Nation-State, New Delhi, pp. 264-265.
13 Andre Beteille, Conflict of Norms and Values in Contemporary Indian Society. In: Peter Berger (ed.), The Limits of Social Cohesion, Conflict and Mediation in Pluralist Societies, Colorado 1998.
14 Partha Chatterjee, Secularism and Toleration. In: Economic and Political Weekly, 29, (1994) 28, p. 1768.

15 Amrita Basu, Hindu Activism in India and the Question It Raise. In: Jeffrey/Basu, Appropriating Gender..., loc. cit., pp. 170-172.
16 Ibid., p. 172.
17 Lata Mani makes this point with regard to the attitude of the Hindu Right's on the Shah Bano controversy in the epilogue to her essay on "Contentious Traditions: The Debate on Sati in Colonial India" in: Kumkum Sangari/Sudesh Vaid (ed.), Recasting Women: Essays on Colonial History, New Delhi 1989.
18 Organiser, 20 October 1985.
19 The last two paragraphs are based on my article "Gender Politics, Legal, and the Muslim Community in India" in: Jeffrey/Basu (ed.), Appropriating Gender..., loc. cit., pp. 78-83.
20 Ratna Kapur/Brenda Cossman, Communalising Gender/Engendering Community: Women, Legal Discourse and the Saffron Agenda. In: Tanika Sarkar/Urvashi Butalia (ed.), Women of the Hindu Right, New Delhi, pp. 82-120.
21 Ibid, p. 171.
22 Nilufer Gole, Forbidden Modern: Civilization and Veiling, Michigan 1996, p. 5.
23 Valentine Moghadam, Introduction: Women and Identity Politics in Theoretical and Comparative Perspective. In: Valentine Moghadam (ed.), Identity Politics and Women: Cultural Assertions and Feminisms in International Perspectives, Boulder 1994, p. 13.
24 See for example the paper prepared by the Anveshi Law Committee, Hyderabad. "Is Gender Justice Only a Legal Issue? Political Stakes in UCC Debate". In: Economic and Political Weekly, 1-8 March 1997.
25 For instance, in the case of the Hindu Succession Act, there were several compromises: the joint family system was retained; retention of coparcenary, whose membership was restricted to males, meant that sons would not only get a share of their father's property but also their own interest as coparcenary in the joint family property; by excluding agricultural land from legislation relating to succession, its benefits were restricted; the unrestricted right of tessellation, i.e., right to make a will, often led daughters to be dependent upon their father's good will for being provided for life. Mad Kishwar, Codified Hindu Law: Myth and Reality. In: Economic and Political Weekly, 29 (1994) 33, pp. 2145-2161.
26 In 1993, a Christian Marriage Act was proposed by the government with the approval of all Christian churches and Christian women's organization. Despite the Christian community's support for changes in divorce laws, the Bill has not yet been debated in Parliament.
27 Flavia Agnes, Women's Movement within a Secular Framework. In: Economic and Political Weekly, 7 May 1994, pp. 1123-1127.
28 Three kinds of interventions were made with regard to legal reforms. First, there were attempts by women's groups all over the country to evolve a common package of laws that are free of gender bias. Second, there is the effort to reform from within communities. Third, a number of judicial interventions addressed themselves to discrepancies in law to reduce inequalities between men and women. For example, a recent Supreme Court judgment gave the widow and daughter of a deceased coparcenary equal rights to property left by him. Another judgment granted a divorced Hindu woman the right to sell, use for income or dispose in any way she likes the land given to her in lieu of maintenance. In another case, the widow was granted full ownership rights of the premises given to her as part of her maintenance. Such verdicts have greatly helped to reduce the existing inequities between men and women in matters of inherited property.

29 Menon, Women and Citizenship, loc. cit., pp. 253-263.
30 This idea was put forward as early as 1945, when it was suggested that the UCC be made optional. After Independence, the Special Marriages Act or the Indian Succession Act offered a number of options. Yet the government did not endeavor to create a machinery for implementing an optional code. Had it done so, it may well have expanded the ground of secular laws, besides building up pressure for reforms within community laws.
31 The proposal includes the following: 1. The need for changes and modifications in the procedures of law to ensure effective implementation. 2. The demand for a system of social security benefits for women. 3. The demand that state take on the responsibility for imparting legal education to women at all levels.
32 The proposal has three features: 1. Comprehensive package of legislation providing equal rights for women in terms of access to property, guardianship, right to matrimonial home, and equal rights in the workplace, anti-discriminatory provisions in recruitment and promotions. 2. All Indian citizens would come under the purview of common laws at birth. 3. All citizens would have the right to choose at any point to be governed by personal laws, if they so desire, while retaining the option to revoke this choice. Reversing the Option: Civil Codes and Personal Laws. In: Economic and Political Weekly, 18 May 1996.
33 Sangari, Politics of Diversity, loc. cit., p. 3386.

The Bharatiya Janata Party and Hindu Nationalism in India

David Taylor

In March 1998, following the collapse of the previous centre-left united front coalition and mid-term parliamentary elections, India saw the induction of its first-ever government headed by the Bharatiya Janata Party (BJP). Atal Behari Vajpayee, who had made an earlier but unsuccessful attempt to form a BJP-led government in 1996, became prime minister. The BJP is frequently characterised as a Hindu nationalist party, and its leaders had played a major role for example in the demolition of the Babri Masjid at Ayodhya in North India in December 1992. There is little doubt that the BJP has close links with other organizations in the same field, for example the Vishwa Hindu Parishad (VHP) or World Hindu Council, which since the early 1980s has been exploiting every means at its disposal to heighten Hindu self-awareness, very often by whipping up anti-Muslim feeling and provoking violent confrontations, as in the aftermath of the Ayodhya demolition. The BJP is often described in India as having a family relationship with these other organizations; the head of the family, or Sangh Parivar, is the Rashtriya Swayamsevak Sangh (RSS), which since its foundation in 1925 has sought to mobilise the Hindu community, or rather the Hindu community as it has tried to construct it, on a programme of national revival. On many different issues the BJP appears to challenge head-on the Nehruvian formulae that have guided Indian policy-makers and politicians over the last five decades. In view of this background, one might have expected the BJP's accession to power to have been marked by major convulsions, in the form on the one hand of large-scale public celebrations and on the other of demonstrations by opposition parties and other groups fearful of the impact of the new government on India's institutions and ideology. The consequences of such opposed street manifestations might well have been violent civil conflict. In fact, however, the celebrations were on a modest scale, and protests were mostly restricted to verbal lamentations on the part of some sections of the intelligentsia.

How is one to explain this apparent paradox of major political change without much public concern? Two initial considerations are important. First, the BJP is not in power by itself but heads a coalition of parties. Although, unlike the preceding United Front where the Janata Dal, the notional core, did not even have the largest number of seats, the BJP has two-thirds of the coalition's parliamentary delegation, it is still critically dependent on a miscellaneous collection of regional parties, often led, as in the case of the All-India Anna Dravida Munnetra Kazhagam (AIADMK), by eccentric and demanding individuals. Indeed, it was only some days after the election results were declared that it was certain that the BJP would survive.[1] This was hardly surprising, given that the party had secured only a quarter of the popular vote, less in fact than the Congress, which despite securing 30 per cent of the vote rightly saw the election results as a major disaster. Even counting the votes of its pre-election allies, it still only held 32 per cent. This points to the second consideration, which is that the BJP came to power through the modalities of the Indian democratic system, and that unless it chooses to make radical changes to that system it can just as easily lose power at a subsequent election. One such change might be to move away from a parliamentary to a presidential form of government, ironically a proposal in the past associated with some sections of the Congress party, but changes in the Indian constitution require a two-thirds majority in both houses of parliament, and it would be extremely difficult to achieve such a result for what would be seen as a partisan move. The party could only implement such a change through some form of constitutional coup. While one would be unwise to attempt to predict the future course of events, such action seems unlikely, both in terms of the desire of the present party leadership to attempt it and of the willingness of key sections of Indian society to accept it.

One could resolve the paradox, therefore, by arguing that the change brought about by the 1998 elections was simply part of the fluctuations of political support that characterise any open and competitive party system, and that the electoral and coalition-building actions of the BJP demonstrate that its ideology is of less importance to itself and to the electorate than appears on the surface. The steady rise in support for the BJP in elections since 1989, including in areas where it was previously unrepresented, reflects incremental change within the political system rather than a challenge to the system itself. This paper will seek to argue that this is a valid insight provided it is not pushed too far. But it should not obscure the extent of the social changes that have led to the decline of the Congress and the rise of the BJP. In responding to these changes the BJP has itself been changed. It is equally important to understand that a concern with what today one calls Hindu nationalism has been present in Indian political discourse since the mid-nineteenth century, and that the victory of the BJP gives greater scope to ideas that have been present in the political consciousness over a long period. The 'common sense' of daily life in recent years has often included a majoritarian and anti-minority element, and this is likely to be heightened while the BJP is in power. Although less noticeable than actions like the nuclear test programme, measures in the educational and cultural field may be just as significant in producing longlasting changes in popular perceptions, which in turn will shape the agenda of other political parties.[2] But these changes too, even though reflective of a longer term debate, are very much bound up with India's present position vis-á-vis processes of globalization. The present article will explore these issues by looking first at the tradition of Hindu nationalist thinking, which was partly masked in the first half of the twentieth century by the success of the nationalist movement under Gandhian and Nehruvian leadership, then at the social and political changes which brought about a new political climate by the 1980s, and finally at the position of the BJP government and the interaction of quotidian political pressures and the ideological project of Hindu nationalism.

I

Important work[3] in the last few years has helped us to rediscover the intellectual climate in India before the articulation of an official nationalist discourse from the 1920s onwards. The old stimulus-response model which inspired even the most well-meaning liberal inquiry into the origins of nationalism can now clearly be seen to be deficient in its understanding of the vigour of Indian intellectual life in the eighteenth and nineteenth centuries. From the earliest moment, the force and power of European colonialism was examined from many different angles simultaneously. For every Rammohun Roy there was a Radhakant Deb, for every Vidyasagar a Brahmobandhab Upadhyay.[4] The same individual could go through strikingly different phases of intellectual outlook, or often present divergent views at the same time.

As part of this examination of European colonialism, and the selective appropriation of themes either directly from contemporary European thought or via the distorting mirror of colonial discourse, the question soon arose of the relationship between group membership, collective identity and 'national' action. The theme of nationality and of a national history was quickly adopted by elite circles, many of whom, like Chitpavan Brahmans in Maharashtra or Kayasths in North India, had long experience in serving as part of earlier state apparatuses. European models and experience had mixed messages to convey to an Indian elite seeking to understand their own dilemma as a conquered and colonised people. After the French Revolution especially, the principle that all residents of a territory should think themselves to be one people with a common history and language (even if many had to learn to speak it for the first time), became widespread. But could groups who did not seem, at least if seen through a lens which filtered out social interaction and left in only a certain form of political and dynastic history, to belong in any way to the historical nation, be allowed a membership which was based on false premises and therefore disruptive and damaging to those who truly belonged?

The confusion over the name to be given to an inhabitant of the subcontinent illustrates the difficulty that many saw themselves facing. Deriving from Persian, the term Hindu could be and was seen as fulfilling precisely this function, in so far as one needed a relational term. In parts of South-West Asia, someone coming from the subcontinent was a Hindu, although often he or she would be Muslim by religious conviction. However, as national descriptions needed more than a purely geographical determination, and as Orientalist scholars such as Sir William Jones were beginning to associate a certain body of texts with the religious beliefs and practices of all those in India who appeared not to be Muslim or Christian, so the term Hindu came to acquire an exclusionary overtone, and also to be bundled with other forms of description and self-identity. Within the area where Bengali was spoken, for example, Hindu and Bengali became more or less synonymous, while to be a Muslim was to be neither.[5]

The precise terms of the emerging discourse on group identity varied somewhat from region to region (and in ways which were to be of political significance later on) and reflected regional traditions as well as local power structures. Nor were neat associations of regional culture with Hinduism ever unchallenged, whether by a Gokhale in West India or by a Surendranath Banerjea in Bengal. Nevertheless, a sense that Hindus were a distinct category defined in terms of possession of a common set of beliefs and practices and with a common history had clearly crystallised by the end of the nineteenth century. Bankim Chandra Chatterji's historical novels show this process at work. Writers began to use the English term "race" in ways which showed how the categories of European discourse had been absorbed and given substance in the context of colonial India. The "imagining" of India which began in the nineteenth century was at the same time the imagining of a Hindu community that transcended the local ties of caste or sampradaya (sect) which had allowed more space for the acceptance of difference.

Alongside the emergence of the idea of an imagined Hindu community came the practical conclusion that the interests of this community needed to be served through organization, *sangathan* in Hindi. This conclusion then took several institutional forms. In Punjab and elsewhere, especially in North India, the Arya Samaj emerged as an organization which worked in the educational field to teach its young students, drawn very often from urban mercantile castes, that European knowledge could be imparted alongside the wisdom of the Vedas, and that the latter took priority epistemologically and metaphysically as well as ethically. The Arya Samaj was also active in polemical debates with Christians and Muslims and embarked on a programme of *shuddhi*[6] which was on occasion to give rise to fierce conflict with the latter. In principle, if less so in practice, the Arya Samaj denied the ontological significance of caste. In Maharashtra Bal Gangadhar Tilak, more traditional in his attitude to caste, but no less fierce in his belief in a glorious past that had been compromised by successive generations of outside invaders, explored ways in which his vision could be imparted through the updating of popular festivals. In Bengal the charismatic figure of Vivekananda attracted a wide following with his message of a "muscular Hinduism" interacting on equal terms with the West.

The Indian National Congress at its foundation in 1885 declared itself to be a wholly secular organization, in the sense that it would never intrude into the domain of the religious beliefs and practices of its members, which in effect it declared to be part of the private rather than the public. At the same time some of its early members wanted to associate themselves openly with moves for "social reform", which inevitably meant challenging "traditional" attitudes rooted in notions of *dharma* or religious obligation. Yet it could not easily maintain such a position, given the intellectual background sketched in above. In fact, in a move which was to foreshadow some recent debates in India, Tilak pulled the rug from under the reformers' feet by insisting on a purely political role for the Congress, while within that arena he called for an assertion of Indian national pride and self-sufficiency that related clearly to a past in which Muslims played no role other than that of aggressors and destroyers. Although Tilak faced considerable resistance from the so-called "moderate" wing within the Congress, and indeed had eventually to leave the organization following the (in)famous shoe-throwing episode at the Surat Congress session in December 1907, it is by no means the case that his views on Indian history and its communal interpretation were limited to his immediate followers. On the contrary, given the prevalent intellectual atmosphere, they were widely shared, even if the way they were articulated together and the way they translated into political strategy varied widely. In Bengal at more or less the same time the partition of the region by the British provoked a storm of protest which brought together virtually the whole of the middle-class and upper-caste Hindu population. Concerns with employment prospects for the many who came from what was to be part of the new Muslim-dominated East Bengal merged with the belief that the essential cultural integrity of Bengal, premised on its religious traditions, was being damaged. While writers and activists like Aurobindo Ghose wrote mistily of the indissoluble link between nationalism and the *sanatan dharma*, others had more practical concerns.

By the 1920s, the Congress under the leadership of Gandhi moved into a phase of active and prolonged confrontation with the British Raj. This project, as is well known, introduced additional layers of complexity into the relationship between religion, community and politics. Gandhi's great effort to bring together India's communities into a common national and social enterprise on a basis that saw religion as a unifying rather than divisive force succeeded in the first instance only to end as a heroic failure. His own ecumenical vision was only partly shared by other political figures within the Congress. It was easy for figures like Gobind Ballabh Pant or Vallabhbhai Patel to remain within Congress, representing there what Christophe Jaffrelot, following Bruce Graham, calls a Hindu traditionalist position.[7] Only after independence, when such men took power, was it possible to see the full extent to which their views on Indian nationhood could easily lead to the casual exclusion of minorities, Muslims especially, although it must of course be remembered that partition stood between them and the heyday of nationalist confrontation with the British.

For others, however, Gandhi's efforts to incorporate Muslim support were seen as fundamentally misguided, indeed as dangerous, and had to be resisted rather than accommodated. Rather than looking for a common spiritual basis, which from this perspective would legitimise the presence of an 'alien' element, i.e. Indian Muslims, the task should be to strengthen Hindu society through building on its strengths in spirituality and using these to eliminate social ills, for example untouchability, and to encourage youths and young men to develop all aspects of their personality, including the willingness to fight and sacrifice themselves for a righteous cause. These themes were not new, of course. As has already been stressed, they grew out of concerns that were articulated from the earliest moment of response to colonial intrusion. However, in the 1920s the changing political situation gave a greater urgency to the debate. In 1923 V.D. Savarkar, a revolutionary nationalist, published a book which he wrote while in prison for nationalist activities. In it he reflected on the essence of Indian or Hindu nationalism, finding it, as the title of the book proclaimed, in the notion of Hinduness (Hindutva). This required no spiritual quest or observance of religious discipline, but was a quality inherent in all those whose cultural roots were in India. Although there was an element of voluntarism in Savarkar's formulations, it was easily compatible with a purely communal approach to questions of citizenship.

Two years later, although not directly linked with Savarkar, another Maharashtrian, Dr K.B. Hedgewar, founded the RSS as an organization which aimed directly at the strengthening of Hindu society by the promotion of the values mentioned above. After Hedgewar's death in 1940, its second leader, M.S. Golwalkar, turned the organization into a major force in most North Indian towns, and articulated its ideology through extensive writings in Hindi and in English. The movement as it grew attempted to inculcate a monastic spirit in its fulltime workers, but these were socially oriented workers who came most commonly from urban middle-class backgrounds and who were very familiar with the capacities of modern, i.e. early twentieth century, technology to transform productive forces and social relations. The work of the RSS was to ensure that India's Hindu majority was not excluded from its benefits by the accidents of history, both past and present, while at the same time emphasising, in the spirit of Vivekananda, that Hinduism had a spiritual message for the whole world.

Although the RSS represents a new departure in the singlemindedness with which its members pursued its goals, in ideological terms it clearly built on the earlier debates and concerns discussed above which reflected the specific concerns of India's middle class in the late colonial period. A defensiveness towards the arrogance of colonial discourse on the innate defects of Indian society led to a social conservatism alongside the desire to reinvigorate Indian cultural, religious and intellectual life. The assertion of Brahminical values as the only basis on which a revitalised Hinduism could be constructed was a defence both against British denigration and against the initial signs of independent social consciousness among lower-caste groups, which were as it happened especially noticeable in Maharashtra, where the RSS was born.

For figures like Golwalkar, therefore, Congress was not part of the solution to the question of national revival but part of the problem. Gandhi's experiments with truth, and his deliberate attempt, one might almost say, to find new weapons for the materially weak but spiritually strong were profoundly mistaken in that they ignored India's national history, a history that had only been interrupted by Muslim and then European incursions. During the 1920s and 1930s, while a strong Hindu traditionalist strand developed within the Congress party itself, another element, more concerned with advancing the interests of a nation defined in terms of a monolithic cultural identity, was asserting itself.

II

After independence, Nehru was able to put together a broad coalition in favour of his programme of modernization, a modernization which went far beyond the merely economic in its vision of an India entering the post-war period as the exemplar of post-colonial pride and achievement. India had the capacity to be the equal of the other members of the new global community, and could lead other colonised countries in a new world order. Questions about the cultural specificity of Indian identity, and its relationship to Hindu values were seen either as irrelevant echoes of the colonial past or as having been transcended by India's new position in the world. "Progress" would sort these things out in the fullness of time. Politically, Nehru's optimism seemed to be justified. The Congress success in the 1952 and 1957 elections could be interpreted in terms of popular response to the Nehruvian vision, and the principal opposition parties that emerged were on the left rather than the right. The Bharatiya Jana Sangh, founded in 1951, appeared to be little more than a sectional party among a limited stratum of North India's urban population. Within Congress, the Hindu traditionalist current had its moment in August 1950 when Purshottamdas Tandon won the party presidency against Nehru's opposition, but he was outflanked and forced to resign, to be replaced by Nehru himself, and the right more generally suffered a blow with the death of Vallabhbhai Patel in December 1950. Despite opposition from important figures in the Congress, Nehru was able to push through major changes to Hindu personal law in the mid-1950s. Although Nehru stood tallest among the advocates of a secularising modernization, there were others who shared his vision and who worked with successive generations of the Nehru dynasty to put it into practice.

How then is one to understand the position in the 1980s, a period when a Hindu nationalist movement seemed suddenly to succeed in putting the advocates of the Nehruvian consensus on the defensive? Hindu traditionalists had always had some influence, and this had not vanished with the death of Patel; Hindu nationalist ideas had been important ideologically from the nineteenth century. The 1980s are nevertheless characterised by a reinvigoration of specifically Hindu nationalist movements such as the VHP. This reinvigoration was accompanied by a significant restatement of Hindu nationalist aims and objectives . These developments have to be seen in the context of socio-economic and political change since independence.

In the 1950s the Nehruvian vision of progress was translated, through the mechanism of the five-year plans and the associated expansion of government activity, into a series of policies designed to maximise self-sustaining economic growth and to spread its benefits through widening the range of opportunity. Education, better health, and selective targeted intervention, notably on behalf of the Scheduled Castes, were to ensure a quicker achievement of equality of opportunity and greater equality of distribution. Some economic growth did take place, both in the public and the private sectors, during the 1950s and 1960s, although at a more modest rate than the planners had hoped. However, the benefits of growth were disproportionately appropriated by certain categories of the population. Such groups notably included the following:[8]

a) Entrepreneurs. Taking advantage of their pre-independence support for the Congress party, they broadly accepted the terms offered to them by the planning process, and found that the latter allowed them to develop without too much fear either of foreign or of new domestic competition. Although individual members of the industrial bourgeoisie were unhappy with some aspects of the regime under which they had to operate, for the class as a whole the situation was not an unhappy one. Corporatist mechanisms put in place as part of the planning process, for example tripartite industry-wide councils between capital, labour and government, imposed no particularly stringent restrictions on their activities.

b) Surplus-producing farmers. This class was initially greatly strengthened by its previous role as the backbone of the Congress movement in many parts of the country, and by its subsequent ability to ensure that land reform, promised since the Karachi session of Congress in 1931, would stop precisely at the point at which it ceased to benefit them. In many parts of the country it was again this class which later benefited enormously from the 'Green Revolution' package of technological advances introduced in the late 1960s and early 1970s, and to some extent continuously since then. However, although in some contexts the farmers did indeed act as a class, for example in lobbying for higher support prices for grain, and no political party in the past or at present would dream of denigrating agrarian interests, at the same time other cleavages such as caste and region came into the picture, not in any essentialist sense, but as representing substantial interests. For example, the Jat farmers of Western Uttar Pradesh, supporters over many years of the late Charan Singh, found that their caste networks powerfully reinforced their ability to dominate the political life of the region.

c) State functionaries. The apparatus of the state in India, although in fact considerably smaller in terms of resources and manpower than in modern capitalist states, has for a number of reasons assumed a greater salience in India than in many other countries. Opportunities for rent-seeking on the part of its functionaries, elected and appointed alike, have been numerous and often tacitly tolerated by the public at large, who benefit from other aspects of the discretion thus implied.

The Congress's ability to remain in power for many years was intimately bound up with its ability to preside over this selective appropriation of the benefits of economic change. By ensuring that at the same time the political system remained open, and that, except for the brief period of the Emergency in the mid-1970s, there was no overt dictatorship by the favoured groups and classes[9], the party avoided large-scale confrontation with opposing political forces. Even when the party began to enter into seemingly terminal decline in the 1980s, the political economy that had developed since 1947 ensured that similar types of party emerged to battle for the space that had been left open. There was a reciprocity between the needs of the ordinary citizen, for whom implementation of policy was as important as formulation, and those of the politicians and political parties in search of the votes that led to power.

One way of looking at the success of the BJP in the recent past would indeed be to absorb it into this framework. There is always space for new entrants into the political arena, given that even the most successful of umbrella parties such as the Congress can only absorb so many politically significant groups. In the first place, the relative power of such groups is always changing within the broader socio-economic context, while political parties cannot always adjust so quickly, and in the second the supply of goods distributed through the political system can never be sufficient to meet all the potential claimants. To the extent that this approach is valid. ideology would lose its explanatory power, just as much as class, and all would be reduced to the ebb and flow of local group interest within a structure that merely reproduced existing class relations.

This approach could be used to understand the ability of the BJP to pick up substantial support in the three general elections in the 1990s from groups that lie outside its "traditional" support base in the urban upper castes. In Uttar Pradesh, for example, divisions among the "Other Backward Classes", the category of the population which has emerged in recent years as politically the most dynamic, has given the BJP a significant foothold among them, signalled by the emergence of Kalyan Singh, from the Lodha caste, as the state's first BJP chief minister. While the largest group among the OBCs, the Yadavs, have tended to support figures like Mulayam Singh Yadav, who confronted the BJP head-on over the Ayodhya issue in 1990, other sections have been more anxious to protect their local position, and have found the BJP a willing partner. Similarly, the Scheduled Caste population has been divided, with the larger groups such as the Jatavs enthusiastic supporters of what is perceived to be 'their' party, the Bahujan Samaj Party, while others, such as the Balmikis, in the past dutiful supporters of the Congress, are now interested in what the BJP has to offer. This has been matched in the past few years by the willingness of individual politicians to switch allegiance to and from the BJP if it suits their purposes. Such behaviour among BJP or previously Jana Sangh members was very uncommon in the past, while from the mid 1960s it had been very frequent among Congress political leaders.

What does this new ability and willingness of the BJP to recruit from other parties' traditional support bases tell us on the one hand about the Indian political system and on the other about the BJP?[10] The answers to both require us to widen the framework of investigation beyond the simple argument outlined above that the BJP has after all been absorbed by the Indian political system (paralleling the way new groups are eventually absorbed into the caste system). In essence, the argument here is that underneath the apparent continuities of Indian politics, social change is generating new political impulses, to some of which at least the BJP is well placed to respond. Take, for instance, the matter of literacy. Although India notoriously lags behind the rest of Asia in terms of basic literacy, this should not blind us to the progress that has taken place. At independence, the assumption was that an ordinary farmer or labourer was illiterate. Now, the assumption is that a young man, and to a lesser extent woman, of whatever class or occupation, is more rather than less likely to be literate. In parallel, and with rapid acceleration in the last decade, the electronic mass media have penetrated almost all parts of the country. Urbanization in the restricted sense of the word has been growing, even if not at the explosive rates seen elsewhere in Asia or Latin America, but important elements of the urban lifestyle are now widespread throughout the country. These processes affect all strata of society from existing urban, upper-caste elite groups to the dalit (oppressed) communities in village and city alike.

To some sections of all of these groups, the BJP under its present leadership offers a form of identity that appears to blend the appeals of modernity without having to abandon more specific ties and networks. Although the party grew out of a tradition which aimed to develop an Indian identity based on upper-caste, Brahminical values, its effort in recent years has been to find means of making these values more readily available to a broader constituency, a constituency which as argued above is keen to respond. The educational activities of the RSS over the past several decades, which have targeted among other groups so-called 'trials', assume importance in this context, as does the Sangh Parivar's skill in using the electronic media to put forward its vision. The work of the VHP in the 1980s, culminating in the successive confrontations at Ayodhya, succeeded in overcoming the previous, more hierarchical approach that had characterised the outlook of the movement.

The BJP's worldview provides what to many are powerful and convincing answers to questions of why India has made relatively little progress in the half century since independence. On the one hand, the party can blame the Congress and parties like it for allowing a corrupt political culture to develop. Its own record, at least until fairly recently, appears clear by comparison. The mechanisms by which this corrupt culture have developed can be assimilated to the BJP's broader narratives. The elite which presided over the newly independent state were a westernised elite who were ignorant of Bharatiya values and aspirations. Unwilling to engage in the arduous task of revitalising a society and nation enfeebled by centuries of outside rule (in the first instance British but previously Muslim), they had taken the easy task of bribing sections of the population to support the Congress. The BJP thus offers an account of the villains of the piece, the interests that serve to block the further rise of previously excluded elements. These villains are the threat within, in other words the Muslim minority, and the threat without, the forces of globalization that undermine India's ability to develop its own economy and achieve self-reliance and strength.

The BJP's account of India's difficulties competes with other narratives, put forward in slightly different ways by the BSP and the Samajwadi Party, which see the upper castes, precisely the groups which have in the past been represented by the BJP, as the prime culprit. The BJP's position is made more difficult, precisely because the alternative narratives have correspond in many ways to the realities that people perceive. The party and its allies, especially the RSS, remain committed to an outlook, inherited from its past history, which is more compatible, materially and ideologically, with the interests of the upper castes.

III

The Ayodhya mosque demolition in December 1992 and the subsequent communal riots in which members of the Sangh Parivar were deeply implicated was a climactic moment for the BJP in several different ways. After a decade in which it had sought to exploit the desire of many middle-class Indians for a new, more assertive identity, it had decided to bring the matter to a head at a time when the other political parties seemed on the decline. It had itself played a part in bringing down the National Front government in the 1989-1991 period, while the Narasimha Rao-led Congress, despite its successes on the economic front, seemed lacklustre and in power only through the vagaries of electoral politics. The 1990 confrontation had allowed the BJP, through the detention of its leader L. K. Advani and the deaths in police firing of a number of its youthful supporters, to portray itself as a martyr for the Hindu cause. In 1992, an exact repeat of such a scenario would have shown it to be weak and indecisive. Instead, with the help of the BJP-controlled local state government, it went ahead and achieved the demolition, symbolically asserting the privileged position within India of the Hindu majority, a majority whose definition the Sangh Parivar sought to control. The riots that followed, spontaneous and organised at one and the same time, were a macabre victory celebration that allowed visceral hatreds and emotions free rein in attacks on the Muslim minority. Yet despite calls from the hardliners to move on to other sites at Varanasi, Mathura and elsewhere, the Ayodhya demolition was a once and for all affair. To repeat it would have been counterproductive in terms of electoral support and would have identified the BJP for ever, both in India and abroad, as a narrowly communal party, committed to sectarian violence.

Without disowning the Ayodhya demolition, the BJP shifted its stance after 1993 to portray itself as a party more broadly committed to the promotion of Indian national interests. The vehicle for this was to hand in the form of a campaign for greater protection for Indian economic interests in the era of globalization and the World Trade Organization. The slogan of Swadeshi, or indigenous production, was one which harked back to the partition of Bengal and could therefore link together aspects of the nationalist struggle with the ideological emphasis of the Sangh Parivar on the desirability of maintaining the purity of India. Many Indian companies felt that the moves towards welcoming foreign capital and technology had left them disadvantaged compared to their foreign competitors, and were happy to support political parties which promised to right the balance. The Enron confrontation in 1995 allowed the state government of Maharashtra, ruled by a Shiv Sena-BJP coalition, to dramatise the issue and to blame a corrupt Congress culture for allowing an American multinational company to exploit the innocent Indian consumer. Issues such as the patenting of seeds by outsiders, to the detriment of the Indian farmer, were also raised. Similar points were also raised by the Left parties, but the BJP was probably more successful in placing them within a symbolic repertoire which evoked India's national identity.

The BJP fought the 1998 elections on three main planks. It criticised the other parties as inept or corrupt or both; it emphasised its own competence to run the country effectively in the interests of all its citizens and deal adequately with defence issues; and it stressed its commitment to protect India's economy in an era of globalization, so that Indian rather than multinational interests were given priority. Although, as mentioned above, it only slightly increased its share of the vote, it succeeded in establishing some presence in virtually every part of the country. Yet the majority that it was eventually able to achieve was only possible with the help of pre-poll alliances with what were mainly regional parties and some post-poll pieces of horse-trading. Implicit in these arrangements was the understanding that the BJP would restrain its more rabid supporters among the Sangh Parivar so as not to embarrass men like George Fernandes of the Samata Party, whose previous political affiliations had been on the left.

Once in power, the BJP had to face the problem of justifying the claims it had made during the campaign, and to do this in ways which would not alienate its allies or erode its own electoral base, which by now was much broader than the hardline supporters of the Sangh Parivar. On the economic front the dilemma the government faced was that the process of liberalization and restructuring introduced by their predecessors in the early 1990s had gone so far that any attempt to change direction in any radical way, for example by tightening controls on foreign investment or by withdrawing from the WTO, would have had a massive negative impact on business confidence. The budget introduced in June 1998 by Yashwant Sinha was on the whole a very cautious affair. The only major step he took to pursue a swadeshi agenda was to raise import duties by 8 per cent so as to compensate domestic industry for the internal duties it had to pay. Measures were also taken to sort out the question of regulating satellite television broadcasting, and steps were taken to limit the impact of foreign media companies. However, these were issues that had long been discussed, and the BJP's position was not very different from other parties.

The most striking and, at least in terms of timing, unexpected measure the BJP government took was to test a series of nuclear devices on 11 and 13 May. Although the party's manifesto had promised a defence review and the probable induction of nuclear weapons thereafter, the timing of the tests was clearly a move aimed at the electorate. By exploding the devices, pushing forward the existing missile programme and insisting that India was now a nuclear weapons state, the government could make a series of interlinked claims. In the first place, the BJP could argue that it had put India in a position to deal with its neighbours from a position of strength. An initial statement by the Home Minister, L. K. Advani, who also had responsibility for Kashmir, suggested that India would use its new capacity to deal more effectively with Pakistani support for Kashmiri militants. Secondly, India had demonstrated the hollowness of the existing nuclear powers' commitment to total nuclear disarmament. Thirdly, it believed that India's demonstrated capacity to achieve nuclear status would be the basis of a new role for it at the United Nations and elsewhere. In practice, the script prepared by the government was difficult to follow, not least because of the ability of the Pakistan government to carry out reciprocal tests. Although the economic sanctions that the US and certain other countries imposed were not beyond the country's capacity to cope with, the more serious problem was that India had underestimated the diplomatic repercussions, not least the fact that it gave Pakistan the ideal opportunity to put Kashmir back on the international agenda. However, one can be sure that the BJP will for some time to come emphasise to the Indian electorate that it was prepared to take the decisive step forward that other parties were not willing to.

The BJP has made a conscious decision to operate within the limits of the Indian constitution and the democratic conventions embodied in that document and in subsequent Indian political practice. Even if this is a largely pragmatic decision (and the BJP would hardly be alone in making its decisions on such grounds), the constraints of the political process in India are likely to ensure that it keeps to its present course. It therefore seems determined for the time being to present itself as a modernising, right-wing party, capable of running the country in a forward-looking fashion. It represents in that respect a long tradition of thinking about Indian backwardness which attributes it on the one hand to the malign role of "outsiders" such as the Muslim minority and on the other to the lack of organization and consciousness among the Hindu population. This tradition can be labelled "Hindu nationalist" and traced back to debates in the 19th century. As India has evolved socially, with newly active groups demanding material and emotional satisfaction from their political representatives, while at the same time the existing elite's own concerns have begun to focus more on India's place in the new world order, the Hindu nationalist answers appear on the surface to offer attractive solutions. However, just as in the past, contradictions are not very far beneath the surface, and are likely to give rise to difficulties sooner rather than later. Whose Hinduism, and who is to represent it are the key issues. While in the past spokesmen for lower caste interests could be loftily dismissed,[11] such an option is no longer available. The terms of ideological discourse in India have shifted irreversibly, while the social changes referred to above have made latent tensions more evident. While displacement activity such as the temple campaigns or nuclear tests can work in the short term, the structural tensions between rich and poor, newly arrived migrants in the city and established elite, between different castes and caste groupings will remain. In developing its future strategy, the BJP will of course look to the tradition of Hindu nationalist thought and action that it has access to through other members of the Sangh Parivar, but by itself this will not be adequate to meet the needs of a major participant in India's democracy. The present coalition politics demonstrates one dimension of the problem the party faces,[12] namely the need to make major policy concessions to its allies.

Even if the party were more secure, however, it would still need to address the question of an appropriate politics for an India in the middle of massive economic and social change.

Notes

1. To form a government in India at the present time requires a notional 273 seats in the Lok Sabha. After the elections the BJP had 177 seats and its pre-election allies 40. For a while it seemed that the BJP would be unable to bridge the gap, but eventually, following the shrewdly judged concession of the Speakership, a major component of the United Front grouping, the Telugu Desam, decided to support the government on the crucial vote of confidence, thus ensuring the government's survival. Subsequently, the Telugu Desam under its leader N. Chandrababu Naidu, has come closer to the government.
2. The early measure taken to change the membership of the Indian Council of Historical Research so as to install new members notable more for their ideological sympathies wit the BJP than for their professional achievements is perhaps symptomatic.
3. Partha Chatterjee, Sudhir Chandra, Sudipta Kaviraj, Tanika Sarkar are among the more important names, but many others could be cited. Younger scholars are also actively engaged in the same project.
4. In addition to works by the authors cited in the previous note, see also David Kopf, The Brahmo Samaj and the Shaping of the Modern Indian Mind, Princeton 1979.
5. As Rafiuddin Ahmed's work indicates, the feeling of difference was mutual: The Bengal Muslims 1871-1906, New Delhi 1981.
6. Purification as a means to reconvert former Hindus who had become Muslims.
7. Christophe Jaffrelot, The Hindu Nationalist Movement and Indian Politics, 1925 to the 1990s, London 1996, p. 83.
8. Among many authors who have written on these subjects, Pranab Bardhan in his work *The Political Economy of Development*, Oxford 1984, deserves special mention. Theoretically, Bardhan's work draws on Michael Kalecki's concept of "intermediate classes".
9. The problem from Mrs Gandhi's point of view with the Emergency was that it drew her close to the interests of the urban middle class, represented by her son Sanjay Gandhi, and cut her off from the concerns of the rural population, including the richer farmers.
10. The argument here is not that the BJP has abandoned its core support, far from it. The BJP enjoys proportionately substantially higher support from the urban upper castes than it does from the rural middle and lower. The point is that the BJP is no longer to be seen as a purely sectional party.
11. See, for example, the recent work by Veena Naregal, English in the Colonial University and the Politics of Language: the Emergence of a Public Sphere in Western India (1830-1880), PhD thesis, University of London 1998.
12. And may by the time this piece appears have brought the government down.

Memories of a Fragmented Nation: Rewriting the Histories of India's Partition

Mushirul Hasan

I

> Today I am asking Waris Shah to speak from the grave,
> To turn the page of the book of love. Once the daughter of the Punjab wept, and you wrote endlessly.
> Today Lakhs [100,000] of daughters are weeping and they are imploring you Waris Shah
> Get up, you who sympathize with our grief, get up and see your Punjab.
> Today there are corpses everywhere, and the Chenab is filled with blood.
> Somebody has mixed poison in all the five rivers,
> The rivers we use to water our fields ...

> When I think of Lahore, I go back to the days of my youth just before the Partition. Life then was so romantic, slow, deep and beautiful. Really, they were good times, they were great times.

> I hope that one day ... displaced families on both sides of the fence will at least be able to freely cross the borders and show their grandchildren where their grand parents had once lived and belonged. The day such a change comes about, I shall be the first to cross the Wagah or Hussainiwallah border posts to take my grand-daughter to Lahore, and show her the home of my youthful dreams - *91, Garden Town*.

The countdown to 15 August 1997, India's fiftieth year of Independence, generated an extraordinary interest in plotting the history of Partition.[1] One wonders why painful memories and traumatic experiences were revived on such an occasion, why the nostalgia and the celebration of the dead?[2] Was it because there was not much to celebrate? Or did the occasion itself finally sensitise sections of the intelligentsia to the painful legacy of a brutal past. Amrita Pritam, the noted Punjabi writer who lived in Lahore before moving to Delhi in 1947 and whose celebrated poem quoted in the epigraph became one of the most influential and representative works of Partition, recalled:

> "What I am against is religion - the Partition saw to that. Everything I had been taught - about morals, values and the importance of religion - was shattered. I saw, heard and read about so many atrocities committed in the name of religion that it turned me against any kind of religion and revolution."[3]

Sure enough, a common refrain in popular and scholarly writings was that the country's division was a colossal tragedy, a man-made catastrophe brought about by hot-headed and cynical politicians who failed to grasp the implications of division along religious lines.[4] For a change, the focus was on the popular experiences of violence and displacement[5], on the impact of Partition on the lives of hundreds of millions, including the trauma of women[6], and the great variety of meanings they attached to the upheaval in and around their homes, fields and factories[7]. Although one should not make much of this shift in emphasis, the inclination to sideline the tall poppies in the Partition debates was in large part an expression of the growing disillusionment with high politics and its post-colonial practitioners.

The mood reflected in popular literature was decisively against the leaders of the subcontinent and their inability to resolve their perennial disputes over power-sharing. Doubtless, the colonial government's role in heightening Hindu-Muslim rivalries and the "communal" implications of Bengal's partition in 1906 were recounted. So also the political blunders committed by Wavell during his inglorious years in the viceregal lodge, the impetuousness of Mountbatten who revelled in his role as arbiter, the destiny of millions sitting light on him, the collapse of the law and order machinery which was kept in a state of readiness to protect the Europeans but not the hapless victims of a civil war, and, finally, the arbitrary demarcation of the border by a British jurist who had neither been to India nor shown interest in Indian affairs.[8] "Nothing could illustrate," commented the senior journalist Ajit Bhattacharjea, "the callous haste with which Partition was pushed through more strikingly than the last-minute arrangements to demarcate the border."[9]

According to the same writer, the onus none the less rested on the Indian leaders, many of whom were primarily interested in ensuring that the transfer of power was not delayed and were therefore "unaware and uncaring of the human cost of cutting a border through the heart of populous provinces"[10]. Illustrating Jawaharlal Nehru's "lack of touch with grassroots reality" and his "self-delusion" that Pakistan would be compelled by its limitations to return to the greater Indian fold,[11] Bhattacharjea recalled what Nehru told the author Leonard Mosley in 1960.

> "We were tired men and we were getting on in years too. Few of us could stand the prospect of going to prison again-and if we had stood out for a united India as we wished it, prison obviously awaited us. We saw the fires burning in the Punjab and heard of the killings. The plan of Partition offered a way out and we took it ... We expected that Partition would be temporary, that Pakistan was bound to come back to us."[12]

With the focus on high politics, the same old story does the rounds with unfailing regularity. The engagement continues to be with the "major" political actors of the 1930s and 1940s, who conducted their deliberations lazily in cosy surroundings and presided over the destiny of millions without their mandate. One is still encumbered with the details of what went wrong and who said what from the time the First Round Table Conference was held in London in 1930. Thanks to the publication of the voluminous transfer of power documents and the works of Gandhi, Nehru, Mohammad Ali Jinnah, Vallabhbhai Patel and Rajendra Prasad, the spotlight remains on the "mystery" behind the protracted and tortuous negotiations triggered by the Cripps offer and the Cabinet Mission.[13] The bitter and acrimonious exchanges thereafter, which have all along dominated the historiography on nationalism, "communalism" and "Muslim separatism", continue to haunt present-day writers. The search for the "guilty men", based on personal reflections/memories or the blunt testimony of the socialist leader Ram Manohar Lohia and the guarded "revelations" of Maulana Abul Kalam Azad, goes on relentlessly.[14] As a result, the historians' history of Partition "is not a history of the lives and experiences of the people who lived through that time, of the way in which the events of the 1940s were constructed in their minds, of the identities and uncertainties that Partition created or reinforced"[15].

These concerns are not so widely reflected in Pakistan, where it is conveniently assumed that the "Partition issue", so to speak, was resolved well before 1947 by the weight of the two-nation theory.[16] The result is for everybody to see. Although Jinnah of Pakistan has been elevated to a high pedestal by the Cambridge-based scholar Akbar Ahmad, he would remain, unless rescued from his uncritical admirers, a lonely figure in the pages of history and in the gallery of nation-builders. If the desire is to come to terms with his political engagement and explain his extraordinary success, it is not at all helpful to press him into service to establish Pakistan's identity as an Islamic state. Likewise, the use of religious symbols, long forsaken by that country's bureaucracy and military establishment, can hardly serve as the starting point for a meaningful dialogue on Partition.

The engagement of several writers in India, though sometimes marred by a majoritarian perspective, centres around "secular nationalism", the main inspiration behind much of liberal-left activism from the 1920s onwards. Their chief concern, though nowadays pooh-poohed in the "post-modernist" discourse, is to examine why the secular elites and their ideologues, whose presence is grudgingly recognised across the ideological divide, failed to mediate between those warring factions/groups who used religion as a cover to pursue their worldly goals and ambitions. While detailing the cynical games played out on the Indian turf by the British, the League and the self-proclaimed "nationalists" of every variety, they do not spare the Congress stalwarts, Gandhi, Nehru and Patel included, for their failure to guide the movements they initiated away from the forces of reactionary communalism.[17] They marshal a wide array of sources to comment on Hindu communalists disguising themselves as Congressmen and preventing the national movement from becoming truly inclusive.

They also point to Gandhi's role in introducing religion into politics, the anti-Muslim proclivities of the Hindu right, led by Patel in the 1940s, the Hindutva agenda of the Hindu Mahasabha, the Arya Samaj and the RSS (Rashtriya Swayam Sewak Sangh), and Nehru's arrogance and haughtiness in dealing with Jinnah and the Muslim League. At a time when the Muslim League was flexing its muscles, India's first Prime Minister is said to have jettisoned the plan for a Congress-League coalition in 1937 and dimmed the prospect of an enduring Hindu-Muslim coalition in Indian politics. Thus the mainstay of the argument is that the country's vivisection could have been avoided had Nehru acted judiciously on this and other *critical* junctures in the 1940s.[18]

Though such impressions rest on questionable assumptions, they cannot be brushed aside.[19] The real difficulty lies with the grand narrative itself and the tendency to generalise on the basis of the actions of a few. While the grand narrative illuminates several facets of the Pakistan story, it fails to incorporate the complexities and subtleties of institutional and structural changes introduced by the colonial government, as also the impact of socio-economic processes on caste, class and religion-based alignments. One does not, moreover, get a sense of why the two-nation theory was floated in March 1940 and not earlier, why and how different forms of identities and consciousness got translated into a powerful campaign for a separate Muslim homeland, why Partition created ten million refugees, led to the death of over a million people, and resulted in sexual savagery, including the rape and abduction of 75,000 women. Finally, the grand narrative does not reveal how the momentous happenings in August-September 1947 affected millions, uprooted from home and field and driven by sheer fear of death to seek safety across a line they had neither drawn nor desired. Clearly, the issue is not whether a million or more died or whether only 3 percent of the country's population was affected by the communal eruption. The essential facts, as pointed out by the chief of the governor-general's staff, were that "there is human misery on a colossal scale all around and millions are bereaved, destitute, homeless, hungry, thirst - and worst of all desperately anxious and almost hopeless about their future".

In order to explore some of these aspects and probe those areas which directly or indirectly impinged on the sudden and total breakdown of long-standing inter-community networks and alliances, it is necessary to locate the Partition debates outside the conference chambers. Without being swayed by the paradigms set by the two-nation theory or the rhetoric of Indian nationalism, it is important to examine why most people, who had so much in common and had lived together for generations, could turn against their neighbours, friends and members of the same caste and class within hours and days. Such tragedies have taken place in the former state of Yugoslavia, but it is unclear why they have gone unnoticed at research centres in the subcontinent, especially in areas worst affected by gruesome violence and migration. Is it because the ghosts of Partition should be put to rest and not exhumed for frequent postmorterms? Or, is scholarship on the subject itself is so woefully inadequate and contentious that it fails to excite the imagination of young graduates?

The perspective and attitudes on such vexed matters are bound to differ, though scholars in Pakistan tenaciously adhere to the belief that the creation of a Muslim nation was a legitimate act, the culmination of a historical process. Perhaps, it is hazardous to contest such inherited wisdom in a society where nationality is still defined, often clumsily, in purely Islamic terms, and religious minorities, Hindus and Ahmadiyas (Qadianis) included, are left to stew in their own juice. Perhaps, Partition does not convey the same meanings in Lahore and Islamabad as it does to some people living in Delhi, Lucknow, Calcutta and Dacca. It is not bemoaned, for understandable reasons, as an epic tragedy but celebrated as a spectacular triumph of Islamic nationalism. After all, why should people inhabiting the fertile districts of western Punjab or the rugged Frontier region mourn the break-up of India's fragile unity or lament the collapse of a common cultural and intellectual inheritance? Some beleaguered *muhajirs* may still want to recall their friendships and associations in Hindustan (*guzashata bada-paraston ki yaadgaar koi*), trace their intellectual and cultural links with Lucknow or Delhi, and occasionally revive memories of a bygone era by dipping into the writings of Saadat Hasan Manto, Ahmed Ali, Josh Malihabadi, Quratulain Hyder and Intizar Husain.[20] Yet the nostalgia for what has already become an imaginary homeland or the identification with Lucknow's grand *imambaras* or with the sufi shrines of Khwaja Muinuddin Chishti's shrine at Ajmer and Nizamuddin Auliya in Delhi is gradually fading away with the passage of time and the passing of a generation. The Badshahi mosque, standing majestically as a symbol of India's secular dream, is as distant and remote as the *Masjid-i Qartaba*, the theme of Mohammad Iqbal's poem. Aminabad in Lucknow or Ballimaran in old Delhi are far removed from the imagination of a generation that has grown up in a different social and cultural milieu.

The differences in approaches and perspectives should not, however, stand in the way of developing a common reference point for rewriting the *histories* of an event that cast its shadow over many aspects of state and society in the subcontinent. Despite decades of mutual suspicions and antipathies that has led to a mindless arms build up and contributed to the backwardness and appalling poverty of the region, it is still possible for the peoples, rather than the governments, to make sense of the poignant writings of creative writers and poets and to reflect on how and why a generation was caught up in the crossfire of religious bigotry, intolerance and sectarianism. Such an exercise can be undertaken without calling into question the legitimacy of one or the other varieties of nationalisms.

For the initiative to get off the ground, it may be useful to revisit the old-fashioned theories on the syncretic and composite trajectory of Indian society and detail, as the writer Krishna Sobti does in her recent interview, the shared values and traditions that had enabled diverse communities to live harmoniously for centuries.[21] It is not necessary to be swayed, as is often the case, by the "nationalist" historians who portrayed an idyllic picture of Hindu-Muslim relations during the pre-colonial days in order to strengthen inter-community ties during the liberation struggle. It is none the less important to underline, despite valiant attempts to uncover the "Pre-History of Communalism", the fusion and integration of the Hindu communities at different levels and the value they attached to religious tolerance and pluralism in their day-to-day living.[22] In so doing, one can put to rest those speculative theories that are designed to lend respectability to British colonialism and offer a corrective to the distorted Islamist or the Hindutva world-views which have, in equal measure, created widespread confusion in the minds of the common people and, in the process, caused incalculable damage to state and civil society.

The conclusions flowing from such formulations are bound to differ, yet the urgency to underline the commonality of interests amongst large segments of the population must be felt in India where Hindutva could well be the new *mantra* of civil society in the foreseeable future, and in neighbouring Pakistan, where ethnic and sectarian strife, combined with deep-seated regional and linguistic cleavage, reveal the limits of an agenda that is tied to wild and imaginary notions of Muslim/Islamic brotherhood or solidarity.

II

The following three impressions are drawn from a period when Hindu-Muslim relations had reached their lowest watermark. The first is of Malcolm Darling, a civil servant in Punjab for many years. During his travel in 1945-46, he found much similarity between the Hindu and Muslim communities in the tract between the Beas and Sutlej and the Chenab and Ravi rivers. He noticed, something he would done on numerous occasions during his long career as a British civil servant, how often Hindus, Muslims and Sikhs had a common ancestor in a village, how a Hindu from Karnal proudly announced that the Muslim inhabitants of the fifty neighbouring villages belonged to his clan and were prepared to return to the Hindu fold on the one condition that the Hindus would give them their daughters in marriage. Although the condition was refused, Hindus and Muslims of the area continued to interchange civilities at marriage, inviting the *mullah* or the Brahman, to share in the feasting. Malcolm Darling wondered how was Pakistan to be fitted into these conditions. "What a hash politics threatens to make of this tract", he observed, "where Hindu, Muslim and Sikh are as mixed up as the ingredients of a well-made *pilau* (rice cooked with fowl or meat)."[23]

Mohammad Mujeeb, the vice-chancellor of Delhi's Jamia Millia Islamia, had a similar experience in Bihar soon after the orgy of violence had taken a heavy toll of human lives. While visiting the grave of a sufi saint on the bank of the river Ganges, he found that the Muslims living in the shrine had already abandoned the place. But soon a group of Hindu women appeared. They performed the same rituals that their ancestors had observed for generations. It appeared "as if nothing had happened that affected their sentiments of veneration for the tomb of a Muslim saint"[24].

Finally, consider the reports of Phillips Talbot, written for the Institute of Current World Affairs in New York on the eve of Independence and published recently in the daily newspaper, *Hindu*. For one thing, Talbot was struck by the countrywide expression of Hindu-Muslim cordiality during the Independence celebrations.

> "For twenty long and bloody weeks after 16 August, 1946, Hindus avoided entering Muslim neighbourhoods and *vice versa*. Communal clashes and deaths were daily occurrences. Yet at the climax of Independence celebrations this week, Hindus and Muslims mixed together freely. Many Hindus visited mosques on the 18th and distributed sweets to Muslims who were observing their Id festival ... It was a spectacular truce, if not a peace treaty, between the two communities. Similarly, in Delhi and Bombay I saw Hindus and Muslims playing hand in hand. Reports of the same nature came from most places except the still-troubled Punjab."[25]

Talbot's own explanation was that the political parties desired peace and friendship between the communities, though he laid greater stress on "the popular revulsion against the constant dislocation and actual fear of life during the last year". "Terror", he added, "is an enervating emotion. I've seen neighbourhoods so distraught by the medieval lack of personal security that they could not think of nothing else. I think that people everywhere used the excitement of the celebrations to try to break the vicious cycle of communal attacks and retaliations. How permanent the change may be is yet to be seen."[26]

Such impressions need to be drawn into the discussions on Partition so that the past is not judged through our recent encounters with Hindu-Muslim violence in India. It is just as important to delineate the multiple strands in the Muslim League movement, underline its complexity, assess its ideological orientation afresh, and explore the mobilization strategies adopted by Jinnah after he returned from his home in Hampstead to plunge into the humdrum of Indian politics. In addition to having greater access to source materials, this is an opportune moment, fifty years after Independence, to revise and reconsider established theories on Partition, introduce a more nuanced discourse, and stay clear of the conventional wisdom that we, the generation born after Independence, have inherited on the theme of "communal" politics generally and the

Pakistan movement in particular. As "old orthodoxies recede before the flood of fresh historical evidence and earlier certitudes are overturned by newly detected contradiction", this is the time to heal "the multiple fractures which turned the promised dawn of freedom into a painful moment of separation"[27].

For example, one of the points adequately documented, though not sufficiently considered in secondary literature, is that not everyone who raised or rallied around the green flag was uniformly wedded to or inspired by a shared ideal of creating an Islamic society. The reality is that many were pushed into taking religious/Islamic positions, while many others, especially the landed classes in Punjab and the United Provinces (UP), used the Muslim League as a vehicle to articulate, defend and promote their material interests. In fact, the intensity of emotions expressed in the 1940s, which is so often invoked in the subcontinent to create popular myths and stereotypical images, had more to do with the political and economic anxieties of various social classes than with a profound urge to create a *sharia*-based society. Today, the issue is not the legitimacy of a movement but to place in perspective the dynamics of power-politics in a colonial context. In fact, a rounded picture of the Pakistan movement is possible only if we are able to contest the exaggerated claims made in the name of Islam, then and now, by the Islamists and the proponents of the two-nation theory.

In sum, the clamour for a separate nation, though pressed vigorously in the post-war years with much popular backing and enthusiasm, was raised not so much by the Muslim divines, many of whom were waiting on the fringes of Indian politics to intervene on behalf of Islam, but by the vociferous professional groups in Uttar Pradesh, Bihar, the princely state of Hyderabad, and the small but upcoming trading and banking communities in Gujarat, Bombay and Calcutta. Interestingly enough, the Muslim landlords of UP were the first to raise the banner of revolt against the League; in fact, the Nawab of Chattari and Nawab Mohammad Yusuf of Jaunpur broke away from the Muslim League Parliamentary Board in April 1936 in order to revive "a mixed party in preference to a Muslim communal organization"[28]. They changed course once the Congress Ministry adopted the UP Tenancy Bill and Nehru and his comrades became more and more strident in their socialistic pronouncements. These men were not concerned to defend the Quranic injunctions which they probably flouted every day of their life. Nor were they interested in the welfare of the poor Muslims, who were victims of their oppression and exploitation. Their chief goal was to defend their landholdings, orchards, *havelis*, palaces and, above all, the nawabi paraphernalia built through the courtesy of their British benefactors. Notice the following conversation between Saleem and his father Hamid in Attia Hosain's (died in January 1998) celebrated novel *Sunlight on a Broken Column*:

Saleem was saying, "In the final analysis, what you are facing is the struggle for power by the bourgeoisie. It is not really a peasant's movement, but when it comes to a division of spoils even class interests are forgotten. For example the four hundred or so *Taluqdars* insisted the British should give them higher representation than the thousands of other landlords."

"It is not a question of numbers alone," protested Uncle Hamid, sitting up and waving his pipe in negation. "We Taluqdars have ancient rights and privileges, given by a special charter, which we have to safeguard ..."

"Yes, yes, of course. One respects tradition. One fights for one's self, one's interests. But you cannot expect the tenants to love you for it."

"That is because so-called reforms are destroying the personal ties between landlord and peasant. Surely a Government and its changing officers cannot have personal relations or traditional ties with the tenants? With whom are the people in constant touch? Their landlords or local political leaders? ..."

"How can landlords but be uneasy at the thought of such reserves of power being vested in officials at a time when it is uncertain what class of persons will obtain political power? ..." (Uncle Hamid)

Saleem could not let an argument die an unnatural death. He began, "What you said, father, about the landlords' fear of abolition is the crux of the matter. This fear for their existence is the basis for the formation of a new parry which is interested in keeping the *status quo* intact, that is favoured by the British and is fundamentally opposed to progressive, national movements ..."

"Words? Theories! Irresponsible talk!" Uncle Hamid burst out. "I am a part of feudalism, and proud to be. I shall fight for it. It is my heritage - and yours. Let me remind you of that. And that you enjoy its 'reactionary' advantages. You talk very glibly of its destruction, but you live by its existence. It is, in fact, your only livelihood."[29]

No wonder, the landed elements in UP, as also the Jamaat-i Islami and sections of the *ulama* connected with the Barelwi "school", Nadwat al-ulama, Firangi Mahal and Deoband, *hitched their fortunes with the Muslim League at different points of time and for different reasons*. Their overall strategy, one that suited the Raj during and after World War II, was to masquerade their hidden agenda and project the Congress, their main rival in the political world, as a "Hindu" party inimical to Islam. Once the League bandwagon rolled on, other aggrieved groups, especially those who failed to secure employment, contracts or seats on regional and local bodies, jumped into the fray as the defenders of the faith.

Still, Pakistan was not everybody's dream. Nor was Jinnah everyone's *Qaid* (leader).[30] In this respect, one should not, as is generally the case with both the *Hindu* and *Muslim* majoritarian discourses, loose sight of the perspectives of those who were intellectually committed to secular nationalism or were actively engaged in repudiating the two-nation theory. Their voices, which have been stifled by "secular" as well "communal" histories, should not be relegated to a historian's footnote. Indeed, the part played by those Muslims, who are patronisingly described as "Nationalist Muslims", the Khudai Khidmatgars in the North-West Frontier region, who were eventually let down by the dispirited Congress leadership on the eve of Independence, the *ulama* of Deoband and the Momins in Bihar, should not be submerged beneath the rationalization of the "victors". Their main contribution, exemplified by Maulana Abul Kalam Azad's exemplary conduct and performance[31], was to keep alive the vision of a secular India These "marginal" voices should be recovered to rewrite the histories of Partition.[32]

For these and other reasons, it is appropriate to ask if the Muslim League movement was as cohesive and unified as is made out to be by some writers in India and Pakistan. If the Congress was faction-ridden and ideologically fragmented, so was the League.[33] This is illustrated by the depth and intensity of jealousies and internal discord in the organization, the regional groupings, the *Ajlaf-Ashraf* divide, the Shia-Sunni strife in many places, and the unending doctrinal disputes between the theologians. Especially the followers of the Barelwi and the Deobandi "schools". Such differences, which are conveniently overlooked in the histories of the freedom movement in Pakistan, were real and not imaginary. If so, it will not do to portray the Muslim Leaguers as earnest and self-sacrificing crusaders or equate them with the *Muhajirs* or *Ansars* of the Prophet Mohammad. What is perhaps challenging, as indeed intellectually rewarding, is to probe those critical areas where the "faithful", despite having projected themselves as a community acting in unison, were themselves so hopelessly split. Such an exercise, far from reducing or tarnishing the reputation of historic figures, would enrich our knowledge and understanding of a complex phenomenon. Arguably, if we know our leaders better and question their reading of the authentic and vibrant histories of shared memories and experiences, we may not repeat their mistakes and errors of judgement which cost the nation dearly at the stroke of the midnight hour on 14-15 August 1947.

III

"The decision about the creation of Pakistan had just been announced and people were indulging in all kinds of surmises about the pattern of life that would emerge. But no one's imagination could go very far ... The sardarji sitting in front of me repeatedly asked me whether I thought Mr Jinnah would continue to live in Bombay after the creation of Pakistan or whether he would resettle in Pakistan. Each time my answer would be the same, 'Why should he leave Bombay? I think he'll continue to live in Bombay and continue visiting Pakistan.' Similar guesses were being made about the towns of Lahore and Gurdaspur too, and no one knew which town would fall to the share of India and which to Pakistan."

In the specific context of the Pakistan movement, the professed ideology of the nation-state itself, though celebrated on both sides of the border, had no significant impact on or relevance to the millions living in India or Pakistan. Contrary to the exaggerated claims made in both the countries, most people were either indifferent to or unconcerned with the national borders or the newly-created geographical entities that were being laboriously created. National borders were political constructs, imagined projections of territorial power. Although they appeared in deceptively precise forms, they reflected, at leat initially, merely the mental images of politicians, lawyers, and intellectuals. Their practical consequences for most people were quite different.[34] Rajinder Sachar, jurist and human rights activist who has spent a lifetime struggling with his memories of Lahore, recalled:

"One day I ran into a Muslim villager who had come to Lahore all the way from Sargodha looking for my grandfather, a well-known criminal lawyer. Poor chap he didn't realise that Partition had taken place and that the Hindus had left. It just shows how long it took for the implications of Partition to sink in."

Indeed, though such people were repeatedly fed with ill-informed and biased views and interpretations about the Other, they were neither committed to the land of Aryavarta nor the *dar al-Islam*. They had no destination to reach, no mirage to follow. Even though the trains had started carrying people to their death-traps, they were unclear whether Lahore, with its splendid Mughal monuments, beautiful gardens and boulevards, would be part of India or Pakistan. They did not know whether Delhi, the city of Mir Taqi Mir and Mirza Ghalib, would remain in Gandhi's India or Jinnah's Pakistan. Manto captures the mood in his brilliant story *Toba Tek Singh*, a character from the lunatic asylum. This is what he writes:

"As to where Pakistan was located, the inmates knew nothing. That was why both the mad and the partially mad were unable to decide whether they were now in India or in Pakistan. If they were in India where on earth was Pakistan? And if they were in Pakistan, then how come that until only the other day it was India?...

Those who had tried to solve this mystery had become utterly confused when told that Sialkot, which used to be in India, was now in Pakistan. It was anybody's guess what was going to happen to Lahore, which was currently in Pakistan, but could slide into India any moments. It was still possible that the entire subcontinent of India might become Pakistan. And who could say if both India and Pakistan might not entirely vanish from the map of the world one day?... Just before sunrise, Bisham Singh, the man who had stood on his legs for fifteen years, screamed and as officials from the two sides rushed towards him, he collapsed on the ground. There, behind barbed wire, on one side, lay India and behind more barbed wire, on the other side, lay Pakistan. In between, on a bit of earth which had no name, lay Toba Tek Singh."

The paradox of how borders simultaneously separate and unite is discussed elsewhere.[35] The significance of Manto's description lies in describing an existentialist reality - the separation of people living on both sides who had a long history of cultural and social contact - and the paradoxical character of borders being a metaphor of the ambiguities of nation building.[36] He was, in essence, offering a way of correcting the distortions inherent in state-centred national histories. then "India" or "Pakistan" were mere territorial abstractions to most people who were ignorant of how Mountbatten's Plan or the Radcliffe Award would change their destinies and tear them apart from their social and cultural moorings. In their world-view, there was no nationalism, religious or composite. They were blissfully unaware that their fate, which had rested in the hands of the exploiting classes for centuries, would be settled after Mountbatten's three days of "diplomacy" leading to the 3rd June Plan, and that the frontiers would be decided by Cyril Radcliffe in just seven weeks and "a continent for better or worse divided"[37]. They had no clue whatsoever that these vain, insensitive and conceited representatives of the Crown, having received the mandate from Clement Atlee's Labour government to preside over the liquidation of the most important imperial possession of all time, would abandon them in mid-ocean "with a fire in the deck and ammunition in the hold". Nobody had warned them how Mountbatten's mentor Winston Churchill had, likewise, sat with T.E. Lawrence and the Emir Faisal in Cairo as Colonial Secretary in 1922 drawing nation states on the map of what had previously been the Ottoman Empire. But, then, how were they to know that the colonial powers divide people and territories when in ascendancy, as also in retreat.

IV

"For a long time I refused to accept the consequences of the revolution, which was set off by the Partition of the country. I still feel the same way;

but I suppose, in the end, I came to accept this nightmarish reality without self-pity or despair. In the process I tried to retrieve from this manmade sea of blood, pearls of a rare hue, by writing about the single-minded dedication with which men had killed men, about the remorse felt by some of them, about the tears shed by murders who could not understand why they still had some human feelings left. All this and more, I put in my book Siyah Hashye." (Saadat Hasan Manto)[38]

Everytime I visited Amritsar, I felt captivated. But the city this time presented the look of a cremation *ghat*, eerie and stinking... The silence was so perfect that even the faint hiss of steam from the stationary engine sounded a shriek ... The brief stoppage seemed to have lingered into eternity till the engine whistled and gave a gentle pull ... We left Chheharta behind and then Atari and when we entered Wagah and then Harbanspura everyone in the train felt uplifted. A journey through a virtual valley of destruction has ended when finally the train came to a halt at Platform No. 2 - Lahore, the moment was as gratifying as the consummation of a dream."[39]

Scores of writers reveal the other face of freedom, the woes of divided families, the agony and trauma of abducted women, the plight of migrants and the harrowing experiences of countless people who boarded the train that took them to the realization of their dream, but of whom not a man, woman or child survived the journey. A Zahid in Attia Hosain's *Sunlight on a Broken Column* or a Saddan in Masoom Reza Rahi's *Aadha Gaon* (Half-a-Village) offer a vivid and powerful portrayal of a fragmented and wounded society.[40] What political debate will never fully do - and the reason we so badly need the literature - is defeat the urge to lay blame, which keeps animosity alive. Only the literature truly evokes the sufferings of the innocent, whose pain is more universal and ultimately a vehicle of more honest reconciliation than political discourse.[41]

Board the *Peshawar Express* or the *Train to Pakistan* to discover the implications of what happened before and after the fateful, midnight hour. Consider the exchanges between Choudhry Mohammad Ali, a well-known landlord of Rudauli in Barabanki district (Uttar Pradesh) and his daughter who left his father to settle in Karachi, or the correspondence of Brahm Nath Dutt, father of the historian V.N. Datta, to capture the poignancy of the moment. Turn to Rahi's Gangauli village - a world where people are seen to be wrestling to come to terms with competing ideologies - in order to uncover how the intricate and almost imperceptible way in which the politics of Partition worked its way into the interstices of people's consciousness.[42] Read Attia Hosain's *Sunlight on a Broken Column* or *Phoenix Fled* to discover how the Pakistan movement split families on ideological lines and created fears and uncertainties in the minds of people. To read her novel and collection of short stories is, "as if one had parted a curtain, or opened a door, and strayed into the past"[43].

Indeed, if the *histories* of Partition are to be rewritten, there are several reasons why we must judiciously draw upon the intellectual resources made available to us by such creative writers. They expose the inadequacy of numerous narratives on Independence and Partition, compel us to explore fresh themes and adopt new approaches that have eluded the grasp of social scientists, and provide a foundation for developing an alternative discourse to current expositions of a general theory on inter-community relations. Their strength lies is representing a grim and sordid contemporary reality without drawing religion or a particular community as the principal reference point. In their stories, the experiences of each community distinctly mirror one another, indeed reach out to and clutch at one another. No crime, no despair, no grief in exile belongs uniquely to anyone.[44] In the words of Krishna Sobti, whose best-known Hindi writings on Partition are *Sikka Badal Gaya* and *Zindaginama*, the fiction written about that cataclysmic event preserved "essential human values"[45]. That is probably why

> "We emerge from the literature with a mistrust towards group solidarity of an oppositional bent. If so, we must emerge at the same time, paradoxically, with a conviction to oppose such mistrust with trust in the goodness of the human life-urge wherever we find it. Indeed, we emerge from the literature as searchers of such trust. If we find it in the solitary dissidence of even a singly person, we feel obliged to offer him or her our companionship. And if we find it stitched into whole communities, we come away not necessarily more pious, but inspired. The literature as a whole seeds pathos for the suffering and inhumanity of the Partition, and related instances of cultural chauvinism, but not merely so. It also sprouts a countervailing protest, a voice of justice that must be the surging of our humanity itself - something greater than our bestiality - within us. In this sense the literature does what religious leaders in each community failed to do: to make communities forces for the affirmation of humanity broadly ... If religious politics worked nefariously in favour of Partition, it was because ecumenical religious politics never developed. We are in a different position than the men and women of August, 1947. Our choices are not limited to exile, death or resignation ..."[46]

In other words, if creative writings can still stir the individual and collective imagination of sensitive readers in the subcontinent, there is no reason why people on both sides of the Wagah border cannot share the anguish of Faiz Ahmad Faiz[47] and, at the same time, echo the optimism and plea of Ali Sardar Jafri in the following lines:

> Tum aao Gulshan-i Lahore se chaman bardosh,
> hum ayen subha Banaras ki raushni lekar,
> Himalaya ki hawaon ki taazgi lekar,
> Phir uske baad ye puchen ke kaun dushman hai?

Notes

1. Some years ago, the historian Gyanendra Pandey complained that the history of violence accompanying Partition had not been written. Recently, Ashis Nandy bemoaned that the finest creative minds of India had maintained a profound, almost cultivated silence about Partition and the bloodbath. Times of India, 20 July 1997. See, also Urvashi Butalia on the "Official Silence". In: Hindu, 21 September 1997. My principal interest in this essay centres around articles published in newspapers, magazines and journals during the fiftieth year of Independence. I have, however, used scholarly writings, mostly published in 1996-97 to comment on the theme of Partition. The Delhi-based weekly newsmagazine *Outlook* brought out a special issue on 28 May 1997. The *Asian Age*, edited by M.J. Akbar, published extracts from books on Partition, personal memories and recollections and interviews. See, for example, the reports of the Reuters correspondent Don Campbell who arrived in India in March 1947 and spent the next 15 months in Delhi. The coverage in the newspaper *Hindu* (Delhi) was also quite extensive. The impressions of Phillips Talbot, an American, were particularly interesting.
2. For example Urvashi Butalia, Blood, In: Granta, London, March 1997; Sunil Mehra, Sufferers and Survivors. In: Outlook, 28 May, 1997, pp. 32-3; Bridging a Great Divide. In: India Today, 18 August 1997; Anita Mukhopadhya, The Last Journey. In: Hindu, 31 August 1997; Ajeet Cour, I've seen rootless trees wobbling and walking. In: Hindustan Times, 4 January 1998 (Courtesy: Nonica Datta); C.M. Naim, Pakistan or Hindustan. In: Communalism Combat, September 1997; India's Unforgettable Divide. In: Guardian, London, 30 July 1997; Iqbal Masud, Dream Merchants, Politicians & Partition: Memoirs of an Indian Muslim, Delhi 1997.
3. Femina, Bombay, 1 August 1997. I am grateful to Nonica Datta for this reference.
4. For example Patrick French, Liberty or Death: India's Journey to Independence and Division, London 1997.
5. See, for example, the scholarly contributions of Gyanendra Pandey, Community and Violence. In: Economic and Political Weekly (EPW), 9 August 1997; id., Partition and Independence in Delhi: 1947-48. In: EPW, 6 September 1997; Azhar Abbas, The Twice Displaced. In: Outlook, 28 May 1997, p. 66. For insights into ethnic violence in Sri Lanka in 1983 that had many features in common with the Hindu-Muslim riots before and after Independence, see S.J. Tambiah, Ethnic Fratricide and the Dismantling of Democracy, Chicago 1986.
6. Butalia, loc. cit.; Ritu Menon/Kamla Bhasin, Borders & Boundaries: Women in India's Partition, Delhi 1998.
7. Mushirul Hasan, Legacy of a Divided Nation: India's Muslims Since Independence London 1997; India Partitioned: The Other Face of Freedom, Delhi 1997 (2nd revised edition).
8. For a critique of Mountbatten, see N.N. Vohra, 91 Garden Town, and F.S. Aijazuddin, Same to Same, from a different perspective, in: Sen (ed.), Crossing Boundaries, loc. cit.
9. Outlook, 28 May 1997. Notice the following letter of Cyril Radcliffe to his son: "I thought you would like to get a letter from India with a crown on the envelope. After tomorrow evening nobody will ever again be allowed to use such stationery and after 150 years British rule will be over in India ... I am going to see Mountbatten sworn as

the first governor-general of the Indian Union ... and then I station myself firmly on the Delhi airport until an aeroplane from England comes along. Nobody in India will love me for the award about the Punjab and Bengal and there will be roughly 80 million people with a grievance who will begin looking for me. I do not want them to find me. I have worked and travelled and sweated - oh I have sweated the whole time." Quoted in: Sunil Khilnani, The Idea of India, London 1997, p. 201.

10   Ajit Bhattacharjea, Cyril's Scalpel. In: Outlook, 23 July 1997, p. 8.

11   Thus the following view: "Looking back 50 years, the haste and self-delusion of Congress and Muslim leaders that contributed to the bloodiest religious cleansing in history emerges with disturbing clarity. Outlook, 28 May 1997.

12   Leonard Mosley, The Last Days of the Raj, London 1961, p. 77.

13   For example, the presidential address delivered by Professor V.N. Datta at the Indian History Congress held in Madras, 1996.

14   Kuldip Nayar, Was Pakistan Necessary?". In: Indian Express, 15 August 1997; id., Partition: An Inevitability. In: Hindu, Special Issue, August 1997. For earlier accounts of who is to blame, see Chimanlal Setalvad, India Divided, Bombay, n.d., pp. 4-7.

15   Gyanendra Pandey, The Prose of Otherness. In: David Arnold/David Hardiman (eds.), Subaltern Studies VIII: Essays in Honour of Ranajit Guha, Delhi 1994, p. 194.

16   This is the common refrain in the writings of Ayesha Jalal and Farzana Shaikh. For his critique of Jalal's work, see Pandey, The Prose of Otherness, loc. cit., pp. 209-10. And for her response, see Secularists, Subalterns and the Stigma of "Communalism": Partition Historiography Revisited. In: The Indian Economic and Social History Review, 33 (1996) 1, pp. 93-103. The tendency to exaggerate the difference in perspectives and to castigate each other for that reason is the hallmark of recent historiography on South Asia. Young and upcoming social scientists, many of whom have not even written their doctoral dissertations, are engaged in polemical writings. They regard this as a shortcut to establishing their scholarly reputation in the West. Ayesha Jalal's critique of my introduction to: India's Partition: Process Strategy and Mobilisation, Delhi 1998 (4th impression), is based on a misunderstanding of my overall argument. Yet, I respect her views and her understanding of a highly complex phenomena which should not, incidentally, be reduced to polemical exchanges among fellow-historians.

17   In a perceptive article, Aijaz Ahmad has offered a powerful critique of "the Congress-inspired mythology". His analysis suggests (a) that the politics of caste and communalism was inherent in the structure of the colonial society itself; (b) that the reform movements usually contributed to solidifying such identities rather than weakening them in favour of ecumenical culture and a non-denominational politics; and (c) that the national movement itself, including the majority of the Congress under Gandhi, was deeply "complicit in a transactional mode of politics which involved bargaining among the elites and a conception of secularism which was little more than an accommodation of the self-enclosed orthodoxies. *Given the immensity of this historical weight, the wonder is not that there was a partition but that there was one*" (emphasis added). Hindu, Special Number, p. 28.

18   The judgement is harsh, although many contemporary observers believed that Jinnah may not have had the space to press his campaign in the United Provinces if the coalition issue was amicably resolved. The Governor of UP felt that way. Harry Haig to Linlithgow, 3 June 1939, File no. 115/6, IOLR. See also my introduction to: India's Partition, pp. 12-5.

19 On the coalition issue, there is unmistakable evidence to suggest that talks for a Congress-Muslim League alliance were initiated sometime in March-April 1937. Although Nehru had opposed "all pacts and coalitions with small groups at the top". (To Abul Wali, 30 March 1937, All India Congress Committee [AICC] Papers, G-5, K.W i, 1937, Nehru Memorial Museum & Library), Abdul Wali of Barabanki (UP) referred to a scheme "being hatched with the help of Pantji [G.B.Pant] and Mohanlal [Saxena] to bring about coalition between the Congress and League parties in the Assembly". To Nehru, 28 March 1937, AICC Papers. The governor of UP reported on 7 April that the League was looking forward to an alliance with the Congress and felt that "at present it looks as if the new government will gradually attract to itself a fair number of the Muslim Leaguers".
20 See Masud Hasan Shahab Dehlavi. In: Mushirul Hasan (ed.), India Partitioned. Vol. 2, pp. 184-95.
21 Interview with Alok Bhalla, in: Sen (ed.), Crossing Boundaries, loc. cit., p. 66. And the comment of J.S. Butalia, a retired journalist: "I was born and brought up in a predominantly Muslim village, Butala. There were 300 Muslim families and only 10 or 15 Hindu homes but we lived in such close harmony that it was difficult to make out who was who. A Hindu-Muslim conflict was something we had not imagined even in our worst dreams. It is with a sense of horror and shame that I look back ... but, finally, I am overwhelmed by nostalgia." Hindu, Special Number, 15 August 1997, p. 32. For Bengal, see Mukhopadhaya, The Last Journey. In: Hindu, 31 August 1997.
22 See the contributions of Rakshat Puri, Muchkund Dubey and Sumanta Banerjea, in: Sen (ed.), Crossing Boundaries, loc. cit.
23 This is quoted in full in: Mushirul Hasan, Legacy of a Divided Nation, loc. cit., p. 168.
24 See Mushirul Hasan, India's Partition: Process, Strategy and Mobilisation, Delhi 1997, (4th Impression), p. 405. For Punjab, see Sobti, loc. cit., pp. 67, 69-70. For Bengal, see Ranabir Samaddar (ed.), Reflections on Partition in the East, Delhi 1997, and the review of the book by Sumanta Banerjee in: Biblio, Delhi, July-August 1997, pp. 40-1; Peter Van Der Veer, Playing or Praying: A Suf Saint's Day in Surat. In: The Journal of Asian Studies, 51 (1992) 3, pp. 545-64.
25 Phillipe Talbot, Thus Independence Came to India. In: Hindu, 4 and 24 August 1997.
26 Talbot filed this report on 10 August 1947.
27 I have borrowed these lines from Ayesha Jalal, Secularists, Subalterns and the Stigma of "Communalism", loc. cit., p. 1.
28 Nawab of Chattari to Hailey, 28 October 1936, Malcolm Hailey Papers, File no. 28c, IOLR.
29 Attia Hosain, Sunlight on a Broken Column, Delhi 1992, pp. 231-3, 234.
30 In this respect, my reading of the Pakistan movement is different from that of Ayesha Jalal.
31 The following impression of Azad by Kanji Dwarkadas is interesting. "Abul Kalam Azad", he wrote, "is dignified and level-headed, but his health is giving way. Jinnah dislikes him heartily and a few years ago he called him the 'show boy' of the Congress and in private conversations Jinnah says much worse things about Abul Kalam Azad." India - April 1944 to November 1945: What Next?, 28 November 1945 (Typescript), George Lumley Papers, India Office Library and Records, London.
32 See Pandey, The Prose of Otherness, loc. cit., p. 214.
33 In fact, Jinnah exhorted various regional groups and other factions to overcome their differences and rival claims so that the Muslim League could concentrate all its energies towards the achievement of Pakistan. "We shall have time to quarrel oursel-

ves", he said, "and we shall have time when these differences will have to be remedied. We shall have time for domestic programmes and politics, but first get the Government. This is a nation without any territory or any government." Quoted in: Khalid B. Sayeed, Pakistan: The Formative Phase, 1857-1948, London 1968, p. 297.

34 These lines are based on Michiel Baud/Willem Van Schendel, Towards a Comparative History of Borderlands. In: Journal of World History, 8 (1997) 2, pp. 211-242.
35 Baud/Schendel, Towards a Comparative History..., loc. cit., p. 242.
36 Benedict Anderson, Imagined Communities: Reflections on the Origin and Spread of Nationalism, New York 1991; E.J. Hobsbawm/Terence Ranger (eds.), The Invention of Tradition, Cambridge 1983.
37 This is a line from W.H. Auden. See Khilnani, loc. cit., p. 200.
38 For my translation of *Siyah Hashye* (Black Margins), see Hasan (ed.), India Partitioned, loc cit., pp. 88-101.
39 Mohammad Saeed, Lahore: A Memoir, Lahore, 1989, p. 94.
40 On *Aadha Gaon*, see Sudhir Chandra, The Harvest of Fear: A Retrospective Critique of Hindu-Muslim Relations in Two Hindi Novels. In: T.V. Sathyamurthy, Region. In: Religion, Caste, Gender and Culture in Contemporary India. Vol. 3, Delhi 1996.
41 Jason Francisco, In the Heat of Fratricide: The Literature of India's Partition Burning Freshly (A Review Article). In: The Annual of Urdu Studies. No 2, Madison 1996, p. 250.
42 Chandra, loc. cit., p. 195.
43 Anita Desai, Introduction. In: Phoenix Fled, Delhi 1988, p. viii.
44 Francisco, loc. cit., p. 250.
45 Sen (ed.), Crossing Boundaries, loc. cit., p. 77; Alok Bhalla (ed.), Stories About the Partition of India, 3 vols, Delhi 1994.
46 Francisco, loc. cit., p. 250.
47 This leprous daybreak, dawn night's fangs have mangled
This is not that long-looked-for break of that day
Not that clear dawn in quest of which those comrades
Set out, believing that in heaven's wide void
Somewhere must be the stars" last halting place
Somewhere the verge of night's slow-washing tide
Somewhere an anchorage for the ship of heartache.

Religion and Group Identity in Present Mongolia

Klaus Sagaster

When speaking of Present Mongolia I am using a term which needs some explanation. Today the name Mongolia is the name of the independent State Republic of Mongolia[1], the former People's Republic of Mongolia, which was called Outer Mongolia as long as this territory belonged to China. The Republic of Mongolia, however, is only one part of the territories where Mongols live. There are three other large political units which can be considered to be Mongol states: 1. Inner Mongolia, which is one of the five Autonomous Regions of the People's Republic of China; 2. the Republic of Buryatia, which belongs to Russia; 3. the Kalmuck Republic, which belongs to Russia as well. When I speak of Present Mongolia I mean all the Mongol States of today.

Over the last few years I had the opportunity to visit the Republic of Mongolia regularly, but I also travelled to other parts of the Mongolian world. Wherever I went, I was confronted with the problem of the identity of a numerically small people, which lives together with other ethnic groups in vast territories belonging to different states. All of them had their own history, and all of them are exposed to the political, social, economic, technical and cultural challenges of the modern world.[2]

Identity is a means of survival. Mongolian survival is threatened in different ways. The communist Mongolian People's Republic was a satellite state of the Soviet Union for almost seventy years. The free and democratic Republic of Mongolia of today is still squeezed between Russia and China. Inner Mongolia is a good example of what would happen if Outer Mongolian borders were opened to Chinese immigration. In the Autonomous Region of Inner Mongolia one Mongol is outnumbered by seven Chinese. Similarly, the Mongolian states in Russia have a very large percentage of Russians. The most serious consequence for the situation of the Mongols living in China and Russia is the progressive loss of their native language. This inevitably leads to the loss of native culture. Native culture does not necessarily contradict globalization, but globalization is a danger to the existence of native culture, particularly when smaller ethnic groups belong to a state dominated by a larger ethnic group, as in Russia and China. Globalization will be realized through the medium of the language of larger ethnic groups, which provides the full range of what globalization includes. It would not be realistic to expect that all knowledge, concepts and practice connected with globalization be expressed through all the languages of a state composed of different ethnic groups. The dominant language will inevitably be the language of the largest group as the linguistic means of globalization. As far as the Mongols are concerned, only in the Republic of Mongolia is the native language, Mongolian, the medium of modern concepts.

By the way, the percentage of Russian and English expressions in present-day Mongolian is far less than the percentage of English words in present-day German. Language as a means of identification also plays a basic role in those areas where Mongols do not enjoy political independence, but it is losing more and more ground.

Another basic means of identification which is gaining more and more ground is religion. The Mongols adhere to three religions: Buddhism, Shamanism and Christianity.[3] The most widespread religion is Buddhism in its Tibetan form which is often called Lamaism. Shamanism, a term used by the Mongols themselves, is the technically imprecise name for their non-Buddhist ethnic religion including ancestor-worship. Shamanistic beliefs and practices have been widely incorporated into Buddhism, but on a small scale they still exist independently, particularly in Buryatia. Christianity was introduced to Inner Mongolia on a very small scale by Catholic missionaries. Orthodox as well as Protestant mission was successful in Kalmuckia and Buryatia. I do not know to what extent Christianity has survived amongst the Mongols in present Russia and China. But there is a very active and successful Christian mission in Outer Mongolia, the present Republic of Mongolia. In this connection it should be mentioned that Islamic missions have also been set up amongst the Mongols. Islam is present in Outer Mongolia only amongst the Turkic Kazakhs, but practically no Mongol believes in Allah. In recent years close contacts were established between Mongolia and Turkey. This resulted in the opening - as far as I know - of two Turkic schools for Mongols in Ulaanbaatar. From what I heard during my last visit to Mongolia it turned out that these schools where not normal international institutions but centres of fundamentalist Islamic mission.

Buddhist missions amongst the Mongols began as early as in the middle of the thirteenth century. The Mongol rulers, confronted with the necessity to introduce a universal religion in order to strengthen the ideological frame of their world empire, made their decision in favour of the Tibetan form of Buddhism. It was the religion of the Land of Snows which particularly suited the religious ideas and practices of the Mongolian nomads. Throughout the following centuries Buddhism became the religion of the overwhelming majority of Mongols. Even the Kalmucks, a confederation of West Mongolian or Oirat tribes who emigrated from Eastern Turkestan to the Lower Volga at the end of the sixteenth century remained Buddhist in spite of the fact that they were surrounded by Orthodox Russians and Muslim Turks. Many Kalmucks emigrated once again during the first and second World War to Europe and America. They established a Buddhist temple in Munich and several temples in Philadelphia and in the small town of Howell in New Jersey. It was in Howell, during a visit in 1975, that I had a very interesting experience about Mongol Buddhist identity. When I made inquiries about Buddhism among the

Kalmuck refugees in America, one of the leaders of the Kalmuck community said: "A Kalmuck who is not a Buddhist is not a Mongol."[4]

This statement was indeed remarkable. The Kalmucks, who have a significant microidentity as Western Mongols in historical, ethnic and linguistic contrast to the Eastern Mongols of Inner and Outer Mongolia and Buryatia, use their religious identity in order to define their macroidentity as Mongols. The same was true in 1990, the great year of political change, when the Kalmucks celebrated the 450th anniversary of the great West Mongolian Jangyar (Jangar, Džangar) epic.[5] I had the opportunity to attend the celebrations which were held between 22 and 26 August in Elista, the Kalmuck capital. When I arrived I saw a group of Buddhist monks at the airport. They turned out to be a delegation from Ulaanbaatar, headed by the highest dignitary of the Mongolian People's Republic, the Abbot of the Gandan Monastery in Ulaanbaatar. The monks had come to Kalmuckia to select the ground for the first Buddhist monastery to be erected after communist destruction. The abbot of Gandan was even one of the official speakers at the public session of the Central Committee of the Communist Party of Kalmuckia in honour of the epic hero Jangyar, who is the most prominent identification figure of Western Mongols. Kalmuck microidentity was again connected to Buddhist identity. But Mongol macroidentity was also reaffirmed. The first foreign speaker at the session was a representative of the Mongol government. He presented a gift of honour which turned out to be a carpet with the portrait of Činggis Khan. This carpet was solemnly displayed to the audience on the rostrum with the members of the Central Committee.

This symbolic action did not take place by chance. The anniversary of the Jangyar epic was preceded by the 750th anniversary of a famous work in Mongolian literature, the "Secret History of the Mongols", which was celebrated from August 14 to 18 in the Mongolian capital, Ulaanbaatar. The "Secret History of the Mongols" is an epic biography of Činggis Khan.[6] The celebration of this work was the turning point of the ideological condemnation of Činggis Khan during the communist period. From now on, Činggis Khan was no longer a non-person, but was officially reinstated in his position as creator of the Mongolian people, founder of the Mongolian world empire and Mongolian reputation throughout the world, as cultural hero and divine protector of the Mongols. The Pan-Mongolian character of Činggis Khan became evident in an exhibition of Mongolian books. Literature from Outer Mongolia, Inner Mongolia, Buryatia and Kalmuckia was arranged around a large painting of Činggis Khan. The religious character of Činggis Khan was apparent in many paintings and drawings shown in a special exhibition and in many publications on the occasion of the anniversary. With regard to the religious character, two kinds of symbolic representation could be observed: symbols related to the cult of Činggis as an ancestor deity and deified hero and symbols relating Činggis

Khan to Buddhist ideas, for example Činggis Khan as a protector of Buddhist religion.

The Secret History celebrations clearly marked two events: the resurrection of Činggis Khan and the resurrection of Buddha in Outer Mongolia. These two events coincided with developments in other Mongolian countries. The Mongols had regained their two most important identification figures: Činggis Khan and Buddha.

Consequently, the ritual veneration of Činggis Khan was reestablished in the Republic of Mongolia, particularly practised by the Mongolian army. More and more monasteries were rebuilt. More and more former monks returned to their former monasteries, and more and more young people, even children, entered the monkhood. The white and the black standard, *tuγ*, of Činggis Khan, already attested in the Secret History of the Mongols[7], became the symbol of the civil and military authorities of the state. The Soyombo, a traditional Buddhist emblem symbolising a complex of religious and secular values, is the main element of the Mongolian flag.[8] It should be mentioned, however, that the Mongolian flag is identical with the flag of Communist Mongolia, with the only difference of the red star which has now been removed from the top of the Soyombo sign. This sign is the first letter of a graphically rather complicated script which was invented in the seventeenth century by the first Grand Lama of Outer Mongolia, Öndör Gegen Zanabazar (1635-1723) as a national script.[9] It became the special symbol of Mongolian independence. The Soviets had obviously not discovered the Buddhist implications of the flag of their Mongolian brothers.

The Soyombo sign is not used in Inner Mongolia. The black and white standard, however, is well-known, particularly in the Ordos country in South-West Inner Mongolia. The *tuγ* standard is the sign of Mongolian identity *par excellence*. Houses where Ordos Mongols live can be identified a longway off: In front of the house there is always an altar table with one or two *tuγ* standards.

The Ordos country has a particularly close relationship with Činggis Khan. It is the traditional area where the so-called Eight White Tents were kept by a special class of priests, the Darqad. The Eight White Tents contain several relics of Činggis Khan and his family. They were originally located in different places but were assembled in a mausoleum built in 1957 by order of the communist government. Since then, with the interruption of the cultural revolution, Činggis Khan has been ritually venerated in the new sanctuary. When I visited this place in 1985, I could see votive flags offered by believers from Inner and Outer Mongolia and from Xinjiang. This again shows the universal character of Činggis Khan veneration. Mongolian historical pride was demonstrated by a huge figure of Činggis Khan in the entrance hall. Činggis Khan was sitting in front of a map showing the extent of the Mongol Empire. It is not surprising that this map was covered with cloth when I paid my next visit to the sanctuary in 1990. Buddhist ritual veneration of Činggis Khan is restricted to a particular place of offering outside the sanctuary. Being an ancestor cult, Činggis Khan veneration is part of the ethnic religion of the Mongols, the so-called shamanism. It must be stressed, however, that priests performing Činggis Khan rituals are not shamans. Other rituals, like the fire offering, are even performed by laymen. The actions of shamans are restricted to certain clearly defined performances.[10] The border between the different forms of ethnic religion and Buddhism is indistinct. As far as I can see, there is no group identity constituted by ethnic religion. The only exception is Buryat shamanism which seems to be openly opposed to Buddhism but without any effect on ethnic macroidentity.[11]

The same seems to be the case with Christianity in Buryatia and Kalmuckia. The number of Christians living in Inner Mongolia is too small to be dangerous for Buddhism and Mongolian identity. Until recently, the same was true for Outer Mongolia. However, the situation has changed considerably since 1990. Mongolia, in an effort to be democratic, allowed all kinds of Christian denominations to enter the country and spread their faith in written and spoken form. Now there are Catholic missionaries, supported by the Embassy of the Vatican, as well as Protestant missionaries, mostly from America but also from Germany. The missionaries attract the particular interest of young people. Having been educated without religion, the younger generation of Mongolia is not very interested in Buddhism which, in its present form, offers very little to a young layman of today. But the Christians offer discussions, social meetings in connection with meals, and instruction in English, the language which opens the door to the western world. There is now even a Christian radio station in Mongolia. Nevertheless, it is too early to speak of a Mongolian Christian group identity in Mongolia.

A comparison of Christian and Buddhist activities does not at all result in favour of the Buddhists. Buddhist monks are not very interested in the religious education of lay people. Only a few books exist on the basic teachings of Buddha and on special topics. In 1996, the Gandan monastery (Gandantėgčėnlin xijd) in Ulaanbaatar, the largest monastery in Mongolia, started editing a religious journal.[12] There are also some religious newspapers, but their circulation seems to be rather limited.[13] From time to time articles on religious topics are published in other newspapers. However, there is no systematic oral instruction of laymen by the monks. The transmission of knowledge follows the traditional pattern of instruction within the families and the tradition of private ritual practice. Public instruction as given by the Dalai Lama in 1994 in the stadium of Ulaanbaatar is an exception. It cannot fill the gap. In general, lay people concentrate on those religious activities which help them to solve the problems of practical life, such as divination, blessings through holy water and holy powder, and paying for religious texts to be recited by the monks in order to protect them against misfortune. For example, the "Essence of Transcendental Wisdom" (*Bilig baramid-un Jirüken*)[14], a short text comprising the essence of Buddhist philosophy, is recited as a protection against all kinds of evils coming from the ten directions of the world. No layman understands the meaning, which is unimportant compared to its magic effect. Even texts which could be understood, like prayers to Buddhist deities, remain incomprehensible for the layman, since they are recited in the Tibetan language and not in Mongolian.[15]

The Tibetan language is the main obstacle to the divulgation of Buddhist teaching amongst the laypeople. Tibetan has been the holy language of the Mongolian Buddhists since the beginning. This does, however, not mean that Buddhist texts were not translated into Mongolian. On the contrary, translation activities started very early.[16] There are Mongol versions of all the basic works of Tibetan Buddhist literature and there is reason to suppose that not only Tibetan, but also Mongolian was used as a ritual language in earlier times. It is very strange that this practice has disappeared completely. It has disappeared to the extent that even simple prayers meant for recital by laymen are in Tibetan and rendered in the Mongolian Cyrillic script. It is completely impossible for laymen to understand the meaning of the prayers.

The use of the Tibetan language is symptomatic for the situation of present-day Buddhism in Mongolia. During the seventy years of communist rule Buddhism suffered not only material but also very serious intellectual, institutional and moral losses. It is not difficult to understand that revival aims at restoring Buddhism in its previous forms, also taking into consideration the traditional Buddhist feelings of the lay population. In 1990 it was clear that, in principle, neither the former monks nor the laymen had lost their Buddhist identity. Even younger people, who were educated as communists and were party members, are now proud of the fact that they still possess the Mongolian or Tibetan version of the famous *Altan Gerel*[17], "The Golden Splendour", a Buddhist text which is particularly dear to the hearts of the Mongols. It turned out that a surprising number of people had successfully hidden Buddhist texts during the Communist period, although this had been rather risky. The revival of Buddhism is also documented by the public memory of great Buddhist personages. When I visited Mongolia in August 1997 I had the chance to attend a festival in honour of Zava Damdin, a high-ranking lama who was a great scholar of Buddhist logics and the author of an important history of Buddhism in Mongolia.[18] Zava Damdin was born in 1864 in the present Central Gobi District (Dundgov' Ajmag). He died in 1937. In 1997 the government of the Central Gobi District organized a belated festival in memory of the 130th anniversary of Zava Damdin's birth. The celebrations were held from August 15 to 18 in the district capital, Mandalgobi (Mandalgov').[19] They included the three traditional Mongolian games (nadam [*nayadum/naadam*]) horse-racing, wrestling and archery and attracted a great number of people even from far-off areas. The festival conveyed the vividness of Mongolian Buddhist identity. Nevertheless, I had the feeling that this identity was in great danger because of its intellectual weakness. I presume that few participants at the festival knew who Zava Damdin really was and that certainly no layman had ever read Zava Damdin since his works were written in Tibetan.

Mongolia is changing fast. It is no longer a remote country, it is no longer difficult to access, but a young state open to the modern world and exposed to globalization. Mongolian Buddhism will only remain a means of identification if it is prepared for intellectual, institutional and social change. Religious identity which includes lay people cannot continue to be based on tradition alone. Lack of social and educational responsibility will seriously damage Buddhist group identity. The door will be open more and more for new identities, for example agnostic and Christian.

But not only Mongolian Buddhism must be ready for change. The same is true of Tibetan Buddhism in Tibet and China, and also in its Indian exile. Tibetan and Mongolian Buddhism in its present form will not be able to face the problems of the modern world. It will become a victim, not a winner, of globalization if it continues to be mediaeval.

Notes

1   Official name: Mongolia.
2   On the problem of Mongolian identity and nationalism see, e.g., Igor de Rachewiltz, The Mongols rethink their early history. In: The East and the Meaning of History. International Conference (23-27 November 1992), Roma 1994, pp. 357-380; Udo B. Barkmann, Bemerkungen zum mongolischen Nationalismus - ein Versuch I. In: Humboldt Journal zur Friedensforschung, 3 (1992) und 1 (1993), pp. 80-91.
3   On Buddhism and Shamanism see Walther Heissig, The Religions of the Mongols, London 1979; on Christianity see C.R. Bawden, Shamans, Lamas and Evangelicals. The English Missionaries in Siberia, London et al. 1985.
4   A particularly interesting study on the Kalmucks, based on a field investigation of the Kalmuck Mongol group in the United States and supplemented by historical source materials, is Paula G. Rubel, The Kalmyk Mongols. A Study in Continuity and Change. Indiana University Publications 64, Bloomington—The Hague 1967.
5   See Arash Bormanshinov, Epic, Kalmyk: "Dshanggar". In: Harry B. Weber (ed.), The Modern Encyclopaedia of Russian and Soviet Literatures (Including Non-Russian and Emigré Literatures). Vol. 6, Gulf Breeze, Fl., 1982, p. 233; more recent literature in Klaus Sagaster, The Prologue to the Jangyar Epic. In: Zentralasiatische Studien, 22 (1989/1991), pp. 287-296.

6   English translations: Francis Woodman Cleaves, The Secret History of the Mongols. For the First Time Done into English out of the Original Tongue and Provided with an Exegetical Commentary. Vol. I (Translation), Cambridge/Mass.—London 1982. (Vol. II was not published); Igor de Rachewiltz, The Secret History of the Mongols. In: Papers on Far Eastern History, Canberra 4 (1971), pp. 115-163; 5 (1972), pp. 149-175; 10 (1974), pp. 55-82; 13 (1976), pp.41-75; 16 (1977), pp. 27-65; 18 (1978), pp. 43-80; 21 (1980), pp. 17-57; 23 (1981), pp. 111-146; 26 (1982), pp. 39-84; 30 (1984), pp. 81-130; 31 (1985), pp. 21-93. Professor de Rachewiltz is preparing a revised translation and commentary. Latest German translation: Manfred Taube, Geheime Geschichte der Mongolen. Herkunft, Leben und Aufstieg Činggis Khans, Leipzig—Weimar 1989.
7   See Igor de Rachewiltz, Index to the Secret History of the Mongols. Indiana University Publications, Uralic and Altaic Series 121, Bloomington 1972, lines 6205 (§ 181), 6733 (§ 193, 7707 (§ 202), 9124 (§ 232), 11620 (§ 278).
8   For the Soyombo emblem see Johannes Schubert, Paralipomena Mongolica. Wissenschaftliche Notizen über Land, Leute und Lebensweise in der Mongolischen Volksrepublik, Berlin 1971, pp. 120-121; Rinčen, Soëmba - ėmblema svobody i nezavisimosti mongol'skogo naroda. In: Rinčen, Iz našego kul'turnogo nasledija. Sbornik statej, Ulan-Bator 1958, pp. 12-16; Klaus Sagaster, Der Weiße Lotus des Friedens. Eine moderne mongolische Interpretation buddhistischer Symbolik. In: Zentralasiatische Studien, 12 (1978), pp. 463-541, pp. 516, 517, 531 (note 76).
9   For this script see Rintschen (= Rinčen), Zwei unbekannte mongolische Alphabete aus dem XVII. Jahrhundert. In: Acta Orient. Hung., II (1952), pp. 63-71; Sagaster, Der Weiße Lotus..., loc. cit., p. 531 (note 76).
10 Recent publications on the cult of Činggis Khan: Elisabetta Chiodo, The Book of Offerings to the Holy Činggis Qaγan. A Mongolian Ritual Text. 2 parts. In: Zentralasiatische Studien 22 (1989/1991), pp. 190-220, and Zentralasiatische Studien 23 (1992/1993), pp. 84-144; Elisabetta Chiodo, The Horse White-as-Egg (öndegen čaγan). A Study of the Custom of Consecrating Animals to Deities. In: Ural-Altaische Jahrbücher. Neue Folge 11 (1992), pp. 125-151; Elisabetta Chiodo, The γaril Sacrifice to the Ancestors in the Cult of Činggis Qaγan. In: I. Baldauf/M. Friederich (eds.), Bamberger Zentralasienstudien. Konferenzakten ESCAS IV, Bamberg, 8.-12. Oktober 1991, Berlin 1994, pp. 618-626; Klaus Sagaster, Die Verehrung Činggis Khans bei den Mongolen. In: Werner Diem/Abdoldjavad Falaturi (eds.), XXIV. Deutscher Orientalistentag, vom 26.-30. September 1988 in Köln. Ausgewählte Vorträge, Stuttgart 1990, pp. 366-371; Klaus Sagaster, Ein Ritual aus dem heutigen Činggis-Heiligtum in Ordos. In: Zentralasiatische Studien 23 (1992/1993), pp. 145-151.
11 On Buryat shamanism see Robert Hamayon, La chasse à l'âme. Esquisse d'une théorie du chamanisme sibérien, Nanterre 1990. There is a rich literature in Russian on Buryat shamanism, cf. eg. T.M. Michajlov, Burjatskij šamanizm: istorija, struktura i social'nye funkcii, Novosibirsk 1987.
12 Labai-yin egesig/Lavajn ėgšig, Burxan šašny sudlal, mėdėėllijn sėtgüül (Journal for Buddhist Studies and Information).
13 Bilgijn melmij (The Eye of Wisdom), edited by the Centre of the Mongolian Buddhists in the Gandan Monastery (Gandantėgčenlin xijd); Bilgijn zul, ed. by the "Three Jewels" Association ("Gurvan ėrdėnė" nijgėmlėg) of Mongolian Buddhists; Suvarga (The Stupa), ed. by the Buddhist "Deeds of Merit" Association ("Bujany üjls" nijgėmlėg).

14 Sanskrit *Prajñāpāramitāhrdaya*, Tibetan *Śes-rab-kyi sñiṅ-po* > Mongolian *Šijrèvnjamba*; short Tibetan form *Śer-sñiṅ* > Mongolian *Šernin*. The *Šijrèvnjamba* is listed among the texts offered for recital during services in Buddhist convents, cf. Mongolyn xijd, dacanguudad xurach xurlyn üné, nèrsijn žagsaalt, tovč aguulga (Prices, List of titles and short contents of [texts offered for recital in] Mongolian monasteries and temples, no. 218). This little booklet has no place-name or date but it was bought in August 1997 in Ulaanbaatar. It describes the "contents", i.e. the purpose for reciting this text, as follows: "'*The Essence of Wisdom*' - to be recited as wisdom which removes through the excellent teaching of the Emptiness bad evils like temporary calamities and illnesses" (*Šijrèvnjamba - Cag zuuryn gaj barcad, övčin zétgèr muu xorlolyg xooson čanaryn dééd surgalyn üüdnéès arilgaxyn bilèg bolgon ajltguuldag*) - For further information on the "Essence of Wisdom" as a means for averting misfortune see Klaus Sagaster, Ein Dokument des Tschinggis-Khan-Kults in der Khalkha-Mongolei. Collectanea Mongolica. Festschrift für Professor Dr. Rintchen zum 60. Geburtstag. Asiatische Forschungen 17, Wiesbaden 1966, pp.193-234, p. 224 (note 24).

15 For example a praise (Mongolian of the Green Tārā: Nogoon Dar'èch/Žavzan pagma dulmaa la dod va šügso, Gètèlgègč chutagt èchijn magtaal oršivoj, prepared for printing by S. Dèmbèrèl, transcribed from the Tibetan original into Cyrillic script by C. Tömörbaatar, Ulaanbaatar 1996.

16 Most probably as early as in the thirteenth century. For the beginning of Mongolian Buddhist translation activities see Walther Heissig, Die mongolischen Handschriften-Reste aus Olon süme, Innere Mongolei (16.-17. Jhdt.). Asiatische Forschungen 46, Wiesbaden 1976, pp. 1-5. The Mongolian scholar D. Tserensodnom (Cèrènsodnom) published the first volume of his Mongolyn burchany šašny uran zochiol (The Literature of Mongolian Buddhism) in 1997. It also deals with early translations into Mongolian (Part One, Chapter II, pp. 83-104).

17 Sanskrit Suvarṇaprabhāsa, Tibetan *gSer-'od*.

18 Zava Damdin (< Tibetan rTsa-ba rTa-mgrin) is identical with Blo-bzaṅ rta-mgrin *alias* Blo-bzaṅ rta-dbyaṅs. For his names, short biography and works see Lokesh Chandra, Materials for a History of Tibetan Literature. Part 2, No. 59, New Delhi 1963, pp. 31-35. Blo-bzaṅ rta-mgrin's history of Mongolia is the *gSer-gyi deb-ther* (Blue Annals), written in 1919. Edited in facsimile by Lokesh Chandra, The Golden Annals of Lamaism being the original Tibetan text of the Hor-chos-ḥbyuṅ of Blo-bzaṅ-rta-mgrin (i.e. Zava Damdin, K.S.) entitled '*Dzam-gliṅ byaṅ-phyogs chen-po-hor-gyi rgyal-khams-kyi rtogs-pa brjod-pa'i bstan-bcos chen-po dpyod-ldan mgu-byed ṅo-mtshar gSer-gyi deb-ther žes-bya-ba bźugs-so*, Śata-Piṭaka Series 34, New Delhi 1964; with a short English biography of Blo-bzaṅ-rta-mgrin on p. V.

19 The official name of the festival was "Festival in commemoration of the birth (lit. shining/dawning of ten thousandfold happiness) of Zava Damdin, the famous representative of Mongolian culture, scholarship and religion" (*mongolyn soël šinžlèx uxaan, šašny nèrt zütgèltèn Zava Damdiny tümèn ölzij gijsnij 130 žilijn ojn bajar naadam*), see the program (*chötölbör*) of the festival.

The French Expedition, Egyptian Satanists and Lady Diana: Globalization and its Discontents

Amr Hamzawy

In my paper, I will attempt to analyse processes of dissociation and appropriation of globalized cultural commodities within two local discourses which emerged at two specific historical moments in Egypt in the context of a general perception of foreign threats to certain central "authentic" values, norms, and ways of life. The first moment occurred at the end of the eighteenth and beginning of the nineteenth century: the French expedition to Egypt and its subsequent occupation for three years, which marked the arrival of European colonial powers to the Middle East. The respective discourse is that of leading al-Azhar scholars who tried to come to terms with the overpowerful Europeans, their modern military and civil equipment, and their universalist cultural message. I will analyze this discourse using the reports of ʿAbd ar-Raḥmān al-Ǧabartī, the famous Egyptian historian who documented the events of the three years between 1798 and 1801.[1]

The second moment took place in the second half of January 1997 in Cairo. It began with the arrest of between 76 (official version) and 100 (unofficial version) Egyptian students who were accused of being members of a satanic sect, organization, or cell said to be created, sponsored and promoted by hostile global powers. The respective discourse in this second case is one of Egyptian journalism, whose producers tried to point out and locate reasons and symptoms of the so-called global threat of Satanism or devil-worship.

Albeit formulated in two different historical phases, I would argue that both discourses defined and exhibited their local-authentic character in ethical, cultural, and especially religious terms. Both negatively appropriated certain global signs, symbols, and discursive messages which were perceived as being related to the threatening cultural Other, and included even those elements which had been accepted in previous historical phases and were locally noncontroversial. I would argue further that the global character of these elements was dissociative. They were located very concretely in the history and geography of the cultural Other. In this context, we witness a tendency to define the cultural Other - be it European, American, Western, or Zionist - variably and multiply in religious terms as Christian, Jewish, blasphemous, secular, or satanic. One can also discern a tendency to purify the local culture, even linguistically, from local nonauthentic components which are perceived as being related either to certain negative aspects of local histories and realities, or to extensions and manifestations of the cultural Other on local soil. Both discourses aimed at preserving and reasserting the authenticity and purity of certain perceptions of the local culture, and were engaged in a process of deconstructing and reconstructing globalized cultural commodities.

Finally, I will be looking at another local and Egyptian media discourse which emerged very recently, namely, during the love affair between Lady Diana and Doudi al-Fayed[2], and after their sudden tragic death on 31 August 1997. It seems to me that the participants of this discourse were dreaming of a local breakthrough on a global level, and thus attempted to religiously and culturally authenticate and organically absorb the global figure Diana, and to religiously purify the local figure Doudi from all traces of the cultural Other, again defined in religious terms. Thus, both Diana and Doudi were appropriated throughout the romantic phase of their relationship in a very positive manner, a fact which opened up the possibility of participating with great enthusiasm and creativity in a global journalistic interest in both figures.

I would argue that local narratives of cultural authenticity and religious purification, which are associated with both negative and positive modes of appropriation and dissociation of global commodities, though methodologically not very sound for those who stand in the rationalist tradition of the Enlightenment, represent a central step in local attempts to cope culturally with the challenges of a global modernity which they did not define. Although their central categories imply cultural essentializations in time and space, these narratives are not one-sided or unidimensional. Their structures are multiple and multilayered and contain several shifting perceptions of the local and the global.

Analytical Remarks

Before moving to my three moments, I would like to make a few analytical remarks on local discourses of authenticity. Conceptual constructions of authenticity and cultural-historical heritage are generally put in a contradictory or dichotomous relation to modernity, although they share with it a number of philosophical and sociological propositions which are centered around the question of how to bring modern man and modern society into a true position toward history. One can argue that this dualistic understanding is related to a dominant Western tradition which constructs modernity against history by means of a conceptual reconstruction of the development of the necessary preconditions of modernity using the methodological concept of ideal types. Modernity is seen here in terms of a fundamental break with its historical antecedents as well as with history as such: In other words, modernity has a position of uniqueness in history. In this context, the universal movement of history is conceived as a process of disenchantment from traditions and religions, a process of continuous secularization.[3] The dominance of this tradition within Western philosophy and social sciences (American modernization theory) has been responsible for the neglect of another tradition within Western modernity, namely that centered around Martin Heidegger and his preoccupation with authenticity. Heidegger defines modernity in relation to the ontological essence of historical being; he understands it as a deeper identification with the present by means of a representation of a past which was made absent by the process of history itself. This movement towards the past entails a process of inventing and elevating a certain understanding or vision of authenticity or authentic tradition as the basis of reconciliation with history, a process of cultural self-assertion in a present situation and an authentication of a certain vision of the past. This interpretation opens up the possibility of conceiving both modernity and the search for authenticity as processes which historically coexist.[4]

Al-Azhar and the French Expedition: 2 July 1798 - 8 September 1801

It seems that Napoleon tried from the very beginning of the invasion of Egypt to couple his attempt to communicate and spread the universal principles of the French Revolution liberty, equality and fraternity, with a respect for Islamic belief and its then central principles and practices in the Egyptian local setting. His first communiqué to the "peoples of Egypt", dated 13 July 1798, was headed by the phrase, "by the name of God, the Almighty, there is no God except Allah, has no son and no partner in his kingdom". Napoleon asserted that the French, who came to Egypt to liberate it from the predominance of the ignorant and stupid Mamluks[5] and to spread equality[6], were good Muslims who worshipped God and respected his prophet, the great Koran and the Ottoman Sultan. He said that the French invaded Rome and destroyed the residence of the Pope, who had been urging and calling upon Christians to struggle against Muslims.[7]

Throughout the first four months, the French respected and promoted local traditions even financially, especially religious festivals and events. Al-Ğabartī writes that Napoleon requested Shaykh al-Bakrī, who was a leading Azhar scholar, to prepare the annual festival of the Prophet's birthday and gave him 300 "French Riyal" for it.[8] Reading al-Ğabartī's notes on this period, one gets the impression that officers, scientists and soldiers of the expedition generally conformed to Egyptian values and norms in their public behaviour. It seems as well that the social and economic reforms introduced by the French were socially welcomed and were not perceived as negating religious principles.[9] The only negative reference in the notes between 2 July and 23 October 1798 concerns a few new taxes, especially on merchants in Cairo, which were, according to al-Ğabartī, collected very nicely.[10]

Napoleon seemed to be very interested in establishing positive contact with the leading scholars of al-Azhar. He addressed them as "the great men" of the *umma* and appointed ten of them to the governing council, *dīwān*, which was headed by Shaykh aš-Šarqāwī.[11] However, the scholars, even those who worked with the French authority, were sceptical and resigned. I would argue that this attitude was articulated in the two forms described in the first section of my paper. The first form was distancing themselves from the clear material-technological manifestations and cultural symbols of the French presence in Egypt. Al-Ǧabartī reports on 1 September 1798 that Napoleon tried to convince members of the governing council to wear uniforms in the three colours of the French flag or to stick French badges on their dress. The shaykhs, with the exception of Shaykh as-Sādāt, directly refused and resisted his pressure.[12] When the French flew a gas balloon over Cairo, an event which fascinated the majority of the city's population, Shaykh aš-Šarqāwī claimed that it was satanic work and accused the French of trying to seduce the population.[13] Secondly, the local discourse was purified from the local, non-authentic extensions of the cultural-religious Other. Al-Azhar scholars identified the French as being Christian and foreigners, and thus their local equivalents were Copts as well as native and Arab Christians and Jews. They began to vehemently criticize the appointment of these groups to governmental councils[14], although this was a phenomenon which was socially familiar and locally accepted in previous phases.[15]

Leading Azhar scholars organized and led the first uprising in Cairo against the French, which broke out on 21 October 1798. During the first two days, Muslims attacked and killed not only French officers and soldiers, but also Copts, other native Christians, and Jews and burned down some of their houses. On 23 October as French cavalry soldiers entered the al-Azhar mosque and killed many Muslims, al-Ǧabartī notes that they were described for the first time as blasphemous.[16] Although Napoleon tried in November to gain minimal acceptance from al-Azhar scholars by granting a general amnesty for religious scholars and by arresting and killing several Copts and Jews (according to al-Ǧabartī for no apparent reason[17]), they kept up and even strengthened their oppositional attitude. Al-Ǧabartī writes that several shaykhs, especially Shaykh Ḥasan al-ᶜAṭṭār, described the governmental councils and the French orders as being non-Islamic. The French, the Copts and other native Christians were accused of corrupting the religious morale of the Muslim population, especially of women.[18] The universalist message of the French Revolution, which the French authority attempted to disseminate through the then most modern communication technologies, namely newspapers and leaflets, seemed not to have been heard. Al-Ǧabartī writes that the most important event of the first year of the expedition was the French decision not to send the annual wrapper of the holy *kaᶜba*.[19]

However, it seems that this negative perception was not shared by all Egyptian Muslims and that there were other local, positive perceptions of the French. Al-Ǧabartī reports extensively on the local fascination with French technology and science, even when these were applied to aspects of the sacred. On 5 December 1798, he writes that he himself visited the "house of the scientists" several times where he saw a "nice big book", the biography of the Prophet containing his picture and pictures of his companions. He honoured this effort and described it as *iǧtihād*.[20]

It seems to me that al-Azhar scholars consolidated their local Islamic discourse and integrated a global Islamic dimension into it in the last two years of the French occupation. Al-Ǧabartī reports on the trip of a few shaykhs to the cities of Mecca and Istanbul where they informed their brothers in Islam of the situation in the "Egyptian lands" and tried to get military and financial support. On the 6 June 1799 he notes that several men from *al-Ḥiǧāz* region came to upper Egypt and fought there against French soldiers.[21] In April 1800, leading Azhar scholars managed to mobilize great sections of the Muslim population of Cairo and led a second uprising against the French, which seems to have given the scholars greater popularity. In his notes on the last months of the occupation, al-Ǧabartī refers several times to al-Azhar as the weapon of the *umma* against Christians.[22]

In the years following the withdrawal of the French, a process of intellectual and religious reassessing of their social and economic reforms and their scientific methods took place. Several religious scholars, who seemed to have found a new political role, were the leading figures. In this context, modern universal ideas of equality, liberty and scientific progress were critically received. Certain negative appropriations of the cultural-religious Other were modified and "modern" political and economic ideas were integrated into a newly formulated discourse of cultural authenticity.[23]

Worshippers of the Devil: Cairo in January-February 1997

On 24 January 1997, the official speaker of the Egyptian Ministry of the Interior announced that the security forces arrested 76 students of the American University of Cairo and the two state universities, Cairo and ʿAin Šams, who were accused of being members of a satanic organization which called itself the "worshippers of the devil". He said that the Ministry of the Interior had several indications that certain foreign states and organizations were involved in promoting the activities of the Satanists. On the next day, the then newly appointed Mufti of Egypt, Shaykh Muḥammad Naṣr Farīd accused them of being apostates and called upon the government to implement religious judgment on them. What followed was highly emotional and religiously oriented public interest on the issue and intensive journalistic coverage which attempted to bring out the secret facts of the organization, its origins, its practices, and its relations to foreign powers.[24]

I would argue that a dominant discourse emerged and was shared by the governmental and oppositional, liberal and conservative press alike. Depending on partial and/or invented information, it negatively located what was conceived as the global phenomenon of Satanism in four different contexts in which multiple layers of the local and the global interact. Firstly, it identified the history and geography of the religious and cultural Other, this time defined as the secular, Jewish dominated West. The "story" is as follows: Modern Satanism started in central Europe in the eighteenth century and was led by rich Jewish families (Rothschild was often mentioned) which aimed at undermining Christian dominance and achieving political power. The first Satanist societies were discovered by the German authorities in 1784 and their members had to flee to Switzerland. Later on, at the beginning of the twentieth century, the Satanists immigrated to the United States where they benefited from the secular atmosphere of the country and managed to reorganize themselves. In recent times, several of these satanic organizations were claimed to have close contacts with international Zionism and the state of Israel. This is the second context. From Israel and through Israeli Intelligence, the Egyptian satanic organization was initiated and sponsored.

The third context is found in the realm of global economic, technological and communication networks which are supposed to be dominated by the West, and again, by international Zionism. It seems to me that a very interesting model of how these networks function was developed and put forward as an explanatory framework. It reads as follows: The Internet and international television channels were disseminating cultural commodities (electronic information, music video-clips, documentaries, movies, etc.) which contain the specific repertoire of Satanism. The sacred books of the organization, such as the so-called "Black Bible" came from the States and Israel. The special satanic clothes and symbols, such as T-shirts with skulls, stars of David, and swastikas were produced in Cairo and Alexandria and sold in small shops in several rich districts; which leads us then to the fourth context: The local one. The Satanists held their black masses and practised their abnormal sexual activities at international restaurants and hotels in Cairo, such as McDonalds and the Hilton hotels which were considered to be material extensions of the cultural-religious Other on local soil.

I think there were other relevant layers of the local context, which were perceived as being either negative aspects of local realities and histories or extensions of the cultural-religious Other. These include the history of satanic ideas and movements in Islam, the anti-religious secular intellectuals of the Arab world, and the current policy of the Egyptian state toward religion.

Several journalists claimed that books by the philosopher and poet, al-Ḥallāǧ, as well as books about certain Sufi movements which worshipped the devil and were influenced by Greek and Jewish mythology were found in the apartments of several members of the organization. Westernized secular intellectuals and Marxists who were, in their view, mobilizing against religion had prepared Egyptian youth for these global poisons.[25] The state was accused, especially by Islamic oriented journalists, of indirectly promoting Satanists by its Westernized attitude and by reducing the time and space given to religious topics in the media as well as in the educational system. I would argue that these local layers were actually part of a local attempt to extend the scope of the discussion on the global threat of Satanism and to integrate other relevant Egyptian public debates such as the controversy between secular intellectuals and Islamists and the confrontation between the semi-secular state and several religious movements.

I will extend my argument to say that the journalistic portrayal of Egyptian Satanists reflected the analysed map of global-local interaction. Hence, the majority of them have in addition to their Egyptian nationality a Western one. All of them studied in Europe or the States for a while or were victims of the secular educational system of Egypt. All of them were in Sinai where they met satanic Israeli female secret service agents. All of them had access to the Internet and international television channels. All of them belonged to rich, secular, Westernized families.

I think that these local processes of dissociating and appropriating the perceived global threat of Satanism within an overarching religious, anti-Western, anti-Israeli, and anti-secular discourse, in which both Muslim and Coptic journalists and writers participated, have had several important social and cultural impacts. Firstly, they led to intensive public interest in global communication networks and local familiarization with modern technologies. Secondly, one can witness the emergence of a, relatively speaking, liberal form of public discourse on issues such as non-marital sexual relations and homosexuality which had previously been taboo in the Egyptian press. Thirdly, in a critical local situation (clashes between Muslims and Copts, Islamist motivated violence, and a severe economic crisis), the discussion on Satanism reasserted the existence of a social and cultural consensus based on common ethical and religious values, shared by both Muslims and Copts. A phenomenon which can be described as a sign of an emerging civil religion. Fourthly, a new public controversy on "other worshippers of the devil" was generated, dealing with issues such as political and economic corruption within the ruling regime, at exactly the moment when the Egyptian state was trying to limit these discussions through new press laws.

Lady Diana and Doudi al-Fayed: the Destruction of a Romantic Dream

As in the case of the Egyptian worshippers of the devil, the universalized love affair between Diana and Doudi, the son of the famous Egyptian businessman Muhammad al-Fayed, led to a highly emotional and intensive coverage in the Egyptian press throughout the two months of July and August 1997, motivated by the fact that one of the protagonists is partially of an Egyptian origin. I would argue that quite apart from their political orientation and the profile of their respective print media, writers and journalists articulated a three-phase explanatory discourse which gained amazing credibility in the Egyptian public sphere. These three phases with their respective discursive constructions, categories, and causalities can be distinguished as follows: The romantic phase which lasted till the shock of Paris on 31 August, the phase of formulation and propagation of different conspiracy theories after the death of Diana and Doudi, and the phase of nationalistic and religious oriented local introversion.

A quick glance at a few headlines of the analysed 900 articles and commentaries which were published in the period between 10 August and 18 September 1997 in 33 different newspapers, weeklies and magazines[26] would suffice to point out the major lines of argumentation in each of the three phases. At the beginning of the coverage the romantic aspect of the relationship between Diana and the Oriental dream prince Doudi was overemphasized. One encounters headlines such as "The realization of a romantic dream: Diana and Doudi get marry by the end of September." In spite of the then well known "racist" campaign against the Fayeds in the British yellow press, producers of the local discourse went on investing a whole range of future hopes in the love affair and creating an ideal picture out of Diana and Doudi in which both of them were actually substituted by the Occident and the Orient subsequently. However, this "historic" optimism came to a brutal end with their sudden death. Across the press landscape we find feelings of bitterness and despair, and attempts to explain the dramatic change with the help of the traditional causalities and explanation frameworks within the Egyptian and Arab popular culture. Both trends were reflected in headlines such as "The anti-Arab racism is responsible for the death of Diana and Doudi", "Diana was killed because of her love for an Egyptian", "Diana died as a Muslim woman", "Is Queen Elisabeth responsible for the death of Diana and Doudi?", and "Did the British secret service kill Diana and Doudi?" Reading such headlines one gets the impression that a certain hysterical condition took over the minds of the Egyptian public sphere and got out of control. Less than two weeks after their death, the local traumatic experience and the psychic crisis seemed to have been forgotten and a process of nationalist and religious motivated "Back to The Roots" was initiated. Thus the observer encounters headlines such as "God's mercy for Diana and Doudi", or in the form of a request addressed to the Muslim community

"Recite al-Fātiḥa (the first seven verses of the holy Koran) for Diana and Doudi". In a collective letter addressed to Muhammad al-Fayed he was asked to leave Britain, return to his homeland, and invest his wealth in developing Egyptian society and the economy as a first step in preparing a new, but supposedly final confrontation with the racist West. The journalists wrote: "The racist Englishmen killed your son. They never respected your great economic and political role. Return back to your country and regain your dignity as an Egyptian."

During the first phase of the press coverage the love affair was locally interpreted as a symbolic Western acceptance of Egypt, the Arab world and even the whole Muslim world. Egyptian journalists expected that a local figure would finally be treated positively in the Western press. The romance between the European princess and the Oriental sunny boy evoked hopes for a better understanding and a positive relation between the Occident and the Orient which could, according to local perception, be established on mutual respect and cross-cultural sensibility. Behind this interpretation was the belief that the "love alliance" would lead to major changes in the British policy toward ethnic and religious minorities (more tolerance) as well as in foreign policy toward the Arab-Muslim world and the Palestinian problem (more sensitivity for Arab demands and Muslim hopes).

This ensemble of hopes projected into the love affair led to the articulation of a different attitude toward the cultural-religious Other, the Christian West. On the contrary, to the predominant exclusionist mode of perception and interaction between the Self and the Other in the previously analysed two cases, was added the emergence of a positive local presentation of the subjects and symbols of the Other and a Western-adjusted presentation of local figures which aimed at maximizing the possibilities of the "historic reconciliation" between the Occident and the Orient. Both protagonists, Diana and Doudi, were deconstructed and reconstructed in a manner conforming to Egyptian traditions and religious oriented perceptions of female-male relationships. The aspect of the non-marital sexual relationship, the fact that they were neither married nor engaged when their affair became public, normally grounds for condemnation in an Islamic dominated setting, was deliberately ignored. Since this aspect was, however, well known in the local context, several journalists reacted by spreading the rumour that the lovers were planning to get married soon. Contrary to earlier commentaries in the Egyptian press on the private life of Diana in which her affairs and scandals were negatively discussed, it seemed as if the journalists had suddenly discovered her worldwide humanitarian initiatives and her inner goodness. Her private crises were reinterpreted as bad luck and/or tragic destiny since childhood.

Complementary to these efforts, the Egyptian actors, Doudi al-Fayed and his family, were partially authenticated, kept, however, their appreciated Western identity in this phase. This meant that as locals who had lived for decades in the Western diaspora they gained even in linguistic terms, a newly invented Egyptian, Arab and Muslim identity. Since the invention of the authentic Fayed-identity was accomplished in such a creative way, it is worth describing it here in detail. The grandfathers of the Fayeds were discovered as great leaders and fighters of the national independence movement throughout the nineteenth and twentieth century. Doudi's father, Muhammad al-Fayed, was depicted as a modern Egyptian Pharaoh who had never ignored his origins, had kept in contact with remaining relatives in Alexandria, and had always tried both morally and financially, to help his diasporic fellow countrymen and brothers in Islam to cope with the entirely different living conditions in the West. The emphasis on firstly his alleged yearly pilgrimage to the holy places of Islam and the Islamic architecture and decoration of his palaces in Europe was meant to project the first indications of an authentic religious identity besides the already established national one. Whereas Doudi was postulated as a modern Arab hero who possessed both the sensuality and charm of the Orient and the rationality of the Occident. Stressing these specific qualities of both cultures can be actually interpreted as an implicit local acceptance of the classic Western perception of the Self and the Arab-Islamic Other. I would argue that this attitude symbolizes an attempt to get discursively closer to the West on any terms in order to protect the imagined historical chance.

However, as the negative campaign against the Fayeds in the British yellow press became known, the maximization of the romantic dream in the form of a possible alliance between the Christians and the Muslims was given up, the category of the Other was immediately reactivated. Emancipated from this projected inter-cultural alliance, both figures, Diana and Doudi, were partially purified from certain Western attributes and consequently locally integrated. In this context, three central tendencies can be identified:

Firstly, the origins and contemporary articulation of the ideology of racism were localized in the history and geography of the cultural-religious Other. The traumatic experiences of the colonial era, the Arab-Israeli conflict, and the recent second Gulf war were quickly reloaded. The West was discredited for being essentially materialist, anti-religious, and anti-Arab. This change in local perception was reflected in several fine nuances in the press coverage such as the explanation of the British authorities' refusal to give Muhammad al-Fayed British citizenship as being proof of wide-ranging racist attitudes in the West.

Secondly, the local construction of the global figure Diana assumed new dimensions. A journalistic rumour that she converted to Islam did the rounds in Egypt. The alleged conversion was propagated as a conscious decision by Diana to save herself from the materialist West. The testimony of an unknown Pakistani *imām* was instrumentalized in this context as neutral and credible confirmation. He is supposed to have said that Diana informed him as early as

1991 about her decision to convert to Islam and revealed to him that she was waiting for the "right man" to guide and protect her on this difficult path. Hence a new religiously connoted historical mission for Doudi was automatically established and compensated locally for the loss of the dream of historical reconciliation with the West. Complementary to the religious assimilation of the global figure, nationalist and traditional modes of absorption were developed. Several writers asserted that Diana was planning to leave Great Britain after her marriage with Doudi and move to Egypt, whose civilization and culture she appreciated. A few others went a step further and claimed that she would disappear from public life after the honeymoon and spend the rest of her life peacefully in the house of her beloved husband. One could argue that from the ideals of Egyptian popular music and oral narratives on love, family and partnership, the global figure Diana was reconstructed as a "traditional" Egyptian woman, dreaming only of her future husband and their shared family nest.

Thirdly, in spite of the aforementioned two adjustments in the local discourse, Egyptian journalists still wanted to convince the West of the golden chance it was losing by condemning the love affair between Diana and Doudi, and to negate the racist attacks on the Fayeds from within a Western sensitive argumentation. Thus Doudi and his father were reconstructed as superb examples for local cosmopolitans. The picture drawn was as follows: Doudi is a promising young man who embodies the true qualities of the Orient, openness, sensibility, charm, sensuality, honesty, and generosity. Due to his education in Europe and his experience as a successful businessman he was able to accumulate and internalize the best aspects of Western civilization, education, rationality and the manners of a gentleman. This hybrid character was best spelled out in this citation: "Doudi owns the charm of the Orient, the darkness of the Egyptians, the language of the Englishmen, and the wealth of the Americans."[27] For these qualities Doudi was perceived as the only man able and willing to help Diana overcome the crisis in her life. This was, beside the previously mentioned historical mission of helping Diana convert to Islam, the second local legitimation of the love affair. The father was presented as one of the greatest men in the economic and political life of Great Britain. Four elements were stressed; he continuously supported and stabilized the British economy at several crucial moments. In the typical manner of an Arab shadow-ruler, he supported the defeat of the Tories in the last election because of his disappointment with the position of the former government concerning his application for British citizenship. He is in the process of establishing a political party for the defense of the political and cultural rights of ethnic and religious minorities Europe wide. Lastly, rumours about his illegal business deals were excluded as racist and Zionist propaganda. On a second level, the importance of the father for Diana's life was produced and projected in such a traditional manner that I suppose the first associations which will spring to the mind of an Egyptian reader will contain well known tragic scenes from old Egyptian movies of the 1930s and 1940s. The relevant scene for our analysis here was constructed as follows: Muhammad al-Fayed sitting beside Diana's father and listening to his whisper, a few moments before the death of the latter. Al-Fayed promises him to take care of his daughter (the local formulation would have been "I will protect your daughter with my eyes"). Diana's father dies. The honest Egyptian stands up and leaves the dark room. From that moment on al-Fayed envisaged Diana married to his son as the best way to live up to his promise. I regard this last element as the third local legitimation of the relationship between Diana and Doudi.

The shocking news from Paris initiated a second phase in the press coverage in Egypt which was characterized by three central tendencies that equally separated the Self from the Other, the Egyptian-Arab-Islamic identity from the Western-Christian one:

Firstly, the local absorption of the global figure reached its peak. The assertion of the majority of Egyptian journalists that Diana was pregnant when she died is tantamount to organic absorption. Since it was assumed that the embryo was Egyptian and Muslim, Diana was purified through Motherhood from all traces of the Other, her original Self. She was integrated into the very organic essence of the local identity.

Secondly, the hybrid and Western attributes of the Fayeds were completely excluded. Local representation of Doudi and his father transformed then from elegant cosmopolitans who were able to unite and compromise cultural contradictions between the Occident and the Orient (rationality and sensuality) to victims of the racist Other and then to defenders of the humiliated Egyptian-Arab-Muslim Self. The exclusion of the Western elements and the authentication of the local figures were articulated along an invented religious identity. The Islamic burial of Doudi as well as Islamic mourning rituals observed at the family palace in London were placed at the centre of the press coverage.

Thirdly, subsequent to the separation between the Self and the Other it became discursively possible, and to a certain extent even necessary, to formulate different conspiracy theories which functioned as explanatory models in order to come to terms with the tragic change. I would argue that three major versions can be discerned:

1. The racist version: Several journalists assumed that the British royal family, Europe and the West would have never allowed a marriage between the white princess with her "blue blood" and a dark Egyptian, Arab and African from the Third World. They would never have permitted that prince William have Arab half brothers and sisters, that names such as Muḥammad or Fāṭima become part of royal reality in the coming century. The planned assassination was the only way out.

2. The religious version: It was based on the assumption that the Christian Occident had killed one of its princesses in order to prevent her from getting married to a Muslim and converting to Islam. Great Britain which assumed, according to the adherents of this version, a leading role in the crusades throughout the Middle Ages[28] and was the major colonizing power in modern times had now returned to its bloody history against the Islamic world. The origins of the religious formulated conspiracy theory were localized in the Orient's negative historical experiences with the Occident.

3. The nationalist version: The respective scenario was grounded on the belief that the Jewish dominated West and the state of Israel assassinated Doudi because he had dared to get closer to Diana. Advocates of this theory argued that the "Jews" feared the love affair and possible marriage would lead to major changes in European policy toward the Middle East and to a strategic alliance between Great Britain and the Arab countries. Therefore they killed both of them. The local invention of evidence for this version was especially creative. Several Egyptian journalists claimed that the paparazis who followed Diana and Doudi on the "black" evening in Paris were Jews and that the Israeli press had actually backed the whole racist campaign against the Fayeds from the very beginning.

One could certainly argue that these are classic explanations which emerge time after time in the Arab-Islamic public sphere when certain wishes or visions could not be realized or were destroyed. Conspiracy theories certainly represent one of the common tools of the defeated and/or humiliated Self to come to terms with its own crisis. However, I think the propagation and public credibility of these theories in the Egyptian press discourse on Diana and Doudi were mainly due to the gradually developed local exclusion of and separation from the West, and the systematic instrumentalization of the unclear aspects of the accident.

Less than two weeks after the phase of conspiracy, feelings of hatred against the cultural-religious Other were transformed into Self-introversion and an attempt to reestablish the "authentic" essence of the local context, now defined as the total negation of the Other. Since the West remained racist, even against someone who was part of its social life and had internalized its cultural values, Muhammad al-Fayed was requested to leave Great Britain and return to Egypt as a first step toward local introversion. The previously mentioned headlines "God's mercy for Diana and Doudi" and "Recite al-Fātiḥa for Diana and Doudi" emphasize the general level of perception within a holistic constructed Islamic community. The we-form gained new integrative and healing potentiality in this context through the elevation of both protagonists to martyrs, whose myth was to become sacred. The local absorption of the global figure and the authentication of the local actors came to an end at this point. The maximization of the we-community and its eternal ontological pain systematically caused by the Other in the form of martyrdom, and the articulation of a local version of the "Clash of Civilizations" in which the collective Self is supposed to abolish the Other and hence liberate itself from its pain, entail a vision of a major break within a perceived negative historical continuity, a sort of triumphant end of history. Processes of hybridization between the Occident and the Orient, between the local and the global were supposed to be terminated and the exclusionary purity of the Self to be reestablished.

The developed analysis in this section shows that local representation of the globalized love affair and death of Diana and Doudi was based on a continuous deconstruction of originally Western but systematically universalized versions and interpretations and on a positioning of the protagonists in shifting local settings. Thus Diana was increasingly locally absorbed and the Fayeds gradually authenticated and religiously purified. Following the romantic phase and similar to the two cases previously analysed, producers of the local discourse on Diana and Doudi operated with categories which depended on an inclusion-exclusion relationship between the Self and the Other and purification of the local context and associated global figures from traces of the cultural-religious Other.

Concluding Remarks

I would like to conclude with a summary of the three main points developed in detail during the course of this paper. Firstly, contrary to economic and financial globalization, processes of cultural globalization have no single geographic centre. They are not based on a one-sided flow of cultural commodities from somewhere to somewhere with a unifying or homogenizing impact worldwide. Globalized cultural commodities are continuously being deconstructed and reconstructed in multiple local contexts. There is a continuous effort to dissociate and reappropriate them through several local actors with shifting perceptions, interests, and modes of representation. Put differently, they are being disseminated in a very pluralistic manner, which leads to heterogeneous social and cultural impacts. Secondly, throughout my paper I tried to sketch out an explanatory pattern of the processes of cultural globalization. If I may sum it up in a few words, I would say that globalized cultural commodities are, in a first step, being localized in the geography and history of a constructed cultural-religious Other, which is to be either locally absorbed or negated in a second step. Thirdly, I claim that local discourses dealing with globalized culture symbols and discursive messages can, despite their essentializations and their hysterical representation of the Other, sometimes pave the way for creative solutions to and modern interaction forms with the pressures of globalization.

Notes

1. It is important to note that al-Ǧabartī wrote a first version of his reports in which the French policy and reforms in Egypt were positively assessed and a second one in which he developed a critical and negative stance to the three years of the expedition. Although it would have been interesting to compare both versions, I am limiting my analysis in this paper to the first version of the reports as published under the title *Al-Muḫtār min tārīḫ al-Ǧabartī*, edited by Muḥammad Qandīl al-Baqlī, Cairo 1958.
2. Both his name and the name of his father became well known to non-Arabic readers in the course of the Western press coverage of the affair, so that it is appropriate to write them in the journalistic way instead of transliterating them.
3. For further information see Georg Stauth, Islam und westlicher Rationalismus. Der Beitrag des Orientalismus zur Entstehung der Soziologie, Frankfurt/Main 1993.
4. Martin Heidegger, Sein und Zeit, Tübingen 1993, pp. 240.
5. A formulation which al-Ǧabartī found very sound. See Al-Muḫtār min tārīḫ al-Ǧabartī, Cairo 1958, p. 270.
6. According to al-Ǧabartī, Napoleon advised religious scholars in each village to seize the private property of the Mamluks in all its forms. Ibid., p. 247.
7. Ibid., pp. 245-7.
8. Ibid., pp. 261-262 & pp. 334-335.
9. Ibid., p. 272.
10. Ibid., p. 257.
11. Ibid., pp. 254-255.
12. Ibid., pp. 262-263.
13. Ibid., pp. 281-282.
14. Ibid., pp. 294-295.
15. Heinz Halm, Die Ayyubiden. In: Ulrich Haarmann (ed.), Geschichte der arabischen Welt, München 1987, pp. 200-216.
16. Al-Muḫtār min tārīḫ al-Ǧabartī, Cairo 1958, pp. 274-276.
17. Ibid., p. 281.
18. Al-Ǧabartī refers to bars, prostitution and public cafés for women and men. Ibid., p. 399 & pp. 422-423.
19. Ibid., pp. 307-315.
20. A very positive assessment of a practice which was then religiously forbidden. Ibid., p. 284.
21. Ibid., p. 318.
22. Ibid., pp. 363-373.
23. For further information see Peter Gran, Islamic Roots of Capitalism. Egypt 1760-1840, Austin-London 1979.
24. The analysis of this section depends on the evaluation of over 1000 articles and commentaries which were published during January and February 1997 in the daily newspapers al-Ahrām, al-Aḫbār, al-Masāʾ, al-Ahrām al-masāʾī, al-Wafd, aš-Šaʿb and al-Ǧumhūrīya, the weeklies al-ʿĀlam al-yaum, al-Usbūʿ, al-Kifāḥ al-ʿarabī, al-Maidān, al-Waṭan al-ʿarabī, Ṣaut al-umma, al-Ahālī, al-Ahrām al-ʿarabī, ad-Dustūr and al-Aḥrār and the magazines ʿAqīdatī, Ṣabāḥ al-ḫair, al-Ḥaqīqa, Rūz al-Yūsuf, Āḫir Sāʿa, al-Idāʿa waʾt-tīlīfizyūn, al-Muṣawwar and Uktūbar.

25 In this context both the lecture of the Syrian philosopher Ṣādiq Ǧalāl al-ʿAẓm on "The Rehabilitation of the Devil" in Beirut in 1966 and the defense of the Syrian Islam scholar ʿAzīz al-ʿAẓma of the Satanic Verses of Salman Rushdie were mentioned.
26 The analysed articles were published in the daily newspapers al-Ahrām, al-Aḫbār, al-Masāʾ, al-Ahrām al-masāʾī, al-Wafd, aš-Šaʿb and al-Ǧumhūrīya, the weeklies al-ʿĀlam al-yaum, al-Usbūʿ, al-Kifāḥ al-ʿarabī, al-Maidān, al-Waṭan al-ʿarabī, Ṣaut al-umma, al-Ahālī, al-Ahrām al-ʿarabī, al-Ḥayāt al-miṣriyya, as-Siyāsī al-miṣrī, al-ʿArabī, ad-Dustūr and al-Aḥrār and the magazines ʿAqīdatī, al-Maǧalla, al-Wasaḫ, al-Ḥaqīqa, Rūz al-Yūsuf, Āḫir Sāʿa, Ṣabāḥ al-ḫair, al-Iḏāʿa waʾt-tilīfīsyūn, Niṣf ad-dunyā, Ḥawwāʾ, al-Kawākib, al-Muṣawwar and Uktūbar.
27 Al-ʿĀlam al-yaum, 2.9.1997.
28 An interpretation which does not correspond to the bulk of historical research on this subject.

Global Influences and Discontinuities in a Religious Tradition: Public Islam and the "New" Šarīʿa

Armando Salvatore

I

The present article tackles the issue of the metamorphosis of religious traditions that occurs in the context of their increasing exposition to influences of global communication. In particular, it focuses on the alteration of the understanding of *šarīʿa* within Islamic traditions, effected by the modernization of state rule, the emergence of a modern press and a modern public sphere, and the process of reform (*iṣlāḥ*) of these traditions that engaged significant portions of the religious and intellectual élite. I will concentrate on developments within the Egyptian arena, and propose a historical screening and an actual diagnosis of *šarīʿa* claims in their multiple normative and regulating aspects.

The Islamic *šarīʿa* (*as-šarīʿa al-islāmiyya*) is the religious norm that Muslims see as the emanation of God's Will (*šarʿ*), revealed in the Koran. It is a consensual view that the grade, intensity and extension of *šarīʿa*'s normative power vary considerably both historically and geographically. By *šarīʿa* claims I mean any demand for the implementation, codification and application of the Islamic *šarīʿa* as the perfect, definitive articulation of divine will and divine norm. My argument will take charge of evaluating the impact of the new rules of global communication within and through modern public spheres on the metamorphosis of this particular moral-legal dimension of Islamic traditions. However, I argue against reducing this process of alteration through global constraints (or - trying to spell out the metaphor of the globe - through the formation of a "world society") to a linear pressure on *šarīʿa* to become a mere tool for the affirmation of a particular identity, or for asserting the belonging to an autonomous legal tradition (a claim of "legal identity"). I will opt rather for interrogating the reasons for the enduring - though quickly metamorphosing - transcendence-bound, specifically religious rationale of *šarīʿa*, as well as for suggesting a reading of why it has been metamorphosed through major breakthroughs in public life during the modern era.

The factors of globalization analysed here are not so much the constraints of the project of state building and state centralization pursued by Muḥammad ʿAlī and his successors in Egypt. These developments are to be explained in the context of an increasing market and financial interdependence of Egypt with Europe, that asked for an efficient mobilization of the working force, and for measures for securing the inner, national control over the whole process.[1] Of more immediate significance here is the globalization of the requirements of legal regulation and intellectual communication in the public sphere that followed the centralization of state authority in the framework of increasing colonial influence, and led to the concomitant reform of the legal and judicial system, as well as to the rise of a modern press. In both cases, and as a common rationale, this process can be defined as the rise of autonomous professionals of law and intellectual communication who were faithful to the new national project, but did not become mere instruments of the ruler's policy priorities, in any case severely restricted by British colonial presence.

This presence was the last chapter of a century-long history of European influence in Egypt, where the French, after Napoleon's military occupation of the country (1798-1801), had been long prominent in lending a legitimacy to modern canons and disciplines of law, education and discourse rationality, by way of acting as advisers and planners in several branches of the administration.[2] However, this was no one-way channel of influence, as Egyptian cultural elites did not partake passively in the new public and intellectual game linking Egypt to Europe during the nineteenth century. Much attention has been devoted to the case of Shaykh Rifāʿa aṭ-Ṭahṭāwī (1801-1871), graduate of the Islamic university al-Azhar, who had a formative influence on the Egyptian public sphere even prior to the rise of autonomous press organs that no longer fulfilled a merely administrative channel of communication, between the 1860s and 1880s. Through his contacts and exchanges with French society and culture, and in particular with French intellectual and legal rationalities, aṭ-Ṭahṭāwī gained fresh intellectual power and legitimacy to implement a richer know-how in the reforms of the country, according to the vision that he was consistently reshaping a renaissance of Islamic knowledge and social power. He was the one who translated the French civil code into Arabic, seeing in it a valuable tool of civilization and state power.

But when we talk about globalization - as here, of the globalization of normative frameworks - a more compelling force is evoked than those at work within the culturally rich and politically tense environment within which aṭ-Ṭahṭāwī developed his intercultural competencies in shaping a proto-national project of social reform. The process of restructuring the understanding and public influence of *šarīʿa* from about the time when aṭ-Ṭahṭāwī died is a good case of how globalizing influences work unpredictably in national contexts, enhance social complexity, and multiply the fields where rationalities of law claim to regulate social transactions. Globalization is a catalyst of complexity in the sense that the control of social reform and transformation to a large extent gets out of the control of the autochthonous ruler, the older and newer intellectual elites, and the colonial power. This complexity is the result of the formation of rationalities specific to subsystems of social action and communication and indifferent to rules of reason valid for all society. Here at stake is in particular the development of an increasingly unbridgeable tension between the reform of the legal system and the visions and ambitions to reform the moral norms of society. The metamorphosis of *šarīʿa* is to a large extent located in this field of tension, and is driven by attempts to bridge the gap. This is a tension not specific to modernising Muslim societies, nor to colonised societies in general. It is a tension inherent in the modernization of normative frameworks and legal institutions within world society at large.

In this sense, globalization cannot be reduced to colonization. Contrary to a popular view of globalization as claiming its opposite process, "localization" – both duly contributing to put order in a fast modernising globe through dialectically matching the microcosms of new communities with the macrocosms of global, autonomous rationalities – the present case study shows the importance of social and normative mediation, a process irreducible to the narrative of a balancing between the global and the local. This mediation is represented here by the idea of a religious reform in charge of rewriting and reactivating religious traditions in new guises under altered global conditions. It will become evident that the activity and goals of reformers cannot be reduced to a localised "response" to imperialism. Their endeavours are inspired by a universal view of reason and law, and this pursuit increases – quite paradoxically, and contrary to the intention of the reformers – the unpredictability and complexity within society.

The approach I pursue in this article escapes the short-cut, "essentialist" temptation to attribute this suffered, and even entropic search for legal effectiveness of *šarīʿa* to its idiosyncrasy to feed into a modern legal system, and dares instead to explain this erratic movement and the lack of covariance between normative aspirations and legal effectiveness by pointing to processes of differentiation and specialization that are typical of modern societies. I will try to illustrate different dimensions of *šarīʿa* claims to normativity and validity (in German *Geltung*), that can only be understood through an analysis of the public sphere and of public contests.[3] Here applicable law plays an important role more for its publicly privileged status of being the law of the state, enjoying the endorsing of institutions that carry the prestige of vested public authority, than for the actual rate of enforcement of the law, towards which many legal and non-legal actors in Egypt would reasonably express a well-dosed degree of scepticism.

We cannot start from the ahistorical presupposition of *šarīʿa* as a mere symbolic shibboleth good for all public contests and for all seasons, where the Islamicity of particular practices or institutions is at stake. It is rather in the framework of a growing, though not necessarily functional, differentiation of the fields of social action and exercise of authority associated with divine rules, that *šarīʿa* acquires new impetus, or at least ambition, to impose itself as a norm regulating other norms, and rationally integrating sectorial rationalities or irrationalities: in other words – as I will try to illustrate in the following – the power and shape of (or the aspiration to deliver) a "metanorm". This is what keeps šarīʿa claims discursively and symbolically well integrated, in spite of the primary dysfunctionality between their social fields of pertinence.

The option of situating the analysis of legal-constitutional processes and public controversies within the transformations in the modalities of transmission of special and general knowledge, as well as in the crafting of arguments effected by the rise, consolidation and structural transformation of what has been termed the "public sphere", not surprisingly summons the work of Jürgen Habermas, and in particular of the first and the most recent among his major treatises (1962 and 1992). To be true to Habermas, from whose work much of the terminology here used is borrowed, his approach considers the rise of law discourse as a typical achievement of Western thought and political history, and exclusive to them, so that a new operationalization of this conceptual apparatus with reference to a context historically extraneous to these accomplishments is, from a truly Habermasian perspective, quite heterodox. More than that, my understanding of "metanorm" here is certainly all too spurious and eclectic from the viewpoint of Habermas' theoretical approach. However, this option can prove useful in order to re-conceptualise the range of moral, normative and prescriptive orders associated with claims for the application, codification or constitutional consolidation of šarīʿa, and its analytic utility will provide the first test for such a heterodox extension.

II

As a first step, we are called to consider the view of a "šarīʿa society"[4], perpetuating itself through subsequent phases of social differentiation well into the era of nation-states. The brutal schematization of successive differentiations, built on the fragmentary research available to us, that I am going to suggest, could make us aware that the construction itself of šarīʿa as a conceptual tool defining an entity-like normative system has been gradual, and not in-built in any particular legal-cultural repertoire residing either in Scripture or in the historic experience of the proto-community (the *umma*) of Muḥammad, his companions, and the first rightly-guided caliphs. "The šarīʿa is a concept with which Islamic thinkers in the formative and classical periods were not concerned."[5]

First, a šarʿī episteme (i.e., the view of a normative authority irradiating from God's šarʿ, the divine will) differentiated from the exegesis of scripture and the original experience of order within the community. Next, the idea of šarīʿa as a definite normative order consisting of punctual prescriptions, differentiated from the general šarʿī episteme, here intended as a possible and increasingly legitimate, though in no way exclusive modality of categorization.

A functioning legal system run by law experts, by jurists (*fuqahā'*, the specialists of *fiqh*) later differentiated from *šarī'a* as a normative order, without this differentiation being complete in pre-modern times. Legal careers did not acquire an autonomous profile from the very first stages of instruction required of jurists, so that they remained bound to the general curriculum in religious sciences.

But there is enough historical evidence that the legal function of at least those religious specialists (*'ulamā'*) engaged as judges, as *qāḍī*s (different to the *muftī*s, who are dispensers of advisory legal opinions, to which I will come back later) became well differentiated from the general function of knowledge and guidance demanded of *'ulamā'*. Modern state-building, before the rise of a public sphere, completed this differentiation by increasingly stripping the formulation-interpretation of law from the hands of formally independent, religiously trained jurists, and made it a competence of state authorities. We know that this transition from jurists' law to national codification sustained by the state's sovereignty in fabricating law is no peculiarity of Muslim societies, but is also familiar to Western history.[6]

More interesting is the fact that in the process of transition, the juridical personnel and institutions nurturing this religious law lost legal competencies to the advantage of new courts set up by the state, but were not disrupted. These religious specialists underwent a process of reform, sometimes unwillingly under the pressure of a state desirous to restrain them, sometimes more actively, through the stimuli of contests in the newly created public spheres, finally by way of an impulse of reform developed by some *'ulamā'* under the double incentive of state-building, and of debates in the public sphere over issues of social welfare and of the common good. As we will see, a new normative view of consensus within the community (the *umma*) emerged in the process.

The classical Western literature on the Islamic *iṣlāḥ*, the current aiming at a "reform" of Islamic intellectual, including legal, traditions, has highlighted the role of leading thinkers, like Muḥammad 'Abduh (1849-1905), in their calling for an adaptation of *'ulamā'* competencies to the new situation.[7] Less stressed - in spite of a certain focus on the "creative" efforts of many reformers - has been that the *iṣlāḥ* contributed not only to setting the agenda of public debates, but to formulating the vocabulary and the rules, yes the meta-language and the metanorm, of the public sphere that was shaped in Egypt between the 1860s and 1880s. This was a process of expansion of the scope of press organs from being mainly the mouthpiece of political authority intent on rationalising communication down the echelons of an ever more complex bureaucracy, to becoming fora of expression of the political and cultural aspirations of an intellectual class in upheaval. In the case of religious reformers (the *muṣliḥūn*), this transformation encouraged them to conceive their *iṣlāḥ* as a reconstruction of divine norm, of šarī'a, to be performed through devoting a much more direct attention to the subject and its disciplining, as well as through recollecting different sectors of canonical observance and obligations around a much stronger notion of the Muslim as an individual, believer *and* citizen.[8] Through this focus, reformers, as we will see, redesigned the normative consensus in the public sphere, in the assumption that they were purifying a religious tradition corrupted by undue innovations, but more immediately whilst sharing the definition of the actual public agendas of the emerging nation-state politics.

In a certain sense, the šarī'a, as it is talked about today in both its morally "personalizable", and legally "systematizable" dimensions, was born out of these transformations. Crucial among them was the gradual de-institutionalization - more than abandonment[9] - of the religious law administered by 'ulamā' trained as jurists (fuqahā') within al-mahākim aš-šar'iyya, the "religious courts", or more precisely the "tribunals of the divine norm" (šar'). The major rupture in the competencies of these courts, before their suppression, and incorporation of their residual functions on matters of personal status in the secular system in 1956, was the institution of al-mahākim al-ahliyya, the "national", or "indigenous" courts in Egypt in 1883. Retrospectively, after their suppression, al-mahakim aš-šar'iyya have been called "Sarī'a tribunals" by analysts and actors alike in Western languages, in what looks like an inverted anachronism, as the view of šarī'a projected into them, a pretended šarī'a regulating subject and system, was much the product of the process that led to the disempowerment of these tribunals. But this process of normalization of the past, of construction of a normative tradition, is not peculiar to šarī'a. Any normative order negates fiercely that it was born at a certain moment in history through an arbitrary normative volition, through power games, via the selection and inscription into tables of commandments, through social differentiation. Law must *never* "begin".[10]

This is why we shall be allowed to see the formation of a "new" normative discourse of šarī'a in the process, called to bridge the gap between the traditionally revered divine norm, to be revived and given a new meaning in the face of the new challenges of modernization of society and the state, and the law, intended as positive, "secular" and issued of state sovereignty, respected and feared as powerful and necessary, but looked at in a quite instrumental way. Law was seen as a tool for regulating fields of social behaviour and for disciplining social subjects, a view that religious reformers largely partook with state authorities. More secular intellectuals looked at divine norm and secular law rather the other way around: they were more immediately fascinated and gratified by the new autonomous lawfulness of a growing state sustained by a vital nation (a process made more complex and dramatic in Egypt by the British military occupation of 1882, that was followed by the imposition of different degrees of control on several branches of the state machinery). These intellectuals - among which most prominent were legal professionals who graduated in state law schools - sought nonetheless a dialogue with religious authorities, and by revering the divine norm in their way were entangled in the same kind of dilemma faced by religious reformers: redefining the relationship between an abstract lawfulness derived from God's commandments that could not be deprived of its divine legitimacy and transcendent reference by a simple fiat of a state authority, and institutional legality.

This differentiation, tension and will of harmonization involving abstract normativity and legal system, lawfulness and law, did not result in loud claims of recuperating the legal efficacy of šarīʿa, and implementing its newly assembled normativity within the system of positive law. The situation lasted until the late 1920s. In the period that immediately preceded the institution of the national courts, the Egyptian Minister of Justice Muḥammad Qadri had worked extensively on a project of codification of šarīʿa, but with the exception of the laws of personal status, on which the religious courts were allowed to keep their competencies in full, the national courts adopted French-style codes, designed to suit a French-style system of tribunals. However, apart from the form and structures of codes and courts that best suited the imperatives of order and control of a fast centralising state (even more so at the moment it faced a traumatic colonial penetration that never reduced it to a "colony"), many elements of šarīʿa were maintained. The decision to keep the influence of šarīʿa on the codes adopted by the national courts at a low profile originated from contingent, not strategic reasons: to provide the new courts with a law already experimented within the mixed courts introduced in 1876 to handle cases where interests of a European power were at stake (and thus overcome consular jurisdiction in cases involving Egyptian citizens), in order not to give the military occupant a pretext for discrediting or manipulating this important tool of state modernization and national independence, and also in the hope of gaining European agreement on the suppression of the mixed courts, themselves considered an unacceptable vestige of foreign influence.[11] The move was probably not intended by any major Egyptian actor as a rebuttal of šarīʿa, but as a convenient step in keeping its influence discrete and invisible during a phase when the task of transforming the corpus of legal regulations recorded in texts of *fiqh* of different schools into standardised, unified codes was still in the initial stage. In this absence of public zeal in upholding the visibility of šarīʿa in the new codes we might want to see, not its dismissal, but a blend of contingent political wisdom and technical shortcomings. With time, the jurisprudence of the national courts even enhanced the šarīʿa tenor of the "French law" applied.

It emerges with sufficient clearness that the reform of the legal system, right at a time of burgeoning national agitation and growing influence of independent public discourse, was not considered obnoxious to šarīʿa's normativity that

Muḥammad ʿAbduh and other reformers were on their way to reconstruct. The immanent rules and rewards of the emerging public sphere, built around press organs representing different political-intellectual trends and not immediately reflecting the views of state authority (either indigenous or colonial), regulated this tension between norm and law and in a certain sense delayed the perception of a possible gap. The accomplishment of a differentiation of the legal system to fit the requirements of the modernising state had been accepted by proto-reformers like Shaykh Rifāʿa aṭ-Ṭahṭāwī. The main novelty of the new public sphere was in the fiction of a normativity prior to norms, a sort of "metanorm" consisting in the constraint to address questions of common relevance according to defined rules of speech, to be appropriated by each would-be public speaker or writer. At this juncture the idea of šarīʿa, of a Godly sanctioned lawfulness, intervened to provide a traditional anchor to the necessary fiction. As I will try to suggest, this is fiction in a theatrical sense, not intended as a new invention discursively and symbolically represented for complying with the needs of the hour, but as a powerful tool of disciplining. The virtue to be staged, without which the metanorm would merely be a theoretical construct, is itself inherited from tradition. Not so, however, the staging tools and scripts, which are truly modern.[12]

This reformulation of šarīʿa has been regarded as a process of reduction of the heritage of *fiqh* (Islamic jurisprudence) to an empty formula approximating "natural law" (Kerr 1966), but this might be true only at the level of an analysis of the contents of reform discourses. However, the redefinition of šarīʿaʾs normativity performed by the *iṣlāḥ* should be evaluated by looking at the procedural mechanisms of the public sphere and the underlying requirements of discipline of a subject desirous to partake in public communication and public affairs. A metanorm is essentially form, procedure, and etiquette of access to public talk grounded on the self's own rectitude. Being all of this, it cannot be reduced to an ideological password.

The rise and consolidation of the newspaper, and in particular of the use of concise argument on matters of compelling actuality and common interest (the editorial), though later obfuscated by the spread of increasingly massifying electronic media, remains until today the marker of the existence and functioning of a public sphere where even topics of concern to specific groups have to be couched in a vocabulary of universal rights and general interest. It has been claimed that printing gave a specific form to the act itself of going public, of publicising the self: the standardised form of printing was itself a metaphor of general accessibility and of concern for the common good. Printing required a strict disembodiment of the speaker, a bracketing of his real self.[13] In Egypt, the articulation of these abstract forms of public normativity faced the emergence and consolidation of a modern legal system as a *fait accompli*. For some decades, the fiction of a "public subjectivity" sustaining šarīʿa as a metanorm nurtured the illusion of a normative continuum between *iṣlāḥ an-nufūs* and *iṣlāḥ ad-dāḥiliyya al-mamlaka*, i.e. between the improvement of the selves and the administrative and legal reform of the affairs of the kingdom. Targeting the moral mode of being of the subject in public, yes, its constructing the public through exemplary observance and admonishment of the fellow believer is the new "essentialism" understanding of the Muslim canonical injunction of "commanding good and prohibiting evil" (*al-amr biʿl-maʿrūf wa-l-nahy ʿan al-munkar*), on which reformers liked to pivot their claims, because fitting a procedural and disciplining kind of normativity, more than a normativity of actual prescriptions.

At a closer scrutiny, and if we leave aside the self-legitimating formulas of "secular" intellectuals, the metanorm is beyond any distinction between autonomy and heteronomy, immanence or transcendence of norm: it can sustain both, and both of them cannot but be sustained by metanorm. It is the product of the globalization of the rules of public communication, a process immune to philosophical preoccupations. Certainly the view of metanorm, for which we are mainly indebted to Habermas, is at the ambiguous crossroad between social analysis and political philosophy, of scrutiny and prescription of the ethics of public communication. Its diagnostic value, however, is in that many of the leading participants in public contentions partake the same ambiguous view articulated by Habermas: and this is why the notion may be more useful for social analysis than it appears at first sight, in as far as it helps to describe the fiction through which a meta-narrative with regulating power is constructed and - often successfully - imposed on large portions of the "public" by a core intellectual elite believing in, and practising, this meta-normativity. If there is any social-scientific usefulness in the construct of public sphere, it is tied to this subtle game of multiple reflections and mirroring fictions incorporated in the notion of metanorm, where the formulators of normative discourse take themselves as the moral standards of public rationality, while discursively - and fictionally - projecting these norms onto a reluctant "society" in need of redemption from submissiveness and repetition.[14]

Metanorm has maybe an ideological, but no functional correlate - down the level of the regulation of disparate social affairs - in legal effectiveness. The modernization of the legal system has led in Egypt to the institution of the national courts (the first tribunals that were neither religious, nor an *ad hoc*, administratively managed instrument of the khedive's power, nor instituted through the pressure of colonial powers for the tutelage of their interests) is coeval with the emergence of a functioning and expansive public sphere. Both processes are rooted in the same intellectual ferment, national agitation, and colonial challenge. The claims of reason and generality embedded in the meta-language of the public sphere found a symbolically powerful correlate in the national courts. However, in spite of national courts and the national press being ideologically cognate, they were not necessarily co-functional. Most of the historical dilemmas of the "new" *šarīʿa* are to be explained through this fundamental dislocation of functions.

To understand the major discontinuities effected on *šarīʿa* by the simultaneous, though differentiated rise of national tribunals and a national public sphere, we should take again, briefly, and from the vintage point of this major transformation, a look back at the dynamics of *šarīʿa* prior to the conditions imposed on its equilibrium and further differentiation by the disjunction between norm (no longer only dependent on "culture" and "tradition", but bound to a preliminary filtering through metanorm) and law. It is important to take account of the vitality of *šarīʿa* as a legal tradition with an immanent rationalising impetus before the reification that turned it into a luring trumpcard for the definition of the rules of public communication, the staging of public virtue, and the construction of metanorm, in order to better understand the discontinuity that later subverted the rules of consensus.

It is the process, unfolding during the seventeenth and eighteenth centuries, through which the divine norm was submitted to a positivization and articulation in textual genres with different functions. In this process, collections of recorded *fatwā*s (non-binding legal opinions, as opposed to binding courts judgements) that were endowed with a generality and authority transcending the particular case that occasioned the legal question, functioned as the hub for the homogenization of doctrine, commentaries and jurisprudence, even if no definite hierarchy was established through definitive criteria.[15] In-built in the process was an older differentiation between moral norm and legal ruling, though not solidly formalised.[16] In this pre-nationalist phase, that is prior to the building of a centralising state, the legal system acquired an autonomous profile via an increasing positivization of law, and due to its de facto - and to a certain extent also de jure - distinction from religious-moral guidance.

This happened in the absence of a doctrinal and practical influence of *iğtihād*, the faculty of finding innovative legal solutions through free reasoning that Islamic jurisprudence had confined to very special cases, and only accorded to particularly talented spirits. Historically speaking, the "gate of *iğtihād*" was never closed, but rather restricted to cases that were not crucial to the actual functioning of the legal system, the more this evolved and consolidated, thereby reducing the margins of individual arbitrariness. In the form of a concerted adaptation of the system to evolving circumstances, innovation was rather allowed through the invocation of the *iğmāʿ*, the consensus, of the jurists. We should situate these operations, and the rules governing them, in the context of an increasing specialization of the legal system. Innovation occurred mainly through the selective device of specifying those cases when *muftī*s (the issuers of *fatwā*s) did not have to feel bound to the *taqlīd* ("imitation, replication") of the opinion of other *muftī*s, but were empowered to invoke the actually binding legal consensus of law experts for introducing elements of novelty into the legal system.[17] Operating a legal system requires adaptive innovation permanently, and the non-personalization of innovative legal operations (in the case of *fiqh*, the non-invocation of *iğtihād*) is a sign of the well-functioning of the system.

In the era of the public sphere, a new emphasis on *iğtihād* emerged along with a previously unknown, emphatically constructed opposition to *taqlīd*, along with a distancing from the *iğmāʿ*, the consensus. Both *taqlīd* and *iğmāʿ* were often perceived by reformers as fostering the *ʿulamāʾ*'s unwillingness to take up the challenges of the modern world. If evaluated from the viewpoint of the pace of reform of the legal system, this position was out of touch with reality, because at the time when the legal system based on *fiqh* was called to cope with these challenges, it was being swiftly deprived of its institutional competencies, without significant objections of the religious reformers.[18] At this stage, however, *iğtihād* was propagated, quite consciously, not as a technical-juridical skill of excellence, or a device for updating the legal system, but as a method to regulate and encourage participation in discussions of issues of common interest, to foster a moral and discursive discipline of addressing such questions, and to establish a new view of lawfulness and a new consensus of communication in the public sphere and in society at large. *Iğtihād* was expanded from a classic method for dilating the normative import of scripture via independent reasoning into a discipline of rational-critical debate in the public sphere, to be practised in such a way to best capitalise on its public impact and establish the legislating authority of reason bound only to the Koran.

The myth of the closing of the gate of *iğtihād*, and the call to reopen it, might have been created by those religious reformers anxious to turn consensus, from an exceptional and exclusive mechanism of infra-scholarly accommodation, into a permanent and inclusive mechanism of scrutiny of the soundness of argument through the judgement of an impersonal, potentially ubiquitous "public". Rašīd Ridā (1865-1935), who inherited, updated and radicalised the project of *islāh* of Muhammad ʿAbduh, went so far, in 1922, to affirm that each Muslim, each citizen should be a *muğtahid*, a practitioner of *iğtihād*.[19] The period between the 1880s and the 1920s saw an "essentialist" implosion of *šarīʿa* from its previous positive, systemic and institutional efficacy, to its pretended authentic, normative kernel. This kernel was reformulated not merely under the pressure of an identitarian syndrome or an obsession with authenticity, but according to the new rules of the public sphere, its metanorm and the "new" consensus. In other words, the rise of a public sphere exerted a strong pressure on the previously still largely unreflected and unreified relation between the normative and legal system, on the one hand, and *one* of the labels through which the system had been, with time, identified (*šarīʿa*). However, the surplus of reflection provided by the transformation whirled through an emptied soil, as the system, the šarīʿa, no longer existed as a vital, self-sufficient set of institutions and discursive traditions. The consequence was an overcompensation of the institutional loss through the production of grand normative scenarios, all around the new land of metanorm.

The project of iṣlāḥ played on a triple register, that is typical of any historical constitution or major transformation of a public sphere. Law as a particular form of regulation of human behaviour and social transactions was instrumentally called to provide the intermediate term bridging the gulf, through the disciplining mechanisms specific to legal enforcement, between two other elements otherwise difficult to compound in practice: the construction of models of personal virtue, and the approach of a metanorm expected to allow for rational communication within the community. The useful fiction of metanorm consists in providing the public sphere and its actors with a unitary vocabulary, a homogeneous normative staging ground. A problem arises when the invocation of law becomes a too ancillary fiction in the game, and slides away of the outreach and control of the heroes of the public sphere, old and new intellectuals.

The perspective on metanorm as the intellectual device for complying with a global conformation, and systemic differentiation, of communication within modern public spheres, sustained by the fiction of a terrain of discussion unbound by inherited social status, is to be taken seriously in order to avoid the impression that the talk about šarīʿa is only a reflection of the wave of popularity of what has been called "political Islam". This is generally depicted as an indentitarian approach to politics based on fundamentalist readings of Islamic traditions, that cannot cope either with the history of the Muslim world nor with the social determinants of the contemporary predicament of Muslim societies[20]: a fundamentalism that sometimes enjoys a theoretical redemption by being classified as the local pendant of globalization[21]. Obviously, the issuing of a metanorm via theory, or a concerted effort at fixing rules of discourse through mere rational-critical argument, is at best a theoretical approximation of an ideal situation. This fiction can only be upheld by a public staging of "virtue" as a condition of access to the formulation of the public good.[22]

III

This is why I prefer not to frame this process of transformation by reference to the simple formula of the "invention of tradition". The process sensibly altered expectations and techniques of regulation of social behaviour through dislocating traditional practices from their institutional loci. The construction of virtue to be detected in public discourse, the focus on the improvement of the individual selves, or šarīʿa as the "straight path" (i.e. a definition of šarīʿa in terms of personal perfection) - further subsumed under the canonical obligation of "commanding good and prohibiting evil" - envisions law in its modern shape as a crucial instruments of regulation of society, but reaches beyond this form of law, into legislating over a portion of the self only accessible through a training of self-discipline inspired by instances of moral guidance, and models of excellence. The ultimate models to imitate are Muḥammad's life and his community. The *imitatio Muhammadi* was a practice deeply rooted in mystical (*ṣūfī*) traditions, but changes its operational formula in the context of religious reform through public discourse: no longer to be pursued through obedience due to a master, or through participation in the collective rituals of the *ṭarīqa* (brotherhood), but through distilling the highest property of divine guidance, consisting in providing the ultimate antidote against human arbitrariness, egoism and particularism, and *therefore* being the most secure token of independent reason. Though this operation, the structures of discipline were relocated from traditional paths of piety and devotion to independent, though rightly-guided endeavours in the public arena for the sake of community welfare. Virtue got a definitely public projection, along with paths of access independent of membership in a particular *ṭarīqa*, through becoming virtual, through nesting in abstract, virtual spaces whose chances of new institutionalization were tied up with national and constitutional politics, and subordinated to their vagaries. Virtue became a risky business.

The point I am trying to make concerns the origin of a "revised", or "reformed" idea of *šarīʿa* that tried to harmonise the traditional, cumulative corpus of legal knowledge and jurisprudence recorded in manuals of *fiqh*, their commentaries, and collections of *fatwā*s, along with the traditional science of its fundaments (*ʿilm al-uṣūl*) on the one hand, and the idea of a centralised legislating and disciplining power that arose and consolidated in the context of the state-building strategies pursued from the beginning of the nineteenth century by the khedive Muḥammad ʿAlī and his successors. The result of the process is a paradox: only after the rise of a public sphere, and the concomitant beginning of a process of codification of law, as well as of a constitutional movement that lent a wide legitimacy to the re-centration of the legal system on the sovereignty of the modernising state, did the talk about *šarīʿa* as a normative and at least potentially legal system, first became intelligible to everybody in the public arena, and, *with time*, popular.

The reconstruction of *šarīʿa*, and its search for law, has at least since the 1920s, after the sunset of the classical *iṣlāḥ* of Muḥammad ʿAbduh, occupied a growing and differentiating range of social and legal actors stretching beyond the restricted elite of religious reformers with a profile of "grand intellectuals", who pursued the easy goal of a smooth and multidirectional convertibility between personal excellence, public-communicative metanorm and legal system. I cannot delve at due length into the crucial passage of the late 1920s and

1930s in Egypt, through which the plurality of levels of disciplining-regulating power involved in šarīʿa claims began to display its tension or even dysfunctionality, but also produced a coherent project of integration of the new šarīʿa into the legal system and of accommodation to its functional requirements. Central to this project has been the work of selection, reformulation and codification of šarīʿa rules performed by ʿAbd ar-Razzāq al-Sanhūrī, and that culminated in the civil code promulgated in 1948.

At the very least, this project is embedded in the view of šarīʿa as a normative system formulated and shaped according to the global, normative requirements of the public sphere, and immediately resting on a project of disciplining the subject, as Muslim and citizen. We see at work the discontinuity effected by the creation of a "public subjectivity" on traditions of religious, moral and legal discourses. Nonetheless, if we do not restrict our perspective to a view internal to the legal system and its functional demands,[23] this is no linear process of globalization and "secularization", even if the main frame of reference is a model of citizenship in the nation-state (with its parliamentary and judiciary institutions) that constitutes the obligatory threshold of access to the normative field where šarīʿa is played on the level of enforcement as state law.

Šarīʿa thus modernized or "secularized" is first of all dragged off the self-perpetuating (though in no way homogeneous and repetitive), linear procedures of "ongoing discourse". However, even in its trend to turn "secular" and, increasingly, to produce "law", šarīʿa has kept an axial transcendent reference to the norm emanating from God's will, transhistorical and translocal, liable to positivization because constructed from the outset as universal and non-particularistic. This šarīʿa can feed into immanent, legally positive normativity, but cannot appropriate the fiction of autonomous or human reason. One can object that this is the self-image of šarīʿa, fabricated by those raising its banner, and that in the ineluctable process of positivization and adaptation to the secular legal system transcendence is no longer such: it only survives in the form of "religious" or even "religious-cultural identity".

To face this objection, let me recall here an important peculiarity of all forms of religious communication, even those reduced to the most external (and even consumerist) display of symbols, so common in the cityscape of today's Cairo, for example in the form of "religious commodities"[24], though this is most clear in the case of those forms explicitly evoking religious lawfulness through the normative power of the word. It is the singular property (that no other form of communication can implement) of turning, via the specific discursive devices of theology, the improbable forms of superhuman agents into actual agents of influence on daily life, models of life conduct, and social transactions (obviously through a wide variety of direct or indirect means, only few of them mediated by "pure faith"). Here we meet a specific function of religious communication, a function it keeps through all major discontinuities effected by normative-communicative revolutions and globalizing influences, like the rise of a modern public sphere. These breakthroughs affect the performance of religion for the whole of the social system, but not its function.[25] Recognising a thread of uninterrupted effectiveness of the function leads some observers to postulate a continuity of "tradition", in spite of an evident upheaval in the institutional arrangements of religious mediation and their discourses, as well as in the interpretative methods, personal disciplines and expressive forms through which subjects approach and appropriate the written word of scripture. Branding the sword of "tradition" and focusing on "traditional practices" updated within a modern or modernising society works sometimes effectively in countering the allegations that formulations of šarī'a claims make a merely "instrumental" use of religious knowledge and know-how, or pay mere lip service to theological constructs. How can one distinguish the instrumental from the pure and straightforward in religious communication? Are we allowed to draw a sharp line between a genuine and a spurious use of these communicative devices?

More than an identitarian, culturalist or "indigenizing" twist of religious discourse (that is, where available, the consequence of an intentional tuning into global politics that rewards with attention those raising the banners of a "culture", and not the conditioned, centrifugal reaction to a centripetal force), the real.breakthrough in the evolution of šarī'a claims has been the new intellectual task of balancing a pretension to a tighter control and disciplining of subjects, necessary for a vital nation to function and thrive, and a progression in the objectification of this pretension into a representation of virtue and excellence, culminating in the mechanisms of "public subjectivity"[26], where the virtuosity of the subject is invested fully in the pursuit of the common good. At its best, the identitarian syndrome is a fall-out of this combined process of subjectification and objectification of religious brokerage, and cannot be invoked to short-cut the explanation of the transformation of šarī'a claims.

The power of invocation of a transcendent reference, even according to such "modernized" modalities that bear some resemblance to the patterns of "republican virtue"[27], can be measured with particular efficacy in public, legal controversies on personal status, not by chance often intertwined with heated debates on the relationship between šarī'a's lawfulness and the state's constitution. Through the whole process of reform of the legal system in Egypt, questions of personal status have been quite unanimously perceived as the kernel of šarī'a's regulating power. The religious courts kept their jurisdiction on matters of personal status until they were folded into the National Courts system in 1956, and the codification on these topics, since Muḥammad Qadrī's *al-aḥkām aš-šaʿriyya*, has been inspired by the corpus of texts inherited from classic *fiqh* (Islamic jurisprudence), duly filtered through selective and eclectic choice between different schools (*taḥayyur*).

In the militant climate that preceded the June war against Israel, during the spring 1967, the Egyptian public sphere, at that time dominated by Nasserist-developmental formulas, was suddenly invested with a dispute on the case of *bait aṭ-ṭāʿa* ("house of obedience"), and on related questions concerning polygamy, procedures of divorce, and the maintenance due to the wife. The *bait aṭ-ṭāʿa* was an issue of personal status involving rights and duties in marriage, focusing in particular on the wife's obligation to return to the conjugal home, the "house of obedience", after she had left for whatever reasons. On that occasion, along with, and in opposition to, a leftist attempt to crack the enduring centrality of *šarīʿa* on matters crucial to the relationship among sexes, and the power and distribution of roles within the family, *šarīʿa* claims were propagated in the context of the necessary preservation of the Muslim family and its sacredness as the hub of social harmony. These counterclaims finally attained, even in government-loyal organs of the religious press, shortly before the outburst of the war, such straightforward formulations as "the people demand an Islamic constitution and Islamic regulations"[28]. This is an example, from a time prior to the era when observers locate a new turn to religion in Egyptian society following the shock of the lost war and the Israeli occupation of Egyptian and Arab territory, of how even the mere task of defending what could appear as the last citadel of legal effectiveness of divine law (personal status law), draws religious actors to raise the banner of *šarīʿa* in order to frame public legality in terms of Islamic lawfulness. The initiative of the ministry of justice that aimed at abrogating the enforcement of *bait aṭ-ṭāʿa* through the police was finally thwarted by a combination of resistance of religious personnel, and the escalating tension in the Sinai that finally led to war, but more than that, it was drawn to publicly declare that the main framework of the debate on issues concerning the family was dictated by the "religious-spiritual values" of the Egyptian nation, enjoying a rank even superior to the "socialist society" of Nasserist inspiration.

The view of *šarīʿa* as being a principal source of legislation became first incarnated in Article 2 of the new constitution promulgated in 1971. This was in no way a mere reflection of a move by the new president, Sadat, aimed at finding a new constituency and legitimacy among the Islamic forces that had been banned from the Egyptian public sphere in the crudest way during Nasser's presidency, in particular after the last wave of repression unleashed against the Muslim Brotherhood in 1965. Coming right at the beginning of a new presidency and an announced new "era", the constitution was the outcome of a longer public debate going back to the last period of Nasser's presidency. The new constitutional provision was a symptom of the growing wave of propagation of *šarīʿa*'s lawfulness in the public sphere, whose inception goes back at least to the mid-1960s, in singular coincidence with the anti-*iḫwān* repressive measures. After all, a similar wording about *šarīʿa* as a major source of legislation had been inserted right at the beginning of the civil code promulgated in 1948. Even more so, and ever since the institution of the national courts in 1883, *šarī'a* had been considered de facto by legislative and even more judiciary organs at large a main source of legislation. Dealing with *šarī'a* as a principal source of legislation was probably perceived in the Egyptian public sphere at large during the 1960s to be quite a conventional, consensual, and politically innocuous topic. This is very much an objectification of *šarī'a*. One can suppose that if carried on further along the same trajectory, the process would have probably led to a neutralization of the disciplining power of those legitimised to raise its flag. However, a new "subjectifying" twist was not there to come as a simple reaction to reification, but by virtue of its very advancement and, by the time of Sadat, by the chance to articulate the new *šarī'a* through media of communication and solidarity-building less subject to the supervision of the state.

It seems to me that the new article of the constitution of 1971, more than contributing to the process of incorporation of *šarī'a* in the positive law of the state, made the meta-normative ambitions of the classic *iṣlāḥ* ever more pervasive and effective beyond the boundaries of the "official" public sphere. Matched by the release of many Islamists from prison, and later by a liberalization of the media market, the new constitutional status of *šarī'a* contributed to a differentiation of religious public spheres during the 1970s and 1980s. As a result, the public staging of a religiously based virtue was progressively able to encompass genres of discourses and to capture audiences well below the level of "grand" intellectual discussions on the "common good". Since then, constitutional matters have represented a stake for evaluating the status of the multiple normativity of *šarī'a* within society, that cannot be reduced to a trend of legal "secularization" of the divine norm. The next step in the process was the amendment of 1980 that religious forces obtained in the same public climate that saw their staging of a campaign to oppose the reform of the law of personal status in 1979. This law entailed some improvements on the wife's rights in divorce procedures, and, in cases of conjugal conflict previously regulated by the *bait aṭ-ṭā'a*, reproposed, albeit in attenuated form, some of the elements of the reform on matters of personal status that foundered during the spring of 1967. The law was included in a presidential decree and was approved by the president-docile people's assembly after heated debates in its deliberating sessions and in the media. The Islamic camp persevered in agitating against the law considered, quite exaggeratedly, as the final blow against divine norm. In 1985 the Supreme Constitutional Court judged the law unconstitutional on procedural grounds. In spite of the non-substantial reasons for this judgement, the decision was widely perceived as a sign of the growing influence of the new Islamic publics.

This is not the place to indulge in a structural analysis of the Islamic public spheres that were re-enacted during the 1970s and 1980s as a flourishing branch of the new mass-cultural market that thrived thanks to the economic liberalization of Sadat's era. Let me just summarise this development in a few words and point to a phenomenon that impinged on the spectrum of levels of legality, without directly affecting the legal system administered and guaranteed by state instances. Different sections of the reconstituted Islamic public were very vigilant in pre-defining a negotiating or foot-dragging attitude towards state instances (or an appropriate blend of both). In terms of their goals and normativity, and of the territories of social and religious action that they wanted to control, regulate and discipline, they grew more and more autonomous, thereby developing a more refined and differentiated strategic attitude towards the state, including state law: an undoubtedly fresh development if compared with the Nasser era, and even with the two decades of most successful social mobilization through the Muslim Brotherhood, the 1930s and 1940s, when state politics was an immediate, forceful frame of mobilization and strategy.

The re-enactment of guidance through exemplary paradigms of virtue (often of autobiographical nature) includes an element that could deter us from being lured into the reassuring dualisms that globalization theory and its cognates propound to our eyes, ever more fatigued at observing and having to disentangle social complexity. Between the disciplining of the believer, and the intervention on a constitutional terrain directly affecting the sovereignty of the nation-state and on the competencies of a restricted political elite of mainly military affiliation, a space of lawful and punctual regulations has been reconstituted through an extension of the range and audiences of the genre of *fatwā*s ("legal advisory opinions"), where individual behaviour is scrutinised and recommendations are formulated that conform to a graduated scale of virtuosity and legality. The residual, but enduring autonomous competencies of jurists and their jurists' law, subtracted to the omnivorous voracity of state legal and constitutional sovereignty, has gained terrain thanks to the growth and transformation of media and audiences in the public sphere.[29]

A *fatwā*'s rubric was present during the 1960s in most religious magazines and journals, and even in part of the official press (*al-Ǧumhūriyya*), but not yet in the electronic media. In the 1970s and 1980s the figure of the radio or TV *muftī* who directs consciences not merely through moral exhortation, but through legal opinions as replies to ad hoc questions (many of them, increasingly, concerning questions of "correct consumption") began to occupy an increasingly public terrain, clearly extending the range of concern of the legal question from the individual who raised it to the whole of an anonymous, but interested audience. At the very least, we should admit that this form of legal-religious guidance, so far not liable to be metabolised into the legal system of the state, is acquiring new functions within a landscape of enhanced normative complexity.

Is this a case of outflanking the legal system proper through the legal specialists affiliated to a particular religious tradition, a revenge of localism against the last powerful wave of globalizing discursive, normative and legal rationalities? In classical Islamic jurisprudence the genre of *fatwā* kept or even increased its centrality in the course of the incremental differentiation of a specialised system of law out of the broader functions of religious mediation, in spite of - or even due to - its modality of binding legal opinions to moral-religious justifications. So the media revival of *fatwā*s should be taken at least as a proof of the popularity and effectiveness of religiously grounded (since involving in the final analysis the transcendence of divine norm and the specific way of operation of religious communication) constructions of a sense of justice and of consensus over the legitimacy of legal regulations among the larger Egyptian public. The relation between this *fatwā*-revival in a strongly mediatised environment and the "new" *šarī'a* should deserve a separate investigation. Here we can just formulate the following hypothesis: while the metanormative reconstruction of *šarī'a* through religious reform, though built on a bid to match subjective disciplining and generalization of access to interpretation and discourse, has privileged, in the final analysis, the moment of reification, the media boom of *fatwā*s reinvests the capital of normative consensus into a program of punctual regulation of matters of personal and interpersonal concern. Moreover, this revival carves out regulating functions for religious specialists that would otherwise be more and more blurred into a generic moral guidance performed from mosque and media pulpits. The transformation of this genre of legal-religious guidance is particularly appealing to those citizens for which nation-state instances (even when reflecting or integrating a *šarī'a* lawfulness) offer at best general frameworks of identification and orientation, but no practicable catalogues of virtue and moral behaviour.

IV

What appears to observers as the normatively ubiquitous but legally fragile presence of *šarī'a* in Egyptian society suggests bits of an argument about the entangled relations between "virtue", law, norm and metanorm, and about some of our habitual deficits in framing the problem. This analysis should be placed in the context of the ambiguous mechanisms of communicating virtue and thereby pinpointing a metanorm that is no peculiar syndrome of the enactment of a *šarī'a* lawfulness in Muslim societies, but rather a modern ambivalence embodied in the tension between normative discourse ethics and functional legal process. So we need a non-static and not merely a discursive view of the public sphere: one that does not simply point to an arena of public controversies, but links it up with processes of social differentiation within a given social context, characterised by inherited institutional configurations of the power of social mediation and disciplining, that in turn grounds and legitimates law.

Next, we should raise the question of how the normative game of the public sphere provides a reservoir of legitimacy to positive law, via the form of normative validity that is common to both, in spite of the fact that the former does not partake with the latter of the instruments for sanctioning the norm. Lawyers have often been and sill are - even more so in the Egyptian case, since the formation of a public sphere[30] - legal and public-political actors, but the transfer of normativity between public contentions and the legal system is not in their hands, though their discourse pretends it.

Part of the basic inadequacy of our understanding of the relationship between law, norm and metanorm lies in the construction of a bifurcation between heteronomous and autonomous reason. This is the consequence of observing how some actors within the public sphere relocate the sources of normativity into an "inner forum", a metaphor for an independent faculty of judgement rejecting any established authority not based on reason. Though appreciating the shift in the model of subjectivity implied by the relocation, the observer should not overemphasise it, but rather appraise it for what it is: a shift of script in the staging virtue, where the protagonist, the subject, the actor, claims to be the author of the script as well. That staging skills and authority are both concentrated in the same subject is an impressive achievement, and this is where the *Aufklärung* derives its fascination and spectacular character. The analyst can be easily dazzled, up to the point of assessing heteronomous forms of reasons only in their capacity to successfully imitate the operations of the autonomous one, thereby approximating the prototype of *Aufklärung* public sphere: a procedure that sustains the patronising view of *iṣlāḥ* manifested by some Western observers.

The construction of autonomous reason has been the job of a bunch of philosophically talented spirits (yes, led by Kant), building up a sort of hyperreflection about how the inner forum generates a public sphere, and which is its relation to the basis of legitimacy of the community at large. It might appear a paradox that looking at "religion" as religious communication is necessary if we want to emancipate ourselves from the metaphysics of an autonomous reason, and to delve into more "profane" domains of social analysis and theory, addressing processes where the invocation of a varied spectrum of authorities is the practical condition for the fabrication of judgements. In one recent article about religion Luhmann comes close to designating its function, in an environment of modern communication, as the one of upholding the very possibility to formulate a metanorm, i.e. to guarantee communication as such in the social system.³¹ In a certain sense, Luhmann seems to say that only the fictionally and communicatively "pure", uncontaminated transcendence of religion (whose presence is not dependent on the public visibility of religion) can provide such a meta-language, such a medium of media. Autonomous systems of normative and moral legitimacy only reformulate the transcendent frame of reference to ground the more general fiction of the autonomy of "society", in itself a very problematic construct, an article of faith, and not just for the sociologist.

Through these transformations and types of constraint, šarīʿa becomes the marker of a field of regulation whose hierarchy is still mainly determined by a competence to articulate transcendence and salvation, and is only within narrow limits accessible to actors not trained in such skills. This is not a contamination or a reduction of the Enlightenment model. It is more likely that it is the other way around. If we are captive of the game of fashioning models without having a theory, then I am there to propose that the model of šarīʿa in modern Egyptian history, in spite of the contamination of colonialism, is less alienated from reality, and is therefore a better model, a more plausible prototype. It suffers less from the syndrome of "irrelation to politics" that Reinhart Koselleck has so masterly depicted for the European Enlightenment³², for the simple reason that šarīʿa plays little with politics in a modern, "absolutist" sense. The reasons for this are practical, but not just in the sense of wishing to keep a healthy distance from modern Mamluks. The ideal tenor of šarīʿa has been greatly enhanced by its becoming a meta language, but its goals are more clear and more modest: at least it is more transparent which class interests, forms of domination and regimes of disciplining, šarīʿa is there to serve. The number of legal actors equipped with the know-how to articulate such religious competence is not indefinite, as it would be if we conceive šarīʿa as the marker of a field of normative struggle and integration sustained by a mainly identitarian mechanism of authentication.

Besides the views of šarīʿa claims as either identity politics or tools for an indigenization (and henceforth normative consolidation) of positive law - or indeed a functional blend of both where the identitarian claims pinpoint the process of consolidation - we should consider these claims, especially to the extent they are distanced from casuistic *fiqh* and its standards of fairness in social intercourse, as legislating over a portion of the self (or of the self-in-community), which partly overlaps, but is not identical with the part targeted by state law. Šarīʿa lawfulness makes the regulation of social transactions dependent on the righteousness of the believer who is guided up the straight path by legitimate religious authorities. The community is a congregation of believers, who attend different grades of reason and virtue along a hierarchy that in principle is given by knowledge and charisma, in fact also (if not mainly) by origin and family belonging, or, in the era of centralising states, by a capacity to invest both types of social and cultural capital in the equipment necessary to climb up the ladder of posts whose prestige is determined by their being networked with various sections of the public.[33]

There is no necessary tension between this view of community and concepts of membership and citizenship resting on legal equality, as well as the generalization of rights and obligations. A conflict might only arise if these criteria threaten to diminish the religious standards of guidance and representation. The structure of a modern public sphere fits well into the Islamic vision in that it combines the specialization of the formulation of virtuous scripts with the de-specialization of access to their fruition. The fiction of a metanorm expressed in Islamic terms is built on the presumption of equality in terms of dignity and capacity to learn and rationally adjudicate, but also on the assumption that these capacities should be developed through appropriate methods of guidance (within which a certain pluralism for the choice of a master, a shaykh, is allowed to the member of the community, along with a responsibility of choosing well) and standards of representation.

Sociologically, we should take into consideration the question of the multiple normative networking of subject.[34] An important part of their life might be oriented towards a vision of being good Muslims, but shifts to other registers, and a modularity of standards of values and patterns of belonging is the rule. This is no token of split minds. Shifting patterns of moral justification are a basic requisite of life in a modern, especially metropolitan context. The strains become powerful if the legitimization of choices in private and public life all have to conform to this vision of being a Muslim. On the other hand, this is no simple fundamentalist or totalising trap, as it might prove very useful for raising claims "as Muslims", for reconstructing a vocabulary of rights and obligations, for promoting the virtues of a template that – it is said - had been well integrated in traditions of learning, teaching and adjudicating disputes, and, more than that, is Godly sanctioned. This is the template of šarī'a, that is no mere intellectual shibboleth, or alternative legal system, or identitarian syndrome, but one major normative playground, tightly mechanically associated with the politics of staging virtue, a religiously grounded virtue, in the public sphere.

That this is a fiction, since an Islamic way of life does not exist as such, as it is at best contingently incorporated in life phases or spaces of social interaction often located outside of those of traditionally religious consecration (first and foremost the mosque), does not diminish its power in filling the gap between metanorm and the enactment of a particular, and at least symbolically recognisable norm. The answers to the question "what is šarī'a" may oscillate a lot, but almost any Muslim claiming to be such would answer with certainty and a fair degree of conviction.

Notes

1 For a pioneering work on this "political economy" dimension of globalization, see Peter Gran, Islamic Roots of Capitalism. Egypt, 1760-1840, Austin-London 1979.
2 Ghislaine Alleaume, Linant de Bellefonds (1799-1883) et le saint-simonisme en Égypte. In: Magali Morsy (ed.), Les Saint-Simoniens et l'Orient. Vers la modernité, Aix-en-Provence 1989, pp. 113-131.
3 Baudouin Dupret/Jean-Noelle Ferrié, For intérieur et ordre public, ou comment la problématique de l'Aufklärung peut permettre de décrire un débat égyptien. In: Gilles Boëtsch/Baudouin Dupret/Jean-Noelle Ferrié (eds.), Droits et sociétés dans lemonde arabe. Perspectives socio-anthropologiques, Aix-en-Provence 1997, pp. 173-194.
4 Brinkley Messick, The Calligraphic State. Textual Domination and History in a Muslim Society, Berkeley 1993.
5 Wilfred Cantwell Smith, The Concept of Shari'a among some Mutakallimun. In: George Makdisi (ed.), Arabic and Islamic Studies in Honor of Hamilton A.R. Gibb, Cambridge, MA, 1965, p. 585.
6 Alan Watson, The Making of Civil Law, Cambridge, MA, 1981.
7 Malcolm Kerr, Islamic Reform. The Political and Legal Theories of Muhammad Abduh and Rashid Rida, Berkeley 1966.
8 Cf. Sāmī ʿAbd al-ʿAzīz al-Kūmī, aṣ-Ṣaḥāfa al-islāmiyya fī Miṣr fī l-qarn at-tāsiʿ ʿašar, Al-Manṣūra 1992.
9 Nathan Brown, Shari'a and State in the Modern Muslim Middle East. In: International Journal of Middle East Studies, 29 (1997), pp. 359-376.
10 Niklas Luhmann, Das Recht der Gesellschaft, Frankfurt 1995, p. 138.
11 Nathan Brown, Law and Imperialism: Egypt in Comparative Perspective. In: Law & Society, 29 (1995), pp. 115-118.
12 Armando Salvatore, Staging Virtue: The Disembodiment of Self-correctness and the Making of Islam as Public Norm. In: Yearbook of the Sociology of Islam, 1 (1998), in print.
13 Michael Warner, The Mass Public and the Mass Subject. In: Craig Calhoun (ed.), Habermas and the Public Sphere, Cambridge, MA, 1992, pp. 378-401.
14 Armando Salvatore, Islam and the Political Discourse of Modernity, Reading 1997.
15 Baber Johansen, Legal Literature and the Problem of Change: the Case of Land Rent. In: Chibli Mallat (ed.), Islam and Public Law. Classical and Contemporary Studies, London 1993, pp. 29-30.
16 Baber Johansen, Die sündige, gesunde Amme. Moral und gesetzliche Bestimmung (hukm) im islamischen Recht. In: Die Welt des Islams, 28 (1988), pp. 263-282.
17 Johansen refers to literature about Syria in the 17th and 18th century. So, though these examples cannot be generalised, they might well convey an interesting picture of the time immediately preceding the rise of a public sphere in an important Arab region of the Ottoman empire.
18 Brown, Shari'a and State..., loc. cit.
19 Rašīd Muḥammad Riḍā, al-Ḥilāfa ʿan al-imāma al-ʿuẓmā, Cairo 1988 [1922].
20 Cf. Salvatore, Islam..., loc. cit.
21 Roland Robertson, Globalization, Politics, and Religion. In: James Beckford/Thomas Luckmann (eds.), The Changing Face of Religion, London 1989, p. 17-18.
22 Salvatore, Staging Virtue..., loc. cit.

23 Kilian Bälz, La reconstruction séculière du droit islamique. La Haute Cour Constitutionelle égyptienne et la "Bataille du voile" dans les écoles publiques. In: Droit et Societé (1998), in print.
24 Gregory Starrett, The Political Economy of Religious Commodities in Cairo. In: American Anthropologist, 97 (1995), pp. 51-68.
25 Peter F. Beyer, Privatization and the Public Influence of Religion in Global Society. In: Theory, Culture & Society, 7 (1991), pp. 373-395.
26 Warner, The Mass public..., loc. cit.
27 Michael Warner, The Letters of the Republic, Cambridge 1990.
28 Maǧallat aš-šubbān al-muslimūn, May 1967.
29 Muhammad Khalid Masud/Brinkley Messick/David S. Powers, Muftis, Fatwās, and Islamic Legal Interpretation. In: Muhammad Khalid Masud/Brinkley Messick/David S. Powers (eds.), Islamic Legal Interpretation. Muftis and their Fatwās, Cambridge (MA)-London 1996, pp. 3-32.
30 Farhat J. Ziadeh, Lawyers, the Rule of Law and Liberalism in Modern Egypt, Stanford 1968.
31 Niklas Luhmann, Die Sinnform Religion. In: Soziale Systeme, 2 (1996) 1.
32 Reinhart Koselleck, Critique and Crisis: Enlightenment and the Pathogenesis of Modern Society, Oxford 1988 [1959].
33 Messick, loc. cit.
34 Luc Boltanski/Laurent Thévenot, De la justification. Les économies de la grandeur, Paris 1991.

Locations of Nation: Mobility and Locality in the Cultural Economy of Lesotho Migrants

David B. Coplan

Scholars who chance to visit Lesotho often acquire the peculiar urge to lavish their professional attentions upon it. As peculiar indeed as Lesotho itself, a tiny, Belgium-sized post-colonial enclave with three unique characteristics among members of the United Nations Organization: It is the only member country entirely surrounded by the territory of another member - South Africa; it has the highest *average* elevation of any member, and it is the only member whose chief export and foreign exchange earner is its own labour.[1] These peculiarities aside, why should such a noticeable number of major studies have been conducted there, and, perhaps more importantly, why should social and political scientists elsewhere take the trouble to read them? What has the situation of this remote African kingdom and its mountaineer-miners and their women, uniquely to tell us?

A number of such studies are significant in the cautionary mode, taking Lesotho as an object example of "if something can go wrong in Africa it will", beginning of course with the country's former hard luck, as an African state, in having for it's only neighbour apartheid South Africa. These include Spence, Weisfelder and Bardill and Cobbe on political and economic dependence, Murray, Gay and Wallman on labour migration and its social costs, and Ferguson on the failures of "development" theory and practice in Lesotho's "donor mode of production".[2] Others, such as Sechaba Consultants, have attempted to balance pessimism of the intellect with optimism of the will, as Gramsci put it, by emphasizing such human positives as remain in the current outlook.[3] Conversely, ethno-historians such as Machobane and Eldredge and historical ethnographers such as Hamnet and myself have rather searched for an internal, cultural perspective on the impact of social and material forces on Lesotho's people, the Basotho, in an effort at least to portray fully their courage, resilience, and adaptability.[4] What all these efforts have in common, perhaps, is the attempt to demonstrate that the Basotho and Lesotho, by their very extremity and peculiarity, throw certain problems of political economy, social transformation, and cultural reformulation in southern Africa into vivid relief.

Such an objective is not unfamiliar to scholars of South Africa itself, given the painfully obtrusive distortions of apartheid and its legacies. Surely the best current example is Mahmood Mamdani's *Citizen and Subject*[5], which attempts (with mixed success) to reintegrate South Africa's political history into a model encompassing the colonial and post-colonial experience of Africa as a whole. Indeed, my own recent attempt[6] to explain why Lesotho has failed as a post-colonial state might be seen as having an illustrative value at the "subject" pole of Mamdani's broad analytical dichotomy. But as once again an exception in search of a rule, Lesotho has been subject to the same political contradictions as other African countries despite self-conscious national cultural unity and the total absence of any divisive "ethnic" factor in internal politics. As Weisfelder put it: "... the paradox of pervasive conflict in one of the few ethnically and linguistically homogeneous African states lends added significance to efforts at penetrating this tangled political thicket."[7] What is most remarkable and worth meditating upon, however, is not simply that the Basotho in their "national" instance have survived colonialism and capitalism, but that as people they have adapted their identities, practices and projects at personal, communal, and national level so many times in response to such severe, numerous, unanticipated, *different* crises and transformations.

Never has this been more true than today (as television documentary narrators like to say), when the utility of Lesotho's continued independence is in doubt, and it's reality may already be more constructed than real. Well, almost never. Several times in colonial history Basutoland (as it was then called) was threatened by annexation to the Orange Free State/South Africa through military invasion or diplomatic fiat, but survived.[8] Indeed, only British colonial desire to rein in and countermand the power of the Afrikaner republics saved Basutoland in 1868, and the cost was high. The treaty ending hostilities set boundaries that permanently left two-thirds of Basotho farmland in the Free State, a situation that made Basutoland truly a "mountain kingdom" and materially accounts for the economic and political under-development that followed. Disastrously, Britain then left Basutoland in the hands of the Cape colonial government, which extended to it policies shaped by frontier racism in South Africa.[9] In 1880 the Cape Government demanded that Basotho turn in their rifles, in line with South African laws forbidding "natives" to carry arms. The result was the Gun War (1880-1881), in which Basotho rebels humiliated Cape forces, retained their arms, and forced the Crown to take over direct governance of the colony. In hindsight, this might be called the Basotho "war of independence", as it enabled them to escape settler colonial rule and to successfully resist incorporation into South Africa after the Act of Union in 1910, and again in 1949, and ultimately to gain complete sovereignty in 1966.

At first, the new independent government of Prime Minister Leabua Jonathan maintained close ties with its only neighbour. As the world turned against the apartheid state, however, Jonathan realigned his foreign policies and Lesotho benefited from external aid and sympathy as one of southern Africa's resistant "Front Line States." But it is partly because Basutoland/Lesotho perforce defined its national identity in opposition to incorporation into white settler colonial and apartheid South Africa that Lesotho's future as a sovereign state is now possibly, to the majority of

Basotho, of questionable value and therefore, in doubt. Other reasons are social and economic. Lesotho cannot support its citizens or the framework of a "national" economy. The social relationships that always existed and then steadily intensified across Lesotho's borders as a result of economic dependence demand a re-imagination and reconfiguration of Basotho identity now that South Africa is no longer The Enemy. The purpose of this narrative is to examine by what means and in what forms ordinary Basotho, and not their political elites, are bringing this about.

A Little History, if I May

First, a few observations on local identity: The Bantu root "-*sotho*" found in Basotho (the people), Sesotho (the language and culture), and Lesotho (the national state) is not, demonstrably at least, very old, and first appears in print only in 1824.[10] The Basotho have never been a "tribe" or defined themselves as an "ethnic" collectivity, but come into being as a *kingdom* and a *nation* through a self-conscious, political process that amalgamated invading, autochthonous, allied, and refugee clan chieftaincies in the Caledon River valley of the northeastern Cape of Good Hope in the early 1820s. By that time, however, the people who were becoming the Basotho (and in some cases, learning to speak what was only then becoming modern Sesotho) were already working as labour migrants on railways and in the towns of the eastern Cape.[11] What this means is that the very emergence of a national identity for the Basotho took place in the context of involvement in global processes of European colonial political economy. Labour migration under the most severe conditions of racial capitalism has thus been a defining, though understandably often denied, quality of Basotho identity for the whole of their national existence.

Unfortunately, the political conception and meaning of *territory* to the "Basotho" in the framework of the pre-colonial chieftaincy has yet to be fully understood. Still, there were widely accepted rules, attached to the structure of chieftaincy in the sub-region, that governed settlement and entitlement among in-migrating groups. In disregard of these indigenous legal norms, the Afrikaner intruders did not admit to becoming subjects of the rulers who granted them permission to till and herd within their realms. Nor even did the whites' own practice of "annexation" retain its European application. In southern Africa, as a missionary noted in 1867, "It does not mean to bring a country and its people under a new Government but to expropriate the inhabitants in order to substitute oneself to them."[12] The settlers desperately required African labour however, and so Moshoeshoe's subjects, if they were young, were coerced or cajoled to remain as servants and workers on white farms. Those who chose to take refuge in lands still under Basotho control were condemned for "retreating before civilization." Moshoeshoe I was not in fact the sovereign of a land, like the King of France, nor even of a people, like the King of the Franks, but of a *range*[13], on which he, his royal kinsmen, his vassals, and their followers alone had the right to plant crops and pasture their livestock. Moshoeshoe's people were bound to him by his ability to preserve and extend that range and to provide them with the cattle that embodied their fealty as a social contract. However poorly or rather situationally defined, areas of Basotho occupation were "eaten up" (*Ma a jeloe*) by the Afrikaners with a rapaciousness that exceeded African comprehension.

The British too, beginning with the Napier Treaty in 1843, enforced a series of agreements which sanctioned the loss of the better part of Moshoeshoe's realm to the Free State,[14] simultaneously reinventing "Basutoland" as a territorial entity. At the close of the Free State Wars in 1868 Afrikaner leaders like Col. Henry Fick were burning out the Basotho from their lands in the eastern Orange Free State that were from then on to be known as the "Conquered Territories", driving them east across the Caledon[15]. It was apparently at this time that the lowlands along the western bank of the river, in distinction to the high upland areas newly occupied by the Basotho, came to be called "Lesotho." This sudden influx not only transformed Basotho society in the western lowlands, it had important consequences in establishing family ties across the new territorial boundaries. The origins of what were to become prominent lowland Basotho families could be traced to the Free State, and networks of kith and kin on both sides continued to offer social support as people crossed and recrossed the uncontrolled colonial border. Ironically, it was just at this time that Basotho began to thrive economically from the new opportunities in agricultural marketing, transport riding, and mine labour that arose with the opening of the diamond diggings at Kimberley. The physical harshness and social degradation that the migrants experienced there set the pattern for Basotho experience of urban South Africa, summed up in the well-known couplet from migrants' *lifela* songs:

Oa tseba ke buoa ka Gemele	You know I speak of Kimberley;
Ke buoa ka Sotoma	I speak of Sodom.

Indeed, it was over the 200 km journeys by foot through hostile territory to the diamond fields and back again that the *lifela tsa litsamaea-naha* songs ("songs of the intrepid travellers") emerged as a distinct genre of male migrants' mobile, double-placed culture.[16]

Inexorably, however, the decentralized monarchical system that was designed for centrifugal expansion became distorted and unworkable, bottled up in a sharply delimited territory and suborned to colonial rigidification. In parallel fashion, British Basutoland was transformed from the region's granary into its labour reserve,[17] as mixed pastoralism gave way to labour migrancy and *de facto* proletarianization. While some of this was due to drought, ecological degradation, cattle disease, and the desire for industrial products, colonialism did much to help. Under pressure from less productive, labour-starved Afrikaner farmers, the British undermined the Basuto agricultural economy by laying severe restrictions on grain exports to South Africa. Additionally, overt racial discrimination, the denial of trading and transport licenses to Basotho, and the imposition of hut taxes all accelerated the process of underdevelopment and labour out-migration. When the fabulous gold fields of the Witwatersrand opened in the late 1880s, Basotho reported there in large numbers to sink the shafts, a labour specialization they have retained up to the present day. Basotho workers say that while King Shaka and his empire are the Zulu national claim to fame, the Basotho opened the South African mines. By 1905, when the paramount chief (King) Letsie II actually visited Basotho in the mining compounds near Johannesburg, labour migrancy was a significant feature of Lesotho's economic and social life, with legal male migrants alone totalling 10,000 out of a population of 400,000.[18]

Two important realities, often neglected in the Lesotho literature, are concealed by such statistics. The first is that a great many migrants used their labour passes and mine contracts merely as tickets of admission to the mushrooming highveld Babylon of the goldreef. Desertions plagued the mine labour recruitment system from the beginning, and many migrants moved rapidly from mine to mine, from mine to urban residence and employment, and from Lesotho to the reef and back again without much effective let or hindrance. The second reality was the role of Basotho women migrants or indeed urban immigrants, despite strenuous efforts by South African, colonial, and chiefly authorities to prevent it. At first, in the late 1800s, most Basotho women only followed the men as far as the border, providing a companionable send-off that became a profitable reception when, their pockets full, the migrants returned from the goldfields many months later. As pastoral agriculture and the rural economy declined during the twentieth century, however, Basotho women began to join their men in significant numbers on the Reef itself, creating settled communities in the urban shanty towns that alarmed South African, British Basutoland, and Basotho chiefly authorities alike. Efforts to uproot them failed completely until 1963, when apartheid "influx control" laws that forbade foreign African women from migrating to South Africa were harshly enforced, and border controls were established at the Caledon for the first time. While many Basotho women were forcibly repatriated, they continued to migrate illegally, as they do even under the new political dispensation in South Africa today. Such migrations were not in many cases permanent, however, and even when they were, Basotho settled in towns within the wide Basutoland-Free

State-Witwatersrand corridor maintained strong ties with their natal homes. Indeed, given their insecure or even illegal status and the horrors of life in the South African urban "native locations", there were compelling social reasons for doing so. The *seoeleoelele* songs of generations of women, mirroring the *lifela* ... of their men, express the hardships of a migratory black female Basotho life. Among these is a text by the famous 'Malitaba (now deceased), the first widely popular, recorded exponent of migrant women's songs:

> Hau oelele! oelele! oelele! Helele I remember handsome
> Makhaba [A lover whose name means "maize fields"].
> That green maize field of our home, men oe!
> He stays at Sekekete yonder[19]
> Jo! A man of Nkoebe's,
> Nkoebe's [at] Sebapala, Mats'ela-ha-beli ["Where you cross twice"]
> Qomo-Qomong at Lesala's place, at the home of the handsome Patsi, Boys of my home, 'Molo,
> Those of my home are still crying, they ask each other, not knowing me, 'Malitaba of Mphoso,
> They ask where I stay oe!
> I was born at Thabana Morena, jo!
> A person of Konote's place,
> Mohale's Hoek at Malebanye's,
> The camp [town] of Mafeteng, at my place,
> I stay at Ntsane's, Nyakosoba [Roma District],
> At Chele's, next to Monyohe, the home of Sanaha [her husband], the man oe!
> Come let's depart, Ntate Sanaha jo! The master of love, greetings!
> Let's take ourselves quickly to Lesotho; I should not die here in Johannesburg,
> Amidst noise there at a funeral where tears are flowing[20]
> Greetings, Betlile, my son oe!
> Helele! Hele! "Mankokosane" ["Mother of water"] the rain is coming. ["Mankokosane" is a song praising rain after a drought]
> I don't play with boys, for I am now a grown woman.
> I always tell them I am not born but compound my mistakes, my child Lenka [the accordion player accompanying her][21].
> When she's there, 'Malitaba of Mphoso, you won't see hardships, things just go smoothly.
> I am not afraid of a giant, even one full of cunning.
> Knives they can clean miss me,
> Sticks swing over my head,

Cracking over my head, Man! the fighting sticks of men[22].
Who can be asked bad news [her death]?
They can be asked of Sanaha [her husband], the man jo! The
master of love.
I always tell them oe! The person from Chele's, well!
I won't stay in Naledi [a section of Soweto, Johannesburg],
Jo! A person of Shale's, well oe!
To your home!
I won't stay in Naledi, Tlali, or Moletsane [all townships
in Soweto], my child;
I say, among cannibals[23] yonder, in Mapetla or Senaoana,
When the State of Emergency was fought[24].
It's finished I'm leaving, time up I am going
Time up I am going;
David [Coplan] you live where?
Roma[25], renowned among the nations!

This song, a lament for people and places in Lesotho from the perceived disadvantage point of Johannesburg, is littered with the names of lovers, husbands, and good men gone bad such as the wistfully-named "Maize-fields," who spends his time hanging about at one of the most notorious vice dens in all Lesotho. Sixteen lines from the end, 'Malitaba sings of the fearful fighting that was commonplace among organized gangs of Basotho workers along the Reef from the late 1940s to the 1960s.

Interlude: to Russians with Love

These gangs were called "russians" as an antonym to their major urban foes, Johannesburg's feared "Americans" gang, and in identification with the post-War Soviet Union. "... the only nation feared by the whiteman in South Africa," as one retired russian told me. The preparation for russianism was rooted in rural socialization and in the Basotho custom of organized stick fighting between herdboys from neighbouring villages. Based on "homeboy" networks from the northern and southern lowland border towns of Lesotho, these gangs transmuted from "self-protection units"[26] defending Basotho on the Reef from the attacks of other ethnic groups and the police, to predatory gangs battling, often for sport, against one another and supporting themselves through every variety of second-rate criminal activity.[27] 'Malitaba herself was lover and wife to a number of russians, as the song recounts. The evolution from vigilantism organized for communal protection to indiscriminate social banditry is a cyclical process common in urban African areas since the late nineteenth century. The Basotho russians are of particular interest, however, in relation to the dualistic model, first proposed by Philip Mayer[28], of "townsmen and tribesmen", urbanite and migrant worker in urban African social structure. At first go, the russians appear to embody one of the most fundamental intended social consequences of "grand apartheid": a perpetually unsettled African population from which neither a self-sufficient rural peasantry nor a permanent urban working class was permitted to emerge. Examined more closely, the russians were attempting to resolve or at least domesticate this contradiction by extending *Sesotho*, the Basotho cultural framework, to the heterogeneous and in their view, uncivilized and un-enculturated urban environment in which perforce they had come to stay. An obvious sign of this attempt was the predatory violence and contempt they directed towards urban location youth, whether or not the latter were in fact social predators themselves.

Although many russians had lost physical links with the land and gone from migrant to immigrant in the urban areas, they still regarded themselves as *Basotho a 'Mankhonthe*, true Basotho sons-of-the-soil. While many migrants maintained a social ideology of a dualistic economy (capitalist vs. patrimonial) and social structure (individualist vs. communitarian), their activity was based upon a struggle for autonomy in a social arena which in material reality always included both South Africa and Basutoland. While russian-ism is held not to function in Lesotho, the destruction of Basutoland's peasant economy led inevitably to the dissemination of similar social values on both sides of the border. Violence, prostitution, and thievery are today all too common in Lesotho, even in small communities, and communitarian values are often more honoured in the breach as class formation, individualism, envy, witchcraft accusation, deceit, feuding, and recrimination come to characterize rural as well as urban life. But this is not how russians, or Basotho migrants generally, talk of things. The transformation of the lusty stick fighting of Basotho herdboys in rural Lesotho into murderous gangsterism both actualizes and symbolizes Basotho migrant constructions of the moral economy of what they see as a bifurcated social landscape. In this construction, Lesotho is the place of civilization and cultural morality (*Sesotho*), while South Africa and particularly the mines and urban areas, are uncivilized Hobbsian social *terra incognita*. So, veterans of these gangs are adamant that russian-ism, along with other countersocial forms of behaviour, was left behind when returning to Lesotho.

In sum, what the russians, both male and female, were doing is "encapsulating" themselves, as Mayer famously put it[29], in an ethnically-based and thus culturally grounded subculture of their own, competing strategically and violently with each other but wrapping their blankets and shaking their fighting sticks and battle axes at settled urbanites and landed Basutoland Basotho alike. Gender relations among russians were an expression of this intent to create autonomy in the cracks of a world ill-fashioned for them by enemies both foreign and domestic. Control of independent women, known as *matekatse*, freely translated as "prostitutes" but literally meaning husbandless transients, was an important competitive russian agenda. This control, however, was predicated upon the re-establishment and defense of normative marital bonds, notwithstanding the common-law nature of the majority of russian domestic relationships. Male and female russians were quite often mutually supportive and independent counterparts. A traditional-style men's *mohobelo* song composed as a russian anthem in Johannesburg takes a female perspective and praises the role of women in supporting the embattled men:

> My boy [lover] when I get out of here, I will depart,
> Leave carrying you on my back [like a baby],
> Boy, when I get out of here, I will depart,
> Fearful for you of the thief-men [city gangs and rival russians].

It should be noted that rather than the *mokorotlo*, the dance songs of war in which each soldier prepared himself to meet death through individualized, extemporaneous movements, the russians chose *mohobelo*, the highly stylized and synchronized dance of male fellowship and team display - a dance of social agreement - as preparation for the fray.

The russian *chanteuse* 'Malitaba attended her husband, a gang leader, at numerous battles in the Johannesburg area during the 1950s and 1960s. Asked what role she played during the actual fighting, 'Malitaba replied, "Why, to carry on singing, to give them courage to win the fight!" Many russian women's songs provide harrowing and piteous evocations of famous faction fights. Identifying with the male russians and the marginal position to which they are both socially consigned, female singers express admiration for these stouthearted men and appropriate images of battle to express women's existential struggles:

> Hae oele oele! You, child of 'MaKhalemang
> [a male russian,
> friend and fellow bar singer],
> Blow the whistle so the russians may fight oe!
> When it's fought it is fearsome,
> When it's fought it is fearsome:
> I can fling off my blankets,
> He! I, the child 'Ma'tsepe oe!
> The loafers' [russians] whistle blower, Khalemang,
> Whistler of loafers,
> Khalemang, you, man of Mokotane's,
> Makotane's at Mantsonyane,
> Lead them into the way (of battle); they know it (well).
> Hee! (so) I seize the black (heavy) fighting stick;

> I'm fighting, I cannot be stopped; I am fighting.
> (Alinah Tsekoa, "Malitsepe")

Interestingly, male singers rarely give russianism more than a mention, and almost never sing about russian battles. The women, conversely, sing about them in detail, praising the valorous and handsome, mourning the fallen, projecting themselves into the fray. Basotho labour migrancy became in itself a culture, integrating a set of social strategies and expressions of which russianism was only one luridly visible part. Ultimately, the russians were suppressed by the police apparatus of the apartheid state, with the cooperation of Lesotho authorities, perhaps a quarter century ago.

In sum, nationalism, like tradition is "Janus-faced"[30] such that whenever people's own categories of discourse refer to the past, they express a political instrumentality. The rich and the poor invent and reify "tradition" as ideology, and thereby give credence to the conception of migrants as "men of two worlds" so popular in both scholarly and public discourse. This dualist view assumes a discontinuity between the structure of social relations, patterns of interaction, and cultural norms of Lesotho and South Africa. Such rigid, unreconcilable opposition would seem ideal for differentiating between Sesotho and *Sekhooa*, the culture of the whites, or *mtheto*, the unwritten code that governs life at the mines. After careful ethnographic examination, however, we suggest the discontinuity between Lesotho and *makhooeng*, the "whitemen's place", is more a putative representation, a fiction useful in both the defense and the revision of Sesotho. With the decline of farming and livestock keeping as viable means of making a living, Basotho migrants no longer in practice treat the environments of the mines and the home villages as two separate social fields. South Africa and Lesotho have become a continuous social world, full of dangers that the migrant must uncover and overcome. As one singer exhorted his comrades in a migrant's *sefela* song:

> Koete ha habo monna ke hohle;   Gentlemen, a man's home is everywhere;
> U nke molamu u k'u itekile.   Take up your stick and ramble[31]

Basotho migrants' conformity to *mtheto* at the mines and to Sesotho at home does not imply any reformulation of his identity as a true Mosotho. Broadly, "Mosotho" is a unified concept in the minds of many migrants that remains a portmanteau wherever they find themselves.

Ambushed Again: From Cyclical Migration to Multiple Dis/placement

Just as the term *matekatse* for barmaids derives from the verb "to wander about," male migrant *lifela* singers commonly refer to themselves *lipapatlele*, "vagabonds," or *likhutsana* "orphans," - and both sexes can be *makholoa*, "absconders" from Lesotho. Migrants male and female, then, have classically pictured themselves as socially suspended in the great cross-border axis of Basotho settlement. Despite all the names of people, places, and (for Lesotho) chiefs who rule them used as self-identification within a firm social geography, these Basotho are eternally mobile, multiply located, and displaced.

Since the early 1970s, as "influx control" and laws regulating foreign workers tightened, mine wages increased, and employment opportunities in Lesotho declined, the phenomenon of the "career migrant" has come to dominate Basotho working-class society.[32] In this scenario, declining numbers of more highly paid, skilled, and experienced male migrants visit home more regularly but spend longer and less frequently interrupted working lives on the mines, while their earnings go to support increasing networks at multiple locations. Those migrant workers who have held on to their jobs show signs of developing into Lesotho's "labour aristocracy." Career mining has increased stratification, heightened social tensions, reduced productivity, and accelerated the disintegration of family life. Career miners are more proletarianized, more prone to alcoholism, sexually transmitted diseases and tuberculosis, and suffer more keenly the hardships of mine compound life[33], but in the current situation they must be grateful to have a "career" at all. Indeed, the latest trend is not to offer retrenched mineworkers their old jobs when they are re-hired, but to employ them as "casual" workers on contracts without security or service benefits and at vastly reduced wages. The worst effects of this new form of labour exploitation were revealed in the aftermath of the horrible Vaal Reefs mine disaster in 1995, when 104 mine workers, half of them Basotho, were crushed to death when a mine locomotive ran off its rails and fell on top of an elevator descending a shaft. The families of many of those killed, it emerged, could not officially receive any benefits or compensation because their men had been "casuals" (an old South African canard) supplied by labour contractors and not employees of the mining company, Anglo-American, itself.

For female Basotho migrants, who work in domestic and other service sectors, "career migrancy" may be even older and more entrenched, since their often uncertain legal status and/or lack of employment security makes it difficult for them to return home often. The migration of Basotho women has increased markedly as the declining South African mining industry retrenches so many of their men folk. Lesotho has lost about 50,000 mining jobs since the heights of the late 1980s, and this has forced many wives to seek work across the border while their unemployable husbands look after whoever and whatever remains at home. In micro-economic terms, this latest "reversal of fortune" has led to a closer integration of male and female migrant social networks spanning the South Africa-Lesotho border. Quite commonly, migrants maintain and mobilize variable, multi-sited family networks in adaptation to rapid changes in the structure of employment. So for example, a married male mineworker (one of the lucky ones) now maintains a rural homestead where his parents farm and perhaps look after his children, his wife rents a room in a lowland town where she wrings some income out of the informal sector, a brother or sister works in a service job in some Free State or Witwatersrand urban area, and he stays on a mine compound near which is a location or informal settlement housing a girlfriend and her children. Except for the girlfriend, people can be rotated among any of these sites as opportunities, social needs, and changing circumstances require. A female migrant may maintain a similar multi-sited network based on service employment, complete with unemployed Lesotho husband and South African boyfriend of her own. Basotho workers, then, have gone from independent peasant pastoralists to tenant farmers and farm workers to oscillating mine migrants and "peasantarians" to mobile network managers of either gender - all in order to survive with the historical consolation prize of an independent "national" state that can offer no basis for survival. The question for us, then, is what do these involuntary transformations mean for Basotho national identity in a globalizing context?

Conclusion: Locations of Nation

Since the Treaty of Versailles, it has become an almost universally accepted proposition that the "self-determination of nations"[34] achieves its full expression only in the form of a sovereign "national" state. Peoples without such states, such as the Palestinians or the Kurds, put their establishment at the centre of their nationalist agenda. So the interesting question arises as to whether Lesotho, the truncated Basotho national state, is not now an obstacle to the political and economic aspirations of the majority of "the nation", who might more profitably relinquish its existence as an independent state.

Basotho migrants are strikingly ambivalent on the issue. The Basotho achieved the rare distinction of defeating or at least holding at bay both settler colonialism and imperial militarism (in part by playing these two forces against one another). For this very reason many Basotho are stubborn in their attachment to the concept of an autonomous Lesotho, to institutions like the chieftaincy (however problematic) that have embodied and defended this concept, and to *Sesotho*, the language and culture in which it is expressed. Lesotho is, by virtue of history, a country. It possesses a distinctive political culture, monarchy, chiefship, land tenure and legal system. So great has been the upsurge in nationalist feeling in the face of the political transformation and turmoil taking place across the border in South Africa, that both the African National Congress and the mineworkers union have had to weaken their incorporationist rhetoric. At present those materially involved in the debate avoid the term "incorporation": the less total and more equivocal word "integration" is now preferred.

Recently the appeal of *Sesotho* as self-identifying "tradition" has revived and strengthened among the powerful and privileged and the dominated and exploited alike. With so much original Basotho territory incorporated into the Free State, and so many Basotho residing in South Africa, cultural symbols and practices have become the most significant markers of national identity. Such representations are constructed on the basis of geographical origins and political allegiances within what remains of Moshoeshoe I's monarchical state. In this sense Lesotho anchors an historical patrimony that extends well beyond its present physical borders. Indeed, Basotho nationalism as an explicit agenda still centres on the demand for the return of the "Conquered Territories," no matter how unlikely its fulfilment. Then again, Basotho migrants may have actually found a way to repossess the Conquered Territories. Like the Mexican immigrants presently re-occupying the American Southwest, they may simply join their compatriots over the Caledon. Ironically, many Basotho who applied for South African Permanent Residence Permits under the terms of the 1995-1996 migrants' "amnesty" policy did so rather as a means to recover resources from the Conquered Territories through access to the free services and pensions that come from legal rights in the economy that Basotho have helped to build. Such applicants have no wish to actually move to South Africa, which they see as a sink-hole of crime, unemployment, and landless poverty; headed for political instability once the dominating presence of Mandela is gone.[35]

No one would question why Lesotho's independent existence is defended by the interlocking military, professional, bureaucratic, and aristocratic elites who have a vested interest in structures of government and patronage, land allocation, the revenues from of migrant labour and now the massive Lesotho Highlands Water Project. But for migrants and other working-class Basotho, the independence of Lesotho represents a profound social and economic dilemma. In the mines, the disadvantages of foreign status have come to outweigh the advantages, as those Basotho who were dismissed and deported to Lesotho during the 1987 National Union of Mineworkers' strike will readily attest. The political integration of Lesotho, bringing with it the rights of citizenship and formal recognition of union membership, is the most reliable road to employment security and labour mobility in a future South Africa. Otherwise Basotho will suffer continued discrimination in the workplace and exclusion from the benefits of programs of land reform and reallocation. As Roger Southall[36] puts it, South African politics determines life in Lesotho and on the mines; it's time for the Basotho to be players in that process, not bystanders in the struggle for their own economic future.

On the other hand, the proud history of Lesotho, with its distinctive institutions, social structure, and resistance to incorporation is a hard thing to abandon. Just as important, *lefatse le la sechaba*; "the land belongs to the nation": a married man is theoretically entitled to pasture and fields for cultivation as "free goods," and in genuine practice to some ground on which to build his house regardless of the privatizing impetus (so far unenforced) of the 1979 Land Act. In addition, the rights to residential stands, fields for cultivation, and pasturage that attach to social identity as a member of a Basotho family, clan, and chieftaincy, as well as that identity in and of itself, represent precious entitlements to a great many migrants, the more so as they have to spend so many hard years away from them. Conversely, many retrenched migrants with whom I have spoken state they would, if necessary, give up their Lesotho passports if only South Africa itself could provide the majority of its own citizens with a life that is stable, peaceful, law-governed, and economically viable. Further, half of those who would prefer to carry South African identity documents still resist the idea of "incorporating" Lesotho into its hegemonic neighbour, just as they prefer not to relocate their families to the work place,[37] even if there proves to be a future South Africa worth living in. "That would mean the end of Sesotho," some protest. This worry indicates that political incorporation is also an identity question: if incorporation is a step forward, then Sesotho is a step backward. By *Sesotho* they mean far more than their "language and culture", or a naturalized set of customs and way of life. It means a personal as well as communal, genealogical, and national history, an identity and its entitlements, reciprocities and their resources, investments of the self and substance, and most materially a communal land-tenure system in which land is still not a factor in the market. This, as one veteran migrant explained, summarizing Sesotho as resistance to market relations, prevents "the white man from owning everything, as he does in South Africa". Without Lesotho, they doubt there can be *Sesotho*. Other migrants have no such concerns, and point out that even if Lesotho passports had to be surrendered upon the issuance of South African documents[38], this would not close off access to the resources of Sesotho or Lesotho. "I can practice Sesotho wherever I reside," shrugged one worker. Another migrant who worked tirelessly to build up his farm stated that he would gladly give up his Lesotho passport, and return periodically to his home as a "foreign" visitor, if it meant the preservation of his mining job in South Africa.

The key point is that Sesotho, taken in its more restrictive local sense as the cultural dialect of Moshoeshoe's Basotho, is the expressive counterpart of a political construct with an internally acknowledged history. It is not a vehicle of an immemorial "tradition" embodying the inherent cultural "genius of a people" as the Germanic idealism of apartheid theory attempted to frame it. From the founding of the nation, migrant labour played a role in this process, in the face of colonial racism, Basotho men drew upon the cultural categories of the South African milieu, job specializations such as shaft sinking, and the insecurities of urban residence to define their own collective identity as Basotho. To float a metaphor: for labour migrants Lesotho is the home port or anchor bay, Basotho the ship and crew, and Sesotho the art and plan of navigation. While the horizons of Sesotho are transnational, Sesotho remains a local referent of a tangible national construct.

When it comes to Lesotho or South African residence and citizenship, Basotho migrants have realized that perhaps there is neither necessity nor advantage in making a choice. Basotho migrants are responding with characteristic adaptability to the dilemma by "working the system". Only 13 months after many had trooped home to vote in Lesotho's own parliamentary poll at Easter, 1993, those who had worked in the country for five years or more obtained voting rights in South Africa's 1994 elections. That precedent was further used by the National Union of Mineworkers (NUM) in October 1995 to lobby for foreign miners' right to live in South Africa. Soon after, the South African Government announced the unilateral granting, on application, of South African permanent residence to any Lesotho migrant who has worked on the South African mines for at least five years since 1986. Vocal protests by Lesotho officials quickly followed, as up to 60,000 Basotho working men could qualify for the "amnesty" as it was called. It was feared that such an exodus would have a devastating impact on the Lesotho Bank in the short run and on the country's economy over the longer term. In April 1996 the Lesotho Minister of Finance publicly requested South Africa to give Lesotho equal attention with its former "Bantustans" in its Reconstruction and Development Program (RDP). Even before this, of course, migrants used various ruses, such as bribery and tax registration, to obtain a legal South African identity and with it, preference in employment and eligibility for benefit packages. Yet contrary to expectations on both sides of the border, only about one third of workers eligible actually applied for Permanent Residence, or about one fifth of the total Basotho mine workforce in South Africa.[39] Those who did retain their Lesotho local passports for unimpeded access to their homesteads in Lesotho, as well as to influence events there. When King Letsie III dissolved parliament in 1994, for example, Basotho mineworkers threatened to flood back over the border to destabilise the country, and to force mine managements to suspend the flow of their deferred remittances to the Bank of Lesotho. Broadly, Basotho migrants' identity has become a matter of strategy and tactics, anchored in the implicit confidence of cultural "disposition" and practice.[40]

Currently, the strategy of multiple bases on both sides of the border seems the best to many Basotho working men and women. Lesotho migrants don't want an either/or residence and investment strategy, but a both/and (Sechaba Consultants 1997: 34). Sadly, this "best of both worlds" idea is based on the recognition of some powerful double negatives. Dualism as a strategy will work only if Lesotho remains a fundamentally different kind of place than South Africa, with different social and economic relations, based on Sesotho. Land rights in Lesotho, for example, are still important as a form of social security, but returning to the land is a fond hope and the migrants know it. Only 10 per cent of retired migrants make a go of it as farmers, and the same was true in Murray's study (Murray 1981) twenty years ago. As Philip Mayer put it then, "the elaborate defences developed by [migrant cultures] have lost their effectiveness once the possibility of obtaining arable land has fallen away"[41]. The Lesotho Government too is scorned as incompetent, corrupt, and uncaring, viewing migrants as oxen and using them as cash cows.[42] Over in South Africa, permanent family relocation near the mines may once have looked good, but now appears to be a trap as retrenchments continue, mines downsize or even close, and once thriving mining towns begin to resemble ghost towns. Some male migrants viewed South African life as socially corrupting and without values. Those who had applied for permanent residence but in fact did not wish to move permanently to South Africa cited the hardships of life there, as well as their fears of being expelled anyway in the long run. Basotho who actually take up permanent residence in South Africa, they said, will find the benefits illusory and the future a "ride on a tiger"[43].

The migrants' self-preserving image as rural yeomen and keepers of the "true cultural knowledge" of Sesotho is tempered by their equivocal attitudes towards the Government of Lesotho as a political institution. The rapid deterioration of governance after March 1993 revealed the election itself as something less than a popular re-affirmation of the "modern" state. The subsequent crises did not evoke widespread popular mobilization because what goes on in the capital Maseru, and even what happens to the monarch, are strangely distant to the lives of most ordinary citizens. The marginalization of the people locally, and of the country in the regional economy and in southern African politics, is as apparent as ever. Faced with learned indifference amongst the predominantly rural populace, the state lacks popular support. Unarticulated, for fear of openly confronting the issue, is people's awareness that the state and nation have grown apart. While the state occupies the attention of its small corps of incumbents and opponents, the population is more concerned with what it means to be Basotho, the significance of Lesotho's particular history today, and the inevitably hard road of future.

Relations between the state and its citizens are by now totally conditioned by the demands of donors, lenders, and the market. Even the 1993 elections eventually took place in response to pressure from donors, who made their success a condition for the resumption of financial aid, suspended in order to pressure the military into holding them. Most rural people look to their local communities on the one hand, and to employment, kin ties, and social networks in South Africa on the other for livelihood, cooperation, and support. To the Government in Maseru they look for unwelcome interference, giving in return, avoidance. Basotho popular nationalism expresses a desire for some historically imagined, possible concordance between state and nation, but the ruling party has been unable to constitute the state in a national image that is satisfying to the people - or even to the party itself.[44]

The state and the rural population do not in fact share the same definition of the nation. To the state, Lesotho is politically distinct, but externally dependent. Except for the wealthiest stock owners and those with ties to the bourgeoisie, rural people want secure homes and independent communities governed by Sesotho: the means of survival at the region's margins. By the twentieth century, *Sesotho* had been rigidified as invariant tradition (Hobsbawm 1984) by a modernizing, colonized aristocracy. Labour migrants and their farming families, however, have for the past 125 years rehearsed much more fluid and responsive notions of Sesotho and kept the mix of forms, laws, meanings, and practices it connoted at the ready for a host of uses. For them, political independence has value only in so far as it protects Sesotho and its resources, a protection the state, regardless of who governs it, in practice seeks to withdraw. While the Basotho nation may like other nations be imagined as a community and "conceived as a deep, horizontal comradeship"[45], the state has not managed to draw this communal idea into its service. Nationalism in Lesotho, as Tom Nairn would have predicted[46], is indeed a compensatory reaction to capitalist penetration. But it is precisely because, as Anderson asserts, "nation-ness is the most universally legitimate value in the political life of our time"[47] that in this case it does not imply support for the state. Lesotho is not the Basotho. The state is now the alien power, the neo-colonizer, the intervener in a chieftaincy that is the last political refuge of Sesotho. This is nationalism out of the eye of the "national" state, and that is why it's strength caught all political parties in the 1993 election by surprise.

Among migrants there is no confidence whatever that the Basotho economic or political elite have any commitment to practising or upholding pre-colonial values of hierarchical reciprocity or communal social exchange. Not surprisingly, it is members of the elites who most pointedly represent cultural and political identity as coterminous, bottling up Sesotho in Lesotho. The failure of Lesotho's new democracy to take hold, let alone prove to be relevant to most citizens' lives, may yet turn the stream of emigration into a flood. The reality is that the Lesotho state has become an interference, albeit a powerful one, in the life of both Basotho communities and their nation. Is Lesotho too peculiar to serve as an example of anything but itself? Or does it's very contrariness point to profound disjunctions between state and "nation" elsewhere in post--colonial Africa and even beyond?[48] How can real space be created in our regional political economy for the social arrangements upon which Basotho workers depend for psycho-cultural as well as material survival? In rethinking both productive alternatives and the creation of a viable agenda for the "nation," it may not be to Lesotho's state institutions that we must look.

Notes

1   While the project began in earnest back at the end of the 1980s, the first water flowed at the end of October 1997.
2   Jack Spence, Lesotho: The Politics of Dependence, London 1968; Richard Weisfelder, The Basotho Nation-State: What Legacy for the Future? In: Journal of Modern African Studies 19 (1981) 2, pp. 221-56; J.E. Bardill/J. H. Cobbe, Lesotho: Dilemmas of Dependence in Southern Africa. Boulder-London 1985; Colin Murray, Families Divided: The Impact of Migrant Labour in Lesotho, Cambridge 1981; Judith S. Gay, Basotho Women Migrants: A Case Study. In: Institute for Development Studies Bulletin, Sussex 11 (1980) 3, pp. 19-28; id., Basotho Women's Options: A Study of Marital Careers in Rural Lesotho. Unpub. Ph.D., Cambridge University 1980; Sandra Wallman, Take Out Hunger, London 1969; James Ferguson, The Anti-Politics Machine, Cambridge 1990.
3   Sechaba Consultants, 1995. Lesotho's Long Journey: Hard Choices at the Crossroads, Maseru 1995.
4   L.B.B.J. Machobane, Government and Change in Lesotho, 1800-1966, Maseru 1990; E. Eldredge, A South African Kingdom: The Pursuit of Security in Nineteenth Century Lesotho, Cambridge 1993; Ferguson, The Anti-Politics Machine, loc. cit.; David B. Coplan, In the Time of Cannibals: Word Music of South Africa's Basotho Migrants, Chicago-Johannesburg 1994; Ian Hamnet, Chieftainship and Legitimacy: An Anthropological Study of Executive Law in Lesotho, London 1975.
5   Mahmood Mamdani, Citizen and Subject: Contemporary Africa and the Legacy of Late Colonialism, London 1996.
6   David B. Coplan/Tim Quinlan, A Chief by the People: Nation versus State in Lesotho. In: Africa, London 67 (1997) 1, pp. 27-60.
7   Richard Weisfelder, The Basotho Monarchy. In: Rene Lemarchand (ed.), African Kingdoms in Perspective, London 1977, pp. 160-189, here p. 161.
8   See Bardill/Cobbe, Lesotho: Dilemmas of Dependence..., loc. cit., p. 14.
9   Sandra Burman, Chiefdom Politics and Alien Law: Basutoland Under Cape Rule, 1871-1884, London 1981.
10 David Ambrose, The Basotho Settlement at Griquatown. In: Lesotho Notes and Records, IV (1973), p. 601-664.
11 Judy Kimble, Labour Migration in Basutoland, c.1870-1885. In: S. Marks/R. Rathbone (eds.,), Industrialisation and Social Change in South Africa, London 1982, p. 119-141.

12 Paul Germond, Chronicles of Basutoland, Lesotho 1967, p. 284.
13 John Comaroff/Jean Comaroff, Of Revelation and Revolution. Vol. 1, Christianity, Colonialism, and Consciousness in South Africa, Chicago 1991, p. 204.
14 See map in: Bardill/Cobbe, Lesotho: Dilemmas..., loc. cit., p. 14.
15 Indeed the Basotho founder, King Moshoeshoe I, ruefully accepting the Caledon as the new effective boundary as the price of British "Protection" from the Free State, renamed this river *Mohokare*, "That Which Is Amidst", as in his famous query *How can they make a border amidst our land*?
16 Coplan, In the Time of Cannibals..., loc. cit.
17 Colin Murray, From Granary to Labour Reserve: An Economic History of Lesotho. In: South African Labour Bulletin, 6 (1980) 4, pp. 3-20.
18 Eldredge, A South African Kingdom..., loc. cit., p. 189, 65.
19 A hotel bar in Maputsoe, Lesotho, notorious for hard-drinking migrants and hard-case prostitutes. Makhaba doesn't really "stay" there: he stays there too long and too often.
20 In Johannesburg, people weep loudly at funerals: because there is inordinate suffering, and because the funeral became a noisy, spontaneous political event in the South African townships during the anti-apartheid struggle.
21 Here the singer tells the accordion player that she didn't have to be taught to mispeak herself in song; her talent is natural.
22 Here the singer is referring to battles among gangs of Basotho gangsters on the Reef during the 1950s and 1960s.
23 The singer compares the violent gangsters of the Johannesburg African townships to the cannibals who were said to terrorize the Caledon valley in the early 19th century. See Coplan, In the Time of Cannibals..., loc. cit.
24 The singer compares the faction fights of the russian gangsters to the fighting which took place when Chief Jonathan declared the State of Emergency in 1970, and violently suppressed the singer's party, the Basutoland Congress Party.
25 Roma, sight of the first Roman Catholic mission in Basutoland and Pius XII College, today the National University of Lesotho, is indeed an international centre.
26 "Self-protection units" (SDUs) were famously part of intra-community political violence in Johannesburg and Durban during the 1980s.
27 See Coplan, In the Time of Cannibals..., loc. cit., pp. 189-199.
28 Philip Mayer/Iona Mayer, Townsmen or Tribesmen, Capetown 1961.
29 Philip Mayer (ed.), Black Villagers in an Industrial Society, London 1980.
30 Tom Nairn, The Break-up of Britain, London 1981.
31 Makali I.P. Mokitimi, A Literary Analysis of Lifela tsa Litsamaea-Naha Poetry. Unpub. M.A. thesis, Nairobi 1982, p. 456.
32 See D.B. Coplan/T. Thoahlane, Motherless Households, Landless Farms: The Social Implications of Changing Employment Patterns Among Lesotho Migrants. In: J. Crush/W. James (eds.), Crossing Boundaries, Cape Town 1995.
33 Jonathan Crush/Alan Jeeves/David Yudelman, South Africa's Labour Empire, Cape Town 1991, pp. 151-152.
34 This phrase is a summary paraphrase of the 14th Point of the "Fourteen Points" brought to Versailles by President Woodrow Wilson.
35 Sechaba Consultants, Riding the Tiger: Lesotho Miners and Permanent Residence in South Africa. Migration Policy Series No. 2, Cape Town 1997, pp. 27-28.
36 Roger Southall, Lesotho and the Re-Integation of South Africa. In: S. Santho/M. Sejanamane (ed.), Southern Africa After Apartheid, Harare 1991, p. 225.
37 See Sechaba Consultants, Riding the Tiger..., loc. cit., p. 17.

38 Despite fears of this kind, there is no regulation preventing Basotho from carrying both sets of identity documents. Lesotho border police, however, often deliberately misinform migrants carrying South African residence permits that they must now get visas to enter Lesotho. The Lesotho government has likewise done its best to obstruct the movement of its citizens by refusing to issue any Lesotho passports in 1997, giving as excuse that they can no longer obtain the special paper on which the documents are printed!
39 See Sechaba Consultants, Riding the Tiger..., loc. cit., p. 13.
40 P. Bourdieu, Outline of a Theory of Practice, Cambridge 1977; id., The Logic of Practice, Cambridge 1980.
41 Mayer, Black Villagers..., loc. cit., p. 50.
42 See Sechaba Consultants, Riding the Tiger..., loc. cit., p. 26.
43 Ibid.
44 Faced with an on-going leadership crisis, the Prime Minister's faction of his own party, the Basotho Congress Party (BCP), "crossed the floor" in July 1997 and formed a new governing party calling itself the Lesotho Congress for Democracy, leaving a now minority BCP to form the official opposition.
45 Benedict Anderson, Imagined Communities: Reflections on the Origins and Spread of Nationalism, London 1991, p. 7.
46 Nairn, The Break-up of Britain, loc. cit., p. 343.
47 Anderson, Imagined Communities..., loc. cit., p. 3.
48 Eric Hobsbawm, Identity Politics and the Left. In: New Left Review, (1996) 27,

Configuration of Space in Central African History
(Work in Progress)[1]

Jean-Luc Vellut

Present day developments in Central Africa have put in the forefront the question of the organization of space in Central Africa. The distribution of vast expenses of that region into modern states, defined by precise political boundaries, is still, consciously or unconsciously determining our understanding of processes in the area today. One speaks of the war in Angola or in Congo-Brazzaville, of large-scale massacres in Rwanda, of political tensions and rebellions in Congo-Zaire. Yet these territorial references have become misleading. Angolan armies fight wars in the two Congos, but are kept at bay in Angola itself. Congolese wars are fought by Zimbabweans, Namibians, Sudanese, Ugandans, etc. Massacres have overflown from Rwanda into the Congo. Angolan and Brazzaville refugees are moving by the thousands into the Lower Congo region of Democratic Congo

The economic situation is confused as well. While there have been unequally successful efforts in the colonial period and in its wake to structure the main political entities around administrative and transport infrastructures, to encourage or regulate internal migration movements with a view to building a national labour market, to consolidate economic spheres of influence as a complement to political control, the present postcolonial era shows a different picture. The rich mining basins of the area (diamond, gold, cobalt, etc.) and their local commercial outlets now function as outposts, at the centre of informal economic zones which spread across all political boundaries. They are oriented towards other communication networks than what the political geography of the area would lead one to believe. Diamond resources of Angola are not controlled by Luanda but find their way into Congo-Zaire. Gold mines in North-Eastern Congo feed Uganda, Rwanda, and the wars staged by these states, both internally and externally. Cobalt resources of Katanga are now channelled through Zimbabwean interests and oil fields of Democratic Congo have passed under the control of a company based in Luanda.

A new economic partition of the area is underway and it challenges the relevance of existing political boundaries. It remains unclear at this stage whether it is activated by local, or by external, global dynamics. But wherever the ultimate centres of decision are, local consequences are glaring. Central African states have lost much of their authority and they only function intermittently, abandoning all semblance of maintaining roads, health, education, agricultural support, etc. In fact, an economy of outposts has come to replace the old territorial organization, restructuring space into centres and peripheries, some of the latter gradually sinking into semi-isolation. Even monetary systems are not unified within a given political space.

Yet it would be wrong to conclude that states have become irrelevant leftovers from the past. Up to now, even though fragilized, states still very much exist in the minds of the people. Reduced to the level of aspiration they still function as arenas for claims to a share in political control, they still command identity feelings, they still represent an anchorage in a shared culture of modernity. It is significant, for example, that there have hardly been calls for dismembering the existing states or recreating new political territories in the region. Occasional movements in that direction from Rwanda or Uganda, for example, do not enjoy any measure of support among their Western neighbours. On the contrary, any suspicion of *reunion* with neighbouring states quickly arouses a sense of outrage in the threatened regions of Democratic Congo which suggests that national identities still underlie political consciousness in the area.

The uncertainty of economic and political spaces in Central Africa derives, in fact, from a situation where several space configurations coexist at different levels. Of course, there is hardly anything in this development which could be regarded as particularly African. Elsewhere too, with the demise of colonial empires, or of centralized political control over multinational territories, a greater awareness of the purely political and ideological character of complex multinational constructions is spreading. Old or new identities are now challenging central control in mosaique states such as Yugoslavia, Russia, and there are many countervailing forces which challenge a naive literal reading of maps in Europe, as well as in Western, Central, or Southern Asia. In several of these regions, political spaces as they appear on the maps of these regions today can no longer claim to represent the ultimate organization of territories. Where they are not challenged frontally, they seem at least doomed to uneasy forms of coexistence with a number of rival claims for spatial organization. When they were drafted, political boundaries expressed ambitions to measure with great precision space and territory. Today, these ambitions are fragilized, borders have become porous and hybrid.

Claims for new configurations are sometimes advanced under the banner of increased democracy which, in practice, leads itself to a variety of outcomes. The central question often boils down to deciding who will be reduced to a minority status and who will enjoy majority status in a particular territory: redrafting borders is never innocent. It is surely a paradox that, at a time marked by ruthless globalization, there is a desperate craving to introduce homogeneity wherever a measure of plurality operates. But the aim of total homogeneity is only a deluding hope which can never be reached.

In Africa too, the fluidity as observed today is new in appearance only. It has known historical precedents, even though they were masked for a long time by the colonial pathos of state-building. To take the full measure of fluidity as it operates there as well as in several parts of the world, it is important to approach it with a clear understanding of existing distinctions between different meanings of space. Taken as a whole, this is a concept allowing the organization of material and information in a coherent body of explanation. Yet, partly description and partly metaphor, *space* covers different meanings. After all, this problem is only partly new and, in Germany in particular, there is a time-honoured historiographical tradition of exploring the link between political organization and other dimensions of the German space, be they cultural, economic, etc. The answers have never been self-evident and they have led to lasting controversies with far-reaching consequences.

A primary sense is geographical. It refers to a structured territory, marked off from its neighbours by facilities of communication, by regular movements between centres and peripheries, by a shared sense of identity which is linked to material geographical realities, measurable on the ground. Communication clusters are essential to this understanding of the structure of a given space (K.W. Deutsch).

In this approach, there is an objective, material dimension to the notion of space. The pathos of political space, with its strictly defined boundaries,. has often obscured other levels of space organization. Space also exists as a metaphor, helping to identify less tangible networks and limits. We can indeed map out a *space* whenever we distinguish an order and a structure which regulates transactions and leads to some rules and a sense of sharing, while maintaining boundaries and limits. Such spaces need not be wholly material in character. Organized markets for primary products might illustrate this point. The production of copper, for example, is geographically determined, and so is its distribution by transport networks, its outlets, its transformation. The financial control of these operations, the price cycles, the relative adjustments between supply and demand, are less material in character. The links with territory are not wholly absent but are nevertheless more tenuous than the production, transport and distribution operations. Yet there is a spatial organization of sorts, as it is possible to map out centres of decisions, of commodity trading, flows of investments, and to situate the main actors and their interconnections. The use of space as a metaphor, as a text to be deciphered and interpreted, can also apply to ideological connections, to artistic currents, to ethnic identities, etc.

There is a last element in the multivocal concept of space: it allows *other* spaces to be defined. Indeed, the wide field of social, cultural and spiritual spaces has as one of its main functions the responsibility of establishing boundaries, of delineating differences, of defining what is *in* and what is *out*, what is friend and what is enemy, the one defining the other. A key proviso, however, is to constantly keep in mind that interpretations of space are born in particular historical contexts. This applies more clearly than elsewhere to psychological or aesthetic appropriations of space as produced in particular cultural environments. None better than Western interpretations of African ecological *milieux* provide a case in point. The modern, romantic, European reading in symbolic terms of the interplay between land, water, light and vegetation leads in the end to the concept of landscape, open or closed, smiling or threatening. Next to geostrategical views, this psychological and artistic reading of African space takes its places among the concepts which led to a reinvention of Africa in the nineteenth and twentieth centuries.

The understanding of space may indeed be one of the key markers of particular cultures, with decisive consequences for a discussion of the configurations of space in historical terms. The difficulties are compounded when we are dealing with a multicultural context. As a consequence, it seems that historians ought to proceed along distinct layers.

A broad periodization of the past seems to provide an obvious point of departure. Within these general contexts, discussion should proceed on two fronts. There is, first of all, the existing evidence for a particular organization of space, as it can be traced on the basis of material, verifiable, sources and of their interpretation by present-day knowledge. Then there is the problem of the organization of space as a metaphorical view which is present in consciousness but only partly in territorial terms.

Great caution should be exercised as there is a danger of insidiously projecting norms and concepts into the past which have, in fact, been borrowed from more recent traditions. The imprudent introduction of metahistorical scenarios into the interpretation of archaeological artefacts has been conclusively exposed by Jan Vansina. Similar dangers lurk in transcultural situations whenever historians, trained in Western traditions, fail to make a clear distinctions between their present-day reading and interpretation of spatial concepts transmitted by their sources and, on the other hand, the interpretation of these concepts as produced in other cultures or simply in other periods in time.

Modern historians have, for example, lent strategical views to the kings of Kongo by establishing a connection between the situation of their capital midway between natural resources sites, like copper deposits, North of the kingdom and sea shell resources in Luanda, far South. This interpretation makes good sense in the industrial and commercial tradition of European urban centres in Europe, as vividly shown by historians like Henri Pirenne and the *Annales* school.[2] But it is as well to remember that this discourse, as applied to Africa, is basically a representation constructed on the basis of Western historical traditions. No Kongo representation of the past, collected since the sixteenth century, has ever included such an overall strategic and economic long-term view of the location of the kingdom. Furthermore, from what we know of other capitals in the Southern savanna area, location of the centres of political power does not allow such precise conclusions in economic or strategic terms. It is, after all, possible that we beg the question by starting with the idea that there *must* be economic and strategic motivations, and then look at a modern map and sift the evidence for possible clues.

For their part, old African kingdoms did not rely on maps, but on an empirical knowledge of itineraries, directions and distances. Broadly speaking, it is probably a safe bet that considerations of local complementarity between different resources offer clues to understanding the choice of a political location. The evidence may be scanty, however, as there is a wide spectrum of possible local applications. Wherever there are complementarities there are also opportunities for tribute and taxation as between water and land resources, between forest and open country. There is also a spiritual complementarity between the world of the seen and of the unseen, of the living and of the living dead. In most cases, of course, there *is* the proximity of a river, there *are* forest galleries and tilled land in the vicinity, there *are* possibilities for bartering fish and game, there *are* salt or iron resources in the area. After all, a degree of complementarity can be found everywhere, including among segmentary as well as centralized societies. In fact these parameters are present practically everywhere and they do not allow the derivation of precise conclusions. These foundations are, however, too fragile to allow lending old political traditions similar geopolitical views to those documented throughout European traditions.

It is not suggested here that there is anything new in this proposed distinction between material evidence, as evidence coming from the past and possessed of a factual character, and, on the other hand, discourses and representations which fluctuate in time and are culturally determined just as material sources are. We are back, in fact, to the basic distinction between *Geschichte als Prozeß und als Aussage* (Dietmar Rothermund). It is suggested, however, that we might be well inspired to explore more fully the consequences of that distinction between space as organized, conscious structures which left solid evidence behind, and space as projects and metaphors which left evidence of a more symbolic character and cannot simply be approached from the particular tradition of the West.

This distinction has consequences for the organization of historical material in African contexts. Historians have been tempted to organize their work along narrow *national* lines, a trend which reflects their own training as well as the organization of written sources. They may also have been unconsciously influenced by homogeneous concepts of space, a trend historically derived in the West from the aspiration to define national spaces as a convergence of hegemonic political, economic, and cultural factors. Even archaeologists fell prey to this temptation of homogeneity. To return to centres of industrial production mentioned earlier such as metallurgy, textile, salt, etc., in ancient Africa, it is, on the contrary, striking that their location did *not* coincide with major centres of power. Linguistic and cultural or artistic traditions are not coterminous with political spaces either. If we became more conscious of the coexistence of several types of central points, political, economic, cultural, etc., and of their lack of overlapping, we might be more faithful to local evidence instead of trying to reconstruct grand schemes and introduce them to the African past. Homogeneity and unity of space may have been present in the political ambitions of state-building in the European tradition, although not everywhere, but we have no evidence of it in the African past.

The present-day fluidity of space organizations in Central Africa and the porous character of political borders in that region invites us to a fresh approach to the evidence, first, in terms of material or cultural sources which can be assessed and confronted with each other, and, secondly, in terms of representations and discourses, both as they reach us from the past and as they underwent evolution through time. Distinction between these perspectives should be kept clear at all times. In the following, we will very briefly sketch some tentative directions for a history of space as organization and as representation in Central African.

Ancient Central African History, 500 - 1500 A.D.

For the present purpose, ancient history may be defined as a period extending between entrenched sedentarization with its accompanying organization of space and, as a *terminus ad quem*, the beginning of a period marked by the opening of communications with Europe and the rest of the world, together with the first availability of written sources. Data for that period are yielded by archaeological excavations, from linguistics, whenever possible combined with cautious use of anthropology.

Evidence indicates the well-established progression of sedentarization by 500 AD. By that time, hunters and gatherers had already coexisted for centuries with agriculturalists and, altitude allowing, with pastoralists. Agriculture had by then become the main food-producing activity but is only gradually displacing hunting and collecting, and in some places never eliminates it completely. This is an early example of a hybrid economy of production and exchange. Cultural areas can be distinguished through the evolution of languages derived from the common Bantu trunks. Material culture shows a great variety of iron and, sometimes, copper metallurgy. Despite the wide spectrum of local fusion and smithing practices, some stylistic areas emerge. A glimpse at the exchange economy may be gained by excavating artefacts, shells, etc., of distant origin. They are testimony to the existence of long-distance trading by the early centuries of that period.

Scholarly interpretation of the evidence has been tempted, however, to derive wide-ranging conclusions from data which are still widely scattered. Hard evidence has often been combined willy-nilly with anthropological theories which prevailed in the first third of the twentieth century, at a time when evolutionary ideology called the tune. The appeal exercised by grand theories and the underlying ideology of homogeneous culture areas have led to a search for the economic and material foundations of ethnic entities in a remote period for which, in fact, we hardly have any data.

The overambitious and ideologically tainted interpretations of early material data are now challenged by a more cautious approach to the evidence, and present day scholars, with archaeologists at the forefront, are arguing for the identification of central points, central in terms of production, of population, and of linguistic diffusion. The identification of such clusters does not entail as a consequence the convergence of all variables into distinct, homogeneous territories. The trend is to admit the existence of overlapping as well as of not-overlapping spaces and to abandon "the notion of culture as recognisable archaeological units" (Colin Renfrew).

The problem of representations of social and cultural spaces which were prevalentin ancient history as well as from that time till now can, of course, only be approached with great difficulty, linguistics and anthropology being practically the only available sources. Early written sources can, however, yield some evidence but only for the very few regions which were directly or indirectly in contact with literate witnesses.

Modern History, 1500 - 1900

This period may be delineated here as including the centuries when sea communications between Europe and Central African coasts are unlocked, when written testimonies give us the first inklings of African oral sources, when names of African individuals and of groups appear in increasing numbers, when social dynamics can be traced with more precision.

Interpretation by twentieth century scholars have been determined by the gradual unearthing of evidence and by new analytical tools. A factual history became possible with the increasing availability of evidence culled from the systematization of archives and libraries, and the introduction of professional research among non-literate societies.

The obstacles were mostly methodological, as, for a long time, scholarly research has proceeded on two fronts mutually ignoring each other. In fact, this division of labour reproduced the colonial binary view of historical societies facing societies without history. It is only slowly that awareness grew of the hybrid character of several social spaces in the area, of the changing character of ethnic identities, and thus of the limited value of territorial maps drafted to delineate with precision ethnic groups and the space they occupied. These representations rested on an *a priori* view of the relative permanence of particular ethnic groups and left insufficient room for a dynamic view of social groupings.

It was with the idea of dynamic processes in mind that research into the social groups which functioned as cultural brokers has sometimes been described in terms of a frontier, modelled on Turner's American frontier. Differences are, however, marked between the two cases, since the African frontier should not be regarded as the vanguard of Western civilization but rather as the expression of a new culture, open to a variety of influences. Along the same lines, the spiritual spaces which developed in some areas of Angola and the Congo gave evidence of 'the' christianization of the imaginary, but also of the africanization of Christianity, constituting of an original "popular religion" (J.K. Thornton).

In the meantime, anthropologists realized that the horizontal mapping by Europeans, introduced as early as the sixteenth century, did not correspond to the vertical views of space widely held in Central Africa. A better understanding of segmentary societies, in the wake of the work by Radcliffe-Brown, paved the way for a better understanding of space conceived in terms of a developing tree, rather than as an area to delineate and control.

The problem of the representation of space by contemporaries of the 1500-1900 period of transition remains ill-explored despite promising beginnings by Portuguese scholars (M.E. Madeira Santos). We are little informed on local representations which deserve a systematic programme of inquiry. The nationalistic character of much of the colonial historiographical production on protocolonial history has, in fact, practically ignored this local dimension, concentrating instead on the heroic character of the political dimension sparked off by the European conquistadors in Central Africa. For these first historians, space was above all political, set against rival European powers as well as against the formless societies of the interior.

From Colony to Postcolony

The partition of Central Africa into political territories delineated with precision is, of course, a major aspect of that period. It is important to realize that political boundaries of the area were not drafted with one stroke of the pen but were rather the result of protracted negotiations and political compromises, and were repeatedly questioned politically and economically : see, e.g., the *Mittelafrika* scheme, the post-World War I plans for major adjustments in the area, the British and French proposals for a redefinition of the boundaries of 1938-1940. The stereotype that African frontiers are artificial should be taken for what is, a stereotype. All frontiers are, of course, artificial and political: Africa is no exception to the rule. However, it is true that rival spaces - linguistic, ethnic, trading networks, shared political or juridical cultures - were not erased but rather overshadowed by the new political boundaries.

In many cases, the existing historiography, with its nation-centred orientation, has served the purpose of consolidating the new modern political units at the expense of a broader regional view. It has stressed the creation of a labour market, of communication networks, of financial and industrial groupings, of cultural policies, all of which were to give coherence and structure to modern political space. In contrast, transnational and transimperial currents have been insufficiently explored. The emergence of a postcolonial and postmetropolitan historiography may open broader perspectives, but this would require a deep reevaluation of the practice of historical research, still narrowly divided into national schools.

Bibliography

Bachelard, M., 1972: La poétique de l'espace. Paris, pp. 191-207.
Benko, G./U. Strohmayer, 1997: Space and Social Theory. Oxford.
Deutsch, K.W., 1966: Nationalism and Social Communication. Cambridge, Mass.
Durand, M.-F./J. Lévy/D. Retaillé, 1993: Le monde. Espaces et systèmes. Paris (Fondation nationale des Sciences politiques).
Foucault, M., 1994: Des espaces autres. In: M. Foucault, Dits et écrits, 1954-1988. Paris.
Halen, P., 1995: L'ouvert et le fermé: une typologie de l'espace centre-africain dans toutes sortes d'histoires européennes. In: Descriptions et créations d'espaces dans la littérature. Etudes rassemblées et présentées par E. Leonardy et H. Roland. Louvain-la-Neuve - Bruxelles, pp. 215-233.
Laïdi, Zaki, 1998: Géopolitique du sens. Paris.
Madeira Santos, M.E., 1998: Nos Caminhos de Africa. Serventia e Posse. Angola Século XIX. Lisbon.
Matoré, G., 1976: L'espace humain. L'expression de l'espace dans la vie, la pensée et l'art contemporains. Paris.
Merleau-Ponty, M., 1945: Phénoménologie de la perception. Paris (reprint 1985), pp. 281-344.
Moles, A.A./E. Rohmer, 1978: Psychologie de l'espace. Tournai.
Renfrew, C., 1984: Approaches to Social Archaeology, Cambridge, Mass.
Rothermund, D., 1994: Geschichte als Prozeß und Aussage. Eine Einführung in Theorien des historischen Wandels und der Geschichtsschreibung. Munich.
Le Territoire. Etudes sur l'espace humain, littérature histoire, civilisation, Saint-Denis, (Publications de l'Université de la Réunion), Paris 1986.
[Turner, F.J., 1893]: cf. Lamar, H./L. Thompson, The Frontier in History. North America and Southern Africa Compared. New Haven-London 1981.

Vansina, J., 1995: Historians, are archaeologists your siblings? In: History in Africa, 22 (1995), pp. 369-408.

Wirz, A., 1994: Die Erfindung des Urwalds oder ein weiterer Versuch in Fährtenlesen. In: Periplus. Jahrbuch für Außereuropäische Geschichte 1994, pp. 15-36.

Notes

1   The present topic is presented here in the form of a few exploratory reflections and will be further explored at a later date. Central Africa is understood here as a broadly defined region centred on the basin of the Congo river and adjacent savanna ecosystems, limited by the Great Lakes region in the East, where there is an ecological and identity frontier which can be traced for the last five centuries. A short bibliography at the end of this work in progress will present the main methodological sources.

2   Breaking away with old privilege granted to political history, Henri Pirenne (1862-1935) was a mayor exponent of the economic and social foundations of European history, as followed from the beginning of its medieval expansion. In 1929, Marc Bloch and Lucien Fèbvre, when founding the *Annales d'histoire économique et sociale*, recognized their debt to Pirenne and invited him to join the editorial board of their journal. *Annales* was to play a leading part for at least two generations of French historians.

The Local and the Global in a Workers' Milieu: The Example of Colonial Bombay

Annemarie Hafner

This paper will deal with the global dissemination of socio-cultural elements through colonial expansion and the capitalist world economy and put the process of globalization in a historical perspective. The core issue is how this process contributed to structuring Indian society and to what extent the interplay of global and indigenous factors resulted in establishing a modern society "with specific features".

In the past three decades representatives of the dependency as the world systems' theories have pointed out the impossibility of studying the history of any region isolated from global economic processes, be it in the West or in the Third World.[1] Today, scholars also generally agree on the impact of global economy on social relations and economic development in India. There is, however, a continuing debate on how Indian society responded to the encounter with the West and how the consequences are to be assessed.[2]

My investigation focuses on the factory workers' way of life in Bombay in the late nineteenth and early twentieth centuries. I prefer to call this way of life "workers' culture", using the term "culture" in a very broad sense. It comprises the entire sphere of life both within and outside of the formal work place. This particular proletarian way of life was the outcome of interaction between global and indigenous factors.

I would like to demonstrate the impact of these factors mainly on two levels: first of all, by examining the regulation of working conditions through factory legislation, and secondly, by analysing changes in daily routine. Finally, I will look at manifestations of internationalism in the proletarian way of life.

The city of Bombay itself owes its existence to events of world-wide dimensions. As part of their endeavour to establish a world empire during the sixteenth century, the Portuguese took possession of seven islands on the West Coast of India. In 1668 the British East India Company began to administer the trading area which had been bestowed on the British crown a few years earlier as part of a marriage contract. As Salman Rushdie put it in his novel "Midnight's Children", this event "set time in motion"[3].

Various cultures, interests and ideas influenced the growth of the city. As a result, many different clusters emerged and distinguished themselves in purpose and design respectively through the way of life of their inhabitants, within the larger unity of Bombay which was gradually assuming an identity of its own. Sharada Dwivedi and Rahul Mehrotra, who aptly entitled their book "Bombay

- The Cities Within", have reconstructed the evolution of this urban conglomerate convincingly.[4]

The further growth of the city and the fate of its inhabitants were conditioned by external events as well as internal aspects. In the nineteenth century, for instance, the American Civil War cut off the supply of raw material from America to factories in Lancashire from 1861 to 1865, making it necessary to import cotton from west and central India. Around about the same time, the inauguration of the Suez Canal in 1869 and the opening up of the Deccan and Konkan regions with a road and rail network provided the necessary infrastructure for speeding up the global and regional transport of goods, and the movement of people. It is a common explanation that the origins of industrialization in India formed part of a steady process of technological diffusion, working gradually outwards from eighteenth-century Western Europe.[5]

The first factory to produce cotton yarn and cotton textiles in Bombay went into operation in 1854. In the following decades most factories were producing yarn for export to the Chinese and African markets.[6] Weaving began to develop as a branch of the Indian textile industry only at the turn of the century when competition from Japanese textile factories increased on the world market. Periods of economic prosperity were accompanied by the rapid growth of the work force which was offered employment in the newly-established industrial and transport enterprises.

During the latter part of the nineteenth century a distinct social group emerged among the population of Bombay. This group consisted of poor peasants from the Maharashtran districts of Satara, Kolaba and Ratnagiri who, from now on, earned their living as wage labourers in the cotton factories and dockyards of the city. It should be noted at this point that industrialization was not simply the consequence of widening flows of exchange and their effect on the development of the forces of production. Historical evidence also points to an understanding of industrialization in terms of the social relations of production in its specific South Asian context.

The textile mills were located primarily in three wards north of the old so-called "native town", and the workers settled in the immediate vicinity. In the mid-twenties about 90 per cent of the textile workers - totalling about 125 000 - had to walk only 15 minutes from their homes to reach their place of work. The new quarters were called *girangaon* which means "village of factories" and it was in this geographically clearly-defined locality that a particular urban-proletarian milieu developed, accompanied by a specific way of life.

Descriptions of working conditions in those early days of factory production in India reveal a picture of extensive exploitation. Faced with Lancashire competition, Indian industrialists struck at the workers and exploited them even more in a struggle for survival. The long working day was particularly exhausting. In the initial stages, working hours in the cotton factories lasted from sunrise to sunset. Later, with the introduction of electricity, the working day was prolonged and lasted for 13 to 16 hours. General rules for regulating breaks and free days were nonexistent.

The labour question gradually became an issue of public concern. The colonial administration approached the problem in a manner which was marked by the conflict of interests between British capital in Europe and indigenous capital in India, between visions of philanthropists and intentions of legislators. Right from the beginning, British cotton manufacturers closely watched conditions of production in the factories of their competitors in India.In the early seventies they had already tried to limit the hitherto unregulated employment of women and children in Indian factories.

Simultaneously, several British philanthropists began to take an interest in the emerging labour question in India. Moves were made on both sides and resulted in 1875 in the first debate on labour conditions in Indian factories in the British House of Commons. In the same year, Lord Shaftesbury, a philanthropist and promoter of factory laws in his own country, tabled the topic in the House of Lords. His arguments included humanitarian aspects as well as the so-called commercial aspect of the issue. He put it as follows:

> "We must bear in mind that India has the raw material and cheap labour and, if we allow the manufacturers there to work their operatives 16 or 17 hours and put them under no restriction, we are giving them a very unfair advantage over the manufacturers of our own country and we might be undersold, even in Manchester itself, by manufactured goods imported from the East."[7]

The then Secretary of State for India, Lord Salisbury, persuaded the government of the Province of Bombay to look into the conditions of the cotton factories. On 23 March 1875 the Bombay Government appointed a commission to enquire into labour conditions. The work yielded no results initially, because seven of the nine members had close connections with local entrepreneurs and felt that legal provisions were unnecessary and would be extremely detrimental to the industrial interests of the country.

This course of events prompted social reformers in Bombay to increase their activities. Hitherto, their appeals for the abolition of child labour in particular had met with no response, either at home or abroad. One of their most prominent representatives, Sorabjee Shapurjee Bengalee,[8] now turned to his friends in Manchester. His appeal for relief was published in September 1878 in the London "Times". Parallel to this, the first independent steps of the Indian proletariat were making themselves felt. A petition to the government signed by 578 workers demanded the introduction of a nine-hour working day as well as one free day per week.[9]

The Lancashire factory owners, the British philanthropists and the social reformers in Bombay were motivated by quite different considerations. Their diverse efforts resulted in the first Indian Factory Act of 1881. The Act prohibited the employment of children under seven years of age and limited working hours for children between seven and 12 years of age to nine hours per day. None of the parties concerned was satisfied with this legislation. In the following decades legislation on wage labour in factories was frequently reshaped.

New protagonists in the struggle for improved factory legislation entered the stage. Thus, representatives of the Lancashire textile factory workers approached the Secretary of State for India in 1889, asking for legislative intervention on behalf of their fellow-workers in India and demanding, in particular, shorter working hours. They felt their own social achievements threatened. Their argument ran as follows:

> "... if the Indian mills were to be allowed to work night and day, Sunday and week days, it was obvious that the working men of this country must be placed under very great disadvantage in competition in the markets of the world."[10]

Finally, international bodies such as the International Conference for the Protection of Labour held in Berlin in 1890 also made efforts to improve labour conditions in industries everywhere.

The findings of various commissions of enquiry as well as the repeated amendments of factory acts in the following decades reveal the close interrelation between international economic competition and political decision-making in a colonial set-up. But there was also a further impetus for the gradual improvement of labour legislation. It came from the trade union movement in India after the First World War, as well as from activities conducted by the International Labour Organization, of which India became a member in 1919. As a result, by 1922 the average daily working hours of Indian factory workers were limited to ten, and each worker was entitled to one free day per week.[11] The eight-hour day was not introduced in India until after political independence.

The limitations of labour and factory legislation in India during the colonial period are well known.[12] I do not intend to dwell on this point here. I took up the issue for two reasons only. First of all, it demonstrates the interplay of global and local factors which surface during the interaction between the colonial state and the national and international institutions. In this context, political measures to control the work process - including steps to protect the interests of the workers - took concrete shape in India. The Founding Meeting of the Indian Labour History Association, held in New Delhi in December 1996, referred to this process and described it as follows:

"Historically, labouring activity was an object of control and repression. In South Asia this was complicated by the insertion of the Indian economy into the strategic and commercial system of British imperialism. The interaction between inchoate forms of capital and traditional institutions over time gave rise to hybridised forms of exploitation and regulatory mechanisms adjusted to the needs of empire."[13]

On the other hand, however, and in my opinion, one other aspect seems to be of equal importance. The evolution of Indian labour and factory legislation, however tardy and hampered by the conflicting interests of those involved, was also an indication of a process which, in the long run, would bring about not a homogenization but at least a greater similarity in industrial labour conditions on a global scale.

Let us now examine the everyday life of the Bombay labourer in search of change, a situation which can be traced to the impact of global processes and ideas. There are certain difficulties to be faced here. On the one hand, the wide realm of proletarian everyday life in colonial India has hitherto hardly ever been studied. In his essay "Toil, Sweat and the City" Sandeep Pendse pointed out that "the culture of the toilers in the city ... is not chronicled".[14] Hence a considerable part of their lives, their mentality, their leisure activities, and their desires and ambitions remain hidden to the eye of the historian.

The circumstances permit only limited and tentative conclusions. On the other hand, as we know only too well, the life of the factory workers was a permanent struggle against poverty. They were compelled to live in distressing housing conditions, to make do with a minimum of food and clothing, and enjoyed hardly any free time. And yet, especially during the twenties and thirties, there were glimpses of improvements in living standards, and changes in behaviour with regard to food, dress and articles of daily use, as well as in the art of recreation.[15]

Up to the middle of this century the food habits of urban wage labourers had changed only marginally and very slowly. Investigations conducted since the early twenties under the auspices of the labour officers of the provincial government of Bombay revealed that there was no change in the consumption of staple food. Rice and pulses were just enough to kill the hunger.[16] As a rule, food was prepared in the worker's household twice a day.

Children were additionally given tea and biscuits as a quick breakfast. Biscuits were undoubtedly one of the first industrially produced food items to be accepted by all strata of the population in India. As far as tea is concerned, one brief remark should be added. Up to the twenties, tea was a luxury item in India which was one of the major tea-growing and exporting countries. It was rarely consumed in the rural areas. In the urban areas, however, it had gradually become fashionable with the middle classes. An article describing the conditions of the children of factory workers in Bombay indicates that "tea is still considered to be an article of luxury by many of the working classes, and on a Sunday which is a rest day they make tea as a change from regular routine"[17]. The consumption of tea by children should, therefore, not be misinterpreted as a sign of prosperity. On the contrary, it was the prohibitive cost of good milk that made tea an acceptable substitute.

Leisure was the area which probably experienced the most vigorous changes through the impact of global ideas and processes. An article published in the Bombay Labour Gazette conveys a comprehensive idea of how mill-hands spent their leisure time around the mid-twenties.[18]

The report presupposes that only men, and not women, were in a position to enjoy a certain amount of leisure in the evenings. Women looked after the children and did the household when they returned home from the factory, whereas men spent their evenings either in tea-stalls or liquor-shops, or simply sauntering around the streets. Playing cards and throwing dice were favourite pastimes. Factory workers also attended theatre performances and particularly enjoyed *tamashas* (a kind of folk theatre). They attended lectures - sometimes illustrated with slides - or evening classes which were arranged by welfare organizations. Workers were fond of kite-flying[19], or going to *akhadas* (gymnasiums), where they practised wrestling or *lathi*-fighting (*lathi* - stick).

The enthusiasm of urban workers for wrestling emanated from an age-old tradition which was referred to in the Indian epics. Activities like wrestling were closely intertwined with other social contexts. Gymnasiums played an important role in the culture of the workers in Bombay. The sports association network was in a position to rally forces to support or break strikes, in favour of political agitation or to protect working-class neighbourhoods during periods of communal clashes.[20] The cotton mill entrepreneurs used the workers' propensity for sport to motivate, but also to discipline, their employees. The Bombay Mill Owners Association, for example, arranged an inter-mill wrestling tournament in 1941 for which 35 factories nominated 86 participants.[21]

In the first half of the twentieth century, workers still basically adhered to traditional patterns of spending leisure time, at least as far as sports and games were concerned. They had not, as yet, begun to play open air or field sports such as football, hockey or cricket. This is all the more noteworthy since cricket had gained great popularity in India at the time.[22] A psychological but not entirely convincing explanation as to why workers had not turned to cricket was that "the taste for personal contests in throwing a ball or shooting a missile in the open field ... is non-existent in India"[23]. The real reason, however, was probably more simple. They could not afford the expenses required for team and field sports.

Another traditional way of spending leisure came from the villages to the city. For quite some time it was common practice for workers to meet twice a week between 8 p.m. and midnight to perform *bhajans*, i.e. to sing religious or mythological songs. However, by the mid-twenties this kind of social gathering had lost its attraction when the cinema gained a foothold in Indian towns and cities as an "instrument of recreation" and "the most popular form of entertainment"[24]. From now on the Bombay textile workers avidly followed the adventures of "The Tramp" or "The Thief of Baghdad" on the screen, too. During the twenties and thirties Charlie Chaplin and Douglas Fairbanks were among the most popular film stars in India, as they were in Europe and America. But Indian cinema-goers also greatly appreciated Indian films; these became popular "particularly with the less cultured classes" as stated in the Report of the Indian Cinematograph Committee for 1927-1928.[25]

The development of the cinema and the film industry in India bears ample testimony to the economic integration of the country into the capitalist world economy. It simultaneously demonstrates how forms of mass commercialised leisure were established within a national framework. This, however, is a separate topic. My intention was merely to show that, with the introduction of the cinema, a step was taken towards establishing a popular culture whose determining features were "modernity" and "consumption". The Bombay factory workers were involved in this kind of popular culture to the extent that they were able to meet certain basic preconditions: consumption requires people with purchasing power.

A number of publications address the international co-operation of Indian trade unions since their inception, from the perspective of the history of the organizations.[26] Recent investigations, however, devoted respectively to social and to cultural-historical issues, frequently neglect the question of internationalist phenomena in everyday life and the political culture of the working class. There is still a need to carry out a comprehensive study on how the alien and indigenous elements, manifest in symbols and rituals, were amalgamated, and how they shaped the distinguishing features of the Indian working-class movement.

Indian workers' local protest actions echoed global economic questions and international political aspects only marginally. Yet, such links were evident occasionally. One example was the general strike in the Bombay textile industry in 1925 when entrepreneurs linked a reduction in wages to the excise duty imposed on them by the colonial administration. The textile labourers were opposed to the 11.5 per cent wage cuts. The Bombay entrepreneurs refused to drop the cuts unless the Government abolished the 3.5 per cent excise duty, introduced in 1894 to protect the English cotton industry. When the colonial government conceded to the demand, the entrepreneurs withdrew their decision.[27]

International solidarity became a reality and was appreciated in instances of extreme distress. During the long-lasting general strikes in the twenties and thirties the trade unions established relief centres to distribute food to the starving, utilising donations to the cause from international trade union federations.[28] At a strike meeting held in 1928 trade union leader S.S. Mirajkar compared the distribution of rice, paid for with these donations, to the tail of the god *Maruti*, known for its unexpected appearance in utterly hopeless situations.[29]

A feeling of belonging to the international workers' movement was first roused in the working people of India at the May Day celebrations. May Day was inaugurated in India in 1923 and by the late twenties had become an annual festive affair in almost all Indian industrial centres. "May Day has become the most important and significant occasion for expressing (its) class solidarity and camaraderie with the international working class"[30], writes Sukomal Sen.

Notes

1 Cf. Immanuel Wallerstein, Incorporation of the Indian Sub-continent into the Capitalist World Economy. In: Economic and Political Weekly, Bombay 21 (1986) 4, PE-28ff.
2 Cf. Rajnarayan Chandavarkar, Imperial Power and Popular Politics: Class, Resistance and the State in India, c. 1850-1950, Cambridge 1998, p. 327.
3 Salman Rushdie, Midnight's Children, New York 1982, p. 106.
4 Sharada Dwivedi/Rahul Mehrotra, Bombay: The Cities Within, Bombay 1995.
5 Cf. B.R. Tomlinson, The Political Economy of the Raj: The Economics of Decolonization in India, London 1979, p. 31.
6 Daniel Houston Buchanan, The Development of Capitalistic Enterprise in India, New York 1934, p. 201.
7 Quoted from: Ahmad Mukhtar, Factory Labour in India, Madras 1930, p. 16.
8 S.S. Bengalee was doubtless the most prominent representative of labour in India, especially in Bombay during those years. What he wanted to do can best be seen in his Draft Bill. The Bill had more than one objective; the regulation of hours, however, was the overriding question. The Draft Bill and a biographical sketch are published in S.D. Punekar/R. Varickayil (eds.), Labour Movement in India; Documents: 1891-1917, Bombay 1990, pp. 209ff; pp. 343ff.
9 See Bipan Chandra, The Rise and Growth of Economic Nationalism in India; Economic Policies of Indian National Leadership, 1880-1905, New Delhi 1966, p. 328.
10 Quoted from: Mukhtar, loc. cit., p. 26.
11 Chamanlal Revri, The Indian Trade Union Movement: An Outline History 1880-1947, New Delhi 1972, p. 35.
12 Annemarie Hafner, Die Arbeiterfrage im Indien des 19. Jahrhunderts; Werdegang, Motivationen und Wirkungen von Sozialreformen im kolonialen Umfeld. In: Gerhard Höpp (ed.), Entwicklung durch Reform; Asien und Afrika im 19. Jahrhundert. In: asien, afrika, lateinamerika, Berlin, special number 3, 1991, pp. 27ff.
13 Dilip Simeon, The Founding Meeting. Indian Labour History Association. In: IIAS Newsletter No. 12, Spring 1997, p. 12.

14	Sandeep Pendse, Toil, Sweat and the City. In: Sujata Patel/Alice Thorner (eds.), Bombay: Metaphor for Modern India, Bombay 1995, p. 5.
15	Kanchan Jyoti, Impact of Colonial Rule on Urban Life. In: Indu Banga (ed.), The City in Indian History. Urban Demography, Society, and Politics, New Delhi 1991, pp. 207-235.
16	The Food of the Worker. In: Labour Gazette, Bombay, 4 (1925) 8, p. 835.
17	The Condition of the Children of Bombay Mill Operatives. In: Labour Gazette, loc. cit., 4 (1925) 8, p. 860.
18	Utilization of the Workers' Leisure. In: Labour Gazette, loc. cit., 4 (1925) 3, pp. 284ff.
19	Claude Batley, Bombay's Houses and Homes, Bombay 1949, p. 38.
20	Rajnarayan Chandavarkar, The Origins of Industrial Capitalism in India. Business Strategies and the Working Classes in Bombay, 1900-1940, Cambridge 1994, pp. 212ff.
21	Wrestling Tournament for Bombay Mill Workers. In: Labour Gazette, loc. cit., 20 (1941) 10, p. 807.
22	Arjun Appadurai, Playing with Modernity: Decolonization of Indian Cricket. In: Carol A. Breckenridge (ed.), Consuming Modernity. Public Culture in a South Asian World, Minneapolis—London 1995, pp. 23ff.
23	Utilization of the Workers' Leisure, loc. cit., p. 284.
24	Report of the Indian Cinematograph Committee 1927-28, Madras 1928, p. 1.
25	Ibid., p. 19/20.
26	Cf. Sukomal Sen, Working Class of India. History of Emergence and Movement 1830-1990, Calcutta 1997.
27	Excise Duty Repealed – End of Strike. In: Labour Gazette, ibid., p. 233; General Strike in the Textile Mills in Bombay City. In: Labour Gazette, loc. cit., 8 (1928) 2, p. 159.
28	Progress of the General Strike. In: Ibid., p. 233; General Strike in the Textile Mills in Bombay City. In: Ibid., 8 (1928) 2, p. 159.
29	State Archives of Maharashtra, Home Department (Special), 543(10)C Pt. A of 1928: Bombay General Mill Strike 1928, p. 131.
30	Sukomal Sen, May Day and Eight Hours' Struggle in India, Calcutta 1988, p. 199.

The "Great" Shoe Question: Tradition, Legitimacy, and Power in Colonial India[1]

K. N. Panikkar

The selective appropriation of traditional cultural practices was one among the many means of hegemonization that British colonialism pursued in India. The incorporation of indigenous mores into the corpus of colonial technologies of control helped to invest the colonial rule with an illusion of continuity and legitimacy. Since appropriation tended to impart new meanings and hitherto unknown symbolic importance to existing practices tradition became a site of contest, often in the guise of what constituted the authentic tradition of the "natives". But behind this facade were articulated, asserted and negotiated several other issues germane to subjection and resistance. This essay is an attempt to explore these issues in the context of the shoe regulation of 1854 and the controversies that entailed.

Clothes and Social Order

In a pioneering study of dress and fashion in French history, Daniel Roche has argued how the complex symbolism of appearances implicit in the pattern of clothing signifies a variety of social and political ideas, such as hierarchy, exclusion and respect.[2] That clothes and adornments have significance far beyond the protective and utilitarian functions and that they reflect social distinctions and cultural identities have been for long a part of Anthropologist's œuvre.[3] A relationship between dress and social order in terms of power, authority, status and class, is apparent. What David Hume observed in the eighteenth century about human body, in a sense, is applicable to dress: "The skin, pores, muscles and nerves of a day-labourer are different from those of a man of quality ... The different stations in life influence the whole fabric."[4] The dress, to adopt the statement of Keith Thomas on human body, is a historical document, reflecting the whole gamut of cultural and social relations in which the individual is placed.[5]

The quality, texture and design of clothes and the modes of wearing them reflected the complex relations within the social order. In all cultures, social distinctions can be broadly discerned by the differences in the mode of dress. Not that alone. Dress often acts as an active agent in the articulation of social relations, though there is no uniform code in all cultures which governs this articulation. In this respect, norms and customs in the West and the East are vastly different. Also the same practice did not carry the same meaning in different cultures. The headgear, for instance. To the Europeans taking off the hat meant a mark of courtesy and civility and a form of salutation. The Hindus hardly removed their *turban* (headgear) in public as it is associated with their honour and rank. Pulling off a man's turban is considered among Hindus a grave insult and humiliation. Turban, in the Islamic world, has a variety of functions: a symbol of spiritual succession, a gravestone embellishment and the carrier of a holyman's spiritual charisma.[6]

The religious, caste and regional variations did not admit of a uniform dress code in India. The practice of covering or uncovering parts of the body also did not have the same meaning to those who belonged to different religions, castes and regions. In Kerala, uncovering the upper part of the body, by both men and women of lower castes, was considered a mark of respect to the members of high castes. The attempt by low caste women to wear breast cloth, under the influence of Christian missionaries, resulted in a major controversy in Travancore in the first half of the nineteenth century. The members of the upper castes viewed it as an infringement of their status.[7] In other parts of India, distinction was maintained through caste-class categorization of dress. But difference on the basis of dress was not demanded from the members of other religious denominations. In Kerala, for instance, Christians and Muslims were not required to remove their upper cloth, even when appearing before their landlords. In fact, conversion to Islam was metaphorically referred to as "wearing a shirt", ending thus the seminakedness imposed by caste restrictions. Thus, there was no single code applicable to the body-cloth relationship which Indians followed uniformly, regardless of religious, caste or regional distinctions.

The body-cloth relationship in India, like in all other cultures, was contingent upon the "prohibitions and commandments" internal to its culture. The negotiation and reconciliation between the internal view of the "native" and the "external view" of the British of these prohibitions and commandments were rendered difficult by a variety of reasons.[8] Among them was the influence of European experience by which the British tended to look for a homologous custom in Indian tradition for the expression of mutual respect in everyday life. Secondly, the British sought to implement a homogenous practice which, given the cultural plurality in India, attracted spontaneous resistance. Thirdly, that the body-cloth relationship substantially differed in public and private space was not adequately realised. Consequently, no reconciliation was possible and the British exercised their authority to implement a practice which the "natives" regarded as an infringement of their cultural rights. It is argued that confrontations arising out of such situations are an outcome of power abuse inherent in domination and subjection.[9] But they were much more than an occasional or accidental abuse of power. Their implications were many: how the colonial power and authority were sought to be structured in society, how the state made its presence felt even in quotidian cultural practices; and how culture evolved as a field of resistance and contest in which cultural nationalism had its roots.

The two hundred years of colonial rule in India which, *inter alia*, based its strategies of control on cultural hegemony, several facets of the cultural life of the people came within the ambit of the above processes. One among them was the right of the "natives" to wear shoes in public places like the government offices and judicial courts - "the great shoe question", as a contemporary newspaper characterized it - which was denied by an order of the Governor-General in Council in 1854 and reconfirmed in 1868. The prohibition was, however, limited to the wearing of "native" shoes. Those who used European shoes and stockings were exempted.[10] The controversy it generated highlighted the cultural apprehensions of the "natives" and their anxiety to preserve their tradition. The colonial rule on the other hand, was keen on appropriating tradition for legitimising its power and authority and at the same time, privileging its own cultural practice as an ideal alternative.

Uncovering the Feet: a Symbol of Respect

An immediate consequence of the Government order was the fairly widespread incidence of friction during the transaction of official business between the lower echelons of bureaucracy and the "natives". The former expected that the shoe regulation would be a means to ensure the public demonstration of respect and submission to the power of colonial authority. To the latter, it was essentially a matter of infringement on human dignity and violence to religious sentiments. Both these perspectives were explicit in an incident at Surat on 24 March 1862 when the Judge of the Faujdari Adalat forbade Manockjee Cowasjee Entee, a Parsee and an Assessor, from entering the court without removing his shoes.

An eye-witness account of the altercation between the Judge and Manockjee published in the *Bombay Gazette*, a pro-British newspaper, on 2 April 1862, was apparently a dramatised version of the incident.[11] Nevertheless, it appears to have captured all essential details of the incident, as Manockjee approvingly appended it to his memorial to Sir Bartle Frere, the Governor of Bombay, as an authentic narrative of what happened. The language and idiom in which the incident was reconstructed in the eye-witness account were themselves significant. They left no doubt about the relative position of the two, not as a judge and an assessor, but as one vested with authority and power and the other as a subject pleading for his rights. The language attributed to the Judge is one of command and his demeanour impatient and intimidating. He was not prepared to entertain any argument, either on law or on procedure, and insisted on unqualified compliance of his orders. Manockjee, on the contrary, used the language of supplicant, registering his objections in a humble and submissive manner. It was a dialogue, if at all it can be termed a dialogue, conducted within the ambit of domination and subordination. The contrast is clear in the following exchange:

> Manockjee: I humbly submit that exposing one's bare feet is something below human dignity and contrary to the sacred ordinances of our scriptures; besides, I have been bound over not to suffer myself the indignity of a pledge, which as long as it does not interfere with the laws, can be respected.
> Judge: Nothing of that here. Take off your shoes or it will be the worse for you. The great Nawab of Sucheen just visited me, and I saw him taking off his shoes. Are you a greater man than him?
> Manockjee: I am only a poor British subject.
> Judge: Then you do not obey our orders.
> Manockjee: Your order I bow to with the greater deference (Saheb-ka-hookoom hamare seer aur anko par hai) but your Honour will oblige by quoting the authority of some law.
> Judge: Law! It is not a matter of law. Don't talk of laws here.
> Manockjee: I respect your order with all the obedience but only on the understanding that by ordering me thus, you disgrace me, wound my feelings and interfere in the discharge of what I take to be a religious objection.
> Judge: I don't care. Beware you interrupt the courts' business, and you will be dealt with accordingly. Do you obey us or no?

Manockjees's refusal to comply with the order of the Judge was based on three reasons. Firstly, Parsees in other towns in the Presidency were permitted to wear shoes while appearing in courts. Both the Supreme Court and Sadar Adalat in Bombay did so. Therefore, the Judge at Surat was adopting a procedure at variance from the norms set by superior courts. This was directly linked to the second objection which raised the question of provision in law on which the action of the Judge was based. Claiming that he was a British subject, he insisted that the Judge indicate some authority of law in support of his demand and whatever law provided he agreed to undergo "with all due obedience". To Manockjee the third objection was more important and fundamental. It related to his religious faith which according to him, did not permit walking with bare feet, not even in temples. Later he collected the opinion of experts on Zoroastrianism in support of his contention and incorporated them in his memorial to the Governor.[12] He held that his religious tenets forbade all those practices which violated human dignity. As a consequence, Manockjee refused to comply with the order of the Judge, as it would amount to a defiance of the dictates of his conscience, a violation of human dignity and a direct contradiction of his religious faith.

The Judge, in turn, did not give much credence to the religious argument of Manockjee. Nor did he care what the courts in Bombay did. He claimed to be the master of what the local practice should be and asserted his right to exercise his authority by implementing the shoe regulation without any exception on religious or social grounds. Manockjee, on the other hand, persisted with his refusal to unshod, as it would compromise his human dignity and religious sentiments. Finally, Manockjee was forced to discharge his duties as an Assessor standing outside the court which in itself was an indignity to which he was prepared to submit "provided human dignity is not violated and religious feelings not meddled with".

In a memorial addressed to the Governor of Bombay, Manockjee elaborated the objections he had raised during the altercation with the Judge. The arguments he advanced were mainly political and religious in nature. The shoe regulation, he contended, was not in conformity with the liberal principles of British administration and a "culpable violation of one of the most prominent rights guaranteed in the celebrated Proclamation of Her Gracious Majesty". He said:

> "... the imperative enforcement of the custom of removing shoes is looked upon by all the various races that inhabit this country as an oppression incompatible with the mildness, forbearance, clemency and justice, by which British rulers of India have rendered themselves so highly popular and endearing."[13]

Manockjee laid greater emphasis on religious objection. The Parsees, according to him, were required by their scriptures to cover the feet in all places which they have scrupulously followed in the past.

> "... in accordance with the spirit of their religion the Parsees have, up to this date, never dispensed with the custom of wearing shoes, (either at home or in public), in any country, though they have had for a long time to pass their days in contact with a bare-footed nation. The rigid covering of the feet is considered by them so essential an element of their faith, that even infants are made to us little slippers no sooner they learn to walk; a child who habitually shuns the wearing of the shoes will never have the ceremony of the sacred thread-investiture performed unto him, until he gets inured to the practice of putting them on."[14]

The departure from this practice by the Parsees in some parts of the country, he believed, was a result of the influence of Hindus and Muslims who did not have such a custom.

The Surat incident was not an isolated event, nor was it the first occasion when uncovering the feet had become a contentious issue. For quite some time it was a part of the colonial discourse of power and was already being negotiated at different levels of political and social intercourse.

Antecedents

The British attitude towards the shoe question was influenced by their early experience in the durbars of Indian rulers. Whatever the initial reasons for the prestige - cleanliness, convenience or respect - unshoding the feet before entering the presence of the rulers was invariably observed in the durbars. During the initial intercourse with Indian rulers British merchants and officials followed this practice without demur. Whenever they went to attend the Indian courts, they observed both the European and Indian practice, by taking off the hat and uncovering the feet.

The "ceremony of taking off the shoes" before entering the durbar was a part of the ritual demanded of the British Residents and Agents accredited to Indian courts. The Indian rulers considered it an assertion of their authority and power and also a recognition of their status and honour. At the time when the East India Company was soliciting trade privileges and struggling to acquire political power, its representatives thought it prudent to submit to these claims. But during the course of the nineteenth century when the relative position of the British and Indian rulers underwent change, such practices became unacceptable to many a British official.

The British Residents and Agents were keen that their demeanour at the durbars reflect the political power the East India Company had acquired vis-a-vis the Indian rulers during the first half of the nineteenth century. After the Mughal Emperor was accorded a pensionary status in 1803 the British tried to re-negotiate their relationship with Indian rulers. An initial step in this direction was the appropriation of the prerogatives of paramountcy earlier exercised by the Emperor. For instance, at the time of succession in Indian states, the Governor-General invoked the Mughal practice of conferring a *Khilat* which symbolised imperial sanction.[15]

Despite the change in the political equation Indian rulers sought to maintain the earlier rituals in their durbars which signified their superior status. The British Residents and Agents were required either to stand or squat on the floor in durbars and unshod their feet outside the audience hall. The British representatives were quite reluctant to concede these demands which often led to disputes and political impasse.[16] In 1833 Maharana Pratap Singh of Udaipur refused to receive the British Agent unless he agreed to remove his shoes and sit on the floor. The Agent was incensed that "the representative of British Government should be subjected to a custom at variance with that of his own country and which puts him on equality with the lowest *mutsudees* in attendance on that chief"[17]. As in all such cases, the government counselled caution and respect of "native" tradition:

"... it is the wish of His Lordship-in-Council that you should continue to observe the ceremony of taking off your shoes at the Durbars of those sovereign chiefs who may expect it as this is the universal practice of the country which is submitted by the highest nobles of their courts and even by the chiefs themselves in their intercourse with one another.[18]"

The practice was observed in almost all other courts as a part of etiquette, despite the resentment and objections raised by local officials. Some of them used the opportunity like the demise of the ruling prince to discontinue the practice.

The experience of this custom perceived as a traditional practice seems to have been a decisive factor in setting the norms to be observed by the "natives" during their intercourse with British officials. Initially, the occasion arose when "native gentlemen" were invited to attend the Governor-General's durbar or entertainment parties hosted by him. Invoking the custom followed in Indian courts, Lord Amherst, the Governor-General during 1824-28, stipulated that Indians unshod their feet before entering his presence. However, it was not strictly followed and in fact, almost discontinued during the Governor-Generalship of William Bentinck.[19] But Lord Dalhousie, under whom British Colonialism assumed an aggressive face, formulated an official code regulating the use of shoes by the "natives". Accordingly, it was stipulated that "all native gentlemen who may attend Durbar either in the Government House or in Court, will conform with the native custom and will be required to leave their shoes at the door". But in the case of entertainment parties, they were given the option to follow "either the native or European custom". If they chose the former, they were required to leave their shoes at the door. Instead, if they adopted the European custom and wore European shoes, it was not necessary to unshod.[20]

The regulation, although initially intended to apply only to the durbar of the Governor-General, was soon adopted by the bureaucracy as what came to be known as "shoe respect" in all government institutions in the British territory. Since some Indians challenged the legality of the extension of this practice to government offices and courts, as Manockjee did at Surat, the scope of the regulation was made applicable to all official and semi-official occasions in which Indians appeared before the servants of the British Government.[21]

The Hindu Intelligencer, a newspaper published from Calcutta, noticed that the decision of the government "seriously agitated the native mind" and aroused "no inconsiderable expression of indignation"[22]. Considering the regulation as discriminatory and insulting, Indians chose to stay away from the durbar of the Governor-General held immediately after the promulgation of the order. Prominent among them were Raja Pratap Chunder Singh, Baboo Prasanna Kumar Tagore, Hara Chunder Ghose, Ram Gopal Ghose and Rama Prasad Roy. Krishna Mohan Banerji, a former member of the Anglophil group, Young

Bengal, although he went to attend the durbar, preferred to return home, rather than comply with the new regulation.[23] The uneasiness of the elite of Calcutta who was part of the cultural world created by the British was quite evident.

Contested Tradition, Multiple Meanings

The public debate between Englishmen and Indians that the shoe regulation and its aftermath entailed revolved around tradition and its meaning as encoded in the practice of unshoding the feet. The British view was that Indians, regardless of religious differences, shared a common tradition of uncovering the feet in both private and public space. This, they held, was analogous to the European custom of taking off the hat.[24] In a letter to the Editor of the *Times of India*, one of them observed that:

"In the eyes of all natives to wear shoes in a room in any one's presence is a most studied insult, and as great a want of manners, as on the part of European gentleman to remain with their heads uncovered."[25]

Such a practice, it was argued, was not confined to private intercourse, but was equally true of public behaviour. The rulers of Rajputana, the Nizam of Hyderabad, the chiefs of Maharashtra and almost all rulers enforced the custom to which both Indians and Englishmen were equally subjected.[26] The experience the British encountered, both in private and public, was proof enough that a tradition of unshoding the feet was honoured in India, regardless of religious and regional differences.

In contrast to this the Indians who participated in the debate highlighted the plurality of tradition and argued that no uniform practice was followed in this case. The Parsees claimed that shoes formed a part of their dress from about four thousand years ago and that they did not remove them even when praying in their temples.[27] This tradition was also respected when they visited the durbar of Indian rulers. Manockjee gave the examples of the Parsees' audience with the princes of Kathiawar and Baroda who received them without unshoding the feet.[28] When some rulers like the Nizam of Hyderabad insisted on removing the shoes, the Parsees adopted some ingenious methods to respect the religious prescription.[29] Manockjee, however, conceded that there were departures from this practice which he attributed to the influence of Hindus who "believed it to be a great sin to take their shoes with them, on consecrated spots, and are very particular about keeping them off when dining or performing religious ceremonies"[30]. The colonial rulers, the Parsees contented, were trying to impose upon them a practice followed by other religious communities and certainly alien to their tradition.

Apart from the differences about the plurality of tradition, the construction of its meaning also differed very sharply. While the British construed it as a practice expressive of respect similar to taking off the hat in Western culture, no such meaning was attributed by Indians. The *Times of India* editorially observed:

> "From time immemorial it has been the fashion of men of the western nations to show respect for each other by uncovering the head. No European gentleman, therefore, will enter a private house, court, or public assembly without removing his hat; and this testimony of respect no well-bred Englishman dreams of withholding in the poorest native house, or native assembly he may enter. Equally certain is it - and let the fact be clearly borne in mind - that the immemorial custom of the East has been to show similar respect by uncovering the feet. The fact that Parsees, as well as Hindoos and Mahomedans, have ever been accustomed to show respect for others in this way, sweeps away at once all the cobwebs of religious stuff that has been imported on their part to this controversy."[31]

This interpretation of tradition was generally shared by those who justified the shoe regulation. One of them claimed that "taking off the shoes as a mark of respect could be traced back for nearly 3300 years among the civilized nations of the East"[32]. Since Indians had rendered this respect to their former rulers and fellow countrymen, there was no reason why it should not be extended to the British. They suspected that Indians were trying to take undue advantage of the liberality of the British which in the light of the prevalence of the practice in the past, would be tantamount to a "studied insult".[33] Hence no concession was conceded.

Indians, however, had an altogether different conception of the meaning of this tradition. According to them mutual respect was not the reason either for its origin or for continued practice. *The Hindu Intelligencer* asserted: "... we have no such formality as uncovering the head or foot or any other part of the corporeal frame as a mark of respect due to another."[34] If practised as a mark of respect, it would have been observed whenever people met each other, either in public or in private. That not being the case - the public meetings, nautch parties and social functions in which people from different strata of society mingled without removing shoes - clearly discounted the idea of respect.[35] The meaning attributed by the British, it was argued, was "out of ignorance of the manners and usages of Indians"[36].

What then did the practice mean? The answer to this question is linked with the explanation for the origins of the practice. The Indians traced them to social and religious factors which either influenced or prescribed a code of conduct. Unshoding before entering the durbar or a public function was a "sheer necessity" due to the "peculiar style of living and furnishing"[37]. On such occasions, since Indians sat on the floor, it was extremely uncomfortable to keep the footwear on. With the use of chairs becoming popular, it was argued, the practice was increasingly dispensed with.[38]

Unshoding the feet within the domestic space had its rationale in the rules of pollution and purity prescribed by religious codes. The Hindu houses generally have a sacred space within them, from which all polluting objects are kept away. Leather, being a polluting object, footwear made of it is left outside the house. At the same time the Hindus had no objection to the use of *padukas* made of wood inside the house, "carrying them in every nook and corner, whether sacred or not sacred"[39].

These reasons led the opponents of shoe respect to conclude that the practice of removing the shoes, either in public or in private, as an expression of respect was alien to the traditions in India. It was, therefore, seen as "a mark of humiliation, such as despots exact from their subjects", an intended insult and oppression.[40] Such an impression was borne out by experience. A Parsee who went to the tent of a British army officer without removing his shoes was scolded and turned out: "You big Scoundrel, why did you come with your shoes in a gentleman's tent? Get out you Scoundrel."[41] The pro-British newspapers used equally insulting language. Advocating stringent punishment to those who violated the shoe regulation, one of them stated:

> "The nigger who refuses to take off his shoes when so far honoured as to be permitted to present himself before a European gentleman *ought* to be slippered - this is our solemn decree."[42]

Despite this racially aggressive attitude the faith of Indians in British liberalism still prevailed. "A Hindu", writing in the *Times of India* bemoaned that "such conduct may become Asiatic despots, but not the sons of one of the most civilized countries of the world and the advocates of liberty"[43].

Culture, Legitimacy and Power

The rationale advanced for demanding "shoe respect" was primarily rooted in its prevalence in traditional practice. That it was not an innovation, but only a continuation was repeatedly emphasised. In other words, the British were only claiming to participate in a traditional practice which was widely observed by the rulers and subjects in the past. Such an appropriation of tradition, given the cultural differences between the colonial rulers and the Indian subjects, lacked cultural authenticity.

In the indigenous tradition, cultural practices were part of a code commonly shared and experienced. The British were not a part of this tradition and more importantly, had their own codes of conduct, evolved in a different cultural milieu. Establishing an identity with indigenous tradition was neither the purpose nor the outcome of appropriation. It was a part of a larger political project of an alien rule to seek legitimacy by invoking the practices of the past. However, making the cultural distinction between the British and Indians more pronounced was one of its consequences.

By permitting Indians to use European shoes and stockings, the British were valorising their own cultural products and practices. The advocates of shoe regulation tried to underplay the cultural implications of favouring the European mode. The *Times of India*, for instance, disclaimed any intention "to impose our fashions of dress upon our native subjects"[44]. But the preferential treatment had its logic rooted in hegemony and power. It tended to make the Western fashion the increasingly enchanting norm for those whom Macaulay envisioned as the "interpreters between us and them" and thus further the process of colonial cultural hegemonization and affirmation of power. The shoe Regulation and its aftermath also indicate how both the appropriation of indigenous tradition and hegemonization through cultural practices were contested and resisted. The emergence of cultural nationalism in colonial India which sought to reclaim and regenerate its cultural resources was partly embedded in such contestations and resistance.

Appendix

(From: Bombay Gazette, 2 April 1862)

The following is a Narrative of the altercation (in Hindoostani) between Mr. Warden, Session Judge, and Mr. Manockjee Cowasjee Entee, Assessor, in the Court of the Surat Fouzdaree Adawlut on the 24th day of March 1862.

Court Peon Seth, take off your boots.
Manockjee: Oh! No.
Peon: Everybody takes off his shoes here.
Manockjee: Never mind, tell your Saheb I shan't.
Sheristedar to the Judge: That Parsee objects to take off his shoes.
Judge: He must take them off. Everybody does so.
Judge turning to Manockjee: Come, take off your shoes soon.
Manockjee: Very good Sir, but let your Honour hear the objections I have against it and then decide.
Judge: You are very disputatious. Have you come here to wrangle with me? I shan't hear any thing.

Manockjee: No, Sir, whatever is legal ought to be heard.
Judge: No, nothing of Law herein. Your interrupt the Court's business, and you shall have to suffer for it.
Manockjee: I respectfully submit I do not interrupt the Court's business; order me to step in, and I shall be very happy to do so.
Judge: Take your shoes off and get in.
Manockjee: I humbly submit that exposing one's bare feet is something below human dignity, and contrary to the sacred ordinances of our Scriptures; besides, I have been bound over not to suffer myself the indignity of a pledge, which, as long as it does not interfere with the laws, can be respected.
Judge: Nothing of that here. Take off your shoes or it will be the worse for you. The great Nawab of Sucheen just visited me, and I saw him taking off his shoes. Are you a greater man than him?
Manockjee: I am only a poor British subject.
Judge: Then you do not obey our orders.
Manockjee: Your order I bow to with the greater deference (Saheb-ka-hookoom hamare seer aur anko par hai) but your Honour will oblige by quoting the authority of some law.
Judge: Law! it is not a matter of law. Don't talk of laws here.
Manockjee: I wonder why I should not. But then I have another very legal objection to raise. I am informed that the Criminal Procedure Act provides that the Summons should be issued to the Assessors at least three days before their presence is required, but I received no such summons. A Peon of the Court called upon me yesterday (Sunday) asking me to present myself before the Court without even mentioning what I was wanted for. This, if I mistake not, is not in accordance with the laws. My presence, therefore, not being legal, I shall be excused today.
Judge: No, I know you do not like serving as an Assessor, and hence this trifling with the Court. You have been summoned just the same as others here. We are not to make a new rule here for you. You interrupt the business of the Court, and you will suffer for it. I order you to take off your shoes at once and get in.
Manockjee: I respect your order with all the obedience but only on the understanding that by ordering me thus, you disgrace me, wound my feelings and interfere in the discharge of what I take to be a religious objection.
Judge: I don't care. Beware you interrupt the Court's business, and you will be dealt with accordingly. Do you obey us or no?
Manockjee: No Sir, I do not interrupt the Court's business. I just wait your orders to step in.
Judge: Come, let us see how you get in with shoes.
Manockjee: No, Sir, of course not until you allow me to do so.
Judge: Do you take off your shoes or no? Say yes or no.
Manockjee: I humbly submit that as long as your Honour do not overrule my religious scruples and show me a law whereby your orders could be justified, I am very sorry I could not act in defiance of the dictates of my conscience, in defiance of human dignity and in direct contradiction of my religion.

Judge: No. You tell us an untruth, your religion does forbid it. You see some Parsees here in the Court, just refer the question to them.

Manockjee: No. Sir, I tell you the simple truth, as far as I know, our religion does forbid this and similar personal indignities. As for the Parsees here the Court may ask them, but every body is not expected to know our religion.

Judge: You represent untruthfully. Whom would you wish us to refer? You make yourself liable to punishment.

Manockjee: I beg your pardon, I believe I am quite right. Whatever the law provides I shall with all due obedience undergo.

Judge: Just name somebody here.

Manockjee: I could not.

Judge: Then who could?

Manockjee: The Court if it likes.

Judge: But you tell us an untruth - there is no religious objection. I know that.

Manockjee: No, Sir, I believe there is and I speak the truth only.

Judge: Do I lie then? Come, sharp, take care and say whom would you have us ask?

Manockjee: I could name no one. Very few have rightly studied our sacred scriptures. Besides you are aware, Sir, that we are allowed to go with shoes on into the Supreme Court, the Sudden Adawlut and every where in Bombay; and if it were disrespectful they would never have permitted it there.

Judge: Talk not of Bombay. Every Parsee takes his shoes off before us and I command you at once to submit to the rule of the Court.

Manockjee: No, Sir, I have religious objections against it.

Judge: That we know not.

Manockjee: But then I do humbly inform the Court it is so.

Judge: (Excited) Stand off, not so near.

Manockjee: Very good, your Honour.

Judge: I order you at once to take off your shoes.

Manockjee: No, Sir, not until you say you overrule my religious objections and care not wounding my feelings as a man.

Judge: Name somebody for us to refer to.

Manockjee: None in Surat that I know of.

Judge: What, no one knows your religion?

Manockjee: No, Sir, none that I know of.

Judge: Not even the Dustoors and the score and half of Modees?

Manockjee: No, Sir, there is no more than one Modee whom the Punchayat used to refer to the former times and he is merely a repository of all our customs and usages. He knows nothing of our Sacred Writings.

Judge: Name any body.

Manockjee: I believe the Son of Eduldaroo of Sunjan, now one of the Dustoors of Bombay and all who are equal to him may answer and solve the question. If you take it no indignity, I am prepared to take my turban off provided you allow me to have my skull cap on.

Judge: What! What! Do you talk of taking your Pugree away? Why, I could not sit with mine on, nor could any person here dare take off his Pugree? Do you condemn the Court.

Manockjee: No, Sir, I just asked if that would suit the Court. Taking off my Pugree would have been a greater insult to myself than to the Court, but I would have submitted to it because there is nothing of conscience or religion involved in it. I hold no respect, or disrespect embodied or disembodied in the shoes, but the putting on of our turban is the greatest of all respects, that we pay. We do not have our Pugrees on when at home but when we go out to see respectable persons we are bound by social etiquette to have it on: whilst we (Parsees) in our social intercourse never take off our shoes before any Parsee however great. In fact the 'abroo' said to lie in shoes is a very novel strange idea with us.

Judge: We do not know of that.

Manockjee: Your Honour may enquire. Besides -

Judge: Stop, go out of the Court at once.

Manockjee: Very good Sir (turns and leaves the Court).

Judge: No, No, No, come back; stand there. Look here, I shall not allow you a chair, you are to stand there and hear the proceedings.

Manockjee: Any indignity I shall submit to, provided human dignity is not violated and my religious feelings not meddled with. I shall stand. (After a short pause to the Sheristedar) ask your Saheb what is the duty of an Assessor.

Judge: You talk of the Supreme Court and the Sudder and still you know not what an Assessor is!

Manockjee: We are not expected to have studied law previous to our coming here, and besides Jurymen and Assessors have not equal powers, I am told. (The Judge explains at length the difference between the Jurors and the Assessors. Manockjee thanks him in return).

Judge: (After the deposition of the first witness was half taken). If you like to sit you could come in without your shoes and there is a chair for you. If you like staying out of the Court, you may sit on the floor.

Manockjee: No Sir, I feel much troubled in refusing your kind offer of a chair, as I could not take off my boots. As for sitting on the bare floor, it is merely adding to the disgrace. If your Honour would allow me any seat whatever, say a goddee, I shall be very happy to accommodate myself upon it, but -

Judge: Enough, Enough, - If you do not want a chair you shan't have it.

Manockjee: Very good Sir.

An eye witness

Notes

1. The response of the participants of the symposium on "Dissociation and Appropriation of Global Processes: History, Religion and culture in Asia and Africa" in Berlin from 23-25 Oct. 1997 has helped the revision of the paper. I have also benefited from the comments of Dr. Neeladri Bhattacharya.
2. Daniel Roche, The Culture of Clothing: Dress and Fashion in the "Ancient Regime", Cambridge 1994, p. 33.
3. Mary Ellen Roach/Joanne Bubloz Eicher (ed.), Dress, Adornment and Social Order, New York 1965.
4. Quoted from: Keith Thomas, Introduction. In: Jan Breman/Herman Roodenburg, A Cultural History of Gestures, New York 1991, p. 2.
5. Ibid.
6. C.A. Bayly, The Origins of Swadeshi (Home Industry): Cloth and Indian Society, 1700-1930. In: Arjun Appadurai, The Social Life of Things: Commodities in Cultural Perspective, Cambridge 1995, pp. 292-293.
7. Robert L. Hardgrave Jr., The Breast-Cloth Controversy: Caste Consciousness and Social Change in Southern Travancore. In: Indian Economic and Social History Review, 5 (1968) 2, pp. 171-187; Dick Kooiman, Conversion and Social Equality in India - The London Missionary Society in South Travancore in the 19th Century, Delhi 1989, pp. 148-153.
8. The idea of internal and external view is as used by Jury M. Lotion/Lid Guisburg/Boris Upenski, The Semiotics of Russian Cultural History, London 1985, p. 30.
9. U.R. von Ehrenfels, Clothing and Power Abuse. In: Justine M. Cordwell/Ronald A. Schwartz (ed.), The Fabrics of Culture: The Anthropology of Clothing and Adornment, The Hague 1979, pp. 400-403.
10. Foreign Dept., 22 Dec. 1854, nos. 263-265, and Home Dept. Public Branch, 4 April 1968, no. 23.
11. For the text of the eye-witness account see Appendix.
12. Manockjee collected the opinion of authorities as Dr. Martin Haugh, Dhunjeebhoy Framjee, Dustoor Hosungjee Jamasjee and also evidence from religious texts. Dhunjeebhoy Framjee stated that "the religious books of the Parsees most emphatically prohibit them from walking barefooted. To cover their feet is not only an immemorial custom with the Parsees, but it is a positive religious Firman (commandment)". Manockjee Cowasjee Entee, Memorial to Sir Bartle Frere, the Governor of Bombay, 5 June 1862. Appendix A (hereafter Memorial).
13. Ibid., p. 9.
14. Ibid., p. 17.
15. K.N. Panikkar, British Diplomacy in North India: A Study of Delhi Residency, Delhi 1968, Percival Spear, Twilight of the Mughals, New Delhi 1969, pp. 32-59; Bernard Cohn, Colonialism and its Forms of Knowledge: The British in India, New Delhi 1997, pp. 106-162.
16. Bharati Ray, Hyderabad and British Paramountcy, 1858-1883, Delhi 1988, pp. 59-60, and Michael H. Fisher, Indirect Rule in India, Delhi 1991, pp. 176-185.
17. Foreign Dept., 27 Sept. 1833, no. 21.
18. Ibid., no. 22.

19 Benares Recorder, 26 March 1853; The Hindu Intelligencer, 9 March 1857. Also see Foreign Dept., 22 Dec. 1854, nos. 263-265.
20 Foreign Dept., 22 Dec 1854, nos. 263-265.
21 Home Dept., Public Branch, 9 March 1857.
22 The Hindu Intelligencer, 9 March 1857.
23 Ibid.
24 The notion of such a homology was very widely shared by those who favoured shoe respect. One of them wrote: "The European custom on entering a person's house is to take off the hat; the Asiatic custom is to take off the shoes; and this custom is as invariable in India as taking off the hat in England." Times of India, 11 April 1862. Also see Bombay Gazette, 14 November 1856.
25 Times of India, 23 April 1862; Bombay Quarterly Review, April 1853.
26 Times of India, 23 April 1862; Bombay Gazette, 4 April 1853, 7 April 1853.
27 Memorial.
28 Ibid.
29 When the dustoor of Poona went to the court of Nizam, he was instructed to remove his shoes. Since he was keen on meeting the Nizam he used "the inconvenient and clumsy" method of placing the *mahajam* (a piece of leather used inside the shoe and as large as the shoe itself) between the naked soles of his feet and the stockings. Times of India, 11 April 1862.
30 Memorial, p. 19.
31 Times of India, 9 May 1862.
32 Ibid., 15 April 1862.
33 Ibid., 23 April 1862.
34 The Hindu Intelligencer, 12 June 1854; Bombay Gazette, 6 April 1853.
35 Times of India, 16 April 1852; Bombay Gazette, 6 April 1853.
36 Times of India, 16 April 1852; The Hindu Intelligencer, 7 March 1857; Bombay Gazette, 15 April 1862, 23 April 1862.
37 The Hindu Intelligencer, 9 March 1857.
38 Bombay Gazette, 6 April 1853.
39 Ibid. and Times of India, 16 April 1862.
40 Bombay Gazette, 15 April 1862; Times of India, 16 April 1862; The Hindu Intelligencer, 9 March 1857.
41 Bombay Gazette, 12 November 1856.
42 Poona Observer, 9 April 1853.
43 Times of India, 16 April 1862.
44 Ibid., 9 May 1862.

Ottoman Women's Reaction to the Economic and Cultural Intrusion of the West: The Quest for a National Dress

Nicole A.N.M. van Os

Introduction

Featherstone in his introduction to a special issue of *Theory, Culture & Society* on global culture, which was later reprinted in bookform, points out that it is not possible to refer to a global culture as something "akin to the culture of the nation state writ large" with a homogenous and integrated character. Instead of a static entity he prefers to talk of globalization as processes of integration and disintegration transcending national or societal borders.[1] A process of integration which leads to homogenization and of disintegration leading to heterogenization at the same time. This homogenization is often equated with Americanization (or McDonaldization) nowadays, but might mean something different in another geographical or historical context. Common is that larger and more powerful polities tend to absorb smaller and weaker polities not only culturally, but also economically and politically.[2] These weaker polities, however, do not always simply accept this absorption. More often they (try to) resist cultural, economic and/or political domination. As a reaction to homogenization, they might want to heterogenize, develop their own cultural, economic and political (id)entity.

According to Robertson this process is inevitably connected with modernization. Sketching the phases in history leading to globalization, he places the beginning of this process in the late nineteenth century. During this period European powers were the largest and most powerful polities in the world. It is therefore no surprise that his "skeletal sketch" is a very eurocentred one. For example, one of the characteristics of the "incipient phase" (approximately 1750-1870s) is the "'admission' of non-European societies to 'international society'"[3]. Homogenization in this context was Europeanization rather than anything else. This was certainly the case for the Ottomans. Modernization for them meant implicitly and explicitly westernization, Europeanization. Both the Ottoman and Turkish words used in this context, *muasırlaşmak* and *çağdaşlaşmak* respectively, indicate this. Both verbs are formed by adding the suffix *laş* to an adjective. This suffix means "to become". The words *muasır* and *çağdaş* literally mean "contemporary, of the same era". Contemporary, however, with whom? Of the same era as whom? For the Ottomans this was Europe. Modernization for them, thus indeed was Europeanization. But in what fields? Originally, the Ottomans, who were losing wars and lands, were only interested in European science and technology. Gradually, however, they were more and more absorbed into the European polity. Economically, politically and culturally they were incorporated into this powerful entity. In all three fields they tried to resist this incorporation and to replace the European elements with *milli,* national, ones.

Arnason points out the importance of culture in this process, because "nationalism defines and justifies power in terms of culture." He does this because, like Smith, he regards the ethnie as the core of the nation.[4] The ethnie, as Smith remarks, could be rediscovered and its existence and (political) power could be legitimized by traditions, invented or "rediscovered" as well. These traditions could be invented to deal with a dilemma which was noticed by Geertz and later also referred to by Chatterjee. Nations drawn into an alien civilization due to, for example, imperialism, recognized the standards they had to adhere to in order to be able to compete with their "superiors" and to become independent of what came from an alien culture.[5] These nations were faced with the choice of following the "Indigenous Way of Life", or "The Spirit of the Age" as Geertz states. The choice between becoming "essentialist" or "epochalist", respectively.[6] According to Chatterjee the result of this dilemma was a double-layered ambivalence. On the one hand, these nations tried to imitate and surpass their "superiors" by accepting standards set by the alien culture that they were at the same time rejecting. On the other hand, traditions which were regarded as "an obstacle to progress" were at the same time "cherished as marks of identity"[7]. Ways to deal with this ambivalence are, for example, to use the standards of the alien culture to show that certain habits of theirs are even worse than indigenous ones, or to demonize these alien habits.[8] This is what Fatma Aliye, a nineteenth century female Ottoman author, did. Although she argued against polygyny, she meanwhile pointed out that the illegitimate sexual partners of men in the Christian world and the children born out of such a relationship were much worse off than the concubine of an Ottoman man, who was entitled to his protection and whose children had the same rights as the children of his official wife.[9] In the same way, she compared the position of Ottoman slaves with that of European servants. The latter, of course, being much worse off, because they could be disposed of at the whim of the employer, while an Ottoman master was obliged to take good care of his slave.[10] Another is indeed the reinvention of tradition, or the rediscovery of a "golden age" during which values, norms, habits, etc. showed a striking resemblance to the values, norms, habits, etc. of the dominating alien culture. Taking up the norms of the alien society thus becomes nothing more than a return to the incorrupted past of the own society and the "modern" and the "own" are reconciled.[11]

Another source of the incorrupted own was the non-urban population. Peasants and nomads were regarded to be untouched by the influence of the modern world and to be more pure. It is with this idea that new traditions are invented with elements borrowed "from the well-supplied warehouses of ... folklore"[12]. Thus, on the initiative of King Otto and Queen Amalia parts of *traditional* outfits from several regions in Greece were used to devise a Greek national outfit after Greece became independent from the Ottoman Empire. So although all these elements were authentic as such and served to give the outfit its legitimation, the combination of these elements was totally new.[13] Therefore, this outfit was not a representative of a national identity but a constitutive. Clothes can also constitute a social identity as is the case with Friedman's *sapeurs* in the Peoples Republic of the Congo. For these *sapeurs,* dressing in their *non-traditional,* Western clothes with clearly visible labels of the great brands was an aspect "of broader cultural strategies of self-definition"[14]. The instituted change in the outfit of Ottoman officials which accompanied the modernization of the Ottoman civil and military institutions can be interpreted as constituting both a social and a national identity. Instead of the traditional garb which had made it possible to distinguish the people of the various religious groups in the Empire, Ottoman officials of all creeds were now uniformly dressed. This convened with the wish of the Ottoman government to create one Ottoman nation in order to prevent the further dismemberment of the Empire due to separatist nationalist movements. Moreover, these outfits were a symbol for the transition to a new and modern order, that of Europe.[15]

Although Friedman stresses the importance of the look people have by dressing the way they do, one can read between the lines that not only the look, but also the fact that the clothes have been purchased abroad, in Paris, is relevant. The choice of where to buy clothes turns the consumer into not only a cultural, but also an economic agent. The purchase of clothes of foreign origin or rather the refusal to do so can thus become a nationalist economic political act. At the end of the nineteenth and beginning of the twentieth century a limited group of Ottoman Muslim women realized that through a conscious purchase of their dresses they could participate in the efforts to diminish the cultural, political and economic influence of the European powers on their country.

The Intrusion of "the West"

Starting at the end of the eighteenth, but accelerating during the nineteenth century, however, the Ottomans had to accept a growing hold of the Europeans over several fields. The Europeans left their mark in Ottoman politics and on its economy. Also, Ottoman culture changed under the influence of increasing European-Ottoman contacts.

Through the larger part of world history people(s) have been in contact which each other exchanging goods and ideas. Long distances were crossed in short tracks or at once. War and diplomacy, on the one hand, and trade, on the other hand, were important instruments for such exchanges. The Ottoman Empire had from its origins at the end of the fourteenth century until the seventeenth century been a feared adversary of the other European powers on the battlefield. European powers regularly sent envoys to Istanbul to secure the support of the ruling Sultan in a controversy against another European power.

The Ottoman Empire was also important for the Europeans in another way. It was one of the crossroads in the trade of goods between east and west. Through the harbour cities goods coming from the east were transferred to the west and vice versa. Although the Ottoman Empire thus was a transit gate for goods and people, its rulers pursued a policy of trying to limit influence from the outside to a minimum in order to prevent society from changing. Classical Ottoman society was, ideally, strictly organized with the Sultan and his entourage at the centre of power. The idea was that change would only mean that this organization would be upset and thus that the Ottoman Empire as such would be endangered.

By the end of the eighteenth century contact between European powers and the Ottoman Empire increased because the latter had several problems, both externally and internally. It had been losing wars against Russia and Austria, its traditional adversaries, which meant that the Empire had also been losing parts of its territories. Moreover, the central government could no longer rely on its vassals. The local notables in its provinces behaved as if they were independent rulers instead of vassals and refused to fulfil their military requirements or transfer the taxes they collected to Istanbul.[16] During the nineteenth century, efforts were made to turn the tide.[17]

Solutions were sought in reforms in the military and administrative fields. To bring the unruly vassals under control the administration had to be centralized. To deal with outside adversaries the military had to become acquainted with the newest technical developments in warfare and diplomatic contacts had to be established. Especially under the Sultans Selim III (1792-1807) and Mahmud II (1808-1839) important steps were taken to carry out these reforms.

For the administrative reforms the France of Louis XVI was taken as an example. For the military reforms the Sultans also looked to Europe. Students were sent to several cities in Europe, while over the years French, British and Prussian instructors were invited to the Empire to educate and reorganize the military. In order to facilitate communication with the European powers and also to remain informed on developments in Europe, permanent embassies in some of the European capitals were established for the first time. The training of administrative personnel lagged behind. In the second quarter of the century personnel for the administration were mainly trained in the so called "translation offices" of the diverse governmental departments and through apprenticeships at the embassies abroad. Only in the second half of the century were more schools opened to meet the rising demand for modernly educated administrative personnel.

What were the results of these reforms? Over the nineteenth century the army and the administration were gradually reformed. However, the problems which these reforms had aimed to cure were only partially solved. The dismemberment of the Ottoman Empire continued. The rebellious vassals of the late eighteenth and early nineteenth century gave way to a new threat to the internal stability of the Empire: nationalism. Initially in the border provinces, but in the course of the nineteenth century also in communities in the heartlands of the Empire which considered themselves to be different from those ruling at the centre because of their religion, language, or other reasons, started to ask or fight for more autonomy or for independence. Moreover, instead of become stronger *vis à vis* the European powers, the latter were able to extend their influence on the Ottoman Empire in several ways.

As written above, the Empire turned to the Europeans and asked for their assistance in the reorganization of the army. As a result the language of instruction at the newly-founded schools was French. Thus a layer of French speaking officers was created. Moreover, the rebellious provinces of the Empire forced the Ottomans to ask for military assistance from their European counterparts. Especially, the troubles with the governor of Egypt, Muḥammad ʿAlī, compelled the Ottomans to seek help from the British. Russia formed another threat which led the Ottomans to look for support from the Western European states. The latter were eager to give their support, but at a cost. The Ottomans had to accept the European powers turning the (Christian) communities into their protégés. This meant that they started to meddle in the internal affairs of the Empire to act on behalf of their protégés. Thus, under European pressure, the Ottomans were forced to extend the rights of the non-Muslim communities living within their borders. The need for assistance of the Ottoman Empire was not only used by the European powers to strengthen their political hold on the Ottoman Empire, but also as a leverage to enlarge their economic grip on it. The Ottoman Empire was forced to sign free trade treaties with most of them and thus became part of an economic system in which the European powers, with Britain at its head, were the unrivalled leaders. The free trade treaties meant that the Ottoman Empire became a partner in the international division of labour, producing raw materials for the industrializing European countries and buying its manufactured goods from them. During the nineteenth century both import and export increased. The former, however, grew faster than the latter. This led to a deficit in the trade balance. After 1900 this deficit grew more dramatically than in the period before. This led to a drain on the finances of the Empire. Moreover, areas which were important for cash crop production in the Balkan were lost, while the change in the old trade routes due to the colonial expansion of the European powers and the building of the Suez canal also meant a loss of income. Incomes which were badly needed to finance the reforms and the wars. The costs incurred by the Crimean war forced the Ottoman Empire to knock at the door of the European powers for financial help for the first time, because the local bankers in Istanbul were no longer able nor willing to lend money to the state. The foreign loans turned out to be a millstone around the neck of the "Sick man of Europe" as the Ottoman Empire began to be called. By the 1870s the Ottoman Empire was no longer capable of paying its debts or even the interest on them. In 1881 the European creditors created the Public Department Administration (PDA), an institution staffed by Europeans which had to guarantee that European investors would get back the money they had invested in a loan to the Ottoman Empire. In due time the PDA actually administered one third of the public income and was acting as direct intermediary between the Ottoman government and potential foreign investors.[18]

Foreigners also invested directly in the Ottoman Empire. These investments were directed by the requirements of trade. This meant that they were involved in the building of ports and railroads which connected the producers of manufactured goods with their suppliers of raw materials and their market.

Since the Europeans preferred to do business with their co-religionists, a bifurcated bourgeoisie was created. Especially in the coastal cities, non-Muslims engaged in banking, trade and industrial entrepreneurship but were devoid of any political power, while Muslims typically aspired careers in the imperial bureaucracy or the military.[19] Another result of the economic developments was that shifts in manufacturing took place. Some branches were almost completely destroyed, leaving whole families to look for an alternative source of income. Other branches such as those producing or processing half products, on the other hand, flourished due to these developments.[20] Moreover, with the improved means of communication and transportation, it became easier for individuals to travel between Europe and the Ottoman Empire[21], to purchase European goods and to learn about European developments.

European, mostly French, books found their way to an Ottoman public. Originally, mostly technical books on warfare, but soon philosophical treaties, novels, newspapers, periodicals, etc. were also read by an increasing audience. For those who could not read these European books, translations were made. The Ottoman intellectuals of the nineteenth century were inspired by what they read and started to publish their own newspapers, periodicals, while Ottoman literature also went through a transformation.[22] In their writings they expressed their ideas not only on the (political) situation of the Ottoman Empire, but also on family life, the position of women in the family and society and other subjects.

With the introduction of European goods and thoughts a kind of dualism was developed in culture: on the one hand, the *alafranga*, on the other hand, the *alaturka*. *Alafranga* represented the modern, Europeanized way of life, *alaturka* symbolized the life-style of past generations. The two, however, were often not completely separated. The traditional and Ottoman Muslim was not always replaced by but coexisted with the European and modern.[23]

However, not everybody appreciated the growing influence of the European powers on the political, economic and cultural life of the Ottomans. Different tactics were employed to diminish their influence.

Reaction to the Intrusion of "the West"

The increasing influence of "the West" on Ottoman economy, politics and its culture gave rise to resistance that took several forms. Although the critics all seemed to have agreed on the need to diminish the European domination of Ottoman politics and economy, there was disagreement on the path to follow in order to diminish this domination. This disagreement seems to have focused on the cultural aspect of the whole and entailed choosing which path to follow: that of the "Indigenous Way of Life" or that of "The Spirit of the Age".

Some of the Ottoman intellectuals argued that the perceived decline of the Ottoman Empire was caused by the Europeans leading the Ottomans astray from the ways of Islam. Although they accepted that it was necessary to take over the technical devices of the West, these conservatist-muslims as Berkes[24] calls them regarded the safe-guarding of the traditional ways as the only means to make the Ottoman Empire capable of facing up to the Europeans again. Their position was strengthened when Abdülhamid II (1876-1909) decided to support pan-Islamism in order to strengthen his position vis à vis the European powers. He propagated himself not only as the Ottoman Sultan, ruler of the Ottoman subjects, but also as Caliph, the religious leader of all the Muslims in the world. In cases where a conflict arose between European colonizers and their Muslim subject, for example, he would intervene on behalf of the latter. By using his spiritual leadership of the Muslims this way he hoped to earn the respect of the European powers and increase his temporal power *vis à vis* them.[25]

On the other end of the scale there were what Berkes calls the "new-Westernists". These "new-Westernists" argued that only by adopting and absorbing European artefacts, culture and ideas, as a whole, and thus becoming completely European (and preferably secular), would the Ottomans be able to fight them on equal terms.[26]

People belonging largely to the latter group were strongly opposed to the rule of Abdülhamid and his Islamic clique. Especially the creation of the Public

Dept. Administration which turned the Ottoman Empire into a puppet of European powers was a reason for criticism. The critics of Abdülhamid's regime came from a group of military and civil officers educated at modern schools founded in the nineteenth century but who had been ousted from the system due to the neo-patrimonial hiring system of the increasingly paranoiac Sultan.[27] Their protests had been smothered by the strict censorship of the Sultan and his vast network of spies. Many of them had been forced to fled the country and to take refuge abroad where they formed centres of opposition. One of the leading centres was in Paris and was headed by Ahmed Rıza, a man who strongly believed in positivism and the necessity of progress towards (Western) civilization through science. His ideas were also reflected in the name the group became known under: Committee of Union and Progress (CUP). After his group joined forces with rebellious military in Thessaloniki they were able to force the Sultan to restore the constitution he had one-sidedly suspended in 1878 in July 1908 with what is also called the Young Turk revolution.[28]

Ottoman Women and Parisian Fashion

While the military and civil servants were forced to dress in a European type outfit, others started to wear these outfits voluntarily to show their "modernity" or "sophistication" or, in other words, one's "familiarity with things European". Women's dress, too, changed towards a more European garb. This development started in the first half of the nineteenth century, but gained momentum in the last three decades of that century, especially in the coastal cities, Istanbul, Izmir and Thessaloniki.[29] These cities had large non-Muslim populations, who were the first to adopt European clothing, but also the Muslims there were more likely to get in touch with Europeans.[30] The wives of diplomats and merchants, and (female) travellers[31] formed a ready source of inspiration for the Ottoman women wanting to dress "modern". The first Muslim women to adopt these European outfits were the women in the palaces of the imperial family and those of the upper-classes.[32] It was in these classes that the wish to be part of European society was first felt.

The males of these families who were educated at modern schools or had travelled abroad also changed their ideas on the education of women. Amongst the elite families it became a custom that the daughters were taught French, English or German, and other European skills like playing the piano. The European governesses hired to teach these young women were another source of information on European fashion.[33] Furthermore, these young women educated in the European languages - French being the most favourable one - were increasingly able to read Parisian fashion periodicals which were available from the shops in the (non-Muslim quarters of the) big cities. Moreover, the Ottoman women's periodicals that started to appear in the second half of the nineteenth century did not hesitate to publish pictures of European women in the "latest Parisian fashion". The (first?) Ottoman fashion periodical, however, did not appear until 1911. This trilingual periodical, La Reine de la Mode Parisienne, was biweekly and appeared in French, Greek and Ottoman Turkish.[34] The display windows of the European (and/or non-Muslim) shops in the fancy parts of a city like Istanbul formed another source for news on the latest developments in the fashion sector.

Some of the women were able to purchase their dresses directly from Paris, the centre of fashion in those days, either by going there themselves or through relatives living there. The less fortunate would go to foreign dressmakers in Istanbul. Another way was to ask the traditionally non-Muslim family dressmaker to sew a dress based on the pictures in the magazines. The cloth necessary for this would be ordered from Paris, bought in the European stores in Istanbul or purchased through the dressmaker. For those who could not afford a tailormade dress, the *pret à porter* from the European stores formed the solution. If necessary adjustments could be made by the seamstresses available at these stores. These stores also sold the accessories to complete the outfit of the modern, westernized woman, like gloves, umbrellas, parasols, stockings, shoes, etc.

European fashion also took a prominent place in the satirical press of those days. The feelings towards the West were clearly reflected in this press in which the Ottoman "nation" as a whole was generally represented as a female. Sometimes, however, the woman symbolized only a part of that nation. In these cartoons the way the woman was dressed was the main indicator of how to interpret the picture.[35] She would be dressed in traditional garb when opposed to the European powers (depicted as males in their supposedly national attire) which are threatening her. When opposed to (religious) conservatism she would be dressed in modern (= European) garb. Or, the European dress indicated her subversive attitude, as an active participant in Europeanization. As such, Ottoman women dressed in Parisian fashion became the symbol for certain groups which collaborated with the West, whose moral norms were corrupted, and who looked down upon or ignored the needs of their own people.[36] Dress, and particularly, women's European dress was important in symbolizing the empire's relationships with the European powers in the satirical press. It was also to play an important role in the rejection of European domination by Ottoman Muslim women.

Women, Fashion and Nationalism

The resistance against not only political and economic domination through the European powers, but also their influence on the Ottoman cultural domain are reflected in the discussions on the "national dress". As was the case with the critics of European domination mentioned above, the participants in the discussions seemed to have agreed on the need to diminish the political and economic influence. The cultural aspect of it, however, raised more controversies.

Although the CUP won the first elections after the Young Turk revolution by getting all but one seat, they decided not to take part in the cabinet that was formed, but to leave these posts to the senior, more experienced members of the Hamidian political establishment. The only CUP member in the June 1909 cabinet was the Minister of Finances, Mehmet Cavid. That it was exactly this post that was to be occupied by a newcomer in politics is no coincidence. It stresses the importance the CUP was giving to the economic situation of their country. In their opinion economic independence was a prerequisite for political independence. The Hamidian regime had proved to be default in this respect, thus the CUP deemed it right to give this post to a newcomer.

Mehmet Cavid held a nineteenth century liberal economic view. Initially, he aimed at solving the Empire's economic problems by gaining capital through the stimulation of free trade and free enterprise and rejection of protectionist measures. Moreover, even if he had wanted to introduce protectionist measures, this would have been impossible due to the agreements the Ottomans had reached with the different European states. The latter were of course not willing to give up their advantageous position. Thus the solution had to come from gaining capital by spending less and saving more.

In an article in one of the first women's periodicals which appeared after the Young Turk revolution in October 1908, Mehmet Cavid called upon the Ottoman women to be frugal and not to spend the money their husbands earned on unnecessary items. By saving money, he argued, women would help the Ottoman Empire to pay its debts. A good housewife, therefore, was a woman who would control her expenses and who would know how to manage a budget.[37]

The idea that purchasing foreign goods had negative effects on the Ottoman economy and should be prevented had already been expressed by Fatma Aliye in a book which appeared in a French translation under the title *Les Musulmanes Contemporaines* in 1894. In the third chapter of this book two arguments are brought forward against buying European fashion that are related to the costs involved. In the first place it was argued that following fashion leads to squander, since dresses were put aside not because they were worn out, but because they were out of fashion. Another argument used was that for Parisian fashion cloth used was the not locally produced but imported. Even though, the narrator argued, locally produced cloth was often more durable, cheaper and of better quality. It could be used just as well for European dresses. She pointed out that by using imported cloth a considerable amount of money was leaving the country, while the Ottomans needed that money so badly.[38]

Women used the same argument also after the Young Turk revolution of 1908. Even before Mehmet Cavid published his article, Fatma Fahrünnisa, a famous female writer of that time, had argued in a newspaper that the expense of following (French) fashions was too high: it not only caused the corruption of family life, but also damaged the national economy.[39] One of the authors in the *Kadınlar Dünyası* (Women's World) claimed that the spendthrift Ottoman women were responsible for Europe being able to extract up to 15 million Turkish pounds out of the Ottoman economy.[40]

Although the aim at first was to prevent money from flowing outside the borders of the Ottoman Empire, the rise of Ottoman Muslim nationalism with the Balkan wars of 1912-1913 led to a shift in the arguments used. As explained above, the developments of the nineteenth century had led to a bifurcation of the Ottoman bourgeoisie. Commercial activities in the coastal cities were mainly in the hands of non-Muslim Ottomans. During the Balkan Wars the rumour was spread that the non-Muslim Ottomans were financially supporting their co-religionists fighting against the Ottomans. This led to a boycott of the shops of non-Muslims all over the Empire. The shift in focus is also visible in the name and goals of an organization founded by women concerned about the economy of the Ottoman Empire. This organization founded in 1913 was originally named Society for the Consumption of Local Products (*Mamulat-ı Dāhiliye İstihlaki Kadınlar Cemiyeti*), but from April 1914 onwards it called itself the Society for National Consumption (*Milli İstihlak Cemiyeti*). The difference seems to be minimal but I would argue that it is indicative of the shift in focus. With *Mamulat-ı Dahiliye* (lit. "internal products") the society was referring to products produced within the borders of the Ottoman Empire as opposed to those produced outside of it. With *milli* ("national"), however, the organization was referring to "Muslim" and "Turkish" as was confirmed by the fact that the organization originally aimed at educating young girls and women in general, but by 1914 had turned its attention to educating poor *Turkish Muslim* girls only.[41] This was indicative of the development towards a more nationalist economic policy that replaced the liberal policy of Mehmet Cavid and which had as one of its aims the creation of a "national", that is Muslim, commercial bourgeoisie.

This meant that by 1914 a good patriotic woman would wear a dress devoid of unnecessary frills, which was made out of cloth produced by, preferably a Muslim-owned, but at least an Ottoman-owned factory, made by a Muslim dressmaker or seamstress, and/or purchased from a Muslim-owned shop. In the course of the years to follow, other arguments were added in favour of the simpleness of their garb. Through continuous war which left so many families destitute, conspicuous consumption was deemed improper. Moreover, not only the war, but also the efforts to create a strong national economy, forced women to turn from being conscious consumers into producers themselves. A dress full of frills and laces would not serve them in such a situation.

However, what should this outfit look like from now on? Fatma Fahrünnisa in the above mentioned article argued that the Ottomans should develop a national dress. Before the Young Turk revolution, she stated, the Ottomans had imitated those they admired and respected. Now the time had come to be admired and respected and therefore imitated, because they had thrown off the yoke of the despotic Sultan, Abdülhamid.[42]

Fatma Fahrünnisa did not indicate whether she was referring to the outdoor or the indoor dress of women when she pleaded for the development of a national outfit. This is, however, particularly relevant especially for Muslim women. Muslim women were supposed to obey the rules of Islam. According to these rules, men who were not part of the immediate family of the woman (basically all men a woman can marry) were not supposed to see certain parts of her body. She had to dress in *tesettür*. However, what parts of the body were not to be shown to these men was (and is) subject to debate.

It is not hard to imagine that the traditionalist-islamists with Abdülhamid at their head acted vigorously against any change in the traditional Ottoman Muslim dress. In the name of the Sultan several decrees were issued which forbade women to adorn a particular outfit. In 1890 the Sultan forbade the black, all-covering *çarşaf* because "[women wearing the *çarşaf*] were immodestly dressed to such a degree that they were 'not covered'". In the imperial decree the reason for its issue was also stated. If women did not dress according to the orders of Allah, which entailed that they should be properly dressed, Allah would damage the individuals and the state both materially and immaterially.[43] Thus this decree forms an example of the ideas which prevailed in the Islamic circles around Abdülhamid II that the loosening of the rules of Islam was one of the reasons for the perceived decline of the Ottoman Empire. Their solution to the problems of the empire, therefore, was a stricter adherence to these rules, one of them being related to the proper dressing of women. That women did not let themselves be directed by these decrees and continued to dress in the way they fancied, however, is clear from another decree that was issued in 1900. Here the gendarmerie was urged to prevent Muslim women from "wandering around immodestly dressed and not taking into account the rules of *tesettür* (covering oneself according to Islam)"[44].

Even after the Young Turk revolution of 1908 conservative forces were able to continue to put pressure on the authorities and make them act against the loosening of the rules of *tesettür*. Between 1908 and 1914 the (religious) authorities published several warnings that the women should not "behave and move in contradiction with the national good morals and ethics"⁴⁵, but that they had to dress according to "the religious orders and national morals"⁴⁶, because these were "habits ... acknowledged and followed by the whole of the nation"⁴⁷. In all three cases it is clear that the term "national" here, was referring to the Muslim community only. The periodicals *Sırat-ı Müstakim* (Straight Road) and its successor, *Sebilürreşād* (Straight Road), which represented the view of the "islamists" supported the authorities in their activities and published several articles on the necessity of *tesettür* for Muslim women.⁴⁸

The authorities also tried to prevent the spread of writings opposing *tesettür*, but were unable to do so.⁴⁹ Arguments in favour of its lifting appeared in the periodical of the strongly secularist Abdullah Cevdet, *İçtihad* (Opinion).⁵⁰ However, by the end of 1913, with the rise of Ottoman-Muslim nationalism, the question of lifting *tesettür* or not was no longer posed. For the majority of women nationality was largely defined by their Muslim identity. Hence *tesettür* was an unquestionable part of their national garb. To what extent the two were regarded as inseparable can be understood from the term *tesettür-ü milliye* (national *tesettür*) which was used by one author.⁵¹ *Tesettür* being accepted as part of the national dress, the question was asked what *tesettür* actually meant. *Tesettür* meant that women had to cover themselves up, but to what degree? What was allowed to be visible and what not? This is the question women asked, not only for ideological reasons, but also for practical ones. They often found to their unpleasant surprise that what was accepted as proper dressing by the police officers in one area of Istanbul, was deemed improper by policemen in another area of the city.⁵²

The issue was picked up by some women writing in the *Kadınlar Dünyası*. A further unknown woman from Üsküdar, a part of Istanbul on the Asian side, brought up the idea that a *moda cemiyeti* (fashion society) should be founded which would develop a national dress. The membership of this society should consist of women with a profound knowledge of Turkish costume history, experienced designers and seamstresses who would turn the findings of the "historians" into a new national design and painters and journalists who should take care of the marketing of the designs.⁵³ A few weeks later another woman pointed to government responsibility to issue clear regulations on this subject and not leave the women to the whim of a local police officer. She asked the *Kadınlar Dünyası* and its readers to come up with some proposals to this end.⁵⁴ Thus the *Osmanlı Müdafaa-ı Hukūk-ı Nisvan Cemiyeti* (Ottoman Society for the Defense of Women's Rights) was founded, which had as its first aim "to create a national outdoor dress for [their] women"⁵⁵. In the following issues of the *Kadınlar Dünyası*, which became the bulletin board for the organization, the society explained its plans to reach these aims. To find out what the "national and religious traditions" regarding women's dress were, research was to be conducted among men and women in Istanbul and the provinces. This way what would be acceptable to the general public was to be determined first and according to the results of this research, designs would be made. Consequently, the *Kadınlar Dünyīsı* had to publish these designs after which the public were to cast their votes in favour of the design they wanted to have as the national dress.[56] Further research showed that the "illustrious orders of Allah" regarding the covering of women, were completely differently interpreted in the Islamic world and that even within the heartland of the Ottoman Empire, Anatolia, a great variety existed, which, according to one author, was indicative of the fact that the rules for covering women were not religiously determined, but locally, or nationally.[57] After this conclusion, the discussion shifted to a very particular part of Ottoman women's outdoor dress: the facial veil (*peçe*). The question whether or not this fell under the commands of Islam was heavily debated by some women. Some of them vehemently argued that this was the case, others denied it and stated that it was exactly this veil which turned them into backward, non-modern beings.[58] After this discussion the search for a national dress suddenly ended. Obviously, the issue of a national dress was too complicated to pursue. Moreover, the outbreak of the First World War put an end to the appearance of most women's periodicals, including the *Kadınlar Dünyası* and thus to a public forum to discuss this topic.

Conclusion

During the nineteenth century the Ottoman Empire was drawn into an economic and political entity that was dominated by the European "modern" nation states. The Ottomans, either forced or willingly, had to become part of that world, too. Dress was only one way to show their "modern worldliness".[59] Thus, when the army and the administration of the Empire were reformed to match their European counterparts, the civil and military officers were forced to wear European dress and uniforms, respectively. Civilians who wanted to show that they were part of the modern world also started to dress in European outfits. In this context Ottoman Muslim women, following their non-Muslim compatriots, were attracted by Parisian fashion, too.

The economic and political domination of European powers over the Ottoman economy and its (internal) politics, however, evoked a reaction. Anti-imperialism and the wish to put an end to the despotism of a Sultan who had been partly blamed for the subservience of the Ottoman Empire to the European powers, led to growing resistance and finally revolution. This revolution meant the start of a search for a new identity, that of a modern, independent, nation state. Such an identity should, Ottoman Muslim women argued, be expressed in the dresses they wore. No longer a copy of the dresses of the

Europeans who tried to keep the Ottomans under their thumb, but their own national dress. Although consensus was reached on the economic aspect of the dress, it proved to be more difficult to agree on the way it should look. The outbreak of the First World War diverted the attention to other subjects and the national dress was forgotten. It was only after the end of one more war, the War of Independence, that the issue of dress was taken up again. This time by a leader who again wanted to make his country part of the modern world. Atatürk, as this leader was called later, thus forced his civil servants, women and men alike, to adorn European-style hats instead of their headscarfs and fez's, respectively. A repetition of what happened a century earlier?

Notes

1   Mike Featherstone, Global Culture: an Introduction. In: Mike Featherstone, Globalization, pp. 1-14 [published earlier in: Theory, Culture & Society, 7 (1990)].
2   Arjun Appadurai, Disjuncture and Difference in the Global Cultural Economy. In: Featherstone, Globalization, loc. cit., pp. 295-310; Smith quoted in: Johann P. Arnáson, Nationalism, Globalization and Modernity. In: Featherstone, loc. cit., pp. 207-236.
3   Roland Robertson, Mapping the Global Condition: Globalization as the Central Concept. In: Mike Featherstone, Globalization, loc. cit., pp. 15-30, quotation 26.
4   Arnason, loc. cit., pp. 216-217.
5   Partha Chatterjee, Nationalist Thought and the Colonial World: a Derivative Discourse, Minneapolis 1993² (1986), pp. 1-3.
6   Clifford Geertz, The Interpretation of Cultures. Selected Essays, New York 1973, pp. 240-249.
7   Chatterjee, loc. cit., pp. 1-3.
8   Deniz Kandiyoti, Identity and Its Discontents: Women and the Nation. In: Millenium. Journal of International Studies, 20 (1991) 3, pp. 429-443.
9   Alihé Hanoum, Les Musulmanes Contemporaines: Trois Conférences, traduites de la langue Turque par Nazimé-Roukie, Paris 1894, pp. 45-67.
10   Ibid., pp. 5-25.
11   Kandiyoti, loc. cit., p. 433.
12   Eric Hobsbawm, Introduction: Inventing Traditions. In: Eric Hobsbawm/Terence Ranger, The Invention of Tradition, Cambridge 1994, pp. 1-14, quotation 5.
13   Linda Welters, Ethnicity in Greek Dress. In: Joanne B. Eicher, Dress and Ethnicity: Change across Space and Time, Oxford-Washington 1995, pp. 53-77.
14   Jonathan Friedman, Being in the World: Globalization and Localization. In: Featherstone, loc. cit., pp. 207-236, quotation pp. 216-217.
15   Roderic H. Davison, Reform in the Ottoman Empire, 1856-1876, New York 1973, 27; pp. 33-34; Bernard Lewis, The Emergence of Modern Turkey, London 1968² [1961], pp. 99-103; Hester Donaldson Jenkins, Behind Turkish Lattices. The Story of a Turkish Woman's Life, London 1911, pp. 121-122; Nurettin Sevin, Onüç asırlık Türk kıyâfet

târihine bir bakış, Ankara 1990, pp. 123-124, 127-128; Fatma Karabıyık Barabarosoğlu, Modernleşme sürecinde moda ve zihniyet, Istanbul 1995, pp. 111-113.
16 Lewis, The Emergence..., loc. cit., pp. 21-39.
17 The information on the bureaucratic and military reforms is mainly based on the following sources. Lewis, loc. cit., pp. 64-128; Erik Jan Zürcher, Turkey: A Modern History, London 1993, pp. 23-79.
18 Çağlar Keyder, State and Class in Turkey: A Study in Capitalist Development, London-New York, pp. 37-42; Emine Kıray, Osmanlı'da ekonomik yapı ve dış borçlar, Istanbul 1993; Zürcher, loc. cit., pp. 66-69.
19 Fatma Müge Göçek, Rise of the Bourgeoisie, Demise of Empire: Ottoman Westernization and Social Change, New York-Oxford 1996.
20 Donald Quataert, The Age of Reforms: 1812-1914. In: Halil Inalcik/Donald Quataert (eds.), An Economic and Social History of the Ottoman Empire, 1300-1914, Cambridge-New York 1994, pp. 888-933.
21 Especially for the British and Americans it became fashionable to travel to the Ottoman Empire due to the "Mediterranean passion" of the Victorian and Edwardian culture. Billie Melman, Women's Orients: English Women and the Middle East, 1718-1918. In: Sexuality, Religion and Work, Ann Arbor 1992, pp. 8-18.
22 Ahmed Ö. Evin, Origins and Development of the Turkish Novel, Minneapolis 1983.
23 Alan Duben/Cem Behar, Istanbul Households: Marriage, Family and Fertility, 1880-1920, Cambridge 1993, pp. 202-210.
24 Niyazi Berkes, The Development of Secularism in Turkey, Montreal 1964, pp. 296-297.
25 Jacob M. Landau, The Politics of Pan-Islamism: Ideology and Organization, Oxford 1994, pp. 37-39.
26 Berkes, loc. cit.
27 Şükrü Hanioğlu, The Young Turks in Opposition, New York-Oxford 1995, pp. 25-26.
28 Zürcher, loc. cit., pp. 90-94; Aykut Kansu, The Revolution of 1908 in Turkey, Leiden 1997.
29 Fanny Davis, The Ottoman Lady: A Social History from 1718 to 1918, New York etc. 1986, pp. 195-196; Nancy Micklewright, London, Paris, Istanbul and Cairo: Fashion and International Trade in the Nineteenth Century. In: New Perspectives on Turkey, (Spring 1992) 7, pp. 125-136.
30 Jenkins, loc. cit., p. 122.
31 Melman, loc. cit.
32 Nancy Micklewright, Late-Nineteenth-Century Ottoman Wedding Costumes as Indicators of Social Change. In: Muqarnas, 6 (1990), pp. 161-174, esp. 161-162.
33 Jenkins, loc. cit., p. 29; Davis, loc. cit., pp. 54-55.
34 Modeblatt, Osmanischer Lloyd, Istanbul, 16 December 1910. Although it did exist for some time I have been able to find only one issue without coverpage (and thus date) in the Istanbul libraries.
35 Nora Şeni, Fashion and Women's Clothing in the Satirical Press of Istanbul at the End of the 19th Century. In: Şirin Tekeli (ed.), Women in Modern Turkish Society: a Reader, London 1995, pp 25-45; Palmira Brummett, Dogs, Women, Cholera, and Other Menaces in the Streets: Cartoon Satire in the Ottoman Revolutionary Press, 1908-1911. In: International Journal of Middle East Studies, 27 (1995), pp. 433-460; Palmira Brummett, Dressing for Revolution: Mother, Nation, Citizen, and Subversive in the Ottoman Satirical Press, 1908-1911. In: Zehra F. Arat (ed.), Deconstructing Images of "the Turkish Woman", New York 1998, pp 38-63.
36 Brummett, Dressing for Revolution, loc. cit.

37	Mehmed Cavid, Kadınlara dair: hanımlarımıza. In: Kadın, Selanik, 1 (26 October 1908) 1, pp. 2-4.
38	Alihé Hanoum, loc. cit., pp. 121-145.
39	Fatma Fahrünnisa, Gönül ister ki... In: Millet, Istanbul, 13 August 1908, pp. 1-2.
40	Emine Seher Ali, Kadınlıkta seviye-i irfan. In: Kadınlar Dünyası, Istanbul, 17 April 1913, pp. 1-2. See also Konferans. In: Kadınlar Dünyası, 19 April 1913, pp. 3-4; Mamulat-ı Dahiliye İstihlâki Kadınlar Cemiyet-i Hayriyesinin beyannamesi. In: Kadınlar Dünyası, 20 April 1913, p. 4; Mamulat-ı Dahiliye İstihlaki Kadınlar Cemiyet-i Hayriyesinden. In: Kadınlar Dünyası, 2 July 1913, p. 4.
41	This section is based on part of my PhD thesis (forthcoming) which is (provisionally) entitled "Their Share in the Struggle: Ottoman Muslim Women and the Nation".
42	Fatma Fahrünnisa, loc. cit.
43	Rukiye Bulut, Istanbul kadınlarının kıyafetleri ve II. Abdülhamid'in çarşafı yasaklaması. In: Belgelerle Türk Tarihi Dergisi, (1968) 8, pp. 34-36, quotation 35.
44	Başbakanlık Osmanlı Arşivleri (BOA), Zabtiye İradeleri, Genel no. 368, Hususi no. 1, 18 Ramazan 1317.
45	BOA, Dahiliye Nezareti: Hukuk Müşavirliği (DH.HMŞ), 17/33, 8 August 1328; BOA, Dahiliye Nezareti: Muhaberat-ı Umumiye İdaresi (DH.MUİ), 121/15, 8 Şaban 1328; Tesettür-ü nisvān, Istanbul, Tanin, 19 August 1910, p. 3; Sittenvorschrift für die muhammedanischen Frauen. In: Osmanischer Lloyd, Istanbul, 30.8.1910, p. 2.
46	Havadisçi, Kadının haberleri. In: Kadın, Istanbul 1 (30 March 1912) 5, pp. 11-13. According to the Österreichische Monatsschrift für den Orient, the reason for issuing this order was the religious fervor which had increased due to the Tripolitanian war with Italy, a Christian state. Cf. Die türkischen Frauen, Österreichische Monatsschrift für den Orient, 38 (June 1912) 6, pp. 101-102.
47	Die Verschleierung der Muhamedanerinnen. In: Osmanischer Lloyd, Istanbul, 1.2.1914, p. 2.
48	Şefika Kurnaz, II. Meşrutiyet döneminde Türk kadını, Istanbul 1996, pp. 48-60, 121-122.
49	BOA, DH.MUİ, 69-2/4, 19 Sefer 1328; BOA, DH.MUİ, 57-1/53, 2 Rebi-yel-evvel 1330.
50	Kurnaz, loc. cit., pp. 48-60, 121-122.
51	Muzaffr, Tesettür-ü milliye-i nisvaniyemiz haqqında bir mutalaa. In: Kadınlar Dünyası, 24 May 1913, p. 3.
52	Bu haftanın vukuatı. In: Musavver Kadın, Istanbul 1 (27 April 1911) 2; Havadisçi, qadının haberleri. In: Kadın, 1 (30 March 1912) 5, pp. 11-13.
53	C.H., Milli Moda. In: Kadınlar Dünyası, 12 May 1913, p. 4.
54	Belqıs Şevket, Kıyafet-i milliyemizi nasıl düzeltmeli. In: Kadınlar Dünyası, 7 June 1913, p. 4.
55	Faaliyet başlıyor. In: Kandınlar Dünyası, 15 June 1913, p. 2; Osmanlı Müdafaa-i Hukuk-u Nisvan Cemiyeti programı. In: Qandınlar Dünyāsı, 12 June 1913, p. 1.
56	Kıyafetimizin ıslahı. In: Kadınlar Dünyası, 12 June 1913, p. 1; Teenni şarttır. In: Kadınlar Dünyası, 13 June 1913, p. 1; İşe başlamalı. In: Kadınlar Dünyası, 17 June 1913, p. 1.
57	Aliye Kıyafet-i nisvan hakkında. In: Kandınlar Dünyası, 15 June 1913, p. 2; Belqıs Şevket, Tesettür ve peçe. In: Kandınlar Dünyası, 27 June 1913, p. 4; Pakize Sadri, Anadolu İhtisasatı. In: Qandınlar Dünyāsı, 21 June 1913, pp. 1-2; Pakize Sadri, Anadolu İhtisasatı. In: Kandınlar Dünyası, 1 July 1913, p. 1-2.

58 Mehpare Osman, Bizde tesettür-ü nisvan. In: Kadınlar Dünyası, 29 June 1913, p. 4; Mehpare Osman, Hukuk-u nisvan cemiyeti. In: Kadınlar Dünyası, 1 July 1913, pp. 3-4; Semiha Peyami, Mehpare Osman Hanıma - tesettür hakkında. In: Kadınlar Dünyası, 1 July 1913, p. 4; Halide Nusret, Kadınlar Dünyası vasıtasıyla Mehpare Osman Hanıma. In: Kadınlar Dünyası, 3 July 1913, p. 4; P[akize] S[adri], Tesettür-ü nisvan. In: Kadınlar Dünyası, 4 July 1913, p. 3; Belkıs Şevket, Tesettür ve peçe; son söz. In: Kadınlar Dünyası, 4 July 1913, p. 3-4.

59 Others were, for example, the participation in world fairs which took place in Europe and America at the end of the nineteenth and beginning of the twentieth century.

Perspectives on Globalization
(Summary of a Round Table Discussion)

The symposium on dissociation from and appropriation of global processes and ideas in Asia and Africa concluded with a Round Table discussion moderated by *Ulrich Haarmann*. Introductory statements were delivered by *Gudrun Krämer, Ute Luig, Shalini Randeria*, and *Joachim Heidrich*. The discussants presented their views on the globalization problematic as well as on some issues raised by participants in the symposium. The entire debate conducted at the Round Table was marked by variegated and even contradictory approaches. The different attitudes were due, at least partly, to the various disciplinary affiliations of the speakers, comprising historians, political or social scientists, anthropologists and economists. But, as *Joachim Heidrich* noted, the discussion also reflected the general state of affairs in so far as the objective process of globalization obviously proceeds faster than our ability to perceive and rationally react to it. The fact that specialists on the Middle East, Asia and Africa proceeding from regional peculiarities endeavoured to tackle this cognitive challenge should make it worthwhile summarizing the main points raised in the discussion.

The exchange of views at this multi-disciplinary forum demonstrated the existence of extremely different, at times even contradictory perceptions of the core issue. The clash of arguments, however, also provoked a creative process of discussion as *Ulrich Haarmann* remarked. *Thomas Scheffler* favoured a rather detached look at the globe. He suggested understanding globalization as the process of the crystallization of the world into a single place. Conceptualizing globalization in this way would require an investigation into the development of the perception of the world as a whole as well as of mankind as a whole. He maintained that concepts of the world transcending ethnic and political boundaries have a long history; they were not restricted to Europe alone and constitute an aspect of the process of civilization. In this connection *Scheffler* suggested paying more attention in historical research to the worldviews of people as manifested in their religions, to geo-centric and helio-centric worldviews. On the other hand, he called for accepting the challenge put forward by concepts of macro-space building, of attempts to build larger economic and political blocs in the world. He mentioned efforts to establish a large-scale institutional order as envisaged, for instance, by Fukuyama's "Communities of Trust" or as represented by the European Union. In his opinion, the history of different regions of the world as a discipline might provide clues for administering them. For this purpose the study of large ancient empires could be helpful. *Scheffler's* approach emphasizes the spatial aspect of globalization. It singles out the history of the vision of the globe while relegating other temporal and historical aspects to a secondary position. His understanding of globalization as globality where the question of a centre does not arise received support from *Henner Fürtig*. *Fürtig* pleaded for dealing with the phenomenon "just as it happens", for concentrating on its operational, technical aspects in order to de-ideologize it.

The topic of the symposium, however, focused on the impact of globalization on peoples and cultures of former colonial or Third World countries and their reaction to it. That is why the majority of the participants felt the necessity to analyze the historical roots of globalization, the sources which feed the ongoing process and the forces which dominate it. This issue is intrinsically connected with the complex problem of modernization. It calls for exploring whether modernization and globalization are interlinked. *Birgit Meyer* suggested in this connection using the term modernity and distinguishing between modernity and the modernization theory. Disagreement prevailed among the participants in the discussion on whether the interrelationship between modernity and globalization was marked by a greater continuity or a greater disjuncture. The different interpretations offered depended on the importance attributed to economic and political or to cultural factors in the globalization process.

One of the key issues heatedly debated was the centredness of globalization. Does globalization signify a phenomenon, which originates from various centres? Or does it represent a global trend which moves "from the West to the rest"? Several participants stressed that a centre and an agency can be identified. Applying economic criteria, the centre is definitely located in the West. Agencies of the process are the global players - multinationals and global institutions such as the World Bank, the International Monetary Fund and the World Trade Organization. Economic globalization is manifested in neo-liberalism and the main driving forces of the ongoing globalization are the highly developed countries which dominate the world market. *K.N. Panikkar*, for instance, questioned the ability of post-colonial societies to participate in the process of globalization and stressed the point that modernization in India could at best benefit a few while it meant marginalization for the majority. In his opinion, the concept of globalization cannot be purposefully applied without taking into account unequal economic and political positions and potentialities of the countries involved. In this connection he pointed out the historical dimensions of the process – structures of relationships which existed during the period of colonialism and which have a continuing impact on post-colonial societies.

Joachim Heidrich equally emphasized the historical roots of globalization, which he considered a recent stage of a long drawn-out and complex phenomenon. It should be seen in the context of the world wide expansion of the capitalist mode of production, which in its final stage brought about a network of multi-dimensional global interlinkages. Since economic processes constitute the springboard of globalization, he argued against detaching the political, social or cultural levels of contemporary globalization completely from the economic sphere. He conceived globalization as an objective process which has to be tackled accordingly. Simultaneously, however, he pointed out the urgency of taking a closer look at the attitude of the people involved in this process and at their endeavours to influence its trajectory.

Several participants emphasized the specific features of cultural globalization. They underlined that manifestations of cultural globalization are comparatively independent from socio-economic factors. *Ute Luig*, for instance, referring to Appadurai suggested looking at globalization as a complex yet disjunctive interaction of economic, political and cultural factors. Differing from the situation in the economic sphere where western economies are still dominant, although no longer hegemonic, in the cultural domain globalization constitutes, in her opinion, a definitely non-linear, non-directional process with a multiplicity of centres. She referred to the example of the viable communication and cultural industries of so-called "Third-World countries", which distribute their services and products around the world (e.g. Chinese and Indian films, African music, Rap, etc.). The cultural flows to be observed were not merely instrumental in bringing about a modernization (westernization) in "Third World countries" but created an impact also on the cultural situation in the West. Multiculturation and cultural hybridity are increasingly assuming world wide proportions and are to be tackled accordingly by the researchers. *Ute Luig* also favoured the globalization paradigm vis-à-vis older theoretical constructs because it does not confine itself to the economic and political sphere but focuses on the cultural, aesthetic and recreational dimensions of social life. *Ute Luig* felt that by studying habits, arts and religious beliefs more thoroughly, processes in non-Western societies could then be analyzed as a creative appropriation of external influences and not merely as a reaction towards Western hegemony. According to *Ute Luig*, the globalization approach distinguishes itself by conceiving the relationship between Western and non-Western countries not simply in terms of domination, inequality and non-simultaneity. It attributes a more important part to the subjectivities of local communities and their contribution to "world culture".

Gudrun Krämer argued along similar lines. She wanted the globalization paradigm not to be too closely linked to colonialism and imperialism. Such an approach, in her opinion, reflected a notion of omnipotence, a clear sense of direction and hierarchy. Assuming that colonialism created the world we are living in, that it shaped societies in the colonial world as well as in the West, was in her opinion just another manifestation of eurocentrism. As a historian and someone working in Islamic Studies she felt convinced that colonialism did *not* create societies and Orientalism did *not* create Islam. Islam existed before

Orientalism; it was changed, was reshaped or reformed in the course of time. *Birgit Meyer*, however, while acknowledging the advantage of shedding the hierarchical concepts of the modernization theory by thinking in terms of globalization cautioned against underestimating the power of the West and the impact of colonialism on indigenous societies. She cited the example of Africa. *Peter van der Veer* also opposed the trend to erase the question of colonialism and Orientalism, an attitude which, in his opinion, often surfaces in Islamic Studies. *David Coplan* raised the same issue – although in a different context - stating very pointedly that battles lost in the field of politics and economics can definitely not be won in the field of culture.

Gudrun Krämer and *Ute Luig* also took up the issue of borders and boundaries, of de-territorialization and re-territorialization within the process of globalization. *Ute Luig* pointed to an obvious tendency of fragmentation of former close-knit groups in Western and non-Western societies alike. Its corollary consists of a politically induced process of aggregation, of building more encompassing structures than the nation state. She felt that in view of the global challenge the local is rated higher because it conveys feelings of belonging and social security. The "cultural home" people are searching for could be old or newly-built by migrants. Migrant communities who participate in two cultures, who live "in-between", may even conceive their position as an advantage.

Gudrun Krämer stressed the historical dimension of borders. She maintained that borders changed like everything else over time and space and she rejected the notion of borders having been demarcated in a completely novel way by the West through military, economic, political and cultural means. She again cited the example of Islam that had a notion of border and territory before the colonizers arrived. She further felt that the notion of borders and of boundaries and how borders are going to be changed merits closer investigation in the context of globalization. The possibility of having "unbounded cultures" in the future evoked her particular interest.

Many participants shared the concern of *Ulrich Haarmann, Gudrun Krämer* and others regarding the striking fluidity of notions in the discussion on globalization and its cultural aspects. *Joachim Heidrich* stressed the necessity to develop appropriate cognitive tools, an appropriate epistemology. *Aise Çaglar* pointed to the methodological consequences of globalization for the various disciplines. She called for a restructuring of research and singled out the particular challenge facing anthropologists.

During the deliberations, the question of globalization as a theory or paradigm, its meaning for the concepts of history, society and culture, for the key notions such as community, state and nation was taken up. In her statement *Shalini Randeria* elaborated on those key notions. Referring, on the one hand, to *Anthony Giddens* and *Roland Robertson*, who treat globalization as an endpoint or the culmination of modernization and, on the other hand, to *Martin Albrow* who considered globalization to be the requiem for modernity, she took a closer look at the relationship between modernity, universalism and globalization. While she acknowledged the existence of definite historical, political and economic links between these processes, she also pointed out differences of approach. Compared to universalism, globalization is devoid of any optimistic progressivism and in contrast to the modernization paradigm does not imply a law-like process. The notion of the deductionality of processes such as industrialization or urbanization is also absent. A de-centred, non-hierarchical and non-normative view of globalization, however, was not only challenged by her, but also by other participants in the discussion on key notions.

There was considerable agreement on the necessity to explore the dialectical character of globalization, which *Ulrich Haarmann* called the binary notions, suggesting the simultaneous occurrence of seemingly contradictory trends: globalization and localization, centralization and decentralization, economic concentration of capital and disorganized capitalism, macro-space building and political fragmentation, cultural homogenization versus heterogenization, hybridization and dehybridization. *Shalini Randeria* underlined the interlinkages of economic and political developments in this connection. The process of concentrating capital in multinational corporations, which is accompanied by disorganized capitalism, flexible work patterns, casualization of labour and dislocation of production has considerable repercussions on the political plane. The mobility of global capital, and the unfettered movement of global finance matches political fragmentation and the decline of the nation state. Globalization needs states, but states whose functions are restricted to the role of district policeman and partner for transnational organizations. At the same time, a withdrawal from the social sector, from social services, is encouraged. The consequences seem to be more disastrous for former colonial countries, a point highlighted also by *Zoya Hasan*.

Zoya Hasan assessed the consequences of the weakening of the nation state for India. The trend resulted in the withdrawal of the state from social transformation, a growing preference for group politics and group claims, religious resurgence, caste and communal politics. She deplored the absence of an adequate awareness of these processes at the political level. Thus - along with *K.N. Panikkar, Surendra Gopal* and others – sharing *Shalini Randeria's* view that globalization involves a new stratification, a redistribution of privileges, but also of poverty on the global, regional and even local levels, *Zoya Hasan* felt that structural inequalities require structural solutions, the redistribution of incomes and the re-allocation of resources. Recently, however, the focus has shifted to the cultural level, to cultural affirmation, to the removal of cultural inequalities and cultural discrimination. The subsequent discussion also answered *Surendra Gopal's* question whether ethnic cleansing should be considered as contradictory to globalization or as its very own product. Arguments were brought forward to show that ethnic cleansing and globalization can indeed go hand in glove.

The cultural aspects of globalization constituted a main topic of the symposium. They also played a major role in the Round Table discussion. *Peter Pels* felt that the days of culture as an analytical term are numbered, one reason being its indiscriminate use in present-day discussions. This happens, for instance, when the term is applied in discourses on multiculturalism or ethnicity. *Armando Salvatore* proposed making the idea of global culture more operative by focusing attention on new kernels of cultural elites who are the shapers of culture either as a commodity or as a possible means for raising claims.

The participants almost unanimously considered a cultural homogenization in the process of globalization as highly unlikely. *Aise Çaglar* cautioned against the inclination to romanticize the diversification and fragmentation of cultures and stressed the necessity to ascertain the frames in which this diversification takes place. She suggested that institutions and values that are involved in the fragmentation process be clearly identified. This approach coincided to some extent with that of *Shalini Randeria* who argued that global structures organize diversity, but organize it in their uniform ways, which might not be immediately apparent.

David Coplan submitted a stimulating proposal for the use of the notion of culture in a reflexive manner. He drew attention to the role played by narratives in the post-modern discourse. The differences in reading the narratives of globalization should itself be made a topic of research. The deliberations during the symposium and at the Round Table actually exemplified those differences in reading. *Coplan* wanted the focus of the discussion shifted from what the global is or what it does to the readings and representations of these processes in the regions of our concern. Even though battles lost on the field of politics and economics cannot be won in the field of culture, he considered peoples' narrations to be powerful motivations that can bring them together in active combinations for evolving new social strategies.

K.N. Panikkar had already taken up the question of resistance to globalization. He hinted at the resistance potential inherent in culture, which - although ambiguous in its nature – could be helpful in averting negative consequences of globalization and might be used by people to assert themselves in the globalization process.

Towards the close the Round Table discussion again reverted to the topic of the symposium the dissociation and appropriation of global processes and ideas in the regions of Asia and Africa. In this connection *Dietrich Reetz* wanted the research efforts directed to the strategies people choose, to the historical, cultural or religious discourses they select, use or revive in their endeavours to meet the challenges of globalization.

The Round Table discussion broadened the perspective on the globalization issues raised during the deliberations of the symposium. Additional questions were posed, suggestions regarding the methodological approach submitted and, finally, lacunae pointed out to be addressed by future research.

Petra Heidrich

Postscript

The Effects of Globalization on Asia and Africa: Related Concepts, Language and History

Ulrich Haarmann

I

This symposium on the impact of global processes and ideas on African and Asian societies was characterized (as would have been the case in any other comparable scholarly meeting) by an irritating multitude of methodological approaches and thematic fields, with the concomitant competing sets of notions. If anyone had expected us to be able to reduce the set of reactions on the globalization phenomenon in non-Western environments to one denominator or suggestive formula, they were disappointed. We accept this confusion and lack of uniformity as an intrinsic attribute of our subject.

In order to get closer to an understanding, we even forthright depend on competing arrays of analytical tools, on differing sets of references, and, most importantly, on the open space in front of us. Research subsists on competing models and concurrent methodologies, particularly in the age of post-modernist scepticism vis-à-vis allegedly perennial scholarly truths.

We should see this conference as one small leg of a promising and rewarding intellectual journey. It began, under the scrutinous eyes of philosophers, politicians and managers, with the public debate on the effects of processes of global coalescence primarily in the fields of economy and culture at large. It has now reached the stage of the study of the repercussions elicited by these summary world-wide processes in different social set-ups. In our case, these are non-Western societies in Asia and Africa that have been moulded for at least one century by the external thrust of European imperialism and by the ensuing indigenous reactions to this menace.

II

The political and historical connotations of the term globalization are multifaceted and even outright contradictory. This word conveys by no means only conveys internationalization and the smooth levelling of distinct traditions towards uniformity. It rather encompasses, as Thomas Scheffler has adroitly stated, three distinct processes, (a) the removal, (b) the relocation and (c) the creation of boundaries. In contrast to the utopian idea of a fully globalized – i.e. a world - culture and economy, globalization (or, in other words, the path towards a fictitious static globality) is dynamic. It carries within itself permanent change. In the case of the nation states, which continue to constitute the political cornerstones of our world system, globalization means both construction and deconstruction, emergence and disappearance. Break-up and merger go hand in hand. Transnational units come into being. Within existing nation states new subunits begin to assert themselves. Localism and regionalism, contested forces of political change today worldwide, impetuously come to the fore. I will have to return briefly to this subject.

A number of parallel, equally dynamic terms (characterized by the "...ation" ending) with a presumably clearer, less ambiguous, profile were proffered in the course of the conference as being closely related - i.e. concomitant, conducive or even coterminous - to globalization. These concepts may therefore serve to clarify the vague and volatile semantic perimeter of globalization. Depending on the discipline and scholarly methodology involved – history, sociology, *Religionswissenschaft*, political science, anthropology, economics – such different putative partial cognates were named. Some of them imply causality, others are merely descriptive.

Without any concern for logical hierarchy this inevitably mixed bag of notions will be discussed briefly. To what degree these most divergent terms may prove viable for our understanding of the whole complex of globalization, has been one of the dominant subjects of the contributions assembled in this volume and of the discussions held during the two-day meeting.

Westernization. The fragility of the equation of westernization with progress towards modernity is mirrored in the indefatigable efforts of non-European civilizations to demonstrate their innate capacity for innovation and scientific acumen. History in particular serves as an arsenal in this defence. These cultures take recourse to their own pre-imperialist, often medieval, achievements in these crucial domains. The heated debate over the potential for enlightenment in eighteenth-century Muslim societies, e.g., bears witness to these concerns.

Alleys towards globalization in past centuries - such as the fertile contacts between Asia and Africa in medieval times (*nota bene* largely with the exclusion of the inhospitable shores and areas of barbarian and underdeveloped western and northern Europe) - enjoy so much scholarly and public appeal because they seem to vindicate equal treatment of such formerly highly advanced, yet now "underdeveloped" regions *also* in the global game of today. It is not just pure coincidence - to mention only two examples - that medieval Muslim descriptions of Indian native religions, Arab travel reports on Russia as well as on West Africa, or the collective memory of the peoples around the Indian Ocean as reflected in the *Arabian Nights* enjoy attention in Middle Eastern public awareness.

Modernization. Whereas westernization carries, at least potentially, strong negative connotations in Asia and Africa because the very term implies manipulation of the collective self by alien forces, non-European "traditional" societies can perceive modernization, in principle, as unambiguously positive. As shown above, strategies of synthesizing indigenous traditions with progress made in Europe or America (often under the aegis of combining authenticity with the technical and scientific culture of today) have been devised. The autochthonous contributions of one's own cultural realm to past and present modernities within world civilization is duly emphasized and at times, by way of compensation, grossly exaggerated. Correlations between the subjugation of one's own land by imperialism, colonialism, and post-colonialism, on the one hand, and modernity, on the other, are not easily accepted.

Secularization. The alleged incompatibility of modernity and adherence to religious faith (based on the argument that only after the fetters of religion were shed is Europe said to have inaugurated its triumphant path to progress and human rights) is a particularly sensitive issue. We need not delve into this much debated subject. Certainly some of the premises of this controversy are up for discussion in the light of the upsurge of religious fundamentalism even in highly developed European and American (as well as Israeli) quarters. Adherents of resurgent Islam and Hinduism will violently reject the idea that their profoundly religious, anti-secularist world view precludes, inhibits or contradicts modernity and human dignity.

Homogenization, heterogenization and hybridization. These analytical terms were a pivotal guideline in the discussions at the symposium. They take up the basic three-tiered phenomenology of globalization mentioned at the beginning: the levelling of differences exacerbates the awareness of otherness, both on a global, a national and a regional plane. Processes of unification vie with those of warding off these pressures and of keeping traditional complexity. The individual stages and eventually the results of these conflicts differ from region to region. They provide an enormously fertile, largely untapped, field of study. Perhaps they can best be conceptualized by the notions of (a) homogenization, i.e. the loss of distinctiveness in the all encompassing ocean of globality, of (b) heterogenization, i.e. fragmentation in the aftermath of the collapse of the existing political system, centered around the nation-state, and (c) of hybridization, a process in which native and alien, i.e. for that matter: global, elements are synthesized.

A particular case for concern is the nation state. As has been said, under the impact of globalizing processes nation states develop in three directions. They disappear (one case is Sikkim in the Himalaya), they merge (North and South Yemen), and they split up, often along lines that were established by colonial powers. The fragmentation of former Soviet Central Asia or, in close vicinity to each other, the division of post-World War II Ethiopia into Eritrea and Ethiopia and of independent Somalia into the formerly Italian south and the formerly British north (= Somaliland) may serve as examples. Ethnicity resurfaces as an alternative factor in the drawing of political frontiers. The dogma that colonial boundaries should be preserved at all costs in order to avoid internecine ethnic warfare in Africa is no longer as stable as it was twenty years ago.

Urbanization, finally, was consistently named as a companion to globalization. Concomitance, however, does not mean conditioning. To which degree urban sprawling, large-scale movement from rural to urban areas, the formation of mega-cities (the largest urban conglomerations are found in Latin America, Asia and Africa), and demographic development can also be interpreted in the context of globalization – these questions remained unanswered and call for new encounters in which geographers of various methodological orientations would also have to play a prominent part.

III

In the discussion on globalization one cultural aspect was raised (in Klaus Sagaster's contribution on Mongolia), but in my estimation did not receive due attention, especially in the non-European context: language. Several questions are paramount and are directly connected with the discourse on African and Asian responses to global dynamics:

Is there a typology to be seen in the variegated African and Asian reactions to the rise of English to become the first truly global *lingua franca* in world history? To what degree are post-imperialist European and American rivalries over the domination of Africa and Asia continued in linguistic garb? French apprehensions over a possible switch of a country like Rwanda (or even Zaire/Congo) from the French to the English speaking world speak volumes. In this contest indigenous African interests do not seem to play any role. It is not fortuitous, if this may be added in this context, that African and Asian leaders such as the Lebanese Charles Hélou, the Egyptian Boutrus Ghali and the president of Benin were demonstratively elected spokesmen of an endangered global *francophonie*. Furthermore, are there strategies of regional linguistic homogenization (facilitated by state media) in Asia and Africa whose purpose is to offset foreign influence and to counter imputed post-imperialist stratagems to divide and rule? Will regional languages, such as Arabic, Haussa or Hindi, with tens and hundreds of millions of native speakers assume parity at least with lesser European languages in global matters?

Language as part of Third World cultural policies provides a particular challenge, not the least – and this takes us back to our meeting - because for satisfactory research on this issue not only social scientists, but also linguists and philologists (if pre-modern linguistic processes are to be investigated) are needed. Through these channels the mutual neglect and distrust of "orientalists" and social scientists can be countered productively.

Within the study of language, *Begriffsgeschichte*, especially the history and changing delineations of political and social terminology, can claim prime concern. Should one strive for a global language and thus consistently translate indigenous terms into European languages, blurring their original meaning? The ongoing debate on feudalism and its impact on world history suggests one example. I am talking about the Arabic *iqtaʿ*, which denotes the transfer of the proceeds of the land as a kind of salary for public servants and the military in the pre-modern Middle East (including the Ottoman Empire). Can this term really be equated (as happens all the time) with the Latin *feudum*, or the English *fief*, i.e. with notions predicated upon the element of personal fealty which plays no role in the alleged Middle Eastern equivalent? On the other hand, is it realistic to expect that native Hindi, Arabic or Haussa words with a distinct meaning can be grafted upon international parlance as new loan-words, just as one has learned to replace colonial geographical terminology (Ceylon, Burma; Bombay) with its (at times evidently alleged or even invented) indigenous correspondent (Sri Lanka, Myanmar; Mumbai)? Amr Hamzawy's paper on the viability and topicality of hallowed Islamic political terms such as the "House of War" vs. the "House of Islam" has made it clear that there is a need for historical studies on linguistic usage.

IV

There was a clear consensus in the symposium that as a category of research history deserves more space in the study of today's globalization phenomenon. This is particularly valid with regard to the legitimation of existing nation states but also transcends this issue. In David J. Coplan's paper on Lesotho, e.g., the historical roots of striking collective sets of behaviour in a contemporary non-Western society were elaborated. Without our knowledge of events that happened a century ago these "national traits" would remain enigmatic to us. We need more research on the indigenous paths taken by Asian and African societies, at first independently of Europe and then in permanent reaction to the West. The *Zentrum Moderner Orient* regards the study of these long-term dynamics of amalgamation and rejection as one of its prime areas of activity.

Contributors

Professor Dr *David B. Coplan*, Department of Social Anthropology, University of the Witwatersrand, Johannesburg

Dr *Anoushiravan Ehteshami*, Centre for Middle Eastern and Islamic Studies, University of Durham

Dr *Henner Fürtig*, Centre for Modern Oriental Studies, Berlin

Professor Dr *Ulrich Haarmann*, Director of the Centre for Modern Oriental Studies, Berlin

Dr *Annemarie Hafner*, Centre for Modern Oriental Studies, Berlin

Dr *Amr Hamzawy*, The Middle Eastern Studies Section, Department of Political Science, Free University Berlin

Professor Dr *Leonhard Harding*, Department of History, University of Hamburg

Professor Dr *Mushirul Hasan*, Department of History, Jamia Millia Islamia, New Delhi

Professor Dr *Zoya Hasan*, Center for Political Studies, Jawaharlal Nehru University, New Delhi

Professor Dr *Joachim Heidrich*, Independent Scholar, Berlin

Dr *Nicole A.M.N. van Os*, College of Arts and Sciences, Koç University, Istanbul

Professor Dr *K.N. Panikkar*, Centre for Historical Studies, Jawaharal Nehru University, New Delhi

Dr *Shalini Randeria*, Institute of Sociology, Free University Berlin

Dr *Dietrich Reetz*, Centre for Modern Oriental Studies, Berlin

Professor Dr *Klaus Sagaster*, Institute for Languages and Cultural Studies, University of Bonn

Dr *Armando Salvatore*, Institute of Social Sciences, Humboldt University at Berlin

Dr *Thomas Scheffler*, German Oriental Society, Beirut

Dr *David Taylor*, School of African and Oriental Studies, London

Professor Dr *Jean-Luc Vellut*, Department of History, Catholic University of Louvain

ZENTRUM MODERNER ORIENT

ARBEITSHEFTE

Nr. 1 ANNEMARIE HAFNER/JOACHIM HEIDRICH/PETRA HEIDRICH: Indien: Identität, Konflikt und soziale Bewegung

Nr. 2 HEIKE LIEBAU: Die Quellen der Dänisch-Halleschen Mission in Tranquebar in deutschen Archiven. Ihre Bedeutung für die Indienforschung

Nr. 3 JÜRGEN HERZOG: Kolonialismus und Ökologie im Kontext der Geschichte Tansanias - Plädoyer für eine historische Umweltforschung (hg. von Achim von Oppen)

Nr. 4 GERHARD HÖPP: Arabische und islamische Periodika in Berlin und Brandenburg, 1915 - 1945. Geschichtlicher Abriß und Bibliographie

Nr. 5 DIETRICH REETZ: Hijrat: The Flight of the Faithful. A British file on the Exodus of Muslim Peasants from North India to Afghanistan in 1920

Nr. 6 HENNER FÜRTIG: Demokratie in Saudi-Arabien? Die Āl Sa'ūd und die Folgen des zweiten Golfkrieges

Nr. 7 THOMAS SCHEFFLER: Die SPD und der Algerienkrieg (1954-1962)

Nr. 8 ANNEMARIE HAFNER (Hg.): Essays on South Asian Society, Culture and Politics

Nr. 9 BERNT GLATZER (Hg.): Essays on South Asian Society, Culture and Politics II

Nr. 10 UTE LUIG/ACHIM VON OPPEN (Hg.): Naturaneignung in Afrika als sozialer und symbolischer Prozess

Nr. 11 GERHARD HÖPP/GERDIEN JONKER (Hg.): In fremder Erde. Zur Geschichte und Gegenwart der islamischen Bestattung in Deutschland

Nr. 12 HENNER FÜRTIG: Liberalisierung als Herausforderung. Wie stabil ist die Islamische Republik Iran?

Nr. 13 UWE PFULLMANN: Thronfolge in Saudi-Arabien - vom Anfang der wahhabitischen Bewegung bis 1953

Nr. 14 DIETRICH REETZ/HEIKE LIEBAU (Hg.): Globale Prozesse und "Akteure des Wandels": Quellen und Methoden ihrer Untersuchung

Nr. 15 JAN-GEORG DEUTSCH/INGEBORG HALENE (Hg.): Afrikabezogene Nachlässe in den Bibliotheken und Archiven der Bundesländer Berlin, Brandenburg und Mecklenburg-Vorpommern

Nr. 16 HENNER FÜRTIG/GERHARD HÖPP (Hg.): Wessen Geschichte? Muslimische Erfahrungen historischer Zäsuren im 20. Jahrhundert

STUDIEN

Bd. 1 JOACHIM HEIDRICH (Hg.): Changing Identities. The Transformation of Asian and African Societies under Colonialism

Bd. 2 ACHIM VON OPPEN/RICHARD ROTTENBURG (Hg.): Organisationswandel in Afrika: Kollektive Praxis und kulturelle Aneignung

Bd. 3 JAN-GEORG DEUTSCH: Educating the Middlemen: A Political and Economic History of Statutory Cocoa Marketing in Nigeria, 1936-1947

Bd. 4 GERHARD HÖPP (Hg.): Fremde Erfahrungen: Asiaten und Afrikaner in Deutschland, Österreich und in der Schweiz bis 1945

Bd. 5 HELMUT BLEY: Afrika: Geschichte und Politik. Ausgewählte Beiträge 1967-1992

Bd. 6 GERHARD HÖPP: Muslime in der Mark. Als Kriegsgefangene und Internierte in Wünsdorf und Zossen, 1914 - 1924

Bd. 7 JAN-GEORG DEUTSCH/ALBERT WIRZ (Hg.): Geschichte in Afrika. Einführung in Probleme und Debatten

Bd. 8 HENNER FÜRTIG: Islamische Weltauffassung und außenpolitische Konzeptionen der iranischen Staatsführung seit dem Tod Ajatollah Khomeinis

Bd. 9 BRIGITTE BÜHLER: Mündliche Überlieferungen: Geschichte und Geschichten der Wiya im Grasland von Kamerun

Bd. 10 KATJA FÜLLBERG-STOLBERG/PETRA HEIDRICH/ELLINOR SCHÖNE (Hg): Dissociation and Appropriation of Global Processes and Ideas: History, Religion and Local Culture in Asia and Africa

In Vorbereitung:

STUDIEN

(Arbeitstitel)

GERDIEN JONKER (Hg.): Kern und Rand. Religiöse Minderheiten aus der Türkei in Deutschland

ELLINOR SCHÖNE: Weltbild und Politik der Organisation der Islamischen Konferenz (OIC) nach dem Ende des Ost-West-Konflikts

Bei Fragen zur Produktsicherheit wenden Sie sich bitte an:
If you have any questions regarding product safety,
please contact:

Walter de Gruyter GmbH
Genthiner Straße 13
10785 Berlin
productsafety@degruyterbrill.com